The Plans of War

The General Staff and British
Military Strategy c. 1900–1916

The Plans of War
The General Staff and British Military Strategy c. 1900–1916

John Gooch
Department of History
University of Lancaster

Routledge & Kegan Paul
London

First published in 1974
by Routledge & Kegan Paul Ltd
Broadway House, 68–74 Carter Lane,
London EC4V 5EL
Set in Monotype Walbaum
and printed in Great Britain by
Western Printing Services Ltd, Bristol
© *John Gooch 1974*
No part of this book may be reproduced in
any form without permission from the
publisher, except for the quotation of brief
passages in criticism

ISBN 0 7100 7830 7

For my mother

Contents

Maps

Foreword

Like settlers moving into unknown territory, clearing the forests, cultivating the soil, trafficking with the natives, so professional historians extend their understanding of the past as they exploit the official documents released year by year for inspection in the Public Records Office. In doing so they do something more important than dispelling ignorance: they correct error. The group-memory abhors a vacuum. Some record of the past automatically establishes itself on the basis of fragmentary memories, partial contemporary publications and the recollections of participants intentionally or unintentionally selected to justify their subsequent actions. The documents may reveal few secrets, but only the mass of detail they provide makes it possible for us to get the more salient evidence into perspective and answer the question which nag at all historians: 'what really happened and why?'

It is difficult even today to consider the decade before the First World War except in the light of the catastrophe that followed. An earlier generation of historians, particularly those whose attitude was moulded by the experiences of the Western Front, found it almost impossible. The debates between Easterners and Westerners on the level of strategy, the appalling mistakes of the British High Command between 1915 and 1917 on the level of tactics, coloured all subsequent appreciations of British pre-war military planning. Figures so politically eminent as Lloyd George and Maurice Hankey, writers with the scholarly reputation of Herbert Richmond and Liddell Hart, saw the origins of the holocaust of the Somme in faulty strategic decisions taken six years earlier which, largely as a result of the activities of General Henry Wilson, committed Britain to an atypical and disastrous 'continental strategy'. This view was to shape political and military assumptions for a further quarter of a century; not always for the best.

Now that the records are available we can see that this interpretation is, to say the least, incomplete. Two historians, Mr George Monger in the diplomatic field and Dr Samuel Williamson in the military, have established new and firm outlines which enable us to see far more clearly what decisions were really taken, in the light of what evidence and arguments, when, and by whom. Their work has already made it clear that one of the most important new elements in the situation was the emergence for the first time of a real British General Staff; and that one of the most important reasons for the influence exerted by that body was the hard work, the intelligence and the able reasoning of its members. The failure of the Navy to produce anything comparable, and the paralysis of the Committee of Imperial Defence as a result of the Navy's refusal to co-operate, made the General Staff, in the pre-war years, a very important body indeed. The views of its members—William Robertson, Edward Altham, Adrian Grant Duff, to name only a few—were no less important in shaping British policy than those of their opposite numbers in the Foreign Office; whose part in re-orienting British policy towards involvement in continental politics has been, until recently, similarly underrated. These men were not fools, and they certainly were not Blimps. The policies they advocated certainly led to unforeseen results; but their advocacy was based not on prejudice, but on hard and, within its limits, clear thinking, after careful examination of possible alternatives. Not, it must be admitted, of *all* possible alternatives. No more than their opposite numbers on the Continent did they consider the implications for the British Army and the British nation of a military deadlock lasting for four and a half years.

John Gooch thus fills with this book a serious gap in British historiography. Beginning where Brian Bond's excellent study, *The Victorian Army and the Staff College*, leaves off, he describes the rise of the General Staff concept, the political hazards that attended its implementation, the personalities of whom the Staff was composed, the wide range of problems which they confronted, the submergence of the Staff on the advent of Kitchener to the War Office in 1914, and its final triumph when William Robertson, always its most powerful member, became its Chief at the end of 1915. Inevitably this is a work as much of political and administrative history as of military, and historians of Edwardian England are likely to find it indispensable. The best compliment I can pay Dr Gooch is to wonder how we ever got on without it.

MICHAEL HOWARD

Preface

As an undergraduate I had the good fortune to be taught by Michael Howard, and it was then that I developed an interest in the role of the General Staff in European history. The German example came first to the fore: an institution deemed so dangerous as to be disbanded after the First World War, and so evil that membership of it could figure in the counts levelled against the defendants in the Nuremburg Trials after the Second World War. By the time that I came to begin research much had been written about the *Grossergeneralstab* and a certain amount about the French General Staff. Nothing, by contrast, had appeared for many years about their British equivalent. So this study had its starting point in an attempt to ascertain how an island democracy established what to many seemed a continental engine of militarism and destruction and how it compared in structure with the examples across the Channel.

It was pointed out to me by Captain Stephen Roskill and by John Barnes that such a study would only be one half of the story, and would have more value if related to the strategies formulated by the General Staff to deal with certain contingencies. It is as a result of that advice that this book falls into two distinct parts, as well as having an introductory chapter and a finale. Chapters 2–5 describe the development of the institution, and chapters 6–9 its role in devising strategy. Arranging the material in this way has meant imposing an order on historical events more artificial than most. To this I can only plead in mitigation that to try to describe both functions simultaneously is beyond my powers and would have resulted in a narrative of unreadable complexity.

A word should perhaps be said about chapter 9, 'France and Germany'. This aspect of British strategy has been more closely studied than any other, and I would not want to claim any merit of originality as justifying its inclusion here. It appears simply because some mention of it is unavoidable if this book is to have balance, and because I have sought to relate two strategies which are not generally closely related when considering this problem. I have leaned heavily upon, and would wish to acknowledge, the work of three historians in doing so: Neil Summerton, George Monger and Samuel R. Williamson. It might be appropriate to remark here that I use the term 'military' throughout in its narrower meaning, that is to say relating to the army as opposed to any other service.

Many people have helped me in the writing of this book. Those who have provided documentary assistance are acknowledged on a later page; I would like here to thank them. My deep gratitude goes to a small group of friends who have provided constant help, advice and encouragement: Michael Howard, Brian Bond, Neil Summerton, Michael Ekstein and Howard Moon. And I can now see why authors express such heavy debts to their wives. Ann has somehow always managed to provide me with the conditions in which to write, and she and Alexander have been a constant source of inspiration.

It goes without saying that responsibility for all errors and interpretations is mine alone.

JOHN GOOCH

Wray

Acknowledgments

I would like to thank Her Majesty the Queen for allowing me to use materials in the Royal Archives. Mr Robin Mackworth Young and the staff of the Royal Archives provided idyllic conditions in which to work. For permitting me to use sources in private collections I am grateful to the following: Captain the Earl Haig; Viscount Esher; Viscount Harcourt; Captain the Lord Mottistone; Lady Constance Kell; Mark Bonham Carter; Mrs Lional Hichens; F. M. P. Maurice; Hector Monro MP; Mrs J. Spencer-Ellison.

The following have helped me to gain access to institutional collections and facilitated my research: A. J. P. Taylor and the Trustees of the Beaverbrook Foundation; S. F. Wise and the staff of the Canadian Forces Headquarters Directorate of History; I. Maclean and the staff of the Commonwealth Archives Office, Canberra; J. G. Rose, Departmental Records Office, Ministry of Defence; A. R. C. Grant and the Trustees of the Centre for Military Archives, King's College, London; J. F. Russell, National Library of Scotland; Brigadier R. T. Thurburn and the Ogilby Trust; J. Atherton and the staff of the Public Archives of Canada; N. Evans and the staff of the Public Record Office.

I should also like to thank the following for their advice and counsel: Sir Philip Magnus-Allcroft; Professor Richard A. Preston; Dr J. W. Spurr; Colonel C. P. Stacey; Professor A. V. Tucker.

Abbreviations

B.D.	*British Documents on the Origins of the War 1898–1914*, London 1926–38
Beav.Lib.	Beaverbrook Library
Bodl.	Bodleian Library
B.M. Add. MSS.	British Museum Additional Manuscripts
K.C.L.	Centre for Military Archives, King's College, London
N.L.S.	National Library of Scotland
O.T.P.	Papers of the Ogilby Trust
P.R.O.	Public Record Office
W.O.Lib.	War Office Library

I
Army and Empire

The decades before the South African War of 1899 were self-confident ones for Great Britain. Although the first stirrings of independence were becoming apparent in the distant colonies, there existed no threat to the Empire of sufficient gravity to place its future in any great doubt. The continental powers were manoeuvring for security within a system of alliances, and did not begin to look outwards to colonial prizes until towards the end of the century. Even then, such possessions were symbols of prestige; not until the balance of power was irreparably upset in Europe was there real danger of war.

Mighty though her responsibilities were, Britain felt herself capable of discharging them all. Commercial success was inextricably intertwined with maritime preponderance, as Mahan would point out at the end of the century, and Britain's navy had long been the most powerful fleet the world had known. The fleet protected the Empire, which in its turn supplied the materials for future industrial growth: this future seemed almost one of geometrical progression to enormous wealth.

As part of this era of Victorian confidence there existed the attitude that, in foreign affairs, Britain was wisest to stay out of diplomatic agreements—one might almost call them entanglements. This was an attitude based upon naval hegemony and maritime position, but supported also by a belief in the capacities of the British army. When, in 1898, Germany made approaches to Great Britain about some form of détente, the military attaché in Berlin told the Kaiser that Britain should keep out of the continental alliance system, since 'we were strong enough to hold our own against either group'.[1] While that statement may have held good for naval engagements, it certainly did not if military action were contemplated.

Britain's island position meant that she missed out on a crucial military development in the middle years of the century. The confined continental powers, in establishing their spheres of influence, had been forced to develop sophisticated military machinery; the German wars of reunification and the Franco-Prussian War had driven home the lesson that warfare in a technological age must be guided by experts. Above all, the instrument of success was the General Staff—repository of strategic doctrine, fount of strategic advice, source of military plans. Lacking this, Britain was in a perilous position in the latter part of the century should it come to war with a continental power. In the period up to the end of the South African War, Britain was living militarily on borrowed time. It was fortunate for her that the ending of 'Splendid Isolation' coincided with, rather than preceded, the realization that the whole issue of strategic planning and direction needed considerable reform.

In 1854 there appeared little cause to doubt the security of Britain's large Imperial possessions. As yet they were not the target of acquisitive European powers, since the competition for a place in the sun was still to come. Nor did it appear that the strategic position in which England found herself warranted any great changes in her defence policy or in the tools with which she put it into operation. The army acted as a small but apparently effective police force and was fully capable of dealing with the disturbances which broke out with almost monotonous regularity in Afghanistan or Africa. Britain's naval supremacy was assured by her large fleet of men-of-war and her reserves of nautical skill and ability; not until the keel of the first iron-clad warship was laid down in France in 1858 was there any threat to her naval capabilities. There was, in fact, no hint of how the new weapons being forged by the industrial revolution were to change and make more demanding the task of defending the Empire, or of how perilous were to become the diplomatic machinations begun by Bismarck.

The Crimean War therefore appeared but a variation of the military expeditions to which Britain was fast becoming accustomed—on a somewhat larger scale perhaps, but essentially of the same calibre. The hardships and disasters of the war came as a salutary lesson as they revealed considerable defects in the capabilities of the War Office. As Sidney Herbert, then Secretary of State for War, remarked, 'We had to create an Army and use it at the same time.'[2] The war came, for England, to a successful conclusion, a fact which helped mask some of the resultant criticism. However, those well placed to observe the working of the system in the field were quite alive to its failures. As one such observer commented shortly after the war, the British Army was effective up to battalion level and no further:[3]

> We have no Brigades, Divisions, or Corps d'Armee in time of peace, no commissariat nor waggon train. The organization of these departments has to be commenced at the beginning of each war, and has been invariably broken up at the end of it. This is the reason that we have been generally unsuccessful in our first campaigns.

Nor was reform to follow, for the army of the nineteenth century was even less prone to profit from experience than that of the twentieth.

Success, an unwarranted sense of national complacency and stern demands for financial retrenchment all combined to prevent any reassessment of the state of England's defensive forces and of the army in particular. The only achievement, and it was not an unremarkable one, was that the offices of Secretary at War, responsible for finance, and Secretary of State for War were merged into one in February 1855 in the person of Panmure. When in 1858 the War Office moved to new quarters in Pall Mall, thirteen separate branches could compete with one another under the same roof.

The stifling effect of a peacetime administration served to prevent any successful reforms, although there were in the decade following the Crimea some eighty-nine commissions and committees.[4] The War Office lay undisturbed until the events in Austria in 1866 brought more clearly to the public eye the necessity for permanence, and perhaps a greater degree of professionalism, in military preparations. The Prussian success was due to nothing so much as its expert General Staff, which had been brought to a peak of efficiency over the previous seven years by the great von Moltke. But in England there was no comprehension of the value of such a body, and a proposal made by Sir Henry Brackenbury at that time for a similar institution was ignored.[5] None the less, it was becoming clearer that the Secretary of State for War needed a responsible source of professional advice to guide him in the creation of defence policy, rather than the hit-or-miss method of asking whomsoever he pleased, as had tended to be the case hitherto. The advent of Edward Cardwell as Secretary of State for War in 1868 heralded

3

a period of some thirty-four years of attempts at reforming the War Office.

Cardwell never really gained the understanding of the army. A successor to his office recalled him attending manoeuvres in 1871 dressed in a frock coat and a high hat, the laughing-stock of those present, both English and German.[6] He was nevertheless concerned about his ministerial responsibility for the War Office, and concerned also that his sources of advice be regularized. He therefore followed the recommendations of Lord Northbrooke's committee of 1869 and split the administrative responsibility into three: the office of the Commander-in-Chief would be solely responsible for the military advice given to the Secretary of State; the department of the Surveyor General of Ordnance was to control supply, transport, construction and *matériel*; and estimates and accounts would be handled by the Financial Secretary's department.

This scheme appeared to some contemporaries to direct too much responsibility out of the purlieus of the military element. None the less, to interpret this as the beginning of a period of dominance by the civil servants which lasted until 1895, when it was replaced by a brief ten-year interlude of rule by the military, would be false.[7] The Secretary of State for War ruled, and continued to rule. As the century progressed, various occupants of that post sought different ways of obtaining professional advice and help in running the different portions of the office. The degree to which they centralized affairs, and thus brought civil servants and soldiers into overt opposition, varied in proportion to the strength of their belief that they had a burden of parliamentary responsibility to safeguard. This became clearer in the succeeding decades. The tripartite structure erected under the provisions of Cardwell's War Office Act of 1870 was a first step in this direction; it also masked the possible dangers of a direct confrontation between the civil and military elements in the War Office which was later to become the predominant factor in any discussions of reform.

Though the Commander-in-Chief now had a statutory responsibility to tender strategic advice to the Secretary of State for War, there was as yet little upon which he could rely to aid him apart from his own intuition. The idea of a General Staff on continental lines had been dismissed, but a specialist department did make its appearance at this time which was later to form the basis for the establishment of such a body in 1904. The initiative again came from Edward Cardwell who, on 1 April 1873, established in the War Office an Intelligence Department including topographical and statistical sections.[8]

The section grew rapidly, and by 1875 it had a staff of thirty-eight. The defence and topographical sections retained general responsibilities while the statistical section, following a basic principle which was to remain unchanged, was divided into sections with different geographical responsibilities. Such was the importance of France and Belgium that they rated all of section A, while Prussia came under the aegis of section D, together with Spain, Portugal, India, Persia and Japan. The colonies and colonial defence appeared rather more pressing and they comprised section B. Two other sections dealt with the other major countries of the globe.

Such was the concept of staff duties then current that the department was assigned no more than the task of amassing information and presenting it upon request. It was this conceptual failure, the almost total lack of understanding of the constructive role which the department might play, which was one of the most severe hindrances in the development of a sophisticated machinery for defence planning. Nor was this lack of initiative confined within the walls of the War Office alone; as Sir Richard Harrison subsequently recorded, 'On looking back at the way in which the Staff duties were carried out [in the Regular Army] I am under the impression that there was plenty of room for improvement.'[9]

The short but important era of reform at the War Office was not capable of sustained momentum, and came to an end with the advent of Disraeli's administration of 1874. The electorate may indeed have been expressing a wish to call a pause in the tide of reforms, albeit subconsciously, with this device.[10] The army moved into what Sir Garnet Wolseley called the six years of peace, to be interrupted by yet another Liberal Secretary of State in 1880. Hugh Childers then modified Cardwell's system whereby battalions had been linked in pairs, one at home and one overseas, and introduced four battalion brigades on a territorial basis. During these years the Empire found itself singularly free of any military threat, and therefore the War Office was absolved from having to do any serious thinking about defence.

The 1870s and 1880s saw Great Britain approaching the pinnacle of her power and prosperity. She lay at the centre of a thriving two-way traffic in which tribute, in the form of raw materials, was brought from the Empire along sea lanes secured by the might of the Royal Navy. In return England exported the 'civilizing' experience of Empire. Yet in a few short years, between 1885 and 1890, this eminently satisfactory state of affairs was to be changed almost beyond recognition. Defence of the Empire was to become 'Imperial Defence', whereby the fleet was to be concentrated for a major naval action within the vicinity of the United Kingdom rather than parcelled out amongst the colonies and naval stations, and the army was to battle for a role in defence and lose.

The first signs of the changes to come appeared in September 1884, when the *Pall Mall Gazette* published a polemic entitled 'What is the Truth about the Navy?' with information covertly supplied by Sir John Fisher. Briefly put, the truth about the navy appeared to be that it was not as invincible as the public had been led to believe, in fact that it was barely capable of defending the Empire at all. At the same time, the colonies were becoming alarmed at the prospect that the Empire might need more adequate defence than it appeared to have. Self-defence had been a heady doctrine begotten as a by-product of the period when the colonies had been granted self-government, reaching a climax in 1868–74.[11] In 1885 Australia and New Zealand began to grow anxious about the degree to which Germany appeared to be penetrating the islands to the north, particularly New Guinea and the Solomon Islands.[12] They were quick to communicate this anxiety to the mother-country.

An intensifying process of examination of the problems of Imperial defence began in that same year with the refounding of the Colonial Defence Committee, which was to last until the creation of the Committee of Imperial Defence, and interested itself industriously in all manner of problems of Imperial defence. In doing so it was to make many enemies.[13] The concern evidenced by the colonies also contributed to a revival of the idea of a Colonial Conference, and the first such conference met in 1887. Australia was quite clear that she needed rather more than she currently had in the way of a naval force, and was sufficiently agitated to agree at the conference to contribute to the tune of £126,000 a year towards a naval squadron in

Australian waters.[14] This was to begin the long wrangle about the degree to which control of colonial and dominion defence forces should be placed in the hands of Great Britain, one in which the navy, because of its very mobility, was to play a key role.

At the same time the foundations of naval defence were being shaken by the dramatic discovery that the Royal Navy could not take the offensive against a blockade mounted by one power alone.[15] The prospects for Imperial defence were alarming. They were magnified by events across the Channel, where the turns of French politics had brought into office the bellicose General Boulanger and, as Minister of Marine, Admiral Hycinthe Aube. Aube espoused the school of *guerre de course*, the raiding of commerce by cruisers to which Britain was now patently vulnerable. Far from being confident that the navy could protect the Empire, the public was beginning to wonder whether the navy could even protect the home island itself.

At just this moment, the army was going through a less well-remarked and less publicized crisis about its own abilities. Sir Henry Brackenbury, now the Director of Military Intelligence, examined the problem of what force could if necessary be put into the field. To mobilize one army corps would mean the purchase of 8,000 extra horses and filling gaps in commissariat, transport, medical and veterinary staff; to mobilize a second would require a further 11,000 horses, and it would possess no Regular artillery, no transport corps and no medical staff whatsoever. Even Belgium, with a population one sixth the size of England's, could field two army corps. The conclusion Brackenbury reached was bleak: 'for want of the departmental services, we cannot place two complete Army Corps in the field, either for foreign service or home defence.'[16]

In the face of this the strategic picture was unprepossessing. Brackenbury saw Russia as the power most hostile to Great Britain, and reported that plans had been obtained of a Russian advance on India via Herat. The possibility of a Russo-French alliance against England was clearly worrying the Intelligence Department since they could see no hope of meeting it, particularly with mobilization in such a parlous state and without any comprehensive defence plans. Moreover, they could add to the fears being expressed by the Admiralty with the statement 'London, the richest town in the world, lies undefended at the mercy of the invader.'[17]

7

Unaware of the immense debate which was about to erupt, the army attempted to resolve the question as best it could. In December 1886 a special Mobilization Committee decided that two army corps was the standard to be aimed at, and they began manfully to attempt a task which eluded many successive secretaries of state. A special post to deal with mobilization was created within the Intelligence Department in 1887, but Brackenbury was fully conscious of the puny powers and weak position of the new department. He wrote to a colleague:[18]

> The more I think the matter over, the more I feel that although we have, in our mobilization scheme, laid the foundations of a great national work, we have only laid the foundations, and that the whole super-structure has yet to be built.

He was confirmed in his pessimism when it became apparent later in the year that there was very little chance of mobilizing one corps for foreign service, let alone two, particularly because of lack of cavalry.[19]

At this juncture, the Intelligence Department found itself involved in one episode in what was a continuing battle with the Treasury throughout the period. The view of the permanent officials at the Treasury about any expenditure by the War Office was clear and uncompromising: 'The Military and Naval departments cannot undertake and execute a new work, however small, without Treasury assent.'[20] This attitude was reaffirmed by Sir Reginald Welby in 1887, when he stated that the Treasury should be very chary of advancing any money to the War Office for its Intelligence Department in view of the recent creation of a Naval Intelligence Department. Welby also deplored Stanhope's request for a 20 per cent increase in the grant to the War Office Intelligence Department on the grounds that it would then be perfect; he warned the Chancellor against the tendency of service officers to create excess places for their comrades.

Goschen, then Chancellor of the Exchequer, was sympathetic to the demands of the services, as many of his colleagues were not. He replied that he had only been in charge of his department for four months, but already: 'I have been rather struck by the uniform and almost constant attitude of positive hostility taken up by various officers of the Treasury towards Naval and

Military Officers generally.' Whether or not all service officers looked upon reforms merely as a chance to create jobs for themselves and their comrades, he felt it unfortunate that this view should be constantly reiterated in internal memoranda. The power of special arguments in individual cases was diminished when they were always being reinforced by reference to 'the innate wickedness of the great services'.[21] None the less, Welby succeeded in preventing any increase in War Office expenditure.

Treasury control continued to exercise the minds of the permanent officials throughout the period. In 1902 Chalmers, then Financial Secretary, prepared a memorandum reminding the Treasury that individual estimates could not be submitted to parliament without Treasury sanction. Such sanction was also necessary even if the War Office wished to transfer money between subheads of the same Vote. Three years later it was Welby again who pointed out that the Treasury had other means of control over military expenditure if it wished to exercise them. Technically all ways and means were voted to the Crown and then placed at the disposal of the Treasury by Royal Order. More important, under section 27 of the Exchequer and Audit Act of 1886 the Treasury had the power to forbid the sanction of any expenditure in an Appropriations account which, in the opinion of the Auditor General, was not supported by the Treasury.[22] Although these powers were never mobilized, the issue of principle behind them affected relations between the Treasury and the War Office and stiffened the former's reluctance to disburse funds to the Intelligence Department throughout the period. Assured that it would never get a sympathetic hearing in matters of finance, the task of the Intelligence Department was made the harder.

Parsimony played a part in the manner in which Brackenbury ran his department, although he also seems to have been lacking in any appreciation of how to make it influential in the wheels of government. The instructions he gave Sir Charles Callwell when the latter joined the office in 1887 serve as a guide to his view of the functions of his officers:[23]

I shan't expect you . . . to be able to answer every question that may arise in respect to your particular work, right off the wheel; I shan't even expect the information to be actually available in the department. But I shall expect you not to be helpless, but to find means of getting that information somehow within a reasonable time. If you keep your wits about you, if you look ahead, if, when anything crops up that you do not know all about you set yourself to find out all about it, if you keep sucking in information into the place and if you see that [it] is properly registered and so made available when required, your particular section will in course of time become a real going concern.

As a system this was not designed to encourage initiative or foster growth from within the department. It is scarcely surprising that few of the officers then within the Intelligence Department were subsequently to distinguish themselves. A general spirit of amateurism prevailed, and was summed up in Callwell's comment that the most agreeable part of the work was the opportunity it offered 'to visit at the public expense parts of the world which one might otherwise never have seen'.[24]

It was against this confused background that, in 1888, a major debate over defence blew up which was to have long lasting effects. The cry rose from the lips of the public, with some support from the press, of 'England in danger' since it seemed that the Royal Navy could no longer defend the home islands. A sizeable school demanded the fortification of London, and gained the influential support of the leading soldier of the day, Lord Wolseley. The political condition of France served to heighten the atmosphere of tension, and there were many references to the Duke of Wellington's celebrated warning in 1847 that 'except under the fire of Dover Castle, there is not a spot on the coast on which infantry might not be thrown on shore at any time'.[25]

Such a claim was not without advantage to the army, for it might ensure them a greater share in national defence and with it a larger portion of the budget with which to effect a badly needed overhaul and increase of the armed forces. The House of Lords gathered on 14 May 1888 to hear Wolseley justify his alarm in numbers so considerable that it was the largest gathering Lord Salisbury could recall. Wolseley's own opinion was that, aside from garrisons for India and the colonies, three Regular Army Corps and six cavalry brigades were needed for home defence alone, and a further two army corps for any planned embarkation.[26]

Shortly after Wolseley's provocative statement, Admiral Lord Charles Beresford resigned from the navy to fight for the introduction of the two-power standard, a device designed to ensure that the British fleet was of sufficient size to defeat the combined navies of the next two largest maritime powers. A school of naval strategists rapidly arose to assert that in fact both problems were capable of the same solution if Beresford's ideas were adopted: the way to protect the Empire and to ensure that any attempted invasion of the British Isles was doomed to defeat lay in the command of the sea. This could only be achieved by a heavy programme of naval building which would ensure that a fleet existed in being of sufficient might to secure that command, should it ever be at risk. The founders of this 'Blue Water' school, as it became known, were the brothers Philip and Charles Colomb; they were soon joined by a galaxy of sailors and academics including Julian Corbett and Professor Sir John Knox Laughton.[27]

It was the misfortune of the army that it had no intellectual thesis to present as a counterpoise, that it had in fact no school of theorists acquainted with problems of a similar size and scope. No political decisions had ever been made about the role of the army, so that few had analysed the possible military roles which Britain might have to fulfil in a continental or European war. Evidence of this insularity was clear in the writings of the day; until 1914 Cardwell's *Small Wars: Their Principles and Practice* was 'the only work with any claim to originality'.[28] Whether or not they could have put up a convincing thesis in the resulting debate, and this is doubtful, the military failed totally to counter the invasion argument. The Naval Defence Act of 1889, which sanctioned an expenditure of £21,500,000 on the two-power standard, clearly indicated that the senior service had triumphed; moreover, the navy had a commercial as well as a prophylactic value, and expenditure on it was the more acceptable in that it would protect the trade as well as the persons of the inhabitants of the United Kingdom.

It was the misfortune of the army that it lost the debate over invasion on all possible grounds. Though some money did go to the construction of permanent fortifications, at a cost in 1888 of £160,671,[29] the great bulk of available finance went to the navy. Yet the War Office was unable to accept the thesis of command of the sea and the ability of the navy to fend off any attempted invasion; they felt they now had this additional responsibility, which contributed to a preoccupation with defence and the prospect of invasion which would survive until 1905. The only guidance they got from the government came in a memorandum from the Secretary of State for War, Edward Stanhope, which appeared in 1888 and put as their foremost role the effective support of the civil power within the United Kingdom. Duties in India, at fortresses and coaling stations and for home defence followed in that order of priority. The probability of employing the army in any continental role was thought sufficiently unlikely to make it 'the primary duty of the military authorities to organize our forces efficiently for the defence of this country'.[30] The reasoning behind Stanhope's ordering of priorities, which was more suited to the conditions of 1818 than those of 1888, is still far from clear; but it did have the effect of stultifying any ideas of constructing a military philosophy for the defence of the Empire. Sir William Robertson subsequently claimed that it was due to Stanhope's memorandum that the 'broad military plans essential for the defence of the Empire as a whole' were not properly examined and drawn up.[31]

Although in many ways disastrous for the army, the debate over invasion in 1888 did have one important by-product. During the course of it, it became abundantly clear that co-operation between the services was almost non-existent. As a result a commission was set up under the chairmanship of Lord Hartington, to enquire into the administration of the naval and military departments and their relations with the Treasury. Hartington's concern was chiefly to secure a more efficient system of advice for the Cabinet and particularly for the Secretary of State for War; in a speech made in 1890 he spoke of the necessity of direct control over the army being in the hands of someone responsible to Parliament.[32] The obstacle to this was the person of the Commander-in-Chief, the Duke of Cambridge. A man of unshakeable resolve and conservative convictions, Cambridge had dominated the administration of the army· for some twenty-five years.

The Commission's second report, published in 1890, was for the army the crucial one. This remarked on the over-centralization on the person of the Commander-in-Chief and the lack of a satisfactory system to enable the Secretary of State to obtain independent advice. It advocated abolishing the former office, and replacing it with a General Officer Commanding Great

Britain, and a greater definition of departmental duties in the War Office. The Hartington Commission was very well aware of the need to secure professional advice for the Secretary of State based upon a consensus of opinion rather than the view of one or more individuals. Accordingly it urged the creation of a permanent War Office Council to give independent advice, the council to consist of a newly created Chief of Staff as well as four senior military officials and four civilian members.

Hartington had grasped the fact that one of the most important factors restraining the development of the high command of the army and frustrating the younger officers was the very presence of the Duke of Cambridge. Such was his weight and influence that, no matter how much his position was modified, as long as he remained in his office at the Horse Guards there would never be the freedom of discussion necessary 'to enable a civilian Minister adequately to decide, rightly and justly the question of War Office administration'.[33]

A combination of factors prevented any attempts to put the recommendations of the report into effect. The popularity of the Duke of Cambridge played a part as did opposition from Queen Victoria and Wolseley, then Adjutant-General.[34] Lord Salisbury did not approve of any alteration in the position of the Commander-in-Chief, while the Cabinet were not disposed to allow the intervention of a Chief of Staff 'in any form'.[35] The Duke showed himself prepared to accept a moderate reform, suggesting that Wolseley's successor be styled 'Chief of the Staff and Adjutant General' and exercise the duties of Chief of Staff to the Commander-in-Chief. To this Stanhope replied:[36]

> I feel sure that the Cabinet would not agree. They have not decided, and they do not now intend to decide upon some of the grave questions raised by the Report of Lord Harting-ton's Commission; and to adopt the totally opposite policy [i.e. that advocated by Cambridge] is a step which they would not now be prepared to take.

As an outcome of the invasion debate, the Hartington Commission had offered a real chance that the War Office might get an up-to-date structure and particularly a Chief of Staff. This in turn could have been a stepping-stone to a General Staff on continental lines and thus to the professional examination of strategy and the evolution of a strategic school of thought. But this innovation had met strong opposition from conservative and liberal elements alike. Even Campbell-Bannerman, who was engaged between 1892 and 1895 in drawing up a plan to lessen the powers of the Commander-in-Chief, was fearful that a Chief of the General Staff would militate against the council idea and might become a 'Pope'.[37] Having lost this chance, the Intelligence Department had to struggle on as best it could.

Brackenbury's successor as Director of Military Intelligence from 1891, Major-General E. F. Chapman, laboured manfully but futilely against the notions of static home defence which were paralysing the army after the invasion debate. His isolation from other departments was so great that he was forced to ask Coleridge Grove of the Mobilization Division to send papers to him so that he could keep track of developments. He was also blocked by lack of money; this coupled with Campbell-Bannerman's lack of appreciation even of the value of building up the collection of maps in the department greatly hindered his attempts to expand the vision of the department.[38]

Chapman strongly opposed the defensive attitude of the War Office, embodied in the plans for fortifications around London which currently occupied so much of its time and energy. He would much rather have spent his money on the field army than on fortifications, yet since he was never consulted over schemes of mobilization for home defence he had little chance to put over this view. He also had a wider view of strategy than many of his contemporaries, and expressed a concern that Britain should always be able to fortify India if a war broke out and to give it further reinforcements if necessary. The interest of the Russians in the bridge building of the Canadian Pacific Railway aroused in him some alarm over possible Russian designs on Turkestan.[39] Yet he was by no means an alarmist, and viewing the advances of the continental armies in 1892 recognized that while they were reaching a peak militarily, especially in Russia, yet there was no diplomatic danger of war in the following year.

Chapman had little respect for the abilities or prescience of Gladstone's cabinet:[40]

The present Govt., I think, means to do as little as it possibly can, to spend as little and to initiate as little as may be, and to carry on on the lines of the late administration except as regards Ireland.

He did make some small advances, initiating a study of raids on a local scale, and ensuring that his officers kept in touch with the army through regular attendance at manoeuvres as umpires. However, such were the limits of his powers that he could do no more than express the hope that at some stage in the future there would be a regular scheme for Imperial defence.

The last decade of the nineteenth century saw rapid and ominous political and diplomatic changes in Europe which were to have great effects on the defence structure of England. As the links between France and Russia were strengthened between 1892 and 1895 the strategic outlook became much blacker. The twin threats of invasion and attack on India together dictated a reappraisal of British foreign and defence policy. It was the diplomatic stimulus which was to be of greatest importance, and during these years England moved out of isolation and into what has been termed a period of uncertainty.[41] However, it still needed the experience of the Boer War to provide the necessary impetus to widen strategic horizons and begin serious strategic planning.

During these years, the 'Blue Water' school of defence theorists were producing a flood of polemic designed to propagate the view that the navy was the foremost and best line of defence for England and Empire alike. Sir Charles Dilke and Spenser Wilkinson collaborated to write *Imperial Defence* in 1892. Their readers were wooed with the satisfying assertion that 'The Ocean is, in fact, a British possession.'[42] It was then demonstrated that a stronger navy would be the panacea for all ills, even for the defence of India which was clearly becoming ever more vulnerable as diplomatic alignments changed: 'In other words, the peace of India depends upon Great Britain having an efficient army at home and retaining the command of the sea.'[43] The army was relegated to the second division of British defence. Its most important tasks were to garrison naval bases and to protect Great Britain against a *coup-de-main*, the only eventuality in which the navy was at all doubtful of success. It then had to fulfil Imperial garrison tasks and wage small wars, counter-attack on enemy territory where necessary, and finally put up a resistance *en masse* to invasion in case of absolute naval disaster.

Of the many works of this type produced in the last years of the century, one more must be mentioned. Bearing the same title as Dilke and Wilkinson's work, it came from one of the foremost proponents of the 'Blue Water' school who was shortly to become influential as first secretary of the Committee of Imperial Defence, Sir George Clarke. As secretary of the Colonial Defence Committee from 1885 to 1892 he spoke from an authoritative viewpoint. Clarke stressed the view that colonial self-government was the ideal but that it should be accompanied by definite links with England, rather as Burke had done a century before. The commerce of the Empire was unapproachable by any rival, and naval strength alone could adequately defend it. The best way to protect that commerce was to mask the enemy fleet in its home waters—and since the enemy then appeared to be France, this meant concentration at home. Clarke offered the persuasive argument that the British were particularly well fitted to adopt such a policy since they possessed 'a natural aptitude for maritime warfare'.[44]

Public opinion was intensely concerned with the question of defence, particularly when couched in terms of such immediacies as the threat to trade and the danger of a foreign invasion. Much popular literature appeared on the latter theme, and was in many ways a vehicle for the 'Blue Water' school to mobilize public opinion in their favour.[45] In 1895 Alfred Harmsworth used the *frisson* of terror it provided to try to get himself elected at Portsmouth; his own Portsmouth *Daily Mail* ran a serial entitled 'The Invasion of Portsmouth' and astonished local residents saw themselves featured by name in its tale of terror. In this case theatrical means were insufficient to get him elected.

It was unfortunate that it was the naval Imperialists who were also suggesting reforms of defence structure which were, by their very source, suspect in the eyes of the army. In 1890 Spenser Wilkinson wrote a descriptive work on the German General Staff designed to demonstrate the necessity for a similar institution in Britain. He was quite certain that it was only by means of such an institution that the necessary professional outlook could be instilled into the army:[46]

> it may be asserted with confidence that the high average of practical ability secured in the superior officers of the Prussian Army is due in the main to the practice of selection, the careful inspection by the superiors at every stage, and to the mature wisdom by which the higher education of the General Staff is directed.

However, neither he nor Dilke had much influence in the War Office. Dilke probably suffered from the unsavoury scandal of his divorce and certainly from dislike within the army of his other recommendations on naval and military matters. The proposal put forward by an all-party group of Dilke, Wilkinson, H. O. Arnold Forster and Sir George Chesney for a Ministry of Defence failed to make any great impression on the army because it threatened to deprive the War Office of what power it had left and hand all over to the 'Blue Water' adherents.[47]

It was because the War Office was profoundly suspicious of the outlook of the Colonial Defence Committee that it by-passed that body repeatedly and even got it dissolved in December 1892. This was clearly a defensive action by the less adventurous members of the War Office; Chapman very much regretted its departure. It was, however, sufficiently well established for its demise to last only one month. At the same time, Balfour pressed for a Defence Committee of the Cabinet as a half-way step towards a Ministry of Defence. The concern of the 'Blue Water' school and their successful propagation of the theories of domination of the sea were instrumental in bringing about a growth of the idea of a central body for defence planning.[48] But it should be stressed that there was no remarkable change in outlook during this period—rather a reordering and putting into practical form of earlier ideas and institutions. The War Office had had a council from 1870, and although it met only sporadically and rarely attained the heights of higher defence policy, the presence of several major parliamentary officials argues a not unsophisticated level of advice even before Hartington's report.[49] It needed only revision and expansion.

It is clear also that the Colonial Defence Committee, in its early years, tended in like manner to concern itself more with organization and procedure than with strategy in any broad sense. When it did turn to problems of Imperial defence it showed a concern over the centralization of Imperial naval forces which was clearly in line with the 'Blue Water' theories of defence and invasion.[50] The navy had a role, and the army had not—in fact the army appeared in serious danger of losing out in every strategic concern to the navy. It was for this reason that many in the War Office strenuously resisted the naval view of invasion, and looked askance at institutions which seemed to embody the 'Blue Water' doctrines. At the eleven meetings of the joint Landing Places Committee between 1891 and 1894 the extent of this headlong clash of strategic philosophies was clearly apparent. The army firmly believed that the more time an invader had the more likely he was to be successful, while the navy contended that ten days was an insufficient time in which to prepare and launch an invasion and that after that time its own strength would render such invasion futile.[51]

The impact of the naval Imperialist school did cause the continued advance of defence institutions, though it did not, as has been claimed, bring about a turning point.[52] In many ways it retarded the development of a co-operative examination of the problems of defence facing the Empire, since the army could not agree with the 'Blue Water' school and thereby consciously relegate itself to second place in everything, not least the allocation of financial resources. It was not until problems of Imperial defence were modified by continental considerations, until Britain emerged from her diplomatic isolation to realize the necessity for continental alignments and the related problems which they threw up, that the army could afford to surrender an old role and adopt a new one.

Moreover, the concept of colonial unity was an illusory one in that it meant no more than the utilization of colonial resources for defence within home waters. It was not until Chamberlain arrived at the Colonial Office on 1 July 1895 that any real desire to further closer union with the colonies became apparent. Lord Salisbury had little sympathy with the aspirations of the self-governing colonies, and for their part they looked suspiciously upon the proposal made in 1900 for an Imperial Council.[53] In so far as Imperial defence implied true Imperial co-operation, it was a myth.

The degree to which the War Office's strategic thinking became dominated by the need to disprove the 'Blue Water' school and take a key role in the invasion issue was clearly displayed in the office of Director of Military Intelligence under Chapman's successor from 1 April 1896, Colonel Sir John Ardagh. His appointment seemed to offer a good chance to advance the work and status of his department: Ardagh had the reputation of being one of the foremost 'politico-military' officers in the army, and an authority on international law. He was also a personal friend of the new Commander-in-Chief, Lord Wolseley, who had replaced the aged Duke of Cambridge the previous year, of the senior officers of the army and of many leading statesmen. But Ardagh became preoccupied with the question of invasion and seems to have had no ideas about the value of a capital staff. In a memorandum on 'Organization for War' prepared in January 1900, he made no mention of the provision or functions of such a staff.[54]

The main preoccupation of the new DMI was to minimize the role of the navy in Home Defence. He advanced the view that wherever a definite locality had to be defended, forts were infinitely superior to ships. They were cheaper, more reliable since they were not subject to the destructive attentions of torpedoes, rams or storms, and their gunfire was more accurate. Ardagh's strategic argument was a subtle one, rather more advanced than the outright hostility shown in the Landing Places Committee. The fleet must have 'absolute and unfettered freedom of movement to pursue the enemy'; this the army could give it through fortifications and a prime responsibility to defend the home island against attack. Moreover, the military must be able to protect the capital against 'such enterprises as an enemy may be able to undertake, in the absence, or temporary disablement of the fleet'.[55]

Ardagh's preoccupation with invasion was a logical one within the framework of the contest between the services for a role in home defence, and was widely shared before and during this period. A colleague had remarked upon this some years before:[56]

Grove [of the Mobilization Department] is even madder than you are on the subject of invasion and is recasting the various schemes from the point of view of the probability of our finding the French army on our breakfast tables with *The Times* tomorrow morning.

When external problems of the Russian presence in the Middle East and the protection of the Mediterranean did impinge upon this preoccupation, the newly created Cabinet Defence Committee proved no help in getting them fully considered. Lord Lansdowne admitted that as he and his colleagues became 'busier and busier with Land Bills and suchlike rubbish' the big questions of strategy facing the Empire slid quickly into the background.[57]

If the necessary width of vision was lacking on many sides, it was also true that financial opposition hindered any development of the functions of Ardagh's department. Frequently the final argument against any necessary improvement was that an increase in the budget would imperil the ministerial majority and be resented in the constituencies. Ardagh held that 'the chain of responsibility extends upwards to the Treasury, the Chancellor of the Exchequer, the Cabinet, the House of Commons and finally the British public.'[58] This argument was only partly true, for the War Office itself could be as great a hindrance as anyone. Ardagh requested £18,000 a year for ten years from the Treasury, and was eventually offered £100. Having other matters to press which it felt more important, the War Office had not passed on the demand.[59]

The weakness of what passed for the army's closest approximation to a General Staff became glaringly apparent on the outbreak of the South African War in 1899. No strategic appreciations or plans worth the name existed; even maps were in perilously short supply. In large part this strategic oversight was a result of the preoccupation with invasion which had ruled the previous decade. The horizons of the War Office had contracted as they fought what they had regarded, and continued to regard, as a desperate battle for money.[60] The sums they were given were certainly insufficient for the tasks they were expected to perform. Between 1896 and 1899 the Intelligence Department was allotted £20,000, of which £2,000 was spent on duties connected with South Africa. It was subsequently estimated that the Topographical Department alone required £17,000 p.a. to perform its duties adequately, in addition to £150,000 p.a. for a topographical survey of the Empire.[61] The pressure of Imperial defence was simply not great enough to produce anywhere near this amount.

Something might have been salvaged from the mass of conflicting ideas and priorities had the War Office reordered its administration to recognize the priorities of efficient defence planning, but it did not. The steady move towards professional advice reached an uneasy compromise with an Order in Council of 21 December 1895 whereby the Commander-in-Chief became responsible for decisions on military matters whilst heads of military departments within the War Office were given increased responsibility and direct access to the Secretary of State. In part this was a belated attempt to follow one of the tenets of the Hartington Commission, that the C.-in-C. was too strong *vis-à-*

vis the Secretary of State. But it contained the seeds of considerable disarray since it meant that heads of department were now simultaneously responsible to both. The War Office now had a board and a Commander-in-Chief, an unhappy amalgam and one with which the Commander-in-Chief was not pleased.

The sad truth was that Wolseley was not sufficiently endowed to cope with the demands which changing diplomacy was making on him. Temperamentally he was out of sympathy with the politicians, whom he disliked for conforming to 'the democratic system of the day'.[62] He was frequently absent from his office through illness, and in any case had no ideas about the value he might get from the assistance of a Chief of Staff. He pitched his complaints at the customary level, arguing that either the Commander-in-Chief should be given full powers or else he should be abolished. Failing to achieve anything by this, Wolseley nevertheless resisted all attempts by his subordinates to avail themselves of their statutory access to the Secretary of State.[63]

The task of fighting a campaign in South Africa brought the War Office up short; all its lucubrations about invasion were set at nought as it became apparent that, through neglect and misunderstanding, it had never formed the machinery necessary to compile a comprehensive strategic scheme for action within the Empire. It was not until December 1899, some months after the war had begun, that any thought was given to the question of security intelligence; then a new section was created under Major J. E. Edmonds, H section, which was in later years to become MI 5. There was also a reshuffling of duties within the department so that the sections responsible for France and Germany were freed from responsibility for any other areas. However, much of the value of this reorganization was lost since, on the outbreak of war, most of the experienced staff officers left to fight in the field. The withdrawal of many of its staff and the presentation of poor candidates meant that the Staff College was unable to make good the losses.[64] Hard work perforce became the order of the day, and one civilian remarked—not without regret—that the days when the War Office was fit for a gentleman came to an end with the Boer War.[65]

A novel situation demanded new men as well as new measures, and on 27 October 1900 Lord Salisbury, who had for some weeks had Lansdowne's resignation before him, offered the War Office to St John Brodrick, adding 'You know the post too well to require that I should expound to you its advantages or its drawbacks.'[66] The new incumbent was all too well aware of what the Prime Minister meant, and accepted the post with the rider that he must have Salisbury's support against the Treasury to reconstruct his department. He then turned to the foremost soldier of the day, and telegraphed to Lord Roberts for his suggestions on the matter of staff. The list of remedies Roberts returned in reply included attracting a better class of recruit, generally raising the standard of military life, and improving the marksmanship of the army. It contained nothing about the necessity, or otherwise, for a modern General Staff or for strategic planning. Brodrick plunged himself into the vexed question of the size of the army and worked on a scheme for the provision of six army corps which he presented to the House of Commons in spring the following year, when it was 'accepted with acclamation'.[67]

Roberts was, however, more aware of the need for reform than he appeared, and on being appointed Commander-in-Chief in succession to Wolseley he offered a new post of Director-General of Mobilization and Intelligence to Sir William Nicholson. Superficially Nicholson, who was subsequently to become the first Chief of the Imperial General Staff, was poorly qualified for such a position. He had never commanded a unit in action nor had he passed through the Staff College, and his entire military career up until 1899 had been spent in India. None the less he accepted the position, and was to prove an immense success, grasping the potential of his new department and willing to fight for it against all comers.

Roberts had an early brush with the Treasury over the new post when, in June 1901, he raised it to an equal status with that of Adjutant-General and proposed an increase in pay from £1,500 p.a. to £2,100 p.a. The Chancellor of the Exchequer, Sir Michael Hicks Beach, was unwilling to countenance such expenditure unless the pay of the Adjutant-General was correspondingly reduced from £2,400 by £600.[68] A compromise was eventually concluded whereby each was paid £2,100 but the episode was a clear indication of the difficulties consequent upon any attempts to expand the branch.

The duties of the new post were defined as part of an Order in Council of 4 November 1901. Under the control of the

Commander-in-Chief, Nicholson was entrusted with the preparation and maintenance of detailed plans for the military defence of the Empire, the preparation of schemes of offensive and defensive operations, the mobilization of regular and auxiliary forces and the collection and distribution of information relating to the military geography, resources, and armed forces of foreign countries and of the British colonies and possessions.[69] The great bulk of these responsibilities was new, and Nicholson threw himself into them with gusto. A week after his appointment he informed Lord Roberts that 'I have ordered a beginning to be made in preparing a scheme of offensive and defensive operations, the first, being to meet such a contingency as a war with France and Russia combined.'[70]

A further stimulus to the development of the department occurred with the arrival on 1 January 1901, as head of the Foreign and Indian Section (2), of Lieutenant-Colonel W. R. Robertson. On his arrival he found only one up-to-date statement of the military resources of a foreign country. By January 1903 he had changed the heads of three of his four subsections, had begun the concentration on foreign military developments and manoeuvres, and considerably increased the volume of translation work. There was also a much greater concern with the planning of campaigns and the consideration of strategic problems, an advance aided by the head of the Strategical Section (1), Lieutenant-Colonel E. A. Altham. Remembered by a contemporary stalking the corridors with measured tread and speaking in a masterful if gruff drawl, his approbation expressed by a pleasant grunt, Robertson was held in universal high esteem.[71]

Nicholson at once sought battle with the Treasury. In November 1901 he requested an addition of eight officers, which would add to the annual cost of £14,760 the sum of £4,356. The Chancellor of the Exchequer, shown the proposals privately, proved absolutely unwilling to countenance them. The following January Nicholson made another request to Brodrick, halving his demands. He pointed to the immense resources of the German General Staff and warned that skimping his department was a false economy. Put to Hicks Beach, the request met with another flat refusal. The Chancellor felt that other unspecified agencies might do some of the work of Nicholson's section, and in any case he expected far too much:[72]

It is not possible, during a war, for an Intelligence department to be occupying itself with 'comprehensive schemes of offensive and defensive operations' (i.e. what at Oxford is called 'research') in the way that it naturally would be in time of peace.

However, Nicholson sought the support of the recent Order in Council, claiming correctly that under it he had been placed in charge of what had previously been no one's business.

With the backing of Lord Roberts, Nicholson made a formal request on 5 July 1902 for an expansion of his department to include eleven additional officers at a cost of £5,680 p.a. This request so alarmed the financial department of the War Office that it recommended a departmental committee to thrash out the question before the next year's estimates were prepared, the sum involved being 'so considerable'. A committee of four was duly formed under the chairmanship of the Parliamentary Under Secretary of State for War, Lord Hardwicke, to examine the establishment of the Intelligence Division.

Nicholson's requests were modest and were supported by witnesses called from within his department. But as outside evidence was called it became alarmingly clear how little the rest of the army understood the value of the division, or indeed of strategic planning at all. Ardagh did give the proposals some support, and thought it not impossible that the Intelligence Division should lay down a plan of campaign which could be followed by a General Officer in the Field. He also envisaged the department developing into 'something like the German General Staff'. The attitude of the other witnesses varied from disinterest to something verging on outright hostility to this idea. The Adjutant-General, Sir Thomas Kelly Kenny, felt that so-called paper schemes were of even less value to British soldiers than to any others because 'our military problems are much more liable to be modified by the accidental circumstances of the particular case'. His opposition to the department bordered on the pathological, and he accused Nicholson of trespassing on his own authority by sending executive telegrams to South Africa. To him, paper schemes were no more than 'pious aspirations': the brain of the army should be the General commanding in the field.

That one of the senoir officials of the War Office should display such a blinkered attitude was bad enough, but it soon became apparent that it was shared by the young field commanders fresh from South Africa. Sir Ian Hamilton gave it as his opinion that it was impossible to foresee political developments and therefore that draft schemes served only as mental exercises and training. Sir John French agreed that the commander in the field should form his own scheme, 'the correctness of which must depend very much on the particular circumstances of the moment, which could not possibly have been foreseen'.[73] Attitudes such as this did not augur well for the army in the decade opening before it, which was to see the rise of strategic problems of a hitherto uncontemplated complexity.

The report of the committee, produced on 10 March 1903, recognized the justice of Nicholson's demands by recommending an increase of three officers and four civilians to his department, at a cost of £5,242. However, civil servants were constitutionally incapable of believing that the army knew best how to arrange its own affairs, and they then went on at length to recommend ways in which the department should be reordered and duties readjusted. The extent to which Hardwicke and his colleagues had accepted the beliefs of the non-specialist witnesses was apparent in the suggestion that the work in the mobilization section demanded officers of superior ability whereas that of the strategical section was less important and required less staff. It was out of the question, they thought, that plans be made and maintained to deal with every contingency with which the country might be faced, particularly since witnesses had cast doubt on the value of such plans.

The committee had gone some way beyond their original brief, and Nicholson quickly let them know that he thought their recommendations both impertinent and irresponsible. The recasting of his department caused him considerable anger, but not as much as the strictures about strategic planning. He responded that these appeared to suggest that, because of the variety and complication of the military problems facing Great Britain, no attention should be paid to such plans until war broke out, when complete responsibility should be handed over to General Officers. Nicholson remarked acidly that this view was 'so entirely opposed to the teaching of military history and the experience of past wars' that it would be interesting to hear the grounds upon which the field commanders had based it. He reminded his audience that certain large questions, among them the defence of the Empire as a whole, the selection of objectives for offensive action, and the strength and composition of forces to carry out such operations were the prerogative of His Majesty's Government:[74]

> Unless matters of this nature are carefully studied at the War Office in peacetime it is extremely improbable that a right decision will be given under high pressure, when there is no time to prepare and weigh the data on which the decision should be based.

The suggestions of Hardwicke's committee he rejected comprehensively.

The attitude taken up by the Director-General of Mobilization and Military Intelligence was wholly justified, and both Lord Roberts and Brodrick admitted it. Serious additions had in any case been made to the workload of the department through the institution of the Defence Committee. Hardwicke, however, was adamant that the principles of organization contained in his report should be adopted, and the issue went accordingly to the War Office Council. There it received scant attention, though Hardwicke did admit that his proposals were designed to effect a complete reconstruction of the department.[75]

Brodrick was prepared to back Nicholson, and go to the Treasury with a request for eleven extra officers at a cost of £5,200 a year. The recommendations were too late for the current year, and so were inserted in the Estimates for 1904–5. But by November 1903 these were running at some £32,500,000, a sum which the Secretary of State acknowledged would have to be reduced. By that time Brodrick was no longer Secretary of State, and the advent of the Esher Committee had thrown the future of the Mobilization and Military Intelligence Department, and with it that of the whole War Office, into the melting pot.

While Nicholson was struggling to maintain something resembling the General Staff which he perceived was so necessary, obstinacy was being displayed in another quarter over the post of Director-General of Military Training. This had existed briefly from 1870 until its abolition in 1892 but, under the stimulus of the Boer War and as a result of the findings of one of the many committees which resulted from it, it was revived in 1902. A proposal to put the new post under the joint control of the Military Secretary, Adjutant-General and Commander-in-

Chief was vigorously opposed by the Adjutant-General: Kelly Kenny was unwilling to let the responsibility slip, and was supported by the King.

Edward VII's argument ran that if the new officer were to report directly to the C.-in-C. it would 'greatly diminish the authority, position and prestige of the Adjutant-General, which have been associated with that office from time immemorial'.[76] He was not without ulterior motive in defending the traditional responsibilities of the Adjutant-General since he intended to appoint his brother, the Duke of Connaught, to the post in the near future. Both the King and his brother were prepared to compromise to the extent of giving up the military education portion of the rubric, provided that the Adjutant-General remained responsible for training the army. If the latter power should also be withdrawn, the Duke informed his brother, then he would not take the post. However, the combination of Lord Roberts and Brodrick proved too powerful in its resolve, and Sir Henry Hildyard was gazetted as first Director of Military Education and Training on 15 January 1903.

This episode, although trivial in itself, reveals the extent to which departmental jealousies could percolate even into royal circles, and thus provide a considerable hindrance to reform. The attitude was widespread and stifling. Moreover, the institution of the new director did little to remedy the situation, for in the autumn of 1903 Rawlinson complained of the dolorous state of the new department and of the War Office in general.[77]

The process which was going on in the War Office under Lord Roberts's eye at the end of the South African War was less that of reform than of tidying up and slowly evolving new machinery. The pressures exerted by Nicholson against the Treasury and Hildyard's appointment did not bespeak a new attitude towards the study of war on the part of the majority of the War Office, still less the institution of a General Staff. There was still a considerable reluctance to employ graduates of the Staff College at the War Office at all. Of a headquarters staff of fifty-two at this time, only seven had psc certificates, and these included neither Nicholson nor Hildyard.[78] Yet the pieces were coming into existence which would be shuffled, redesigned and expanded to create the General Staff.

Roberts was well aware that there existed no doctrine, no school of thought upon which regimental officers might call when training their troops for action. Existing manuals frequently contradicted each other on the most fundamental principles, and therefore he ordered the preparation of a work laying down doctrine on the tactical employment of all arms. A small committee was formed consisting of Hildyard, Rawlinson and Lieutenant-Colonel H. H. Wilson, with the influential Major Gerald Ellison as secretary, which duly produced a *Manual of Combined Training* and a *Staff Manual*. These were later to form the basis of the manual with which the army went to war, *Field Service Regulations Part II*.[79]

As a result of this experience, Ellison addressed a memorandum to the Commander-in-Chief in which he proposed a system on Wellingtonian lines, whereby the Quartermaster-General was head of an operation staff and the Adjutant-General the 'organizer' of the army. Ellison was one of the small band of soldiers who had attended Imperial manoeuvres in Germany and had thus gained first hand experience of the German General Staff. This experience made a deep impression on him, as he remarked afterwards: 'The billeting and commissariat arrangements, the construction of bivouacs . . . the high level of military education . . . above all the amazing thoroughness of the Staff arrangements—every factor attested war efficiency in the highest degree.'[80] Recent experience had made it all too plain that the British military machine could claim no such efficiency, and Ellison realized that the only way to achieve it would be to create a General Staff on the continental model. His suggestions were absolutely opposed by the Adjutant-General, Sir Thomas Kelly Kenny, on the customary grounds that they would reduce his powers. None the less, he forwarded the paper to Roberts, who accepted it. Ellison was just beginning to work on his new scheme when he became swept up in the restless activity of the Esher Committee.[81]

The reforms undertaken after 1899 were in large part a response to the lack of co-ordination and foresight revealed in the earlier phases of the war. *Ad hoc* measures served to paper over the cracks in the fabric, but it was clear that two major faults existed at the highest levels of army administration—the want of an adequate professional consultative agency and the failure of communication between soldiers and politicians. Without greater co-ordination strategy and diplomacy could never be linked. As early as January 1901 the Conservative Party considered itself pledged to an enquiry into the conduct of the war, and Brodrick avoided an immediate enquiry in June 1902 'only by strenuous personal insistence in the Cabinet'.[82] But in October of that year Royal Warrants instituted a commission of enquiry into the preparations for and conduct of the South African War which was to unleash a period of eighteen months of violent change and in the process to modernize the army almost beyond recognition.

Notes

1 Lt-Col. J. M. Grierson to Sir F. Lascelles, 18 January 1898, *B.D.* I, no. 62.
2 Quo. H. Gordon, *The War Office*, London, 1935, p. 49.
3 G. P. Evelyn, *A Diary of the Crimea*, London, 1954, p. 136.
4 C. M. Clode, *The Military Forces of the Crown*, vol. II, London, 1869, p. 394.
5 Sir H. Brackenbury, *Some Memories of My Spare Time*, Edinburgh, 1909, pp. 38–9.
6 Royal Archives. Brodrick to Knollys, 24 July (1901?). R.A W22/25.
7 W. S. Hamer, *The British Army: Civil Military Relations 1885–1905*, Oxford, 1970, p. 30.
8 W. V. R. Isaacs, 'History of the M.I. Directorate', 1957, unpublished. Mss. War Office Library, A.O.11.14, p. 6.
9 Sir R. Harrison, *Recollections of a Life in the British Army*, London, 1908, p. 243.
10 J. S. Omond, *Parliament and the Army 1642–1904*, Cambridge, 1933, p. 126.
11 N. Gibbs, 'The Origins of Imperial Defence' [Lecture], Oxford, 1955, p. 4.
12 *The Cambridge History of the British Empire*, vol. III, Cambridge, 1959, p. 236.
13 J. Ehrman, *Cabinet Government and War 1890–1940*, Cambridge, 1958, pp. 9–11.
14 J. E. Kendle, *The Colonial and Imperial Conferences 1887–1911: A Study in Imperial Organization*, London, 1967, p. 9.
15 *Cambridge History of the British Empire*, vol. III, p. 243.
16 Brackenbury to Q.M.G., 14 April 1886. W.O. 33/46.
17 General Sketch of the Situation Abroad and at Home from a Military Standpoint, 3 August 1886, p. 22. W.O. 33/46.
18 Brackenbury to Ardagh, 13 October 1887. P.R.O. 30/40/2/1.
19 Memorandum by Capt. P. Lake, 12 November 1887. P.R.O. 30/40/13.
20 Hamilton Papers. Duties and Organization of the Treasury of the United Kingdom, 21 November 1879. T./168/15.
21 Hamilton Papers. Memo. by Goschen, 21 May 1887. T./168/8.

22 Hamilton Papers. Treasury Control, 23 May 1905. T./168/8.
23 Sir C. E. Callwell, *Stray Recollections*, vol. I, London, 1923, p. 305.
24 Sir C. E. Callwell, 'War Office reminiscences', *Blackwood's Magazine*, vol. CXC, August 1911, p. 158.
25 R. Cobden, *The Three Panics*, London, 1884, p. 14.
26 W. Verner, *The Military Life of H.R.H. The Duke of Cambridge*, vol. II, London, 1905, p. 343.
27 H. R. Moon, 'The Invasion of the United Kingdom: Public Controversy and Official Planning 1888–1918', vol. I, Ph.D. thesis, London, 1968, pp. 33–40.
28 J. Luvaas, 'European military thought and doctrine 1870–1914', M. E. Howard (ed.), *The Theory and Practice of War: Essays presented to Captain B. H. Liddell Hart*, London, 1965, p. 81.
29 J. K. Dunlop, *The Development of the British Army 1899–1914*, London, 1938, p. 13.
30 *Ibid.* Appendix A.
31 Sir W. R. Robertson, *From Private to Field Marshal*, London, 1921, p. 92.
32 O. Wheeler, *The War Office Past and Present*, London, 1914, p. 244.
33 B. H. Holland, *The Life of Spencer Compton, eighth Duke of Devonshire*, vol. II, London, 1911, p. 323.
34 G. E. Buckle (ed.), *Queen Victoria's Letters 1886–1901*, vol. I, London, 1930–2, pp. 582–4.
35 Ponsonby to Cambridge, 5 April 1890; and Stanhope to Cambridge, 28 April 1890. Quo. Verner, *op. cit.*, vol. II, pp. 356–7.
36 Stanhope to Cambridge, 6 June 1890. Quo. Verner, *op. cit.*, vol. II, p. 360.
37 Hamer, *op. cit.*, p. 142.
38 Chapman to Brackenbury, 21 October 1892. W.O. 106/16.
39 Chapman to Roberts, 4 October 1892. W.O. 106/16.
40 Chapman to Roberts, 19 October 1892. W.O. 106/16.
41 J. E. Tyler, *The British Army and the Continent 1904–1914*, London, 1938, pp. 13–14.
42 Sir C. Dilke and S. Wilkinson, *Imperial Defence*, London, 1897, p. 34.
43 *Ibid.*, p. 132.
44 Sir G. S. Clarke, *Imperial Defence*, London, 1897, p. 104.
45 I. F. Clarke, *Voices Prophesying War 1763–1884*, Oxford, 1966, pp. 107–61.
46 S. Wilkinson, *The Brain of an Army*, London, 1890, p. 105.
47 Dilke and Wilkinson, *op. cit.*, pp. 186, 192–5.
48 L. Trainor, 'The Liberals and the formation of Imperial defence policy 1892–5', *Bulletin of the Institute of Historical Research*, vol. XLII, November 1969, p. 199.
49 Records of the War Office Council, 1870–90. W.O. 163/1–4.
50 Minutes of Colonial/Oversea Defence Committee, 10 June 1897. Cab. 7/7/105.
51 Moon, *op. cit.*, vol. I, p. 84.
52 Trainor, *op. cit.*, p. 200.
53 Kendle, *op. cit.*, pp. 19, 33.

54 Organization for War, January 1900. P.R.O. 30/40/13.
55 Home Defence, 18 January 1897. P.R.O. 30/40/14.
56 Fleetwood Wilson to Ardagh, 15 August 1889. P.R.O. 30/40/13.
57 Lansdowne to Ardagh, 24 September 1896. P.R.O. 30/40/2.
58 Army Reform, 1900. P.R.O. 30/40/13.
59 Cd 1790, Minutes of Evidence taken before the Royal Commission on the War in South Africa, vol. I. Qs. 4978, 5011–3.
60 Roberts Papers. Nicholson to Roberts, 24 November 1903. Box X 20926, file N2.
61 Cd 1790, *op. cit.*, Qs. 5126–32, 888,881.
62 Wolseley to Ardagh, 19 July 1892. P.R.O. 30/40/2.
63 Sir E. Wood, *From Midshipman to Field Marshal*, vol. II, London, 1906, p. 251.
64 A. R. Godwin-Austen, *The Staff and the Staff College*, London, 1927, pp. 236–7.
65 J. G. Ashley, 'The Old War Office and Other Humours', unpublished MSS. W.O. Library A.O.11.1, p. 41.
66 Salisbury to Brodrick, 27 October 1900. P.R.O. 30/67/5.
67 St John Brodrick (as Lord Midleton), *Records and Reactions 1856–1939*, London, 1939, p. 139.
68 Hicks Beach to Brodrick, 12 June 1901. P.R.O. 30/67/7.
69 Cd 1792, Appendices to the Minutes of Evidence taken before the Royal Commission on the War in South Africa, app. 41, no. 11, p. 281.
70 Roberts Papers. Nicholson to Roberts, 8 May 1901. Box X 20926, file N2.
71 W. V. R. Isaacs, 'F.-M. Sir William Robertson', n.d., unpublished MSS. W.O. Lib. AO11.14, pp. 4–6, 8.
72 Hicks Beach to Brodrick, 15 February 1902. P.R.O. 30/67/9.
73 Appendix IV to Hardwicke Report, pp. 43–6, 48, 53, 55. W.O. 32/367.
74 Minute, Nicholson to Roberts, 19 March 1903. Hardwicke Report, p. 8. W.O. 32/367.
75 Minutes of Proceedings and Precis prepared for War Office Council, 4 May 1903. W.O. 163/6.
76 Edward VII to Brodrick, 17 January 1903. P.R.O. 30/67/18.
77 Sir F. Maurice, *The Life of General Lord Rawlinson of Trent*, London, 1928, p. 83.
78 Appointments to Commands and High Staff Positions made from 1 January 1901 to 30 November 1903. Cab. 17/14.
79 Sir G. F. Ellison, 'Lord Roberts and the General Staff', *Nineteenth Century and After*, vol. CXII, December 1932, p. 729.
80 Sir G. F. Ellison, 'From here and there', *The Lancashire Lad: Journal of the Loyal Regiment*, 3rd series, no. 45, July 1933, p. 8.
81 Additional evidence of Roberts's appreciation of the value of a General Staff, which had often been ignored or denied, may be seen in Roberts to Sandars, 23 January 1903. B.M. Add. MSS. 49725.
82 Roberts Papers. Brodrick to Roberts, 11 June 1902. Box X 20931, file B5.

2
The Triumph of Lord Esher

When faced with what seemed an intractable problem of government, the tendency of Victorian England was to put it to some form of committee. Where the problem was sufficiently grave, it came before a Royal Commission and received rather more publicity, though frequently the one form of examination had as little result as the other. By the time that the result of such enquiries were made known their findings were often *passé* and were not guaranteed a sympathetic audience. Catalogues of disaster were in any case far from the best means of obtaining reforms since public and politicians alike tended to feel that the worst was passed and that hunting for scapegoats was a degenerate and ungentlemanly pursuit.

Superficially, the Elgin Commission offered a new departure since the events on which it was to report were so momentous. However, the commission considered itself tightly bound by its rubric which required it to:[1]

> inquire into the military preparedness for the war in South Africa, and into the supply of men, ammunition, equipment and transport by sea and by land in connection with the campaign, and into military operations up to the occupation of Pretoria.

Since they chose not to depart from their brief in any way, the report of the Elgin Commissioners was chiefly valuable as a military history of the war, though it did lay bare some of the deficiencies in the organization and running of the War Office. In the course of an extremely rigorous investigation, the nine members of the commission sat for 55 days, saw 114 witnesses and asked 2,200 questions.

As the examination into the antecedents of the war progressed, the parlous state of the Intelligence Department was clearly revealed. Sir John Ardagh described his functions as in the main of a limited executive nature, and even L. S. Amery of *The Times* was moved to remark on the paucity and poverty of the Intelligence services in the field: 'they were fewer than the men I employed myself as "Times" correspondents, and I should have been ashamed to send "Times" correspondents anywhere, or even a commercial traveller, with the sums of money they were given.'[2] Moreover, the work which the Intelligence Department did complete was hindered by the rivalry which had grown up between the Commander-in-Chief and the Civil Departments. As an instance of this, it was revealed that the Secretary of State for War received notice of Intelligence reports about South Africa from his opposite number at the Colonial Office.

It soon became clear that the question of the role and status of the Intelligence Department, and with it the future of a 'thinking' branch for the army, was inextricably bound up with the structure of the War Office as a whole. On this the Commissioners felt able to make little comment or criticism due to the involved and complicated nature of the question and to the fact that everything was then in the process of change as the Clinton Dawkins Committee examined this specific problem. As far as operations in wartime went they sided with Brodrick who remarked that during the war, 'practically the whole War Office had worked to such a degree that it would have been impossible to attempt a fresh organization . . . when the pressure was so severe'.[3]

One innovation made during the course of the South African War had worked particularly well: the Army Board which had come into existence on 13 July 1899 represented, for the first time, the collective opinion of the War Office. In 1900 its functions were taken over by the War Office Council, where all subjects were discussed by civilians and military face-to-face. The idea had been Brodrick's own, to overcome the attitude that the two halves were 'two antagonistic bodies sitting constantly and keeping a check upon each other'.[4] It was a distinct and noteworthy advance in harmonizing the conflicting elements within the War Office, and was to be expanded by Esher into the Army Council. But at the time it was only a temporary measure, resting on nothing more secure than a memorandum from the Secretary of State which could be withdrawn at any moment. To preserve its position, an Order in Council was required defining more closely the position and duties of its members. This was the sum of the commission's consideration of War

Office organization, and as such might well have been consigned
to oblivion had it not been for the presence upon that body of
one singular personage. Reginald Balliol Brett, second Viscount
Esher, was uniquely placed to ensure that some concrete changes
emerged from the *travail* of the enquiry. Esher, the possessor of
acute intelligence and a mind of Renaissance scope, had gained
a deep interest in defence problems as private secretary to the
Marquis of Hartington from 1878 to 1885, and coupled this with
experience of the House of Commons as Liberal member for
Penrhyn and Falmouth 1880–5. He was acquainted with all the
leading political figures of his age, and on personal terms with a
great many of them. However, Esher had no taste for a life of
service in the public eye and always regarded himself as the
personal servant of the monarch. His friendship with the Prince
of Wales was consolidated by his tenure of the position of secretary
of the Office of Works (1895–1902), which necessitated frequent
journeys to Windsor to advise on renovations.

It was therefore natural that, at the moment when the Elgin
Commission first began to take evidence, Esher should write
to the King giving him a brief account of the hearing, and humbly
offering to keep up the chore should it be thought desirable. The
King did think so, and there followed a stream of letters giving
précis of the views of the various witnesses. Though in the main
of a serious nature, Esher occasionally enlivened them with
flashes of humour, notably in the case of General Brabazon, who
had commanded the Imperial Yeomanry in South Africa. Esher
informed the King that he:[5]

> did not display profound knowledge of the raising, nor of the
> war service, of that Force; but he electrified the Commission
> by a recital of personal experiences on the Afghan Frontier,
> and his theories of the use of the cavalry arm in war.
>
> The General laid special stress on his life-long mistrust of
> the weapons supplied to the cavalry, and of his preference for
> shock tactics by men armed with the Tomahawk. He drew
> graphic pictures of a cavalry charge under these conditions,
> so paralysing to the imagination of the Commissioners that
> they wholly failed to extricate the General or themselves
> from the discussion of this engrossing subject.

More serious was the information that in a marksmanship
competition held in the Aldershot Command the previous year

the twelve best shots had fired 1,210 rounds at targets from 210 yards to 2,600 yards distance, and had scored a total of ten hits. As Esher drily remarked to the King, 'It was not thought desirable that this record should appear in the printed evidence.'[6]

Esher was sufficiently dissatisfied with the Elgin Report to append to it a note pointing out the main defects of the War Office: the want of co-ordination between the various branches, the consequent weakening of the influence of the Secretary of State, and the absence of a proper system of inspection to ensure that the government's policy was carried into effect. He also indicated where a solution might be found—in the establishment of a board along the lines of the Board of Admiralty:[7]

> It may be truthfully contended that the sound administration of the Admiralty results from the system under which the First Lord determines all naval questions in council with his principal advisers, after formal discussion, and is thus enabled to approach the treasury, the Cabinet, and Parliament with the force of professional opinion behind him.

Esher recommended the abolition of the office of Commander-in-Chief and the adoption of Hartington's proposal for a General Officer Commanding the Army, responsible to the Secretary of State for its efficiency.

The Elgin Report was received by the press with general approbation. *The Times* ran a summary of the findings on 26 August 1903, as did most of the other newspapers, and selected extracts appeared in the weeks following its publication. There were, however, signs that a dangerous complacency was again setting in. The editor of the *Whitehall Review*, writing on 3 September 1903, offered the opinion that 'the one great consolation about it is that the country now knows the worst'. The main lesson appeared to be that the Liberal reign had ended just in time in 1895; having taken over a weak War Office Lord Lansdowne had done his best and stood freed from any blame for subsequent events. Public response was mixed, with retired civil servants emerging to defend the War Office administration and requesting that the washing of dirty linen in public should cease. Effective reform of the War Office and the creation of a General Staff were by no means the inevitable consequence of the publication of the Elgin Report.

Balfour's administration was in fact rapidly becoming preoccupied with more pacific if no less controversial problems.
Grasping the thorns of Education, Licensing and the Irish
question, and concerned about the formation of a French *entente*,
the government was in the throes of a crisis. Even the Secretary
of State for War himself was chiefly concerned to bring about his
scheme for the provision of six army corps. By a strange chance,
it was the apparently unrelated question of Tariff Reform which
was to prove instrumental in the creation of a completely new
structure for defence administration.

It was in a sense fortunate for Esher that the government was
in an unstable state in the summer of 1903. The question of
Tariff Reform had been the cause of an ever-increasing rift in the
Unionist Party which resulted in the resignation of five Ministers
of Cabinet rank. This presented Balfour with a serious crisis, and
at that moment St John Brodrick offered his own resignation.
Lord Roberts wrote to Brodrick in August 1903 informing him
that he could no longer continue as Commander-in-Chief under
the old conditions, since he foresaw greater independence for
himself as head of a board on Admiralty lines. Brodrick subsequently recorded his feelings: 'To fight for the Commander-
in-Chief against the War Commission and the King, if Roberts
himself was a convert [to a Board system] was useless.'[8]

Brodrick was partly motivated in his action by his strained
relations with the Crown, for he never got on well with Edward
VII.[9] Also he was being subject to advice from Esher that his
position was untenable. Brodrick was certainly not manoeuvred
out of office by Balfour in order to facilitate reform of the War
Office on the lines suggested in Esher's note; when, early in
September, Brodrick asked the Prime Minister whether he
intended such a reorganization, Balfour expressed 'some doubts'
as to its value. He did foresee the necessity of surveying the
situation, and asked Brodrick to prepare memoranda to this
end.[10]

The memoranda were duly prepared, but they were Brodrick's
last, for on or about 14 September he proffered his resignation.
In time he came to feel considerably aggrieved at Esher's role
in his departure from the War Office, and not without some
justice. Earlier in the year Esher had warned the King that
before any effective changes could be made in the War Office
'very strong opposition will be encountered from the Secretary

of State and from the Commander-in-Chief'.[11] He was not entirely correct in this assumption—Brodrick had had a hand in the reconstruction of the Defence Committee of the Cabinet which became the Committee of Imperial Defence—but his opinion certainly affected the King's attitude.

Brodrick went on to a valuable career at the India Office, consoled by Lord Curzon:[12]

I do not know what your feelings are at leaving W.O. If I were you they wd. be those of undiluted satisfaction for it is a place where the most strenuous endeavours meet with the smallest return, and from which little is to be got save vituperation.

He always regretted the manner in which he had left the War Office, but he was too well cast in the mould of the Parliamentary Secretary of the 1890s (which he had been) and too little aware of the significance of continental events to have been able to bring about reforms of the calibre of Esher's.

The King now became anxious to make a non-political appointment to the newly vacated Office; and who better to take on the task of modernization than the expert and devoted Esher. On his arrival at Balmoral on 21 September, Esher was at once pressed by the King to take the office. He refused, for characteristic reasons which he later explained to his son:[13]

I am purely selfish in the matter, and I really do not think that I can bring myself to sacrifice all independence, all liberty of action, all my 'intime' life, for a position which adds nothing to that which I now occupy.

Esher proved impervious to the considerable pressure subsequently put on him by Balfour and by Edward VII, but scented his chance. He was prepared, he allowed, to head a three-man commission in order to carry out changes in the War Office.

Having stuck firmly to his suggested compromise, Esher escaped from Balmoral on 26 September. Eight days later the War Office was offered to H. O. Arnold Forster, sometime Parliamentary Secretary to the Admiralty. The offer was accompanied by the suggestion of aid from a small committee, possibly composed of Esher, Admiral Fisher and Sir John French.[14] Arnold Forster accepted the post but disagreed with Esher's idea of a board. To his brother he wrote that it was 'not the time, and these are not the circumstances, I would have chosen for the commencement of such a task'.[15] His subsequent experiences in the office were to confirm him in his jaundiced view.

Esher's proposed committee was a startling departure from the bureaucratic norm. Here was a body appointed specifically to achieve reforms—moreover, reforms of its own devising and not ones dictated to it. It was unique in its standing, but it was also the target for severe military disquiet. The first names firmly proposed were Esher himself, Sir John Fisher, then Commander-in-Chief of Portsmouth Dockyard, and Sir Henry Brackenbury. The first two were fervent navalists of the 'Blue Water' school, and it became the preoccupation of the War Office to prevent such a composition if at all possible. The manoeuvres which followed revealed the depth and extent of inter-service hostility at this time.

In the first place, the King felt that perhaps the Secretary of State for War should be a member of the committee since he would have to put the committee's recommendations into practice.[16] This was definitely not what Esher wanted, and Balfour steered Arnold Forster off the nascent committee. Arnold Forster now became increasingly obstructive, insisting that all requests for witnesses and evidence should go through him and that the terms of reference be such that he could approve of them. In the event, this procedure did not take place.

There was never any doubt that the committee should contain a naval member, nor that Sir John Fisher was the ideal choice. Energetic and brilliant, he had the aura of iconoclasm necessary to break down the encrusted carapace of the War Office. This qualification was reinforced by his successful reforms of the Mediterranean Fleet some three years earlier.[17] Arnold Forster spoke for many besides himself when he wrote to Balfour: 'I am quite certain that no name will command so much confidence with the public as Sir John's and I think therefore that all doubt as to his serving should be removed.'[18] Fisher's superior officers were less enamoured of his presence and both Prince Louis of Battenberg and Lord Selborne, respectively Director of Naval Intelligence and Secretary of State for the Navy, tried to dissuade him from serving. They put heavy pressure on Fisher and their move only failed when Balfour and the King's private secretary, Lord Knollys, combined to stop Fisher's letter of resignation from reaching the King.[19]

To complete the planned triumvirate, it remained to add a soldier, and this was to prove the hardest task of all. Writing to Balfour's private secretary, Arnold Forster encapsulated the problem: 'The man', he wrote, 'would not only be a good man, but the public must think so.'[20] The King at first supported the candidacy of Sir John French but when dissuaded from this by Balfour suggested as surrogate Sir George Clarke, then Governor of Victoria.[21] There were, however, strong objections to Clarke; he might, Balfour pointed out smoothly, be required for the War Office after reforms had taken place and in any case he was a long way away. The King therefore turned to Brackenbury as the military member; but by 16 October Fisher had made it clear that he objected to serving with the Director-General of Ordnance. His reasons, and they were not without weight, were that no one at that time or at any time previously on the staff of the War Office could possibly command public confidence and that he personally found Brackenbury difficult to work with.[22] Fisher's presence on the committee was deemed infinitely more important than Brackenbury's, so that the latter's candidature was irrevocably weakened.

The lot then fell to Lord Grenfell, a soldier with a distinguished record in the South African War and with the added qualification of being politically somewhat colourless. The idea was Balfour's and he justified it with a typical example of his philosophical logic—Grenfell filled in every respect the requirements for the military member:[23]

> who shall neither be strongly identified with any particular military clique, nor with the existing War Office administration—who shall be popular with the soldiers and give confidence to the public, who can be trusted to work cordially with his civil and naval colleagues.

Unfortunately, Balfour was forcing Grenfell into a mould which was not acceptable to him or to others.

Everything appeared to be satisfactorily settled on the basis of Esher, Fisher and Grenfell when Sir Thomas Kelly Kenny, the Adjutant-General, heard of the arrangement and stormed into Buckingham Palace to insist upon Brackenbury being a member. He feared that Grenfell might be unable to put up a defence against the 'Blue Water' theories of his colleagues, and that a radical reorganization of the War Office might result along lines which would make that body conform to the Admiralty's stance. Brackenbury was a partisan of the traditional ideas of War Office organization and would therefore make a much better representative. The King had a strong regard for Kelly Kenny and was prepared to listen to his criticisms because he believed, wrongly, that the Adjutant-General belonged to the advanced school of military reformers.[24] During the interview Kelly Kenny had Fisher brought to the Palace and after a heated discussion a compromise four-man committee was agreed upon which would include both Grenfell and Brackenbury.[25]

The proposed committee which was to cut rapidly through the dead wood at the War Office now showed signs of becoming a more cumbersome and less effective machine. Esher hastened to inform the King, through Lord Knollys, of the dangers of such a compromise: the two soldiers might disagree and a minority report might result, which would be fatal in a committee of the kind proposed. He cared very little which one was selected but 'I would readily accept *any one*, rather than any two.'[26] Balfour likewise swung quickly into motion to defend a tripartite division as 'peculiarly adapted to the smooth and rapid elaboration of a practical scheme'. He reiterated the twin dangers posed by Esher, so exactly that there was probably some collusion between the two, and recommended a return to the original plan of Grenfell.[27]

King Edward VII, though he felt he could defend his choice of Brackenbury, was prepared to give way and accept Grenfell. However, after displaying considerable indecision Grenfell refused to serve, probably due to pressure exerted by the Adjutant-General. Suggestions of a civilian or the Commander-in-Chief were discarded, so Arnold Forster returned to the idea of Clarke: the soldiers might not like him, but it was owing to their scandalous intrigues that he was necessary.[28] Next day Esher told him that the King now saw that a determined attempt had been made by the military to get the new committee into its hands. The post was offered with general approbation to Clarke, and by 5 November he had accepted—'no doubt the better man' wrote Esher 'but 12,000 miles away'.[29]

Clarke was certainly highly qualified for membership of the triumvirate. Having passed out first of his year from the Woolwich Academy, taking ten prizes and a gold medal, he had entered the Royal Engineers in 1868 aged twenty. Early but important work on fortifications had been succeeded by a period of Secretary to the Colonial Defence Committee (1885–92). He became a publicist of note, producing *Imperial Defence* in 1897 and numerous articles on army reform.[30] More important, he was a navalist of conviction and therefore unlikely to upset the smooth functioning of Esher's committee or to jeopardize the unanimity of its outlook. It would be hard to envisage a better choice from this point of view.

The news of the Committee's appointment appeared in *The Times* on 7 November 1903. Its terms of reference were reported as being 'to advise as to the creation of a board for the administrative business of the War Office, and as to the consequential changes thereby involved', and in the first leader the news was greeted as an indication both of the government's realization that speedy action was necessary and that they had correctly perceived the most important area for reform.[31] The military correspondent of *The Times*, Charles à Court Repington, was to prove a valuable publicist for Esher's ideas, and the paean greeting the creation of the committee seems to have been his first contribution to the triumvirate's progress.

The old War Office might have appeared to capitulate over the issue of the personnel of the War Office (Reconstitution) Committee but it made one last attempt to block the appointment of a secretary. This was a post which required knowledge, ability and tact, as well as a *rapport* with the aims of the trio; and L. S. Amery suggested Colonel G. F. Ellison as the obvious candidate. Ellison has left an interesting account of his first meeting with Esher:[32]

> Early in November, 1903, I was at work in my room at Winchester House, St James Square, when a well-groomed, youngish looking man [Esher was then 51] entered unannounced and introduced himself as Esher. He told me an enquiry into the organization of the War Office had been decided on, and he asked if I would care to act as the secretary of the Committee conducting the enquiry. . . . I replied that, if serious business was intended, nothing would give me greater pleasure, and we left it at that.

Esher decided at once that Ellison was the man he wanted: he was capable, dry and reserved, and since he knew few people there was little danger that he would talk. 'He looks', added Esher, 'like a German General Staff Officer.'[33]

Arnold Forster agreed to the move, and in the absence of Ellison's direct superior, Kelly Kenny, both Nicholson and the acting Adjutant-General agreed to release him. However, on 13 November Kelly Kenny returned to his office somewhat aggrieved at his failure to 'pack' the Reconstitution Committee, and flatly refused to release Ellison.[34] He was well aware that his subordinate disagreed absolutely with his own views of army organization. Through Lord Knollys Esher mobilized the support of the King, feeling that unless he was successful in gaining Ellison's services it was 'goodbye' to the committee.[35] This proved decisive, and Ellison's appointment was announced in *The Times* on 18 November.

Two months elapsed between the announcement of the formation of the committee and the arrival of Clarke from Australia to join it; barely a month later it published the first part of its report. This speed was startling to contemporaries, who were accustomed to the lengthy sittings of the Elgin Commission. It was possible chiefly because this committee differed from all previous ones: Elgin's evidence had supplied the fulcrum upon which it would apply the lever. In addition the committee was marked by an uncharacteristic degree of unanimity amongst its members, and in any case a number of major decisions were made before Clarke ever arrived.

As early as January 1903 Esher had felt that the solution to the army's problems was a board system on Admiralty lines, each member having individual responsibilities for some aspect of the service's functioning and the members collectively having the over-all responsibilities for internal policy.[36] If Esher's mind was made up, Sir John Fisher was no less convinced of the need for root and branch reform. He revealed his feelings in a characteristic letter to Balfour's private secretary:[37]

> *I am absolutely certain we can make a good job of the War Office!* but a drastic change is imperative, *we must be ruthless, relentless and remorseless* and there must be no mincing matters. And all the Committee's resolutions *must be swallowed whole*, no leaving out a single one of the ingredients of the pill! or the patient won't be cured!

Fisher envisaged an outline board with five major divisions: 'War Organization', comprising defence, intelligence, mobilization and strategy, together with sections for personnel, *matériel*, finance and civil matters, each under the direction of a 'Military Lord'. Beneath this would lie a substructure of directors having 'the entire management and control' of their own departments subject only to their superintending member of the board.[38]

The old guard of the War Office believed, mistakenly, that very little decisive action could be taken before Clarke's arrival at the end of December, and Brackenbury consoled Lord Roberts with the thought that he had six weeks in which to recover from an inflammation of the lung before the committee met. However, Esher's was the guiding hand and he had already formulated the basis of reconstruction with Fisher—'A peace organization, sound and elastic for war'.[39] Also by late November his own ideas of the strategic role of the army were clear: the largest demand likely to be made upon it was in the event of a war with Russia in India. Since Esher lacked strategic doubts, his task of reorganization was so much the easier.

Although Esher and Fisher had begun work on the task of reconstitution independently of their committee, they were certainly not working in a vacuum, isolated from military opinion. A letter of congratulation from Douglas Haig in India confirmed Esher's existing train of thought in complaining of the want of continuity in ideas and direction at the highest levels: 'schemes seem to be hastily taken up without due consideration of what the ultimate effects will be, and then quickly another scheme is started to cover the shortcomings of the former one so that we have confusion worse confounded.'[40] Accordingly Esher started with the summit of the edifice, and formulated the requirements for the whole structure of defence policy on the basis of the need for much greater co-operation between the two services and between the military forces of the Empire. The need was to strengthen the existing defence system by making the Committee of Imperial Defence into a Privy Council Committee and including Dominion and Australian representatives.

Esher was tentatively seeking an institution corresponding with the great German General Staff in concept, but rather adapted to the needs of a maritime empire. He found it in the suggestion of a permanent Secretariat for the CID to fulfil one of the accepted tasks of a capital staff—to theorize on war. Although clearly thinking of a 'supra-departmental' defence staff, Esher concluded that this would as yet be impracticable:[41]

For a Great General Staff on the German model, i.e. independent of the War Office, material in the shape of a number of highly trained staff officers does not exist, and even if such a department were desirable or possible for Imperial purposes under our *present* institutions, it could only be the growth of years.

He proposed for the new Secretariat the name 'Department of Scientific or Theoretical War Problems' to distinguish its functions from those of the General Staff, a semantic distinction which was to be the cause of much subsequent confusion when the roles of the two later began to overlap. As he imagined it, the General Staff would have responsibility for practical staff work at the highest level.

The conviction that some at least of the functions of a capital staff should lie within a permanent 'Department of the Defence Committee' gained ground in Esher's mind during this period, and the case was made out late in December. Esher realized that the progressive increase in the work done by the recently reconstituted CID necessitated establishing a department under the personal control of the Prime Minister to deal with it. There was an element of deception in the device since any overt imitation of a capital staff would probably arouse a great deal of public hostility, but Esher admitted that it would in fact, though not in name, constitute 'a Great General Staff suited to our Imperial requirements'.[42] Under the guidance of a secretary with a trained strategical mind, the task of the new body would be to consider from the broadest possible viewpoint all questions of Imperial defence; to do so it must have powers, which might well prove contentious, of obtaining information from the two services and preparing documents for the consideration of the CID.

The body that Esher proposed was a new departure in government, and one which might well have repercussions on the accepted notions of ministerial and Cabinet responsibility; it certainly placed a new power in the hands of the Prime Minister. The possibilities of doubts arising on such constitutional scores worried Esher infinitely less than the danger of tainting this novelty with any teutonic flavour:[43]

All reference to Germany, and the methods of Continental powers, are best avoided, as opening the door to the observation that the circumstances of our Empire are so different from any other, that all comparisons are misleading. This argument, and it is sometimes fallacious, invariably carries convictions.

Proposals were then made regarding the conditions of service of the future Chief of the General Staff, taking care not to simulate the German model too openly. In order to accommodate this there was some overlap between the offices of secretary to the CID and CGS, but Esher had covered his tracks so well that this did not become apparent for some time.

A pliant Clarke arrived in England on 28 December 1903, having already agreed that there must be no difference of opinion or principle among the committee, and it began interviewing selected persons the next day. But before it began its official work Esher had written to the Prime Minister indicating that its major recommendations would be a Secretariat for the CID and an Army Council, which should be set up as soon as possible to work out the details of the scheme.[44]

The triumvirate, as it rapidly became known in political circles, worked in a cloak of absolute secrecy and with a speed which startled contemporaries. Sir Neville Lyttelton accounted for this rapidity in the judgment that 'that Triumvirate knew its own mind, and in an incredibly short time the War Office had been reorganized'.[45] Since no evidence was ever published, the actual workings of the committee remained shrouded in mystery and speculation.

The committee did not take formal evidence for a number of reasons. Already there existed an almost embarrassing volume as a result of the Elgin Commission's deliberations; and in any case the committee sought more personal opinions which it might be difficult to defend in print. To this end the cloak of anonymity was calculated to produce more forthcoming witnesses. Thus informal discussions took place, with brief records kept by the secretary of the chief points. The interviews were in fact conducted chiefly in order to confirm in the trio's minds their own opinions on a number of limited points.

Working from rooms in the Office of Works, overlooking St James's Square, the committee saw eighty witnesses in forty-four days. A few, among them Sir Redvers Buller, volunteered to appear; others were less eager. Viscount Wolseley felt unable to present himself before Esher and his colleagues, but did embody his views in a lengthy letter. It encapsulated the conservative unimaginative approach of many past incumbents of top military posts. The great drawback to a board, Wolseley felt, was that the country could never be certain that the army was in a fit state to take the field.[46]

> To satisfy the Nation on this point, the Commander-in-Chief—a non-political personage—should be obliged to submit to Parliament when it assembled and when it is about to separate, a certificate of the most carefully worded nature as to whether our Store Houses contain everything which the whole of our Military Forces require for purposes of immediate mobilization.

It was precisely this concept of the duties of the senior military officials—to insure that the army was ready down to the last gaiter strap—which Esher had to dispel and to replace with a wider attitude of strategic awareness.

The committee cast its net widely to interview all the key serving officers at the War Office, and were concerned chiefly to clarify small points or confirm their own suspicions. Thus Sir William Nicholson did not make his place in the committee's eyes at all secure even though it was apparently he who put forward the idea of a fully fledged General Staff on the German model.[47] Much of his advice was followed but he was not thought a fit agent to initiate such a change. The Military Secretary, Colonel J. S. Ewart, was called on three separate occasions as well as being requested to furnish detailed memoranda on such matters as accelerated promotion and the working of linked battalions; on one such occasion he recorded enduring 'a severe heckling', but no change was subsequently made in the functioning of his department.[48]

Henry Wilson was interviewed, and advantage was taken of the presence of Douglas Haig in England; the latter comforted Esher with the opinion that his measures had the support of the younger members of the army and wanted only a little time to succeed. Exceptionally interesting evidence was given by the military correspondent of *The Times*, Colonel Repington, the main burden of whose verbal report was that Lord Kitchener ought to be the new Chief of General Staff and that only a cabal of 'old military women' was keeping him out. Of more value was a confidential paper sent by him to Esher giving an assessment of the quality of the current Intelligence Department. Of a staff of thirty-two officers only twelve were worth retaining, notably Colonels P. H. N. Lake, Robertson, Callwell—'an able theorist'— F. J. Davies and Lieutenant-Colonel G. Milne (subsequently CIGS 1926–33). Of the general situation he commented: 'I confess that before I went into this matter for you I was not aware how many fifth-rate men had crept in.'[49] However far it may subsequently have deteriorated, there was nothing wrong with Repington's judgment in 1904.

While interviewing witnesses, the Esher Committee was also trying to resolve the vexed question of nomenclature. Although apparently trivial, this was much more complex than it appeared. A terminology had to be adopted which was new to reinforce new duties of officials, and yet awoke no chords of a German tone. It also had to meet with the approval of the King, who gave as much attention to such matters of form as the wearing of orders and decorations in the right sequence as he did to larger questions of policy. Esher had hoped to change the name of the War Office itself to indicate its new function but failed to do so. More difficult was the question of the name for the proposed First Military Member of the Army Council, for which the committee suggested the term Quartermaster-General, used in a Wellingtonian sense to indicate the functions of an operations staff. Clarke objected to using the term 'Commissary General' for the third military member, in charge of *matériel*, and Ellison suggested switching the term Quartermaster-General to this official. This met with the King's outright opposition, as he strongly wished to retain the older term for the first post.[50] The term 'Chief of the General Staff' was then suggested to the King, and after some persuasion by Esher he capitulated early in February. Already pressures were moving the committee along the path to something like the German example.

The various members of the committee were by now expressing their conviction that the measures they were about to recommend should be adopted and put into force before parliament met in February. Fisher feared that unless this happened Kelly Kenny and others would combine to sabotage their report in parliament; his information had come from Arthur Lee, MP, Civil Lord of the Admiralty.[51] Esher was equally concerned that the first recommendations be accepted and carried out as soon as possible because:[52]

first . . . it would be almost essential to work out the detail in consultation with the new and unprejudiced (let us hope) occupants of the offices to be created, and secondly, because it is only by compartments—so to speak—that any practical reforms can be enforced.

The King was equally anxious to get Cabinet approval and publication as long as possible before the opening of parliament.

Esher's committee was remarkable in the annals of reform not least for the extensive and largely unremarked executive powers it exercised. Esher's remarks and Repington's comments on the Intelligence Staff illustrate the dual nature of the War Office (Reconstitution) Committee, for whilst interviewing witnesses and drafting recommendations it was also considering the potential of certain officers to fill the newly created posts. Esher was in close contact with the King from the start, and it appears to have been Edward VII who first suggested that Sir Neville Lyttelton be Chief of the General Staff and First Military Member. The committee were dubious. Fisher reported in no uncertain terms on meeting the candidate at a dinner party: 'I sat for two hours next to Lyttelton and thought him the dullest dog I'd ever met! We don't want dull dogs for this new scheme, we *must* have *youth* and *enthusiasm*.'[53] Esher had his own views, which tallied with Fisher's, and his own candidate, Sir John French. He had perforce to admit that French was not the cleverest man but argued his attraction as being the most successful British soldier to date: '*He has never failed*.'[54] In view of his record as CIGS and wartime commander, and his undeniable lack of high-powered intellect, the critical importance of Esher's committee in making military careers is well illustrated in French's case. French filled the naval Imperialist bill completely since he was sympathetic to a much closer union between the two services and to the navalist outlook. He even made a private speech expressing the hope that one day the two services might merge into one, a sentiment which was anathema to the bulk of the army.[55] The extent to which French was *persona grata* to the Admiralty was made abundantly clear by Fisher:[56]

Sacred.

1st Military Member—Sir John French because he never failed in Africa (the grave of military reputations). He is *young* and *energetic*, has commanded the *First Army Corps*

so far with conspicuous success and *has the splendid gift* of choosing the right men to work with him (vide his Staff in South Africa, the best Staff out there) and as 1st Military Lord it would be his special function to prepare the Army in the Field for fighting and who therefore better to command it when war breaks out as the functions then at the War Office would disappear and be transferred to the Commander-in-Chief at the seat of War. Further, he is an enthusiastic and 'out and out' believer in joint Naval and Military opera-tions as the proper species of manoeuvres for this Empire. In this belief he is almost solitary amongst all the Generals, who all want to play at the German Army.
'Plump for French and Efficiency'!
Every vote given against French is a vote given to Kelly Kenny!

French's candidature came to an end when the King refused to countenance his appointment. None the less, the favourable reactions of Esher and Fisher greatly furthered his career, as also for Haig, Grierson and Sir F. W. Stopford. The latter, a nonentity when given office and an unhappy choice for field command, directly owed his advance to a paper written for the committee on the organization of the 1st army corps.[57]

Divided on the question of a Chief of the General Staff, all three members of the committee were united in agreeing that Sir William Nicholson must go. Fisher referred frequently and in hostile terms to 'Old Nick' and Clarke too regarded him as something of an intriguer; their hostility was doubtless based on Nicholson's opposition to navalist ideas. Esher made one of his rare errors of judgment in concurring over Nicholson; he felt him to be 'too grasping' as well as not possessing an original mind. The question of personnel was sufficiently delicate for the King to express to Esher the desire to 'talk over academically with him' those who were to be appointed before any formal recommenda-tions should be made.[58]

Nicholson's influence at the War Office made him the chief obstacle to the 'clean sweep' desired by the triumvirate, and by 27 January 1904 the possibility of his remaining on was so great that the trio had to make a stand at a small Cabinet that day. Esher also wrote to Balfour on his colleagues' behalf barely veiling a threat to resign if Nicholson were to remain.[59] Balfour was not to be hurried into action by such threats, and his reply was characteristically bland: personally he had no doubts that the Cabinet would opt for a complete change of top War Office personnel, but if Esher had evidence to the contrary then the Prime Minister would not press him to waste time in continuing his work.[60]

The committee, mollified by this view, returned to the question of the four military members and their 'best' list now consisted of Lyttelton, Stopford, Sir Charles Douglas and Sir James Wolfe Murray. Selborne surrendered his support of Nicholson, whom the King now also opposed on Esher's recommendation, and French gave a fuller statement of Stopford's qualities which together led to the final list on 1 February—Lyttelton as Chief of the General Staff, Sir Charles Douglas as Adjutant-General, H. C. O. Plumer as Quartermaster-General and Sir James Wolfe Murray as Master-General of Ordnance. Stopford would be one of Lyttelton's Directors; as Fisher explained to Sandars:[61]

> this would avoid having to make Stopford a General. French told me confidentially the other day that though he was devoted to Stopford, yet he was an awful pessimist and too much given to detail. These are not bad qualities in the second man but are fateful in the first man.

Stopford's performance at Suvla Bay in August 1915 fully bore out French's assessment.

The first part of the report of the War Office (Reconstitution) Committee was published on 1 February 1904. In a covering letter its members pinned their faith to the recently reconstituted Committee of Imperial Defence to fulfil the main functions of a General Staff on an Imperial scale. To guarantee the permanence of the CID and its adequate functioning it was suggested that the Prime Minister should preside over it and have absolute discretion over its membership. To buttress this, the triumvirate suggested a permanent Secretariat which should call the Prime Minister's attention to strategic problems of defence, to the condition of the country's armaments and to 'the relation which the latter should bear to the former if the King's Dominions are to remain secure'.[62]

The seeds of possible disarray were thus planted from the outset. The 'General Staff' which the triumvirate envisaged the CID as becoming would have no permanent membership and was moreover aimed predominantly at Imperial requirements. To accompany it, a Secretariat was suggested which would occupy an anomalous position, having duties which cut across the boundaries of the naval and military staffs, whilst the latter remained in existence independently of the new grafting. Neither stood in a clear relationship to the General Staff proper. And the whole system was designed for Balfour: a Prime Minister with more than a passing interest in defence problems, and the personality and intellectual capacity necessary to guide the operations of such a complex and cross-cut series of powers and responsibilities. The drawbacks inherent in the system were not to be revealed until it passed into less interested hands for guidance.

The report reassured its readers lest they felt an alarming resemblance between the proposed Secretariat and CID and continental General Staffs; since Britain's was predominantly a great naval, Indian and Colonial Empire its problems were of a very different order from those of a continental power. The cornerstone of such an edifice must be a permanent nucleus of the CID consisting of a secretary and at least six assistants. Charged with considering all questions of Imperial defence from the point of view of the army, navy, India and the colonies, from which areas the assistant secretaries should come for a period of two-years' service at the Secretariat, the duties of the Secretariat as enumerated by the committee comprehensively summed up those of an Imperial Defence staff.

Well aware of the instability of the War Office, of the degree of centralization in the hands of the Commander-in-Chief and of the vague definition of responsibilities of military officials, the committee turned in the second portion of their report to the manner in which these weaknesses could be overcome and the position of the Secretary of State for War in the Cabinet strengthened. It was proposed to place the Secretary of State on a similar footing to that enjoyed by the First Lord of the Admiralty in that all submissions to the Crown should be made by him alone. To aid him in this task it was proposed to establish a supreme administrative body at the War Office, to be known as the Army Council and to consist of seven members: for the military, the Chief of the General Staff, Adjutant-General, Quartermaster-General and Master-General of Ordnance and for the civilians the Secretary of State for War, Parliamentary

Under-Secretary and Financial Secretary to the War Office. For the first time a system of collective responsibility for military policy was to be enjoined upon the War Office.

One of the many novel features about Esher's report was the uncompromising suggestion that new measures demanded new men, unencumbered by tradition, to put them into force. The personal qualifications of the new officials were, it was emphasized, as important as the reconstruction of the administrative machine: 'men of exceptional ability can obtain fair results from a bad system, but under a good system, personal shortcomings produce the minimum of disadvantage, and they are, moreover, easily detected.'[63] The third section of the report dealt with the creation of an Inspectorate to ensure that policy formulated by the Army Council would be put into force in the army. The powers of inspection formerly in the hands of the Commander-in-Chief would be transferred to an Inspector-General of Forces, whose task it would be to review and report on 'the efficiency of officers and men, on the handling of troops, on the standard and system of training, on the suitability of equipment and generally on all that affects the readiness of the Forces for war'. For once an analogy was drawn with the effective use of such an office made by the Germans. The report concluded by pressing that all their recommendations be put into force as soon as possible.

Esher's recommendations did not come entirely as a surprise to Balfour. A draft had been sent to him early in January and he had at once seized on its greatest weakness—the confusion between the duties of the General Staff and the Secretariat. The Prime Minister foresaw the danger of 'two Headquarter Staff, who, from the very fact that they are two, and not one, will tend to polarise into a kind of natural opposition.'[64] He was also unsure whether, were a Moltke available, he would under the new system be First Military Member and Chief of the General Staff or secretary to the CID. The draft had also reached Sir William Nicholson, who pungently expressed the opinion that the staff envisaged for the Secretariat 'could in no way be regarded as an expert staff' since their proposed two-year period of service was far too brief. Nicholson was astute enough to recognize the danger of overlap between the functions of Secretariat and General Staff, and had the strongest reservations about its being empowered to advise on defence questions at all.[65] In reply to Balfour's letter, Esher offered the belief that the staff of the

'Permanent Office' of the CID would not reduplicate work or create friction between Service Intelligence Departments, and justified it with the curious assertion that the former had a collative and the latter a collective function. If a Moltke were available he would not be made secretary of the CID, for Moltke took and must always take the field.[66] In the event the CIGS never did so.

Publication of the report was greeted with rapture by *The Times*. A first leader inspired by Repington described it as: 'one of the most important State documents issued in the present generation. With thoroughness, conclusiveness and precision it represents something entirely different from the emasculated compromises that make up the majority report of the ordinary committee or commission.'[67] For readers of the newspaper the report excited much less interest. A sporadic correspondence involved only 'old hands' from the War Office and dealt with financial matters. Parliament, when it reassembled, gave it a similar reception; in the debate on the address on 2 February Campbell-Bannerman took advantage of Balfour's absence to deal with fiscal policy.

Throughout this period Balfour was absent from office through illness and it was this, coupled with a desire to achieve reform rapidly and not to have to submit to the harrying of the Opposition, which led to the constitutional device now to be employed. The announcement to the press of the names of the members of the Army Council was accompanied by the information that they would be appointed by Letters Patent under the Great Seal. In conjunction with the use of Orders in Council, this meant that the whole issue of reform was not to be put before parliament for comment.

Arnold Forster made his formal submission to the King on 29 January 1904 and the names appeared in the press ten days later. The changeover in personnel was made with celerity, largely because in hearing evidence Esher's committee had had one ear cocked for likely candidates for new offices. Sir James Grierson recorded his experience of this process on 5 February:[68]

To town at 10.6 in compliance with a wire from Ellison. He, Sir J. Fisher and Sir G. S. Clarke there, and I was offered head of operations section . . . with £1500 a year and rank of Major General if possible, if not, of Brigadier General. I said I would do as I was ordered and would come if I was wanted and was much flattered.

A similar experience occurred to Henry Wilson, who was offered and accepted the Directorate of Staff Duties.

Sir William Nicholson, who had become the prime target of Esher's triumvirate, was replaced without warning on 11 February, an event which had such an effect upon him that Robertson felt he was never the same man again. A similar experience reportedly occurred between Hildyard and Stopford, the new Director of Military Training.[69] All the changes in personnel were seemingly at Esher's instigation, yet all took place before the actual duties of the Directors of the General Staff had been finally drafted—an indication of the committee's determination to push reform through fast. The new personnel were in fact to be used to help compile the second and third parts of the report.

Some disagreement between Clarke and Fisher preceded the drafting of the second part of the report. Clarke felt there should be only a brief homily on the responsibilities of the new Directing Staff, whilst Fisher pressed for a more thorough discussion. Esher as usual intervened, feeling it neither wise nor possible to frame exhaustive regulations; general principles only should be laid down for the Army Council, after which it should be left to work out details for itself. He was over-cautious about the dangers of conflict with the new body, chiefly because he was unwilling to leave it wholly to its own devices. His own feeling was that the triumvirate should stay on as a committee of reference until the end of the year to examine and advise upon the working of the new system.[70]

News of Esher's extensive activities finally reached Arnold Forster and on 13 February he complained strongly of its making appointments without reference to himself.[71] But by this time things had slipped beyond his grasp. Many important General Staff posts had already been filled; French had begun to discuss divisional appointments with the committee; and Wilson, Ellison and Stopford were discussing the distribution of work among Directors of the General Staff. Clarke was delighted at the pace of reform, and wrote jubilantly to Esher: ' "A Chief of the General Staff" at last. We have done what the D. of Devonshire and the most powerful Commission ever assembled [i.e. the

Hartington Commission] failed to accomplish. Time has its revenges.'[72] There were, however, severe disadvantages in this method of procedure which were not to become apparent for some time.

The second part of the Esher committee's report was published on Monday 25 February. It laid down the duties of the Army Council and also established the principle of administrative decentralization by placing more financial responsibility in the hands of divisional commanders. Promotion and selection of officers was also dealt with, and the fourth and final section attempted to determine 'fully and clearly' the duties of a General Staff. This was prefaced by a note of caution, to the effect that it would take some time before such a body could be adequately trained. Historical examples buttressed the assertion that a General Staff with a clearly drawn constitution and clearly defined tasks in peace and war was essential to the continued well-being of the Empire. The actual division of work within the department followed the *bureaux* system of both French and German General Staffs. The Director of Military Operations bore responsibility for the collection of strategic information and the preparation of plans of offence and defence. His work was complemented by the Directorates of Staff Duties, broadly responsible for the education and instruction of the army, and of Military Training whose functions were self-explanatory.[73]

The pyramidical structure evolved beneath the CGS thus represented a redeployment of existing strength, together with the creation of new branches to redistribute the weight of responsibility. The Directorate of Military Operations was the old Directorate of Mobilization and Military Intelligence, its functions expanded and clarified. At the same time the formation of two other departments left it free for pure thought and investigation on a strategic scale. The keynote of the system was the concept of specialization and division of labour. Yet the organization remained tight and controllable, at least in theory, since all its work was channelled into the Army Council via the Chief of the General Staff. The major omission in Esher's construction, and it was one of considerable importance, was to ignore the question of relations between the General Staff and other government departments.

In one crammed paragraph details of service were outlined which were to cause considerable debate.[74] The General Staff was to be recruited 'mainly' from the Staff College, with a maximum of four years' service. This last should qualify an officer for accelerated promotion 'in all cases'. Distinctive dress for the General Staff in peace and war was held to be essential, as was the necessity that the CGS keep entire responsibility for the administration and distribution of the General Staff.

The report of the Esher committee had demanded that the army be brought precipitately into the twentieth century, and the recommendations regarding the General Staff were to do just that. The triumvirate clearly envisaged a *corps d'élite* with avenues of promotion to senior commands being primarily *via* service on the General Staff at the War Office. The implication, at one point put into print, was that it would be General Staff officers who would in time of war direct operations in the field. Equally there was the inference that some branches of the staff would be in abeyance during a long war, which was to prove a severe handicap in 1914.[75] The whole structure was gifted with immense influence and its performance rested ultimately on the energies, vision and abilities of the CGS. Events were to prove that a structure which needed a Moltke would not necessarily get one.

The publication of the second part of the report evoked some protest, both at its contents and the methods used to bring them into force. The most explicit criticism came from a former Secretary of State for War, St John Brodrick. He complained that the Cabinet had been given insufficient time to consider the principle of a council or the names of its members. The latter had been 'given to the Cabinet at the end of a long sitting and we were forced to make any comment on them then and there'.[76] There was some truth in Brodrick's criticism, since the Cabinet was informed that either the committee's principle of removing all officials in the War Office *en bloc* must be accepted or else they would stop work. Balfour was sufficiently aware of both the political capital and the military benefits of Esher's work to be reluctant to risk the prospect of defeat on this issue. Thus Brodrick failed in his attempt to have the report discussed in Cabinet point by point.

There was criticism of the Prime Minister's use of Orders in Council and Letters Patent to bring the new system into force, and the obvious reluctance of the administration to submit the scheme to the scrutiny of the House of Commons also drew Sir

Henry Campbell-Bannerman's disapprobation. On two successive days he demanded to know why the report was in the hands of the press before it was in the hands of the House.[77] In a debate on 7 March on the Estimates the Leader of the Opposition demanded to know the history of 'this strange committee' and suggested that its conduct represented an infringement of constitutional practice. As Balfour was absent, he received no satisfactory explanation.

Such was the obloquy directed at the government and at Esher that, in the covering letter to the third and final part of the report, the committee felt constrained to justify themselves and the Prime Minister. They were doing no more than adopt and develop the principles laid down by Lord Hartington, they reminded their readers. They also remarked on the rarity of a Prime Minister who possessed such aptitude and intelligence in defence matters as did Balfour; hence the need for continuity in the study of defence questions given by the secretariat. The report itself dealt in detail with the responsibilities of the newly created Inspector-General of Forces, who was to act as the Army Council's watch-dog, and the duties of the General Staff in the field.

In this, the last part of their report, the committee expounded their philosophy of reform and in so doing unconsciously revealed all the inherent weaknesses in their creation. Their object had been to avoid details as far as possible and to erect 'a strong and well knit fabric which can be elaborated by others'.[78] The whole was designed as a carefully balanced compromise between devolution of responsibility and clear over-all direction of policy. The final paragraph contained an attractive, if over-sanguine, prophecy of the future:[79]

The Defence Committee, assisted by a small Secretariat, will deal with questions of National Defence, and will foresee Imperial requirements. The General Officers Commanding in Chief, assisted by the General Staff, will be able to concentrate their energies upon the training and the preparation of the Forces of the Crown for War. The Major Generals in the eight Districts will be able to devote themselves to administration. The Inspector General and his staff will watch over the working of the military system, and bring to light its defects. Lastly, the Army Council, freed from routine, will find the time and the means to direct military policy, to foresee military requirements, and to frame the measures of organization, the neglect of which in time of peace entails disaster or ruinously expensive improvisation in war.

The Opposition tried once more to raise the issues contained in Esher's reports. On 28 June Campbell-Bannerman rose to remark that the House was startled by the revolutionary proceedings being applied to the War Office. He was strongly critical of the ethos behind the report and directly accused the government of evasion, of failing to make clear their own views on the report.[80] Balfour replied urbanely that this was not the place for a debate on the army—the subject had again arisen during the motion to adjourn. The report was not thereafter raised in the House; during the debate on army Estimates Arnold Forster's idiosyncratic scheme to alter the structure of recruiting was of far more immediate interest to members. Thus the General Staff was never subjected to the rigours of close scrutiny by the House of Commons. Such scrutiny might have revealed the inherent weaknesses in the report; it would certainly have resulted in a dilution of Esher's schemata. On balance, therefore, Balfour was wise to resist it.

By the time that the third part of their report was published, the first recommendations of the Esher committee were being worked out in detail by the incumbents of the new posts at the War Office. The committee formally wound itself up on 25 May 1904 and received from the Prime Minister an elegant expression of gratitude for its labours. Douglas Haig also congratulated Esher on his success in interesting public and politicians alike in the army, believing that 'things seem on the right road for efficiency'.[81] This hope was to prove somewhat over-optimistic. Two of the committee were to be forced to continue their interest in the General Staff to compensate for the lack of interest displayed by the politicians; the selection of the first officers for the General Staff was to prove far from ideal; and in the longer term the confusion of roles between Secretariat and General Staff, inherent in the report, was to work against maximum efficiency. But Esher and his colleagues were overwhelmingly successful in achieving their main task; they had laid down the basic structure of the General Staff and had defined its main task as the preparation of the army for war. Of equal importance with the change of structure was the change in outlook required of the army, which was now liberated from the confines of nineteenth-century administration. The effect of this redirection upon it, and upon the war planning already under consideration, remained to be seen.

Notes

1 Cd 1789, Report of His Majesty's Commissioners appointed to inquire into the military preparations and other matters connected with the War in South Africa, p. 1.
2 Cd 1791, Minutes of Evidence taken before the Royal Commission on the War in South Africa, vol. 1, Q. 20443.
3 Cd 1791, op. cit., Q. 21733.
4 Cd 1789, op. cit., pp. 140–1.
5 M. V. Brett and Viscount Esher, Journals and Letters of Reginald Viscount Esher, vol. 1, London, 1934–8, pp. 362–3.
6 Esher Papers. Esher to Edward VII, 29 October 1903. 'South African War Commission Letters'.
7 Cd 1789, op. cit., p. 144.
8 St John Brodrick (as Lord Midleton), Records and Reactions 1856–1939, London, 1939, pp. 156–7.
9 Sir F. Ponsonby, Recollections of Three Reigns, London, 1951, pp. 126–7.
10 Balfour to Brodrick, 8 September 1903. B.M. Add. MSS. 49720.
11 Royal Archives. Esher to Edward VII, 21 May 1903. RA W24/94a.
12 Curzon to Brodrick, 5 October 1903. B.M. Add. MSS. 50074.
13 Brett and Esher, Journals and Letters, vol. 2, p. 14.
14 Arnold Forster Diary, 4 October 1904. B.M. Add. MSS 50335.
15 Mary Arnold Forster, The Right Honourable H.O. Arnold Forster: A Memoir by His Wife, London, 1910, p. 225.
16 Esher Papers. Knollys to Esher, 28 September 1903. 'War Office Reconstitution Committee 1903–5'.
17 A. J. Marder, The Anatomy of British Sea Power, Hamden, Connecticut, 1964, pp. 395f.
18 Arnold Forster to Balfour, 16 October 1903. B.M. Add. MSS. 50335.
19 Esher Papers. Fisher to Esher, 12 November 1903. 'Sir John Fisher 1903–5'. Copies of Selborne's and Battenberg's letters, dated 19 October 1903, may be seen in Royal Archives RA W30/24, 25.
20 Arnold Forster to Sandars, 19 October 1903. B.M. Add. MSS. 50335.
21 Knollys to Balfour, 9 October 1903. B.M. Add. MSS. 49683.
22 Arnold Forster to Balfour, 16 October 1903. B.M. Add. MSS. 50335.
23 Balfour to Edward VII, 23 October 1903. B.M. Add. MSS. 49683.
24 Royal Archives. Edward VII to Brodrick, 15 October 1902. RA W23/48.

25 Arnold Forster Diary, 26 October 1903. B.M. Add. MSS. 50335.
Fisher to Sandars, 26 October 1903. B.M. Add. MSS. 49710.
26 Royal Archives. Esher to Knollys, 27 October 1903. RA W30/31a.
27 Memorandum, 28 October 1903. B.M. Add. MSS. 49698.
28 Arnold Forster Diary, 2 November 1903. B.M. Add. MSS. 50335.
29 Brett and Esher, *Journals and Letters*, vol. 2, p. 30.
30 Sir G. S. Clarke (as Baron Sydenham), *Studies of an Imperialist*,
London, 1928, pp. 120f.
31 *The Times*, 7 November 1903, pp. 11, 12.
32 Sir G. F. Ellison, 'From here and there', *The Lancashire Lad:
Journal of the Loyal Regiment*, vol. IV, no. 3, August, 1937, p.
114.
33 Royal Archives. Esher to Knollys, 12 November 1903. RA W30/31f.
34 Esher Papers. Ward to Esher, 13 November 1903. 'Army Letters
Vol. 1.'
35 Royal Archives. Esher to Knollys, 15 November 1903. RA W30/31g.
36 Royal Archives. Esher to Knollys, 20 January 1903. RA W38/64.
37 Fisher to Sandars, 22 October 1903. B.M. Add. MSS. 49710.
38 Notes for Consideration, 7 November 1903. B.M. Add. MSS. 49710.
39 Esher Papers. Esher to Fisher, 19 November 1903. 'War Office
Reconstitution Committee 1903–1905.'
40 Esher Papers. Haig to Esher, 26 November 1903. 'Army Letters
Vol. 1'.
41 Memorandum by Esher, 2 December 1903, p. 2. Encl. with Esher
to Balfour, 30 December 1903. B.M. Add. MSS. 49718.
42 W.O. (R.) C., p. 1. 20 December 1903. Cab. 17/14.
43 *Ibid.*, p. 2.
44 Brett and Esher, *Journals and Letters*, vol. 2, pp. 34–5.
45 Sir N. G. Lyttelton, *Eighty Years: Soldiering, Politics, Games*,
London, n.d, (1927), p. 270.
46 Esher Papers. Wolseley to Esher, 18 January 1904. 'Army Letters
Vol. 1'.
47 M. Caillard, 'The War Office fifty years ago', *Army Quarterly*, vol.
LXXI, 1955–6, p. 58.
48 Ewart Diary, 27 and 29 January 1904.
49 Esher Papers. Repington to Esher, 4 February 1904. 'Army Letters
Vol. 1'.
50 Royal Archives. Edward VII to Balfour, 30 January 1904. RA
W30/64.
51 Esher Papers. Fisher to Esher, 8 January 1904. 'Sir John Fisher
1903–5'.
52 Esher to Balfour, 3 January 1904. B.M. Add. MSS. 49718.
53 Esher Papers. Fisher to Esher, 17 January 1904. 'Sir John Fisher
1903–5.'
54 Royal Archives. Esher to Knollys, 16 January 1904. RA W39/21.
55 Royal Archives. Speech, 24 November 1903. RA W30/34.
56 Esher Papers. Fisher to Esher, n.d. (c. 18 January 1904). 'Sir John
Fisher 1903–5'.
57 Esher Papers. Notes on the Organization and Administration of the

1st Army Corps, 21 January 1904. 'War Office (Reconstitution) Committee Vol. 1'.

58 Esher Papers. Knollys to Esher, 17 January 1904. 'Lord Knollys 1903–4'.

59 Brett and Esher, *Journals and Letters*, vol 2, p. 39.

60 Esher Papers. Balfour to Esher, 27 January 1904. 'The Prime Minister 1903–5'.

61 Fisher to Sandars, 28 January 1904. B.M. Add. MSS. 49710.

62 Cd 1932, Report of the War Office (Reconstitution) Committee (Part I), p. 1.

63 *Ibid.*, p. 11.

64 Balfour to Esher, 14 January 1904. B.M. Add. MSS. 49718.

65 Royal Archives. Observations on the Letter and Report dated 11 January 1904, addressed by the War Office Reconstitution Committee to the Prime Minister, on the subject of the creation of a Staff for the Committee of Imperial Defence and the duties proposed for that Staff, 4 February 1904. RA W32/38.

66 Brett and Esher, *Journals and Letters*, vol. 2, p. 37

67 *The Times*, 1 February 1904, p. 9.

68 D. S. MacDiarmid, *The Life of Lieut. General Sir James Moncrieff Grierson*, London, 1923, p. 206.

69 Susan, Countess of Malmesbury to Ardagh, 13 February 1904. P.R.O. 30/40/3.

70 Esher Papers. Clarke to Esher, 14 February 1904. 'War Office Reconstitution Committee 1903–4'.

71 Esher Papers. Arnold Forster to Esher, 13 February 1904. 'Mr Arnold Forster'.

72 Esher Papers. Clarke to Esher, 15 February 1904. 'Sir George Clarke Vol. 1'.

73 Cd 1968, Report of the War Office (Reconstitution) Committee (Part II), pp. 21–5.

74 *Ibid.*, p. 24.

75 *Ibid.*, p. 23.

76 Brodrick to Balfour, 29 February 1904. B.M. Add. MSS. 50072.

77 Hansard, 4th series, vol. CXXX, 29 February 1904, col. 1224; 1 March 1904, col. 1368.

78 Cd 2002, Report of the War Office (Reconstitution) Committee (Part III), p. 29.

79 *Ibid.*, p. 31.

80 Hansard, 4th series, vol. CXXXVI, 28 June 1904, col. 1503.

81 Esher Papers. Haig to Esher, 23 March 1904. 'Army Letters Vol. 1'.

3
Division and Debate

Esher's report had created a framework within which to create a British equivalent of the great continental General Staffs, and to bring to British strategic deliberations the expertise and ability which marked their activities and which had hitherto been conspicuously lacking. However, as the War Office came to debate the particulars and details of the new body deep differences of opinion grew up over the precise nature of the professional qualifications required, the question of whether General Staff work should receive especial reward and the status of the army's main academic qualification, the psc certificate which marked successful completion of the Staff College course at Camberley. On the one hand there were those, among them Sir George Clarke and Henry Wilson—himself a future CIGS—who wanted to see the General Staff as a body quite separate from the rest of the army and containing its most able officers. On the other, the conservative faction greatly feared the rise of the Chief of the General Staff to a position of supremacy within the army as the result of such an élite formation and doubted the wisdom of narrow professional qualifications as isolating their holders from many important trends and requirements of the army in general.

The first indications of the intensity of debate to follow came with the reception of Esher's recommendations. Lord Curzon regretted the clean sweep of 'old traditions, old officers and old everything' at the War Office and expected the new system to produce no fruitful results.[1] From India, a cautious Kitchener informed Lord Roberts, 'I must say I look forward with some considerable misgivings to our next war' and felt that Esher's committee had made recommendations which were far too confused.[2] Lord Roberts himself foresaw competition and then friction between the Secretariat and Service Intelligence Departments. Although some officers did send in their papers as a result of reading the report, the younger and more adventurous ones appear to have greeted the report with delight.

One reason why reception of the sweeping changes was so

good in some quarters was the choice of the new officials which accompanied it. Sir James Grierson's appointment as first Director of Military Operations was particularly applauded, with contemporaries remarking on his popularity, knowledge of the German army and friendly relationship with the French. Grierson gave an early indication of his awareness of the strategic problems confronting the Empire, and of the need to create the forces necessary to combat them, in his first summary of the priorities of military needs: 'I . . . consider that our first care should be to be able to mobilize the expeditionary force maintained at home, and which would number approximately two Army Corps.'[3] Perhaps the weakest choice among the major officers of the nascent General Staff was that of its chief, Sir Neville Lyttelton. The third of eight sons of Viscount Cobham, he had seen active service in Canada, Egypt and the Sudan before serving for three years in the Mobilization Section at the War Office (1894–7) and then in South Africa. Prior to his appointment as CGS Lyttelton had been Commander-in-Chief in South Africa, where he had reportedly been noteworthy chiefly for his ability to beat everyone at lawn tennis at the age of 58.[4] Lyttelton appeared to possess the wide range of experience necessary for the new post, as well as having a brother in the Cabinet and being on good terms with most of the influential members of society, yet from an early date doubts were expressed about his suitability for the job. Repington warned Esher that 'Lyttelton, good man as he is, knows practically nothing of great problems of Imperial defence and less than that about the problems which confront foreign strategists'.[5] He was to be proved correct. Clarke too wondered whether the new CGS would prove sound, but felt sure that had Nicholson remained in office there would have been 'no chance of a reasoned policy'.[6]

Sir Frederick Stopford was appointed Director of Military Training, and for the remaining post of Director of Staff Duties, Henry Wilson pushed the claims of Lieutenant-General H. D. Hutchinson, an unknown Indian army officer. Recognizing that he was himself too junior to occupy such an influential position, Wilson calculated that Hutchinson would be sufficiently pliable to leave him a free hand within the branch.[7] He recorded, happily but not strictly accurately, in his diary: 'It is getting known that I am running the General Staff.'[8] Wilson was dangerously over-convinced of his own influence, for he returned from a short staff ride at York to discover that Stopford was attempting to obstruct his choice of DSD as well as poaching responsibilities from the Adjutant-General and the Staff Duties Directorate. Wilson carried the day against Stopford, whose ideas he castigated as 'quite parochial and *very* Adjutant-General sort',[9] but the result of this early fracas was to split the General Staff, and the War Office. On one side, backing Esher's blueprint, stood Wilson and Grierson, fitfully supported by Sir Neville Lyttelton, and on the other Stopford, Sir Charles Douglas, who replaced Kelly Kenny as Adjutant-General in 1904, and a number of others.

The rising tide of internal debate which began to lap at the heels of the reformers was reinforced by an early, and ominous, brush with the Treasury. Since the latter had not yet sanctioned new appointments to the Staff Duties branch the War Office had no power to pay for two new officers there. The matter was referred to the Army Council which failed to reach any decision on it.[10] Following the matter up, Wilson then discovered that the Treasury had successfully persuaded Lyttelton to reduce the proposed cost of the General Staff by £17,000, and this in the only area of army expenditure where Arnold Forster was prepared to defend an increased cost. Wilson endeavoured to persuade the members of the Army Council that this was an issue of sufficient gravity for them to threaten resignation rather than submit to the proposed financial stringency. Having only just been installed in their new posts, and about to commence battle with Arnold Forster over his proposals for a short-service army, the Army Council ignored Wilson's pressing attentions.

By midsummer Clarke was feeling distinctly dubious about the prospects of the new organization and of the General Staff in particular, which he felt to be 'in danger of shipwreck'. He was more than ever convinced that military necessity dictated the need for better informed direction of military policy:[11]

> The only possible means of raising the educational standard, and the military efficiency of our Army is to have a highly trained G.S. to leaven the mass of ignorance from the top downwards. The more I study the S.A. war, the more I see that Staff incompetence, muddling and disorder lay at the very root of our humiliations.

It was Clarke's opinion that with such a staff as he envisaged the bill for the South African War might have been lightened by some £50,000,000.

Clarke's apprehensions soon spread as it became apparent that the new thinking branch of the army was not at the stage of vitality which might have been expected of it. Esher, becoming ever more impressed by the qualities of Sir John French of whose Staff Tour in the Thames Valley in August he wrote an enthusiastic account, felt the contrast between him and Lyttelton—'a good fellow, but vacillating and devoid of inspiration'.[12] Even the Secretary of State for War, who was revealing ever more esoteric opinions and character traits, was moved to record that it would be a good thing to get rid of the CGS 'who does not intend to work, and who is not at all capable'.[13]

The truth of the matter was that the recommendations of Esher's triumvirate were about to suffer the fate of many other reports and commissions, and become submerged in the welter of administrative cross-currents and personality conflicts to which the new War Office was as much a prey as the old one had been. Clarke's indefatigable determination kept the project in motion during these weeks. He subjected Esher to a bombardment of letters and notes all of which emphasized that the army must be impressed with the fact that the General Staff was a thing to be strived for, the 'Blue Ribbon' of the service. Only then, and only after some time, would the system raise the whole tone of the army and turn out generals 'who have thought about war'.[14] The first essential was for Lyttelton to publish an Army Order explaining what the General Staff was to be, something which he appeared loath to do.

If military interest in the new body was lacking, it was matched by a lack of concern on the political side also. Arnold Forster saw his role solely in terms of revising the structure of the army in order to accommodate some form of short-service force and thus make available the reserves which would naturally result from it. To do this entailed the concoction of an exceedingly complex system of 'double recruiting' to provide both a long- and a short-service force together. So preoccupied was he with this that the Secretary of State had practically no time to devote to anything else.[15] In point of fact, his occupancy of the post and his reputation alike would have been more secure had he realized the lasting benefit which would result from laying deep the foundations of a real General Staff. Since Balfour no longer betrayed any interest in the General Staff as such there was no political stimulus to its proper development; the only people both able and willing to foster its interest were Clarke, Esher and Henry Wilson.

Dissatisfaction with the resident members of the General Staff began to mount, and the names of alternatives to circulate with greater frequency. The most popular of these surrogates was Sir John French, whom Arnold Forster regarded as 'the one soldier who really puts the fighting efficiency of the army before all other considerations'.[16] French, however, had no wish to go to London and was adamant that Lyttelton should remain CGS. Considerable dissatisfaction was also being expressed about the Directorate of Military Operations. Clarke, by now secretary to the Committee of Imperial Defence, felt that Grierson's performance in that body was disappointing; also his presence obviated the necessity for Lyttelton to 'get up his subjects'.[17]

Although manifestly unwilling to enter the War Office, French did at this time influence the development of the General Staff on the issue of qualifications for General Staff employment. The so-called 'Lawson case' became a brief *cause célèbre* within the army, at some cost to the CGS and Army Council whose authority was slightly diminished. Esher had pressed upon Sir Neville Lyttelton that French be allowed a free hand with the 1st Army Corps, which he now commanded, and had advised the latter to stand firm in this intention.[18] Following this advice, French requested that his ADC, a Major Lawson, be appointed Brigade Major to his 1st Cavalry Brigade. This was to be a General Staff post and Lawson possessed no psc certificate. Lyttelton, Stopford, and Sir Charles Douglas had no objection to this dilution of the General Staff; those who did were Arnold Forster and Ewart, prompted by Wilson and the Commander of the Staff College, Sir Henry Rawlinson, or so French believed. Nicholson had suffered as a result of being a *protégé* of the outgoing Commander-in-Chief, Lord Roberts; Wilson and Rawlinson did so in this instance, since French clearly bore a similar hostility towards them:[19]

> Now *both these fellows* did much harm in Roberts' time. They are very clever and were R's special 'Pets'. They are now *trying it on again* and, if the Army Council are to

retain the confidence of the Army these two young gentlemen must have their wings clipped.

French was determined to make this matter a personal one and pressed Lyttelton to retain the right to appoint selected officers to the General Staff without a psc; otherwise, he argued, the army would be deprived of the services of many able and experienced officers. Lyttelton felt obliged to bring such a momentous matter before the Army Council.

The Lawson case encapsulated the problem of whether or not the new General Staff was to be a *corps d'élite* composed of the best brains in the army, with a consequent domination over the upper reaches of the service. Clarke adhered firmly to the 'Blue Ribbon' notion, and was currently refusing to appoint to the CID an Assistant Secretary who did not have a psc. The question was therefore referred to the committee currently at work, under the chairmanship of Lieutenant-General H. D. Hutchinson, determining the structure and qualifications of the new General Staff.

The Hutchinson committee, which was lobbied by Esher and Clarke during its deliberations, recommended that no modification should be made to the existing rule requiring a psc for General Staff service in order to accommodate Lawson. They also made no secret of the fact that they discounted French's preference for soldiers experienced in the field:[20]

> The Committee consider it very doubtful indeed whether ability displayed on the staff in the field should be regarded as qualifying officers for staff employment. They consider that field experience is not so valuable as the higher educational training which will be necessary in the future for the General Staff of the Army.

The Army Council concurred in this view, which merely stiffened French's resolve. He accused Hutchinson of criticizing the wording of his orders on manoeuvres and of other, but unspecified, 'intolerable interference'. Direct intervention by Arnold Forster gave Lawson his post. In doing so, Arnold Forster was supporting French as opposed to Lyttelton, for he recorded the previous day in his diary that 'French is worth ten times what the CGS ever was or ever will be'.[21]

Arnold Forster's dissatisfaction was echoed by Wilson, who recorded in his diary towards the end of October: 'I quite dispair of N.G. ever rousing up and making a stand as regards the General Staff. He and Hutch[inson] are wholly lethargic, and I fear the General Staff will come to nothing.'[22] As this was being written, Lyttelton's future as Chief of the General Staff lay in the balance.

In July 1904 Arnold Forster had drawn the attention of the four military members of the Army Council to a letter from the King in which he expressed 'in very clear terms' his desire that members of the headquarters staff of the army should not make controversial speeches on public occasions.[23] This structure was adhered to for some months until, early in December, Lyttelton suddenly departed from it. In the course of a presentation of prizes to a Volunteer battalion at Leicester the CGS was given an introduction which suggested that he held a post corresponding to that of the former Commander-in-Chief. According to *The Times*, Lyttelton was moved to respond thus:[24]

> I don't think the position of the Army Council is fully under-stood in the country. I don't know that I know very much about it myself yet, but I do know this—that we work in what I may call watertight compartments.

This sentiment was clearly at odds with the whole philosophy behind the creation of the Army Council, and Lyttelton went on to liken that body to a corporation and to remark that its members might congratulate themselves since as such it had 'no soul to be saved and no body to be kicked'.

Lyttelton's utterance did not pass unnoticed. Clarke wrote at once to Esher drawing his attention to 'this amazing utterance' and also pointed it out to Balfour. In a somewhat cooler vein, Esher wrote to the Prime Minister's secretary that the speech was 'foolish and undignified' but, after considering seven possible candidates, admitted the great difficulty of replacing the CGS.[25] Arnold Forster was even quicker to sense the slight to his own office and demanded an instant explanation from Lyttelton. In the event of one not being forthcoming, he warned the errant CGS he would feel that his continued presence on the Army Council would not be for the benefit of the public service. He also informed Balfour that he regarded the continued association of the CGS and himself on the Army Council as quite out of the question.

If Lyttelton had been foolish in embroiling himself thus, he showed adroitness and diplomacy in extricating himself from his embarrassing position. A letter to *The Times* submitting that he had merely sought to correct an erroneous but widespread interpretation of his position was followed by one to the Secretary of State expressing his formal regret at the terms he had used at Leicester. The gracefully placatory note on which he concluded gives some indication of the reasons for his political survival to the end of his term of office:[26]

> The fact is that I began public speaking too late in life to become a safe speaker, and I blunder into things which a more experienced hand would avoid instinctively, and in future I shall do as little of it as I possibly can. I am very sorry for the annoyance I have caused you.

Arnold Forster, who had earlier remarked on the fuss made over a 'popular cricketer with good connections', was won over by his apology and reassured Lyttelton that now that the incident was closed he would find the Secretary of State a staunch supporter.

Lyttelton managed to survive his impolitic utterances, although Edward VII was considerably annoyed by his indiscretion. That he did so was due in the final analysis to Balfour's unwillingness to support the demands of Arnold Forster to sack him. Balfour's attitude was due in part to the complete lack of interest which characterized his attitude towards the General Staff, and also to the fact that Esher had made him well aware of the absence of a viable alternative to Lyttelton. Lyttelton himself certainly recognized the power wielded by Esher in such matters, for he wrote to him to explain his actions two days before he did so to Arnold Forster.[27]

Despite the dilatoriness of the CGS some progress was made at this time in determining the shape of the General Staff. In November 1904 the Secretary of State was presented with the report of a small committee which had been examining the question of General Staff appointments 'and certain other matters' under the aegis of Hutchinson. The DSD and his colleagues felt it incumbent upon them to offer some compromise between 'Blue Ribbon' views such as those held by Clarke and the school which held that the General Staff should be in no way distinct from the Adjutant-General's staff or any other. Thus they recommended that no separate General Staff corps be formed, that officers on the various staffs should be interchangeable, and that good service in other branches should be a distinct recommendation for employment on the General Staff—all measures designed to quell the disquiet and jealousy felt by the 'old guard' at the War Office when they looked at the potential power of the new institution.

Having made a gesture to the conservative opinion in the army, Hutchinson's committee then proceeded to make clear their view that the new branch must become the senior one in the War Office. A psc certificate was essential for employment on the General Staff 'except in very special circumstances', and in any case no one below the rank of Major should be eligible. Appointments, which were to be in three grades, should be for four years without the possibility of extension and good service during those years should give Majors and Lieutenant-Colonels a strong claim to a battalion. Symptomatic of the determination of the General Staff to employ the best available officers was the suggestion that selected officers be attached to headquarters for twelve months on leaving the Staff College to gain an insight into the working of the various branches. Also appointments to the General Staff, when posted, should not carry the option of refusal. The committee concluded by recommending the General Staff wear a distinctive but not heavily expensive uniform—they suggested cross-belt and pouch on all orders of dress—and expressing the hope that if their ideas were carried out General Staff officers would in time hold the majority of important posts.[28]

The findings of the Hutchinson committee were clearly considerably in accord with the ideas of Esher and Clarke. The aim was to make the General Staff a highly qualified and respected body, and to use it as a school for most future holders of high army office—hence the emphasis on interchangeability. Some of its recommendations did ape the German General Staff; in particular, the suggestion that good General Staff service give a man a strong claim to a battalion came close to the Prussian system.[29] This served an important dual function: it kept General Staff officers alive to feelings and potentials at battalion and regimental level, as well as familiarizing regimental officers with their opposite numbers on the staff and hence preventing possible division and resultant mistrust.

Although the élitist formula being proposed was more dilute than the Prussian system it was still too strong for some of the more conservative elements, and in a note appended to the

Hutchinson report two of its members, Generals H. S. G. Miles and H. M. Lawson, argued strongly for mixing experience with innovation by selecting General Staff officers from those who had served in the administrative branches. Their justification for this attitude revealed a strong distaste for the idea of the 'Blue Ribbon' General Staff:[30]

> It seems clear to us that, if the recommendation in this memorandum is not adopted, the General Staff will suffer from lack of administrative knowledge which cannot fail to be prejudicial to the Service, especially when such officers reach the higher posts, and the efficiency of the Administrative Staff will be lowered: because the better class of officer may decline appointment thereon in the hopes of being ultimately selected for the General Staff.

Without such a manner of selection, they argued, the General Staff would lack homogeneity, and the result would be jealousy and friction.

Looking ahead to the performance of the General Staff during the First World War, and particularly at the charge most frequently levelled at it that it lacked acquaintance with the troops on the ground and the state of conditions in the front line, it is clear that there was something to be said for the view that wide experience was necessary to make an efficient and effective General Staff Officer. There was even contemporary evidence to support Miles and Lawson: Colonel W. H. H. Waters's report on the Russian General Staff found them to be highly educated theoretically but faulty in practice. Its members were certain of very rapid advancement, becoming General Officers at about forty, and as a result 'their assured career is apt to render them self-satisfied'.[31] However, in the climate of the day there was a real danger that unless the proponents of the General Staff stuck intransigently to their demands for a distinctive branch containing the intellectual élite, the new department would sink beneath the tide of administration and bureaucracy and thereby fail utterly to bring about the revolution in the quality of strategic thought which was so necessary.

Reception of the report was therefore varied. Wilson recorded in his diary that if the General Staff were dealt with according to the recommendations, it would cease to exist; Clarke felt that

Hutchinson and his cohorts had erred in detail rather than in principle.[32] Clarke was stimulated by the report to approach the Prime Minister on the shrewd political ground that his Secretary of State was a danger to him; many of Arnold Forster's proposals would never pass the Commons and the government's position would be the stronger if they could point to military reforms already begun, of which the General Staff was one. Arnold Forster should thus be set to work on this and leave alone the more thorny issue of fitting the militia into his recruiting scheme.[33] Wilson chose to tackle Lyttelton, charging him with failure to make any advance in the constitution of the General Staff since he had achieved office. Neither approach was marked by any demonstrable change in the attitude of its recipient.

Although no great progress was being made in Whitehall the new General Staff was becoming established within the army. Many of the junior officers of the old Intelligence Department were incorporated into the new General Staff. An immensely important innovation occurred with the holding of the first Staff Conference and General Staff Ride early in January 1905. This was an exercise which had long been carried out by the German General Staff and had contributed much to their expertise. It enabled the Chief of the General Staff to assess the progress and potential of his various officers, and also offered the opportunity to evolve strategic doctrines within the forum of common debate. The first British Staff Ride followed the German pattern closely, combining a series of lectures with practical exercise and the writing of appreciations and orders. In at least one case, that of Sir George Aston, the task of giving such a lecture resulted in the knowledge being born in on its author that he was profoundly ignorant about his subject.[34]

The lack of interest in the Staff Ride was an index of how far the nascent General Staff had to go to reach the stage of professional interest shown by its German counterpart. Henry Wilson felt that the work had been rather poor and Lyttelton too lax at the late night conferences; however, he had reasons of his own for feeling pleased with the innovation: 'It was entirely my idea, carried out entirely on my lines, with my criticisms etc. throughout and I was a little nervous as to how it would go, but I am very pleased with the result.'[35] However, a Staff College instructor, Colonel Lonsdale Hale, felt constrained to write a lengthy letter to *The Times* to discount the apparent view of most officers that it had been 'little more than the indulgence of someone in power in a harmless whim'. Hale pointed out that periodic gatherings of this kind could eliminate the three great weaknesses in the Staff: the failure of professional knowledge to keep abreast of increasing scientific advances, the uncertainty that training would be modified to meet the requirements of this progress and the loose connections between Staffs at Headquarters and in commands.[36] Wilson's Staff Ride had in fact provided both a test of the power of members of the new General Staff to appreciate and deal with military situations and a model which the various commands might imitate. In the years before the outbreak of the war it was to contribute greatly to the increase of professionalism within the army.

As the General Staff Ride was being inaugurated, and as the Secretary of State for War was admitting that however much it would benefit the army to be rid of Lyttelton, 'the difficulty is to find anyone to take his place who is conspicuously better',[37] the proposals of the Hutchinson committee came before the Army Council. The report, which was summarized for the Army Council by its secretary, Sir Edward Ward, had grown a prodigious 'tail'. A rider had been added to it, as a result of the Lawson incident, admitting that it might from time to time be considered advisable to appoint to the General Staff officers who 'without a Staff College certificate develop special qualifications, or who have acquired special experience which fits them for some branch of the staff'.[38] Lyttelton and Sir H. C. O. Plumer, the Quartermaster-General, both felt that the prospect of a battalion as a reward for good service on the General Staff, far from attracting the prospective entrant into the General Staff, would be a positive deterrent since it was such an onerous office. Sir Charles Douglas, safeguarding the interests of all administrative branches as well as his own Adjutant-General's department, was concerned that special promotion should not begin to operate until the General Staff was composed of officers at present holding administrative posts. There was therefore no consensus of opinion about any aspect of the structure of the new body within the Army Council and in the face of this Lyttelton would have been best advised to stick to his policy of the 'Blue Ribbon' type and use the divisions amongst the rest of his fellows to steer it through. Instead he admitted the unfairness of a policy of accelerated promotion for those who had entered the General Staff and thereby opened the door to attenuated discussion of principles. This postponed the proper establishment of the General Staff for over a year.

The question which seems chiefly to have exercised the minds of those considering the formation of the General Staff, and which typified the problems facing it, was one raised in an aside of the Hutchinson report. It had been remarked that it was detrimental to the efficiency of the service that practically no substantive Lieutenant-Colonels were employed in command of units and brevet Lieutenant-Colonels only created in wartime. This left a hiatus in the table of ranks which proved a great drawback in such times as the army found itself in action. To overcome this Lyttelton suggested promoting Majors to half-pay Lieutenant-Colonels after three years General Staff service, thus leaving one year to find them commands or re-employ them. Douglas opposed such a policy utterly, feeling that it would result in a large number of officers seeking this mode of advancement rather than face the 'more troublesome and responsible task of commanding a unit'.[39]

The whole issue of the General Staff came before the Army Council on 16 January 1905. Although in theory only discussing certain administrative arrangements in the functioning of that branch, all the members of the council realized quite well that they were in fact debating the place of the General Staff within the army, and particularly *vis-à-vis* the other departments at the War Office. In most cases it was agreed to follow the recommendations of the Hutchinson committee. But this did not mean that Lyttelton now had a free hand to start off the General Staff as he wished, for the most vital decision, on the question of accelerated promotion, was postponed. Wilson felt, with some reason, that the latter had killed the General Staff and on hearing the news recorded: 'It is very disheartening, and although it doesn't matter to me personally, I feel very lonesome and angry tonight.'[40] It was probably this news which prompted the DMO, Sir James Grierson, to write: 'I don't myself think we are getting on as quickly as we might, but still a lot has been done of late and a great deal of it is not, and cannot be, apparent to the world at large.'[41] With sublime and misplaced confidence Arnold Forster felt highly optimistic about the progress of the General Staff in his summary for the Cabinet of the previous year's work.

The complete change in personnel the previous spring had been accomplished 'without undue friction'. After careful consideration, he reported, the character, composition and functions of the General Staff had been established; he drew particular attention to the principle of interchangeable staffs within the War Office.[42] In making this statement Arnold Forster was merely gilding the outline presented by Hutchinson before the details had been fully drawn. He was also labouring under the disapproval of the Crown: the previous autumn, the King had complained at not being 'in any way consulted' about the details of the General Staff scheme which he understood to be 'practically settled or at all events in an advanced stage towards completion'.[43] In truth, Arnold Forster had little enough interest in the scheme and therefore little to report to the King.

The most assiduous partisans of the General Staff were far from well pleased when they looked back over the first year of its existence. Sir George Clarke felt that younger officers such as Wilson had caught the spirit of the thing but Lyttelton was hopeless, Grierson a failure and Stopford 'only a Chief Staff Officer of the bad old type craving after little administrative details with no grasp of his important duties'.[44] He emphasized that a General Staff as they had envisaged it was the only way to bring brains to the fore and prevent the rise of the 'swash-buckling officer with luck and no brains' to positions of power. As it was, Clarke felt that the CGS had been 'sat upon' by the Army Council over the Hutchinson report (which he had), an instance of the bad administration which they hoped to have remedied.[45] A trained and select General Staff offered the only chance of ensuring that troops were properly handled in the field; the question was how to bring it into being.

By a strange coincidence the Commons became at this time briefly curious about Vote 1A of the army Estimates, which included Staff appointments, as a result of being asked for a Supplementary Estimate of £55,000. Arnold Forster was attacked by McKenna and Churchill, who charged him with failure to achieve a promised reduction, and was forced to admit that the War Office 'had anticipated that they would have made greater progress than had actually been accomplished'.[46] The attack became more direct when, on 28 March, Courteney Warner challenged whether value for money was being obtained from the new General Staff.[47]

> Surely, in any alteration of the Army consideration should
> be given to things that were useful while reducing more
> expensive items. Take for instance the new Intelligence
> Department. It was a very expensive item. Every one was in
> favour of a good General Staff; but there was an impression—
> he gave it for what it was worth—that it did not do the work
> it had to do.

He also reported rumours in military circles that the efficiency
of the General Staff as a whole was not what it ought to be, and
demanded an assurance that this was not merely a paper scheme.
There now existed a very real opportunity for the Commons to
follow up this attack and press for the definite establishment of
the General Staff. Whether through lack of interest or pressure
of other interests, they never did so.

Symptomatic of the parlous state of the new General Staff in
the absence of confirmed and influential patrons such as Clarke
and Esher was the state of the recently instituted Directors'
meetings. One of the characteristics of the War Office before the
Boer War had been that one department rarely knew what
another was doing for weeks, or even months, after the event. It
had therefore been decided to remedy this situation; the three
Directors of the General Staff (DMO, DSD and DMT) would
have regular meetings with the Directors of the other branches
of the War Office. As a means of pooling information and solving
common problems this was a failure, and gradually died out.[48]
Sir Charles Callwell recorded that the chief feature of these
meetings was the perpetual ranging of the General Staff against
the administrative staff, but one manifestation of 'a good deal of
passive obstruction from powerful quarters' which hindered the
development of the General Staff.[49]

It was not until March that Clarke turned his attention again
to the General Staff. When he did so, his opinion of the major
figures remained unaltered with the exception of Grierson,
whose 'knowledge of the German system enables him to understand our meaning'.[50] That General Staff work was being
inadequately performed was borne out by a letter Repington
wrote to Esher after the latter had sent him some papers prepared
by the General Staff: 'They appear to me, from a first glance,
rather jejune. I hoped they would say where we want to go and
why we want to go there. The question is not considered from a

sufficiently lofty standpoint.'[51] Even allowing for Repington's hostility to some at least of the military 'establishment', the degree of corroborative evidence supports his contention. To Wilson the only answer was for Nicholson to come in as CGS; otherwise he saw 'nothing but years of chaos in front of us'.[52]

Such was Lyttelton's procrastination that the next stimulus to the development of the General Staff came entirely from outside his department. In order that the recommendations of a committee under Bromley Davenport on rates of staff pay could be given effect, the secretary informed the Army Council that a warrant must first be issued formally constituting a General Staff. Prior to this certain decisions must be arrived at, the most important of which was the question of accelerated promotion or some other form of preferential treatment for General Staff officers. A draft recommendation from the Hutchinson committee suggested that reward be commensurate with rank, Colonels or above being promoted and regimental officers rewarded by brevet promotion or half-pay Lieutenant-Colonelcies. The Army Council refused to agree to these suggestions but offered nothing in their place.

The 'obstructionist' lobby was gaining strength during these months as a result of the dilatoriness of Lyttelton and the pre-occupation of Arnold Forster. One of its members even tried to win over the irascible Clarke. In a letter to him, General Miles remarked that when he arrived at the War Office in June 1904 the General Staff had appeared to him to contain young men who merely happened to be available, no attempt having been made to select them. Their attitude, to which he greatly objected, was that they were on the staff for life. Miles feared that they would gradually absorb a large share of the administrative work in both the War Office and the commands. He argued forcefully that, in contrast, officers should experience all sides of staff work; then, by a winnowing process, the men who rose to the top would have knowledge of all sides of administration.[53] It was unfortunate that, though the arguments of Miles and his fellows were eminently reasonable, their motives were highly suspect.

Arnold Forster's attempt to resolve the dilemma was a re-newed effort to replace Lyttelton as CGS in which he was en-couraged by overhearing Esher at a dinner party urging his removal. On 4 May he approached the only feasible alternative,

Nicholson, who indicated that he would be happy to accept the post if offered it. The next day Arnold Forster tackled Lyttelton, informing him that there was strong evidence that he had almost stopped working and that his office was suffering from neglect and incompetence. He offered Lyttelton command of the Gibraltar garrison, shortly due to fall vacant, and hinted broadly that if he did not accept it the next government would probably throw him out.

Esher's dinner-table aside had not been lightly made. He was himself becoming ever more concerned at the failure of his hand-picked Moltke and turned to Sir George Clarke to sound out feelings on Nicholson as a possible alternative. Clarke's reply was illuminating. He distrusted Nicholson for four main reasons: he did not 'run straight'; he would create internal and external friction; lacking Fisher's genius, he would certainly try to make himself C.-in-C. like Fisher; and he would resume his practice of 'leaking' information to Spenser Wilkinson.[54] In essence, Clarke disliked Nicholson because he was patently not in sympathy with the naval Imperialist 'Blue Water' approach to defence questions in which Clarke himself so firmly believed and which he was attempting to impose on the Committee of Imperial Defence. He did, however, agree with Esher that there was another side to the balance, and that under Nicholson the General Staff would stand a better chance of being made into a strong body.

Considerable pressure was now exerted in the first serious attempt to remove Lyttelton. Arnold Forster approached Alfred Lyttelton, Balfour's Colonial Secretary, who refused to do anything to upset his brother. Lyttelton himself, coolly impervious to veiled threats, refused the Gibraltar Command on 9 May. Esher meanwhile informed Balfour through his private secretary that he and the King were agreed in thinking that Lyttelton ought to go: 'I feel very strongly that in the CGS *competence* i.e. a strong character and the most recent and wide theoretical experience are necessary. Amiability and gentlemanly qualities take a second place.'[55] Clarke also pointed out to Balfour that work on the General Staff was languishing.[56] It might be imagined that Balfour, approached by an old friend whose value he recognized to the extent of pressing him to take Cabinet office and by one of his closest professional advisers, would have heeded these warnings and endeavoured to impart some vitality to the

General Staff. There is no evidence that he took any steps whatever as a result of these letters.

A strong lever did, however, exist to help Esher and Arnold Forster in their task in the shape of the report of the Butler committee shortly due to come before the Army Council; this dealt with irregularities in the sale and refund of stores to contractors after the South African War, when Lyttelton had been C.-in-C. South Africa. Lyttelton was prepared to stand out during the deliberations on the report but not to resign. The Secretary of State for War therefore attempted again to rid himself of his personal burden, this time by charging that he now lacked the support of his chief military adviser on a crucial matter. He sent the Prime Minister his views and a copy of the letter he proposed to send to Lyttelton asking for the latter's resignation on these grounds. Balfour was reluctant to assent to the move. He replied that since the matter was now before a commission there was no obvious reason why Lyttelton should not 'give him all the work he wanted'. 'Is it', he queried, 'your view that every body should resign whose conduct is now *sub judice?*'[57]

News of the political intrigue against Lyttelton soon became well known in the army. By the end of June the affair had become such common currency that questions were being asked in the House as to whether or not Lyttelton had in fact resigned. However, as a stimulus to further activity the public clamour over the General Staff was much less effective than was a series of articles from the pen of the military correspondent of *The Times*, Colonel Repington.

Playing skilfully on Arnold Forster's deep concern with his own reputation, Repington urged him to create a modern General Staff if he wished to immortalize himself. Deploring the half-hearted efforts of the Hutchinson committee, he pressed for consideration of the German system as the one with the most recent and redounding successes to its credit; also its principles were clearly expounded for all to read in the works of von Schellendorff, Verdy du Vernois and Wilkinson.[58] In a second article Repington put forward his own blueprint for a General Staff. He recognized the need for a school of generalship and an established military doctrine. He also disabused his readers of any notion they might have that such a General Staff as was required had already been formed: 'Bits of the framework of a great General Staff system at headquarters have been juxtaposed awaiting the attention of the master builder. But the General Staff which must man, organize, direct, and inspire remains to be created.'[59] His own proposals were, first, that the CGS should be the most able and experienced soldier in the army and that his appointment should be permanent as long as he was successful. Next, General Staff appointments should be made mainly from men who had done well at Staff College or in the field and all should be on one list, including England, India and the colonies. Finally he argued that before appointment all officers should spend up to three years at Headquarters or on instructional work or special missions. Repington's ultimate aim was clear and uncompromising: 'Eventually, the majority of all high commands in peace and in the field, and all places on the operations staffs during a campaign, should be filled by men who have gone through the General Staff training.'[60] This was the stimulus Arnold Forster required. Realizing that he could hope for nothing constructive from Lyttelton, he wrote on 30 May to Henry Wilson asking for his views on the whole question.

Unfortunate as Wilson's later political activities may have been, he undeniably possessed the gift of clear and trenchant exposition and this showed clearly in the uncompromising answer which he gave. Wilson commenced with the twofold object of the General Staff: to gather together the ablest men in the army and, by a system of promotional inducements, to ensure that they always controlled the army's fortunes; and to form a school of thought at least equal to that of any other army. Lacking the latter, the Secretary of State acted without the 'carefully balanced opinion, after mature thought and deliberation, of a collective body of experts'.[61] Hence continuity of policy was impossible. The answer, urged Wilson, was to give the CGS absolute control over the General Staff and relieve him of all routine work so that he might be the Secretary of State's sole adviser on strategy. The General Staff as a body should be composed of the pick of each year's Staff College graduates and must be granted accelerated promotion.

Here was a clear expression of the 'Blue Ribbon' view of the General Staff, and one which of necessity based complete reliance on the qualities of the Chief of the General Staff. As one of Lord Roberts's *protégés* there is little doubt that Wilson was counting on another of that school to succeed to the post, namely Sir William Nicholson. It is interesting to note that when, in 1917, Wilson found himself serving under a different chief (Sir William Robertson) he was quite ready to abandon the notions he had propounded some twelve years earlier.

The fundamental question which split the War Office remained unresolved: was it to be the man or the job which had General Staff status? General Miles felt that confusion over this issue rested primarily on a pejorative connotation attaching to the term 'administration', although he probably did his cause little good in attempting to resolve the difficulty: 'Administration is sometimes spoken of as if it were pure indoors office work. But it is not so; there is no better practice than drawing up large bodies of troops in ceremonial.'[62] He pointed to the plethora of work which fell to administration—discipline and efficiency of units, equipment, camp and barracks—and to the fact that a good General Staff officer at Headquarters might lack the experience necessary to perform such tasks.

Miles's aim was to prevent feelings of jealousy and inferiority on the part of administrative officers, who served under the Adjutant-General. It was this that lay behind his suggestion of a general list of officers fit to perform General Staff duties, coupled with accelerated promotion. His concern that the General Staff should not outpace the other departments in the War Office was not merely the response of one worried individual but was symptomatic of widespread concern. Sir Charles Douglas was at the same time concerned to see that appointments be the reward of merit wherever found. The theme of security of tenure, continually reiterated by the administrative staff, was illustrated in his proposal that once on a common list officers should remain there permanently unless removed for inefficiency. He wanted everyone to have a hand in the selection of that first list—Army Council, Selection Board, and Commander-in-Chief India—in order to ensure that its members had the widest possible experience:[63]

It is impossible, in my opinion, to separate administration from command in our Army, and if in the future our superior commanders are to be drawn in the main from the General Staff list, it is essential that they should have gone through the mill both in the general and the administrative staffs, and also have commanded a unit of the arm to which they belong.

These minutes stimulated Lyttelton to form another small committee consisting this time of himself, Hutchinson, Miles and Lawson, to consider the whole issue again. The recommendations which resulted show clearly how much Lyttelton fell under the influence of the 'administrative' view of the staff. The General Staff list should show, by seniority, all officers thought by a consensus of opinion to be qualified for service thereon; the initial selection was to be made from that list by the CGS and would be mainly though not entirely drawn from officers holding psc certificates. The nub of the question was again the problem of accelerated promotion and here the committee arrived at a somewhat complex solution. In the first instance, i.e. where a Captain was appointed Major of the General Staff, the problem might be resolved by using an 'unattached' list or cross-promotion to a different regiment. The step from Major to Lieutenant-Colonel should be substantive and, where the reward for good General Staff work, at least two years quicker than the average period. It was left to the discretion of the CGS to recommend a Major for a period of regimental duty if he was felt to be out of touch with the troops or to remove an officer's name from the list at any time.[64]

The long-drawn-out discussions about the General Staff had meanwhile stung Esher into action. Some time in mid-June he approached Clarke with the suggestion that the old triumvirate might reunite to produce a supplementary memorandum on the General Staff. Clarke responded eagerly: the thing could be done in a week and might well clear the air and get General Staff started.[65] The resulting paper was wholly the work of these two; Sir John Fisher's contribution was limited to the caustic advice 'For goodness sake keep out "Old Nick" '.[66]

The memorandum appeared on 28 June 1905 as a CID paper above the signatures of Esher, Fisher and Clarke. They complained, not wholly correctly, that since the issue of their report a year earlier no steps had been taken to lay down the conditions of General Staff employment or to provide for the supply of highly trained officers which constituted the greatest need of the army. They recognized that they were themselves partly responsible for this delay:[67]

That little or no progress has been made in this direction may be due to the fact that we purposely refrained from making detailed proposals and preferred to lay down general principles which would serve as a guide for the preparation of a definite scheme.

With a clarity absent from the original report the memorandum divided General Staff work into two distinct categories: at the War Office a special department charged with studying and advising on military policy and collecting and collating the necessary information and on Command Staffs specially trained officers 'with defined duties in war and in peace'. To reach the necessary state of efficiency and readiness for war the CGS was to lead a steady development of the methods and training of the General Staff and constantly to check officers' progress by means of Staff Rides and tests.

The aim of the triumvirate's recommendations was this time much more clearly apparent: to ensure that the General Staff played a full role in all matters connected with defence. Hence the statement that:[68]

[It] should, as in Germany and Japan, provide the means of raising the intellectual standard of the Army, and of watching over and tending its needs at all points. At the same time it should apply a continuous test of the capacity of officers, not only for discharging General Staff duties, but for high command.

A third but no less important aim was to create and consolidate military opinion on sound and generally accepted lines, that is to form a military doctrine.

To further these aims Esher and his colleagues believed it essential that the General Staff contained the best brains in the army, that advancement be by merit and study but that it should not be allowed to become a 'class apart'. As a beginning it was suggested that a list be drawn up of those officers who had performed what might be considered General Staff duties 'with unquestioned success', and who could therefore be regarded as qualified for such employment. Ability alone was to be the criterion for inclusion in the list; and to ensure that no ineradicable mistakes were made, most first appointments should be probationary. Eventually educational qualifications to enter the Staff would be exceptionally high: regimental rank not below Captain, a full course at Staff College and a special report by the Commandant on an officer's fitness to discharge General Staff duties.

The memorandum concluded:[69]

The experience of South Africa has proved to demonstration that the army suffers from the want of a trained General Staff. The Japanese have created such a staff, with the result that huge forces have been handled in the field with conspicuous success. Great Britain alone of great military Powers has neglected to make this essential provision. In the earnest hope that this vital defect may be remedied before we are again called upon to conduct large military operations, we venture to urge that the measures suggested should be taken without further delay.

As ever, Esher had been careful to ensure that advice had been taken from the younger military generation before voicing his thoughts. Suggestions made by Ellison were incorporated and a draft of the paper was sent off to Rawlinson, then Commandant of the Staff College. He felt that the whole subject was of 'vital importance to the future welfare and efficiency of our army' and suggested a 'senior Course' at Staff College for General Staff officers of about forty so that they should keep themselves '*au courant* with the latest ideas in military science and the Art of War'.[70] Douglas Haig was also consulted and felt that 'more stress might be laid on training the Staff for *every description of service* in view of *Imperial* needs'.[71] In view of his subsequent role in creating the Imperial General Staff, this concern of Haig's is illuminating. So too is his ordering of the main qualities that a staff officer in the field should possess:

1 Courage, health, personal magnetism.
2 Decision, self-reliance, reasoning power.
3 Technical knowledge and a skill of imparting it.

The publication of the memorandum did not, of course, guarantee its adoption. In order to stir up the Secretary of State for War into some activity on this score Esher visited him personally on 15 July to give him a copy of the paper. Arnold Forster sounded Esher out on the possibility of Royal hostility to the suggestion of Nicholson's replacing Lyttelton, and Esher took the opportunity to try to put some resolve into his host:[72]

Lord Esher thought it his duty to state his strong conviction that, whatever personal opinions Your Majesty might entertain as to the fitness of Sir Wm. Nicholson for the post, Your Majesty in such a matter, could leave the responsibility to Your Majesty's Ministers for the advice which they might think fit to offer Your Majesty, and that Lord Esher felt sure Your Majesty would not anticipate this advice by expressing any opinion.

Esher certainly intended to leave the Secretary of State with the impression that he would sway the King and Balfour to support a replacement of Lyttelton by Nicholson should this prove necessary; but Arnold Forster was congenitally uncertain, and recorded in his diary after the visit: 'I never really know what this clever and agreeable man is driving at. Whether he actually intends to help me or not, I am still quite uncertain.'[73] This was a cry which numbers of Esher's acquaintances might well have echoed.

Esher's personal initiative coupled with the appearance of his paper seem to have succeeded in impressing on Arnold Forster the need for action over the General Staff, for early in July he called Henry Wilson to him for a private interview. In the course of that *tête-à-tête* he told Wilson that his paper on the General Staff question was 'the most able, lucid and instructive paper by far that he had read on this subject', and went through it thoroughly with him.[74] He soon realized that the key to a proper organization of the General Staff, in default of securing a more active head than Lyttelton, lay in the very directorate charged with such development, the Staff Duties Directorate. Hutchinson was clearly inert, so he wrote to Sir John French seeking his advice on the post. French concurred in the assessments of the current DSD and added:[75]

General Haig, on the other hand, is intimately acquainted with the British Army, and has a good knowledge of the Indian Army as well. His rank is sufficient; he has had wide experience both in war and in peace; he is possessed of a very high order of intelligence; and no one in the army that I know of has greater Staff capacity.

This was the beginning of a campaign to bring Haig into the General Staff into which Edward VII himself entered early in August.

As much as ever, the main problem remained one of instilling some activity and energy into the topmost position in the General Staff. There was within the British army at least one figure with a reputation for administration at home and success in the field; accordingly Esher sounded out Lord Kitchener in India as to whether he would take the post. The ground-bait that Esher laid out was tempting: an increase in salary and a Field Marshal's baton. He also emphasized, flatteringly, the need for 'an electrifying agency, applied with your special vigour' to jerk the system into life.[76] Kitchener replied to these blandishments with a polite but firm refusal: 'I think I know what I can do as well as my limitations—I can I believe impress to a certain extent my personality on men working under me, I am vain enough to think I can lead them: but I have no silver tongue to persuade.'[77] In the meanwhile pressure was building up to appoint Haig as DSD to replace Hutchinson, a scheme propounded by French and Esher and strongly supported by the King.[78] In this Edward VII was following the advice being given him by Sir John French, who was rapidly becoming *persona grata* in royal circles. French's actions were not, however, solely motivated by the impersonal requirements of the service. Haig's appointment as DSD would obviate the need to replace Lyttelton and thereby prevent his replacement as CGS by Sir William Nicholson, whom French disliked. Of the latter proposal he informed the King: 'that his choice would not be the best he could make and would probably not be approved by those soldiers who were best qualified to form an opinion.'[79] No change occurred as a result of these machinations, and Esher was left to lament on the paradox of Hutchinson's appointment: as an 'Indian' he was not deemed suitable for a Home Command yet he was DSD.

A few days later the issue of the constitution of the General Staff was once again placed before the Army Council; the decisions it reached on this occasion, after wrestling manfully with the problem, represented something of a victory for the conservative school of older officers in the War Office. Lyttelton was to prepare a definition of Staff duties and the qualifications presumed necessary for their performance which was to be forwarded to Members of Council 'with the object of assisting them in preparing lists of officers whom they deemed qualified for employment on the General Staff'.[80] The general principle of accelerated promotion was accepted but once again 'the question of the extent and nature of this promotion [is] to be deferred for further considerations'. The decisions that a psc would not be a *sine qua non* and that no separate General Staff corps would be formed were reiterated.

These conclusions, which represented something of a triumph for the '*Adjutantur*' school, deeply depressed Clarke, who wrote to Esher: 'The bad traditions of the WO seem likely to triumph in the long run, and little will remain of our carefully constructed edifice in five years. It needed tending carefully by someone who understood it.'[81] He particularly disliked selection of officers by individual qualifications which he regarded as deliberately designed to bring in 'AG people and others who ought not to be on the GS'.

At last Arnold Forster seriously turned his attention to the problem of the General Staff. He was undoubtedly influenced both by the personal appeals made to him over Douglas Haig and by the decisions just reached by the Army Council; and he was also beginning to realize that his much-vaunted new recruiting scheme would never come to fruition in the face of the almost unanimous hostility being shown towards it. Patently influenced by Wilson's note of 6 June, he now put his own thoughts on paper.

His definition of the objects in view in forming a General Staff was identical with that given earlier by Wilson, and he also complained of a lack in continuity in policy and action. This he blamed on the individual advice tendered to him instead of the 'carefully balanced opinion, after mature thought and deliberation, of a collective body of experts'.[82] He seemed unaware that this amounted to an accusation of dilatoriness against himself. Assuming that the principles he enumerated were accepted, it remained to set up the machinery by which they could be carried out and in which the CGS must play a leading role. Arnold Forster was in no doubt that that officer should have complete control over the General Staff and be the sole strategic adviser to the Secretary of State.

The concrete suggestions he had to make included a first appointment on one year's probation in all cases, this list to be approved by the whole Army Council; all subsequent recommendations for promotion or selections were to be made by the CGS. But of much the greatest importance in immediate terms was the issue of accelerated promotion for the army generally, utilized to promote General Staff officers, or a known policy of promoting as a matter of course all officers placed on the General Staff list or regarding good service on the General Staff as a special recommendation for early accelerated promotion. Recognizing that some special inducement would be necessary to attract the most intelligent and hard-working officers to undertake what would be arduous tasks, Arnold Forster favoured a combination of the second and third proposals: accelerated promotion for officers actually on the General Staff after the satisfactory completion of each term of service and provided the officer was considered sufficiently meritorious to be retained on the list for further employment. He also disagreed that administrative experience be a necessary qualification for employment and pleaded instead for a wide definition of General Staff duties so as to leave the CGS as much latitude as possible. In the meantime, Lyttelton now had sufficient guidance to enable him to make out final proposals.

Lyttelton received the Secretary of State's memorandum with protests of admiration, not knowing that it emanated from Henry Wilson, and proposed to carry it out in its entirety. The draft instructions he then drew up caused Wilson to explode, 'I have never seen anything more futile, more senile, more miserable than N.G.'s minute.'[83] His response was brief and slashing: assuming agreement that a General Staff was to be formed, good service upon which would be rewarded with some form of accelerated promotion *after* work had been carried out, that General Staff duties would be clearly defined and that the CGS would have absolute responsibility over the selection, formation and instruction of the General Staff, then two things followed. There must be an establishment of officers for the General Staff; and the CGS could not reward officers in any other department but his own. Wilson was in effect pleading for a precautionary stage when promising officers would be gathered together to see how they performed, before anything firm was done about publishing a list of General Staff officers:[84]

> It will be obvious therefore that any list of officers now made must be entirely of a provisional nature, and therefore should *not* be published. The reason being, that until an officer has been on the General Staff it is impossible to say whether he is fitted or not for the duties, and whether he is good enough for accelerated promotion.

Under Wilson's schemata, no accelerated promotion would be granted to anyone for at least the first three or four years; by that time the army would have grown accustomed to and accepted the idea that officers who 'have such high qualifications, who have been so systematically trained and so carefully watched, should be recompensed by accelerated promotion'.

Although Wilson did not know it, his efforts were being aided by the two most convinced protagonists of the General Staff. There was now an added spur to action: it was becoming apparent that the days of the Unionist government were short and fears were expressed in several quarters about the fate of the defence machinery under a Liberal administration. Paradoxically it was this predicament which resulted in Balfour's retention of the unfortunate and touchy Arnold Forster at the War Office when it would have been wiser to be rid of him: Sandars, the Prime Minister's private secretary, explained of Arnold Forster that 'he only exists because the days (of Govt.) are short and evil'.[85]

Clarke was strongly convinced of the necessity of the new body: 'If we are to have great Generals and men capable of training the Army for War we must keep the minds of our Officers off administration.'[86] The Prime Minister proved rather more difficult to persuade as to its value. At one point during the Morocco crisis Clarke had appealed directly to the Prime Minister to utilize the General Staff to solve a strategical problem. Writing in mid-August, he requested a General Staff study of the problem of the violation of Belgium by either of the belligerents during a Franco-German war. It was only after several reminders that Balfour consented, and the paper at last appeared on 23 September.[87]

Esher too felt the lack of a specialized Staff as they had envisaged it and tried at least twice during September to awaken Balfour to the need to press on with its formation. Writing at his request on issues of army reorganization raised by Roberts's campaign for national service, Esher concluded that the lack of a General Staff was the fundamental deficiency: 'Were such a body in existence you would find that those other questions would fall into their natural place of mere platitudes of military organization.'[88] Later, in considering the expansion of the Committee of Imperial Defence to review all strategic questions, Esher made the point more strongly in urging that machinery be set up to free the CGS entirely from administration so that he could concentrate on the General Staff.[89]

The efforts of Esher and Clarke met with no response from Balfour, who took no action on the issue. Clarke could write with some justification at the end of September: 'I should say the whole question could have been disposed of in a fortnight. It has taken nearly nine months and has not yet reached the execution stage.'[90] The military 'conservatives' at the War Office fought on in an endeavour to prevent the General Staff being the principal, if not the sole, avenue of promotion to the higher ranks in the army. A minute from Sir James Wolfe Murray at the end of September reiterated these points.

Pressure to push the issue of the General Staff continued unabated. Brodrick wrote to Balfour from the India Office suggesting that a forthcoming vacancy at Madras might be filled by Lyttelton, thereby relieving a troublesome situation at the War Office. On 10 October Arnold Forster sent his General Staff paper to the Prime Minister with the remark that it was 'now or never. We can commence this General Staff and we ought to do so.'[91] In view of the opposition he foresaw, he requested an assurance of Balfour's agreement—nothing more. One day later Clarke sent Balfour a memorandum on the CID which contained the following observation: 'Its one weakness arises from causes lying outside its constitution. Until a trained General Staff has been created, military opinion on great questions of National Defence will necessarily be crude and inadequate.'[92] He plaintively reminded the Prime Minister that the Esher committee had drawn attention to this need, but no remedy had been applied. Balfour's own creation—the Committee of Imperial Defence— seemed at risk; the question was, would this stimulate him to action?

The Prime Minister was sufficiently impressed by the volume of activity about him to send Arnold Forster's memorandum to Clarke for comment. In reply, Clarke urged him to get the affair properly started; all that was needed was a properly worded Army Order and the Prime Minister was the person to make Arnold Forster stir himself. In reality Clarke was being less than fair to the Secretary of State for War, who had awoken to the need for action. With strong opposition from the majority of the military members of the Army Council, a CGS whom he could neither induce to act nor remove and strong opposition in the Commons for his two-tier system of recruiting, Arnold Forster's request for Balfour's assistance was a desperate cry for help.

Balfour took no action as a result of the flood of advice on the need to start the General Staff, and the issue died away. Arnold Forster tried several times in the course of November to remove Lyttelton to the Scottish Command but failed. He then began to take matters into his own hands and set about preparing his memorandum of 16 August for the press. Lyttelton's reaction was a typical one: he agreed at first to such a course, but shortly afterwards changed his mind and felt the issue should go back to the Army Council. Arnold Forster thereupon decided to write privately to Repington to assure him that draft instructions for the formation of a General Staff did in fact exist.[93] In the meantime he sent his memorandum to the CGS virtually unaltered as instructions for the commencement of the General Staff. Hutchinson began to write up the proposals.

There followed a confused incident. Wilson recorded leaking the minute to the press on 21 November on Arnold Forster's instructions.[94] It duly appeared in *The Times* the next morning, when Arnold Forster recorded in his diary that this had occurred despite instructions to the contrary given to Hutchinson. None the less he felt publication was all to the good.[95] Arnold Forster telegraphed Lyttelton expressing his 'amazement' at the early publication, and this was shown to Wilson on 23 November. In view of Arnold Forster's almost pathological indecisiveness, and of Wilson's habit of leaking information to Bonar Law over Ulster in later years, the most probable explanation of the incident is that Arnold Forster indicated his intention to publish something—though perhaps not everything—in the future and Wilson decided that no harm would be done by anticipating direct instructions a little.

The appearance of the instructions in the press met with King Edward's displeasure, since he had specifically requested a draft of any order before publication.[96] However, the minute was generally well received and particularly so by the military correspondent of *The Times*. Commenting on it some days later, Repington remarked that it would have been better accompanied by an Army Order or Warrant setting out the proposed organization. But he congratulated Arnold Forster on 'a serious and statesmanlike attempt to graft upon the somewhat rebel British stem the greatest product of the school of Moltke'. He accepted the principles of individual merit determining a place on the General Staff list, of the refusal to form a General Staff corps and of accelerated promotion with approbation. His conclusion, however, highlighted one of the weakest points of the structure:[97]

> we must first catch our Moltke before we pickle him, and a really great Chief of the General Staff, endowed with the tact, experience, ability, and, if necessary, ruthlessness, required for the fulfilment of such an onerous task, and rendering him worthy of continuance in the exercise of his functions through a long term of years, is not to be discovered without diligent search.

It was with this point in mind that, on 23 November, Arnold Forster formally offered Lyttelton the Scottish Command, shortly due to fall vacant. Lyttelton refused, although he was well aware of the possibility that the next government might try to get rid of him. Wilson was dismayed and determined to postpone any action on the General Staff until after the fall of the Unionist government which was clearly imminent. Early in December Balfour's administration went out of office.

Indolence on the one hand and preoccupation on the other had resulted in small achievement during Arnold Forster's period of office. Facing an increasingly hostile House of Commons and a conservative and unadventurous Army Council, the Secretary of State for War had awoken only late in his period of office to the need to force the issue over the General Staff. There was much truth in his comment to Edward VII on laying down office that 'I have had to attempt a task which the most gifted, the most influential, the most experienced and the most popular of men might have shrunk from.'[98] Arnold Forster's failure reflects the failure of Balfour to concern himself with a body of exceptional importance, not least to his own beloved CID. Where a question aroused Balfour's intense interest in, and talent for, political and strategic analysis he could act quickly and impose unity on warring factions. Particularly was this the case with the invasion question. The General Staff aroused in him no spark of enthusiasm; thus the credit of its foundation fell to Haldane.

Notes

1 Curzon to Brodrick, 17 March 1904. B.M. Add. MSS. 50075.
2 Roberts Papers. Kitchener to Roberts, 4 February 1904. Box X20930, file K5.
3 The Strength and Efficiency of the Military Forces of the Crown, 12 March 1904. B.M. Add. MSS. 50300.
4 Edmonds Papers. General Staff, War Office Intelligence Division, 1904–6, p. 6. K.C.L.
5 Esher Papers. Repington to Esher, 9 February 1904. 'Army Letters vol. 1'.
6 Esher Papers. Clarke to Esher, 23 March 1904. 'Sir George Clarke Vol. 1'.
7 Wilson Diary, 3 and 18 March 1904.
8 Wilson Diary, 24 March 1904.
9 Wilson Diary, 11 April 1904.
10 Minutes of Proceedings and Precis prepared for the Army Council, 28 April 1904, pp. 25, 162. W.O. 163/9.
11 Esher Papers. Clarke to Esher, 13 June 1904. 'Sir George Clarke Vol. 1'.
12 Royal Archives. Esher to Knollys, 6 September 1904. RA W39/48.
13 Arnold Forster Diary, 20 September 1904. B.M. Add. MSS. 50340.
14 Esher Papers. Clarke to Esher, 29 August and 6 September 1904. 'Sir George Clarke Vol. 1'.
15 A. V. Tucker, 'Politics and the Army in the Unionist Government in England 1900–1905'. *Report of the Annual Meeting of the Canadian Historical Association*, 1964, pp. 105–9.
16 Arnold Forster Diary, 5 November 1904. B.M. Add. MSS. 50341.
17 Esher Papers. Clarke to Esher, 7 November 1904. 'Sir George Clarke Vol. 2'.
18 M. V. Brett to French, 21 August 1904. Quo. E. G. French (ed.), *Some War Diaries, Addresses, and Correspondence of Field Marshal the Right Honble. the Earl of Ypres*, London, 1937, p. 102.
19 Esher Papers. French to Esher, 8 September 1904. 'Sir John French Vol. 1'.
20 Minutes of Proceedings and Precis prepared for the Army Council, 1904, p. 357. W.O. 163/9.
21 Arnold Forster Diary, 21 December 1904. B.M. Add. MSS. 50342.
22 Wilson Diary, 18 November 1904.
23 Arnold Forster to the Military Members, 25 July 1904. B.M. Add. MSS. 50305.
24 *The Times*, 12 December 1904, p. 6.
25 Esher to Sandars, 12 December 1904. B.M. Add. MSS. 49718.
26 Lyttelton to Arnold Forster, 16 December 1904. B.M. Add. MSS. 50342.
27 Esher Papers. Lyttelton to Esher, 15 December 1902. 'Army Letters Vol. 2'.
28 Report of a Committee on General Staff Appointments, 23 November 1904, *passim*. B.M. Add. MSS. 50321.

29 Baron Stoffel, *Rapports militaires écrits de Berlin*, Paris, 1870, pp. 97–136.
30 Report of a Committee on General Staff Appointments, *op. cit.*, pp. 7, 8.
31 Report on the Campaign in Manchuria, p. 123. B.M. Add. MSS. 50334.
32 Wilson Diary, 24 November 1904. Esher Papers. Clarke to Esher, 29 November 1904. 'Sir George Clarke Vol. 2'.
33 Clarke to Shute, 14 December 1904. B.M. Add. MSS. 49700.
34 Sir G. Aston, *Memories of a Marine*, London, 1919, p. 246.
35 Wilson Diary, 11 January 1905.
36 *The Times*, 17 January 1905, p. 9.
37 Arnold Forster Diary, 11 January 1905. B.M. Add. MSS. 50343.
38 Minutes of Proceedings and Precis prepared for the Army Council, 1905, Precis no. 168, p. 106. W.O. 163/10.
39 Minutes of Proceedings and Precis prepared for the Army Council, 1905, p. 100. W.O. 163/10.
40 Wilson Diary, 16 January 1905.
41 D. S. Macdiarmid, *The Life of Lieut. General Sir James Moncrieff Grierson*, London, 1923, p. 208.
42 Summary of Year's Work, 31 January 1905. B.M. Add. MSS. 50316.
43 Royal Archives. Knollys to Arnold Forster, 22 October 1904. RA W25/112.
44 Esher Papers. Clarke to Esher, 15 January 1905. 'Sir George Clarke Vol. 3'.
45 Esher Papers. Clarke to Esher, 27 January 1905. 'Sir George Clarke Vol. 3'.
46 Hansard, 4th series, vol. CXLII, cols. 227, 228, 2 March 1905.
47 Hansard, 4th series, vol. CXLIII, col. 147, 18 March 1905.
48 A. C. Pedley, 'Notes on the Days that are Past 1877–1927, pp. 111–112. W.O. Lib. A.O.11.1.
49 Sir C. Callwell, 'War Office reminiscences', *Blackwood's Magazine*, vol. CXC, 1911, pp. 165–6.
50 Esher Papers. Clarke to Esher, 19 March 1905. 'Sir George Clarke Vol. 3'.
51 Esher Papers. Repington to Esher, 2 April 1905. 'Army Letters Vol. 2'.
52 Wilson Diary, 6 April 1905.
53 Esher Papers. Miles to Clarke, 29 April 1905. 'Sir George Clarke Vol. 4'.
54 Esher Papers. Clarke to Esher, 6 May 1905. 'Sir George Clarke Vol. 4'.
55 Esher to Sandars, 15 May 1905. B.M. Add. MSS. 49718.
56 Clarke to Balfour, 20 May 1905. B.M. Add. MSS. 49701.
57 Balfour to Arnold Forster, 24 June 1905. B.M. Add. MSS. 49723.
58 *The Times*, 18 May 1905, p. 4.
59 *The Times*, 24 May 1905, p. 4.
60 *Ibid.*
61 Quo. Sir C. Callwell, *Field Marshal Sir Henry Wilson; His Life and Diaries*, vol. 1, London, 1927, p. 63.

62 Minutes of Proceedings and Precis prepared for the Army Council, 1905. Memorandum by General Miles, 9 June 1905. Precis 249, app. 1, p. 487. W.O. 163/10.

63 *Ibid.*, Memorandum by A–G, 14 June 1905. Precis 249, app. II, p. 491. W.O. 163/10.

64 *Ibid.*, Meeting of a Conference Assembled . . . to consider the Formation, Promotion and Allottment of Duties to the General Staff, 26 June 1905. Precis 249, app. III, pp. 493–6. W.O. 163/10.

65 Esher Papers. Clarke to Esher, 19 June 1905. 'Sir George Clarke Vol. 4'.

66 Esher Papers. Fisher to Esher, 26 June 1905. 'Sir John Fisher 1903–1905'.

67 The General Staff, 28 June 1905, p. 1. Cab. 17/14.

68 *Ibid.*, p. 2.

69 *Ibid.*, p. 5.

70 Esher Papers. Rawlinson to Esher, 7 July 1905. 'Army Letters Vol. 2'.

71 Haig to Esher, 18 July 1905. Cab. 17/14.

72 Royal Archives. Esher to Edward VII, 15 July 1905. RA W39/84.

73 Arnold Forster Diary, 15 July 1905. B.M. Add. MSS. 50349.

74 Wilson Diary, 10 July 1905.

75 French to Arnold Forster, 16 July 1905. Quo. French, *op. cit.*, p. 108.

76 M. V. Brett and Viscount Esher, *Journals and Letters of Reginald Viscount Esher*, vol. 2, London, 1934–8, pp. 94–6.

77 Esher Papers. Kitchener to Esher, 14 August 1905. 'Army Letters Vol. 2'.

78 Haig Papers. French to Haig. 6 August 1905. N.L.S. H. 334.E.

79 Royal Archives. Memorandum by French, 6 August 1905. RA W26/82.

80 Minutes of Proceedings and Precis prepared for the Army Council, 9 August 1905, p. 47. W.O. 163/10.

81 Esher Papers. Clarke to Esher, 21 and 25 August 1905. 'Sir George Clarke Vol. 5'.

82 Memorandum by the Secretary of State for War upon the Formation of a General Staff, 16 August 1905, p. 1. B.M. Add. MSS. 50321.

83 Wilson Diary, 26 August 1905.

84 Minute, 27 August 1905. B.M. Add. MSS. 50321.

85 Esher Papers. Sandars to Esher, 28 April 1905. 'The Prime Minister 1903–1905'.

86 Esher Papers. Clarke to Esher, 31 August 1905. 'Sir George Clarke Vol. 5'.

87 See below, p. 280.

88 Esher to Balfour, 3 September 1905. B.M. Add. MSS. 49719.

89 Esher to Balfour, 16 September 1905. B.M. Add. MSS. 49719.

90 Esher Papers. Clarke to Esher, 22 September 1905. 'Sir George Clarke Vol. 5'.

91 Arnold Forster to Balfour, 10 October 1905. B.M. Add. MSS. 50321.

92 Note on the Imperial Defence Committee, 11 October 1905. B.M. Add. MSS. 49719.

93 Arnold Forster Diary, 13 & 17 November 1905. B.M. Add. MSS. 50352.

94 Callwell, *Field Marshal Sir Henry Wilson*, vol. 1, p. 63.

95 Arnold Forster Diary, 22 November 1905. B.M. Add. MSS. 50352.

96 Esher Papers. Knollys to Esher, 22 November 1905. 'Lord Knollys Vol. 2'.

97 *The Times*, 25 November 1905, p. 6. Reproduced in C. à C. Repington, *Imperial Strategy: by the Military Correspondent of The Times*, London, 1906, p. 165.

98 Royal Archives. Arnold Forster to Edward VII, 6 December 1905. RA W71/14.

4
The Machine Constructed

Of the period of Unionist government which ended in 1905 Sir John Fortescue wrote that for four years there was 'unprofitable discussion; and then the task of setting the nation's military house in order was taken in hand by Richard Burdon Haldane'.[1] Haldane is justly acknowledged as one of the greatest of Secretaries of State ever to have directed the affairs of the War Office, and it was his creation of the Territorial Army which has done most to enhance his reputation. However, in creating a General Staff he had merely to complete the actions of his predecessor. The situation confronting him was best summed up not by Fortescue but by one of his contemporaries:[2]

> Pieces of the framework of a General Staff had been juxtaposed awaiting the arrival of someone to fit them together. . . . But the soul was wanting, and a great work of reform was necessary to create the efficient General Staff and the High School of generalship from which Prussia had profited so much. It remained for Mr. Haldane to complete Arnold Forster's work.

Just as in the earlier months of its existence, personal interest and enthusiasm were to play the greatest role in the development of the General Staff. As control passed from Haldane and Nicholson to Seely and French that interest was to decline, with unfortunate results.

No one was more alive to the potential offered by the change of administration than Esher, and as soon as the major offices of state were filled he arranged for Ellison to be appointed Haldane's private secretary. He recorded his success jubilantly: 'Of course nothing could indicate more clearly the "nobbling" of Haldane by our Committee!'[3] Ellison was greatly experienced in the debate over the General Staff and was well qualified to tutor Haldane in military matters, a task which he undertook at once. The last days of December 1905 were spent at Haldane's country home in Scotland pacing the billiard room by the hour, Haldane on one side of the table, smoking the best cigars procurable, Ellison on the other. It was chiefly as a result of this tuition that Haldane became an enthusiastic supporter of the idea of a General Staff, though afterwards prone to take sole credit for it.[4]

Esher followed up this success by sending Haldane a copy of his earlier memorandum and an explanatory letter in which he clarified his views on the peculiarities of the British army which forbade a slavish imitation of the German model. A volunteer army and the need for expansion in time of war demanded not a list of posts designated 'General Staff' but a list of names of officers qualified to hold General Staff posts.[5] Haldane was thus fully informed from the start of the views of the Esher *côterie*.

Political changes betokened changes in the War Office also, or so Repington perceptively felt. He forecast that Haig would at last replace Hutchinson and that a general strengthening of the extant General Staff side would take place; most significantly, Sir William Nicholson would be brought back to replace Plumer: 'The idea is that generals who dislike Nick may get accustomed to him as QMG and that later he may take NG's place.'[6] This prognostication was absolutely accurate, and Nicholson's arrival was greatly to strengthen the hand of Henry Wilson, his close friend. Whether it was Robertson and Wilson or Haldane's cousin Aylmer Haldane, an officer in the Intelligence Branch, who engineered Nicholson's appointment remains debatable.[7] Certainly Haldane left Nicholson in no doubts as to his intentions when he called the future CGS to ask for his assistance on 13 December:[8]

> He said he was very anxious to have my assistance on the Army Council. The Govt. were not prepared to remove Lyttelton from his present post and the only appointment which he could at present offer me was that of Q.M.G. . . . he gave me to understand that, when an opportunity occurred, he would endeavour to make me Chief of the Staff.

Nicholson was to contribute much to the General Staff and was to prove in some respects a difficult man to handle. Haldane was, however, fully aware of the character of his latest recruit; when Ewart, the Military Secretary, remarked that he was perhaps the most powerful personality in the army Haldane replied, 'Yes, perhaps too powerful.'[9]

Further changes Haldane was not prepared to make. When, early in January 1906, Esher tackled him about the prospect of Haig succeeding Hutchinson, Haldane replied that there was as yet no question of getting rid of the DSD as Lyttelton was very attached to him and 'I have to go wary'.[10] His first reaction to the War Office was to complain to Campbell-Bannerman that the state of things at Pall Mall was chaotic, which doubtless afforded the Prime Minister some amusement. Haldane was, however, far from overcome by the magnitude of his task. Resourceful and independent, he had no intentions of accepting uncritically suggestions about any military matters even when they emanated from one as knowledgeable as Esher:[11]

> The Esher Report is far from being like a Holy Writ. But for the present it does to work under. The broad object which impresses itself on my vision is the fatal confusion which arises if the General Staff get immersed or even entangled in administration. . . . I am busy trying to impress the principle of division of labour on my Generals.

There were others seeking to influence Haldane on the urgency of the General Staff question besides Esher and Ellison, chiefly the indefatigable Clarke. He concocted a memorandum of his own on the issue and sent it directly to the Secretary of State. After reviewing the failure to establish anything approaching a General Staff on the continental model and the revelations of ineptitude resulting from the South African War, Clarke urged an increase in the supply of trained staff officers and the complete separation of General Staff duties from administration. He concluded by hinting darkly that certain officers in high positions were unfit to conduct major operations in the field and that failure to establish a school of military opinion would have disastrous results.[12]

Haldane assured Clarke and Esher that he agreed with their principles as set out in the letters and memoranda sent to him.[13] Esher remained sceptical about the Secretary of State's receptivity, and was particularly concerned since the representatives of the General Staff on the CID were proving much weaker in argument than their naval colleagues.[14] It was also becoming apparent that the competition between CID and General Staff inherent in his report was rapidly approaching actual conflict. He confided his misgivings to Clarke:[15]

> As we have created it, the G.S. is going to be our Franken-
> stein. I can see that clearly. The Defence Committee should
> have been the G.S. for our Empire, with merely an 'Intelli-
> gence Branch' for the W.O., developed through the com-
> mands.

Heavily disguised though it had been, Esher felt that the German
model was going to be their curse. It was, however, too late to
turn back and begin again. Clarke remarked consolingly that
though they might blame themselves for Lyttelton 'who has
been a disastrous first C.G.S.' yet their principles were sound
enough and would eventually prevail.[16]

The manner in which the General Staff was plunged headlong
into strategic planning literally before it formally existed did a
great deal to hinder its proper development, so that a hasty and
in many respects unfortunate machine was created around it.
The first months of Haldane's office were particularly burden-
some in this respect: the General Staff were preoccupied with the
threat of war with Germany as a result of the Algeciras conference,
and were discussing plans of campaign and higher appointments.
It was at this time that the decision was taken to place Sir John
French in supreme command of any British expeditionary force
which might be sent overseas.[17] Looking at the scene from India,
Kitchener was moved to comment on the 'miserable lot . . . the
soldiers of the so-called General Staff' whom he affected to despise
beyond measure, an attitude which he never altered. There was
none the less at least one development which Esher and Clarke
viewed favourably: Haldane had practically settled things for
Haig as Hutchinson's successor.

Even in his absence Haig occupied a peculiarly influential
position in the General Staff; Esher for one felt that he alone
possessed the combination of talents required to put the organization, and the army, on its feet. Esher wrote to Haig at the end of
February offering him the post of DSD if he wished it, and
commenting at the same time on the poverty of Lyttelton's
performance at the CID. Early in March he repeated the offer,
adding that the King earnestly hoped he would accept the
appointment. He gave his reason bluntly: 'Lyttelton requires
guidance. He is a most excellent good fellow, but Providence did
not endow him with a clear brain. "Defence questions" as they
are called, are in a hopeless muddle.'[18] Haig replied accepting

the post if offered—it was to be as DMT in the first instance since Haldane felt unable to get rid of Hutchinson immediately.

Haig's arrival at Whitehall was not due chiefly to Haldane's foresight, as the latter afterwards made out.[19] Esher had pushed the issue even though Lyttelton was 'not very anxious' to have Haig as DMT.[20] Repington speculated on the new appointee:[21]

Will Haig ever make a Moltke? I should have thought that he began to study too late in life, but really I do not know. Circumstances will eventually disclose our Moltke to take N.G.'s place. I suppose it will be Nick to start and then we shall have to discover somebody.

Haig's appointment would have lasting effects on the General Staff; however, Haldane was by no means under the sway of his many advisers and counsellors, and himself provided drive and a sense of urgency which had previously been absent.

In his first debate on army Estimates on 8 March 1906 the Secretary of State for War indicated that he was determined to follow up the work of his predecessors in the matter of a General Staff. He paid an elegant tribute to the Esher committee, and praised Balfour's government for carrying out its principles and laying the foundations. It would not be his fault, he fervently assured the House, if continuity with that policy was not observed. This, the longest and most explicit statement hitherto made by a Cabinet Minister on the subject, caused the member for Tower Hamlets, Sir W. Evans Gordon, to press for similar privileges for British as for German General Staff officers so that 'the very cream of our officers might be induced to qualify themselves in that way'. The general mood of the house was sympathetic to these views.[22]

To accompany a more favourable attitude in parliament, it seemed that progress was now being made at the War Office. A draft Army Order passed through the hands of Haldane, Clarke, Ellison and Repington for consideration and amendment. The revised version sent back to Clarke was still sufficiently unpalatable for him to explode to Esher: 'This whole performance makes me sick. Oh for one month of power.'[23] He returned it to Haldane with a lengthy critique which made three main points. In the first place, it was essential to withdraw patronage from the CGS in the sense that he should not be allowed to draw up and add to the list of General Staff officers alone. His reason was that the army would distrust the exercise of such important powers by Lyttelton, a view which had first been put to him by Repington. He also felt that non-publication of the list would be a grave mistake, and that the list of General Staff posts should be short.[24] This posture was totally at odds with Wilson's concept of autonomy for the CGS and presaged further debate.

For his part, Esher was coming round to the view that the problems surrounding the creation of his General Staff were underlain by fundamental deficiencies in military education and therefore in the outlook of many contemporary soldiers. In a long letter to Lord Knollys he expounded his ideas on the position of a staff officer:[25]

> Our staff system is old fashioned, and unsuited to modern conditions . . . for Staff work which is now designated as 'General Staff', a special training is required, and officers who are qualified for the work ought to 'Specialize' for it, and be subjected to a long and continuous training.
>
> There is not one man on the Army Council, and very few among the Directors at the W.O. who have ever attempted to think about the work they now have to do before they were appointed to their present posts.

As Esher aptly remarked, if such a system were applied in the Treasury the result would be chaos.

Others besides Esher were becoming aware that the new General Staff required some new educational qualifications and that professionalism had to be interpreted in wider terms than hitherto. Sir Edward Ward, secretary to the Army Council, presented a memorandum early in the year stressing the need for specialization in military administration. It was a sign of the changing outlook within the army that he could openly cite the classic work by Bronsart von Schellendorf, *The Duties of the General Staff*, to support his contention that special training was needed for military administration. Ward put forward a scheme based on six months at the Staff College followed by a course at the London School of Economics during which students would study accounting and business methods, public finance, commercial law and statistics.[26] Ward approached the Director of the school, Halford Mackinder, who proved receptive to the idea and submitted a draft syllabus of his own.

An added fillip was given to the scheme in August 1906 when

the report of the South African War Stores Commission was published and revealed gross mismanagement on the part of certain staff officers. This led the King to express the wish that: 'something will be done in the way of training officers to business methods and that this report will not be laid on the shelf and forgotten as so often happens.'[27] Haldane was himself less than sanguine about the prospects for this new departure in military education; however, the Army Council accepted the necessity for special training for officers conducting the administrative business of the army. During December 1906 Haig was busy with the 'School of Economics' in his new capacity as Director of Staff Duties; his proposals were approved by Lyttelton on 3 January 1907 and shortly afterwards the first course began with an official reception.[28] Within a year the whole subject had been transferred out of his control and passed to the Quartermaster-General, so that what might have been a valuable expertise was largely lost to the General Staff.

These developments lay a long way in the future during May 1906 when Haldane's draft was circulating amongst interested parties. The Army Council were becoming convinced that the whole of the tendentious issue of accelerated promotion should rest with the body which made all recommendations about senior promotions, the Selection Board. Wilson was aghast at this prospect and warned Nicholson that it must be opposed. Nicholson pitched his case shrewdly. He pointed out that although it was proposed to add the four military members of the Army Council to the Selection Board, they could easily be outvoted by the seven local Commanders-in-Chief who composed the Selection Board under the chairmanship of the Inspector-General of Forces. At a meeting of the Army Council on 9 June 1906 Nicholson played skilfully on the apprehensions of his colleagues about their position within the army and succeeded in convincing them of the need to avoid being swallowed up by the Selection Board. Wilson recorded, with some accuracy, that if a General Staff were ever founded it would be thanks to Nicholson 'and no thanks whatever to N.G. who has played a most miserable part throughout'.[29]

Nicholson was trying to avoid domination of the General Staff by other agencies, and by late June he had succeeded. A compromise was agreed whereby the CGS, and in India the C.-in-C., would recommend selected officers to a reduced Selection

Board. Wilson was certainly not displeased with this outcome and as a result of it a draft order announcing the formation of the General Staff was approved by the Army Council on 10 July 1906.

During the summer of 1906 the most explosive issue in military affairs was not the General Staff but the proposal made by Haldane as part of his reorganization of the army to reduce the Brigade of Guards by two battalions. Tempers grew heated over this issue, not least at Buckingham Palace. In this atmosphere there was a danger that the new proposals about the General Staff might pass unconsidered, and Esher for one was determined that this should not occur. Accordingly he wrote to Lord Knollys giving his opinion that the danger about the new arrangement was the extent to which Lyttelton retained patronage in his own hands:[30]

> That he should have a voice, even a prominent one, in the selection, I can understand, but that he should have the *sole* responsibility, after the framing of the List, for adding to it, would be very badly received, I feel sure, by the Army.

Esher also gave it as his opinion that all proposed appointments should be first approved by the King.

This skilful intervention had its desired effect: for the first time the King entered directly into the discussions over the General Staff. In a personal letter to Haldane he gave it as his opinion that to dispense with the advice of the Selection Board and the Army Council in drawing up the first list would be most unwise. Equally, echoing Esher, he found it hard to believe that Lyttelton desired the personal weight of responsibility which the draft order threw upon him and indeed thought that he ought not to have it. No man, 'however capable and distinguished', could know enough of the officers scattered around the various commands to be able to draw up a list on his own.[31]

At this moment the publication of the report of the War Stores Commission led Lyttelton to tell Haldane that he was willing to resign since he had been Commander-in-Chief in South Africa during the period under enquiry. The *Blue Book*, published on 10 August, exonerated higher officials of anything more than stupidity but estimated the cost at roughly a million pounds. However, this was not the issue over which to force such an important resignation, nor was Haldane altogether averse to having such a pliant CGS, so Lyttelton remained at his post.[32]

Haldane's exceptional ability to synthesize all that was best in the works of his predecessors never showed more clearly than in the case of the General Staff, and the requisite impetus to its formal creation was now imparted by his own hand. He wrote afterwards of these weeks: 'This body, which had hitherto existed only in the War Office, I had developed and established throughout the Army by an Army Order and a memorandum written by myself personally and published in September 1906.'[33] These were somewhat exaggerated claims: the Army Order had been seen and amended by Clarke, Wilson, Nicholson and Esher before it was finally published, and the accompanying memorandum was written not by Haldane but by his military secretary, Colonel Ellison.[34] None the less he had shown the interest which his predecessor had lacked.

The memorandum accompanying the Army Order of 12 September 1906 explained in simple terms the principles behind the formation of the General Staff 'on lines well understood in most foreign armies'. A Liberal government felt the need to reassure the public that there was no question of aping continental military habits just as much as a Conservative one and accordingly a passage from von Schellendorf was quoted describing the British staff as limited to officers holding commands and their administrative staffs. But the British army had to be prepared to make the transition from a small to a large war, both in terms of size and complexity of operations, which demanded a specialized planning and directing staff—a General Staff.

The public was assured that such a body was just as important in peacetime as in war, lest it feel that the military were over-eager to anticipate hostilities. It was only by such means that the Prussian army had kept abreast of the developments of railway and telegraph and had therefore been capable of inflicting such a rapid defeat on the Imperial army in France in 1870. The task of the General Staff thus appeared as twofold: the collection of information, the observation of scientific advance and the study of possible theatres of war on the one hand and on the other the evolution of theories based upon changed conditions and the consequent modification of training and organization: 'In other words it is the business of the General Staff at Army Headquarters to ensure that the Military System in every part is always up to date, and that military science in all its branches receives adequate recognition.'[35] Perhaps the most important part of the philosophy which Haldane was expounding was that in the course of time the majority of high commanders would come from the ranks of those who had served in the General Staff.

Implicit in the development of the General Staff as an intellectual élite within the army was the growing isolation of its members from the day-to-day requirements of soldiering. In an attempt to prevent this, pabulum was inserted into the paper on the lines of the need to keep General Staff officers in touch with the army at regimental level by periods of service with troops; however, this was almost a dead letter from the moment it appeared in print. Haldane concluded his peroration with the broad hint that there were greater things to come; perhaps the self-governing colonies might be prepared to participate in an Imperial body based on the General Staff, reluctant though they were to brook interference with the finances and administration of their own forces:[36]

> Should such an ideal ever be realised, the new General Staff will become a real bond of union between the widely-scattered military forces of the Empire, giving to them all common ideas even in matters of detail, so that, if ever the need should arise, they could readily be concentrated to form a really homogeneous Imperial Army.

In contradistinction to his plans for the General Staff, the aims of Haldane's general reorganization of the army were highly nebulous. The design of the instrument was plain enough: 'The Regular Army, organised into an efficient "striking force", would be the cutting edge of a blade forged out of the entire nation.'[37] The strategic purpose was less clear. Haldane's memorandum about the General Staff revealed that he was in the first instance merely seeking to make more effective, and in time to widen, the forces available for Imperial defence with no particular theatre in mind. This was the reason why his famous reorganization of the army was not based on the traditional concept of army corps as was that of other powers; the divisional organization was adopted precisely because it was more flexible and therefore better able to deal with other contingencies.[38]

Haldane's attitude to military organization was undoubtedly

influenced by his trip to Berlin in August 1906, when he saw much in German methods that commended itself to him. A long conversation with Count von Moltke, Chief of the German General Staff, in which the latter approved the proposed divisional organization, reassured Haldane that there was little to fear from deliberate German aggression. Moltke's view, he reported, was that a war with England would be: 'for them, as for us also, a fearful calamity because it could not be short, whichever won and would mean slow exhaustion while America helped herself to the trade of both of us.'[39] Haldane was probably not wholly taken in by the pacific statements of von Moltke, but his re-organization of the army was certainly directed at other possible situations besides a war with Germany. He was assisted in working on his gleanings of German policy by Haig, who from this moment seems to have become one of the most enthusiastic exponents of the idea of an Imperial extension of the General Staff for its own sake.

To accompany Haldane's explanatory memorandum, the Special Army Order of 12 September 1906 finally established the General Staff on a basis which was to undergo only minor modifications up to 1914. It was marked by a clarity and precision of style which made misunderstanding almost impossible and by the clear imprint of a definite purpose. Thus from the start the task of the Staff at headquarters was clearly defined:[40]

> to advise on the strategical distribution of the Army, to supervise the education of officers, and the training and preparation of the Army for war, to study military schemes, offensive and defensive, to collect and collate military intelligence, to direct the General policy in Army matters, and to secure continuity of action in the execution of that policy.

The order went on shrewdly to combine the two schools of thought about the General Staff which had riven the War Office for the preceding eighteen months. Thus from the one was abstracted the scheme of a specific list of posts to constitute General Staff appointments and from the other a special list of officers qualified for such employment, to be termed 'The General Staff List'. This latter was to be drawn up and periodically revised by the Army Council and not to be published.

On the vexed question of qualifications a psc was to be the

general rule, with at least eight years' service, but administrative experience would be considered. A diplomatic formula was found to overcome the anxieties expressed earlier by the King:[41]

> At home and in the Colonies appointments to the General Staff will be made by the Secretary of State for War from the General Staff list after taking the advice of the Chief of the General Staff. Such appointments, except in the case of Staff captains and brigade majors, will be submitted to the King for His Majesty's approval.

'Approved service' on the General Staff would be rewarded with accelerated promotion. In sum the structure represented the original model as proposed by Esher but expanded in function and specialized in organization, something more openly akin to the German model but adapted to suit British circumstances.

Haldane had plainly been imbued with a renewed zeal to bring British military organization up to date after his Berlin trip. To Esher he wrote that a complete change of outlook within the army was necessary: 'we must begin to move in the direction of making brains and the modern spirit, and not seniority, the qualification for directing positions in the Army.'[42] However, his time was becoming increasingly taken up with preparations for the formation of the Territorial Army and as a result the General Staff was to be left to its own devices.

The publication of the Special Army Order coincided with a major change in General Staff appointments which was to be of great importance. Douglas Haig, by now a Major-General, succeeded Sir Frederick Stopford as Director of Military Training on 24 August 1906. To aid him in his new duties he had the benefit of a detailed report on the Directorate of Military Education and Training of the Japanese army which, with the German, was the example most often cited by the proponents of the General Staff. It was an example which he was to adopt and adapt.[43] Haig was also well aware of the need to bring into operation a system, particularly of finance, designed to suit the likely situation 'i.e. a great war requiring the whole resources of the nation to bring it to a successful end.'[44]

Haig was to play a major role in drafting the Territorial Army scheme and in the preparation of *Field Service Regulations Part II*. His arrival was accompanied by that of another influential figure in the General Staff, for on 6 October Major-General

Spencer Ewart replaced Sir James Grierson as Director of Military Operations. Ewart was Haldane's personal choice and both he and Haig replaced officers whose four-year terms of office had not yet run out. Also in October 1906 Sir William Robertson's term as head of MO2 ran out and he was posted to Aldershot; it is indicative of the changed spirit at the War Office that it was no longer thought possible for one officer to oversee such a large part of the Military Operations Directorate and it was split into a European and an Asiatic section under the respective charge of Colonel Count Gleichen and Colonel Aylmer Haldane.

Haig soon found that there were still obstructions to any great changes at the War Office—'There are many jarring interests here and even Haldane seems carried away at times by *theories* which are impossible in practice and by political reasonings' he wrote to Esher.[45] His fellow newcomer, Ewart, was meanwhile making a favourable impression. Clarke informed Esher of his advent:[46]

> I have had Ewart here today and we had an interesting talk. Unless the Office atmosphere changes him, his relations with us [i.e. the CID] here will be of the most satisfactory character, and certainly better than in the Grierson period, Ewart has the bigger mind.

Ewart tactfully arranged to give priority of attention to any question which Clarke felt to be pressing, which made him eminently acceptable to the secretary of the CID. The Staff Duties Directorate remained the weakest department but Ewart set a valuable precedent when he instituted weekly meetings of the three General Staff Directors in mid-October and Aylmer Haldane suggested a monthly review of current books for the staff which was in time to grow into the *Army Review*.

The generation of General Staff officers which marked the onset of Haldane's term of office were to add greatly to the efficiency and impact of the General Staff, although by their very professional outlook they were also to contribute to its growing isolation within the army. There was, however, one hindrance operative throughout this period which underlined the ambiguous nature of a professional qualification in the army and thereby affected the recruitment of the lower ranks of the General Staff for some time. This was the practice of the Staff College of granting a psc although confidential reports strongly recommended that an officer be not employed on the staff. The directing staff at the Staff College were unable to make up their minds what to do about the weaker candidates: whether parts of an officer's confidential report should be read out to him to explain his lack of General Staff employment or whether his psc should be withheld. Sir Henry Rawlinson, then Commandant of the Staff College, held to the latter course of action but for rather idiosyncratic reasons: 'It cannot do an officer any good to be told officially that he is not quite a gentleman, however well chosen may be the language. And this is really what it comes to in most cases.'[47] As the DSD was at that time facing a number of cases involving such officers the issue was clearly an important one. Its outcome would determine the value of the psc as a professional qualification and with it the validity of the army's system of higher education. This dispute quickly formed itself on the familiar lines of General Staff versus the rest. Both Kiggell, the Assistant DSD, and Wilson, now Commandant of the Staff College, felt that officers should be told of faults only if they were capable of rectification. Sir Charles Douglas, the Adjutant-General, felt that in all cases an adverse report should be made known to the officer concerned and Lyttelton bowed to this view in the face of opposition from his own staff. The precise status of the psc remained opaque until 1911 when Sir William Robertson, who succeeded Wilson at the Staff College, came up with a solution which separated the personal report which determined whether or not an officer should be suggested for the General Staff from the award of the psc. Only then did the nature of the professional qualification become clear and in any case by that time appointments were made by personal recommendation and not by the possession of a piece of paper.

During January 1907 the final decisions were made on the grading of General Staff officers, following a suggestion by Nicholson, and in the same month the General Staff was installed in the newly completed War Office in Whitehall—the first time all the military departments had ever been under one roof. One result was that members of the Intelligence Department enjoyed much better health than when they had been at Winchester House; subsequent demolition of the latter building revealed that the infamous 'Winchester House throat' had been due to the presence beneath it of a large cess-pit.

In January 1907 Wilson gave his first address to the Staff

College as its new Commandant and revealed that he was well aware of the pitfalls confronting an isolated General Staff. His chief point was that it was 'impossible to be a good General Staff Officer or Superior Commander unless one is possessed of Administrative knowledge'.[48] This and other attempts to encourage prospective General Staff officers to gain a wide range of experience largely failed as, up until 1914, officers preferred to go to the General Staff rather than to administrative branches since the prospects of promotion were much better.[49] Although this militated against the more widely experienced officer which some had hoped to see it had the positive benefit that the more able officers were channelled into the staff. There was a considerable degree of concurrence in the belief that after the issue of A.O. 233 the General Staff was both more 'brainy' and more industrious than ever before.[50]

Events in London made Kitchener doubt the advisability of creating a General Staff, a sentiment which augured ill for the future.[51] It was true that small but irritating frictions existed within the General Staff: Aylmer Haldane felt that Count Gleichen was blocking his scheme to convert the book review started the previous year into an army monthly run by the General Staff. Lyttelton attended Haldane's speech introducing the army reorganization scheme and was unable to remember much about it except that he disagreed with most of it; he began to take more time off from his duties to visit Lords and the Oval. It was in this environment that the news began to percolate through the War Office in the spring of 1907 that Sir William Nicholson would in all probability be the next Chief of the General Staff.

There were still considerable doubts about Nicholson's capacity to fill the proposed office despite the fact that he was the personal choice of Haldane. The King felt that he was unpopular with the higher officers in the army and that 'not being a Leader in War he does not command the confidence of the Army'. Esher thought the answer lay in strengthening the position of the Inspector General of Forces to make him the real trainer of the army and its possible leader in war, in which case Nicholson would be perfectly suitable as head of the administrative machine of the army.[52] This was a significant departure from his earlier concept of the role of the CGS but in any case his influence over the development of the General Staff now sharply diminished.

Likewise Clarke, who was thinking in terms of a National General Staff with the CID Secretariat at its centre, was shortly to turn his attentions to the Governorship of Bombay.

From the earliest days of the Committee of Imperial Defence the General Staff, or what then passed for it, had an impact of sorts on strategic policy. In its new form it now began to have an influence also on the formulation of military policy in general. The Secretary of State for War paid it an elegant tribute in introducing his reorganization proposals:[53]

> In passing I may say that we are realising the enormous advantage of the General Staff. Without the General Staff it is impossible to work out and to solve these problems. We used to operate in a slap-dash way in the old days, and the result was confusion. The General Staff is the brain of the Army, which thinks out these problems; and it is to the General Staff that we owe the organisation which I am going to describe and to suggest as the means by which the requirements are to be fulfilled.

During the course of the year the General Staff devilled away on new proposals with little interruption from the rest of the War Office. The smooth functioning of the machine sharply pointed the contrast between the Directors and their Chief, and in September 1907 Haldane proposed a complicated switch in order to rid himself of Lyttelton. Lord Grenfell was to vacate the Dublin Command with a Field Marshal's baton and become chairman of the London Territorial Army Association; Lyttelton could then go to Ireland to replace him and 'our machine at Whitehall would be reformed early instead of in May'.[54] Esher secured the King's approval but the scheme fell to the ground when Lyttelton refused the proffered post.

Despite the deadweight of Lyttelton there was a reforming spirit moving within the General Staff. Early in November Haig discussed with Haldane and Lord Roberts proposals to alter the functions of the Director of Staff Duties and Director of Military Training. The vital meeting took place on 8 November:[55]

> Sir N. Lyttelton took papers which I gave him last night showing proposals for rearranging duties in D.S.D. and D.M.T. on the lines that all education (except Staff Coll.) pass to D.M.T.—and War Organisation to go to D.S.D. By

this means D.S.D. will have sufficient officers to work out 'Principles of Employment of Troops' and other fundamental questions which hitherto have been ignored. Sir N. gave papers to S. of S. stating that they summarised *his views*.

The CGS signed a minute to Haldane authorizing the change in duties on 9 November, and on the same day Haig succeeded Hutchinson as DSD. His former post went to Colonel A. J. Murray. This move was clearly designed to place Haig in a position where he could wield sufficient influence to design and enforce new manuals and training procedures on the army. It did not go unremarked in the General Staff: Aylmer Haldane remarked in his diary that the new DSD was 'trying the old game of getting everything into his hands and is backed up by Ellison'.[56] The net of patronage fashioned and cast by Esher during his enquiries into the War Office was now in full operation.

For Haig, 1908 was an energetic year. As well as work on the Imperial General Staff and a prolonged illness in April and May he worked out and tested the army's first modern training manual, *Field Service Regulations Part II*. Papers containing the draft scheme were handed to Haldane on 20 March 1908 and during the following summer Haig and his assistant, Colonel L. E. Kiggell, worked on plans to test *FSR (II)* in a Staff Ride. Haig seems to have been too enthusiastic in his designs, for Ewart was forced to object in his capacity as DMO that the scheme gave away too many secrets and Haig had to modify it.[57] Haig was able to submit his manual to the test of a Staff Ride thanks to the provision made by Haldane in each year's estimates for money to be expended by the General Staff on exercises and manoeuvres at its complete discretion.[58]

The organization and conduct of the Staff Ride reveals the painstaking care which Haig took over his branch and its work. Preliminary war games were held at the War Office on 16 and 21 October to familiarize officers with the problems, and the tour met on 26 October for five days. It was attended by sixty-nine officers from the War Office and the various Commands and included Major-General J. C. Hoad from the Australian Commonwealth Forces as an observer. The scenario was war between Scotland and Holland on neutral ground. Orders for advance and arrangements for maintenance were issued by the players, whereupon the directing staff communicated the resulting 'situation' and the next move was worked out, and so on until the end of the tour. A wide range of problems confronted the players including disembarkation, entraining, accommodation, detraining and concentration and each branch was tested minutely. Conferences every evening discussed problems and solutions arrived at during the day, and a general conference took place on the last day at which the Director-in-Chief, Sir William Nicholson, explained the principles on which the more important problems should be solved.[59]

The records of the final conference indicate a very real enthusiasm for the Staff Tour and its aims among participants. Questions which arose touched on the relative positions and powers in the field of the Quartermaster-General and Inspector-General of Communications and Railways and the degree of communication of intentions and information in orders. Lack of co-ordination was revealed as a major problem and resulted in the congestion of the army for several days. The Ride was thus valuable in raising points which sorely needed clarification and in revealing weaknesses in the practice of the staff; it was also decisive in securing the adoption of *FSR (II)* for after two more meetings the proofs were finally agreed on 23 December 1908.

The Staff Ride had followed the example of another innovation earlier in the year, the first General Staff Conference held in January 1908. This was the first gathering to go over in any detail the relationship of the General Staff to military training. It was attended by thirty-six staff officers from the commands and the War Office and Sir William Robertson led off with a statement of his role at the Aldershot Command—to lay down the principles on which the troops should be trained, to bring to notice points which called for special attention and to maintain uniformity as regards tactics and training. Officers from elsewhere indicated that they, too, regarded their duties in a similar light and Colonel J. E. Edmonds briefly described continental practice. Lyttelton concluded the morning's discussion by remarking that it was 'very gratifying to see what steady progress had been made in the duties confided to the General Staff'.[60] The second day's discussion was devoted to the organization of manoeuvres and umpiring and was again led by Robertson. Subsequently there was a discussion of draft chapters of *FSR Part II* conducted by Haig, in the course of which he pointed out that during the South African War three different systems of organization had been in use at three different headquarters, and a general discussion came out strongly in favour of the preparation of common manuals.

On the last day of the conference there was a thorough analysis of the education and training of officers for General Staff duties before, during and after Staff College. There was general agreement on the baneful influence of the 'cramming' system and some discussion of the examination system at Camberley. In the course of debate Robertson expressed the belief that political matters should be avoided in the training of the General Staff since in practice policy in any given contingency was usually furnished by the Foreign Office, and if not 'it was assumed, but it was never discussed by the General Staff'.[61] Haig then read a paper emphasizing the need for a uniform approach on questions of strategy, tactics, organization and training. He argued forcefully for discussion amongst General Staff officers at all levels, the results to be tabulated, culminating in a debate held before the CGS by senior officers of the General Staff. This was indeed to happen later in the year. Lyttelton characteristically remarked that 'the foregoing was a full statement of his views'.[62]

As a result of Haig's efforts the Staff Conference became a regular occurrence and one which offered a valuable forum in which to discuss and assess new doctrines and strategic principles. It also offered a chance to influence the development of the military forces of the dominions. Thus representatives from Australia and New Zealand attended the Staff Conference of 1909 at which Nicholson initiated discussion of various aspects of *FSR Part II*. However, although the discussion proved useful in clearing up doubts as to what had been in the DSD's mind on particular points, the over-all value of the sessions to the General Staff as a whole is questionable since the technique of debate was mishandled. Nicholson made no attempt to sum up each part of the debate before proceeding to the next topic and no officer below the rank of Colonel took any part in the discussions. Twenty of the fifty-four officers attending were of the rank of Lieutenant-Colonel or below.

Subsequent discussions on the Territorial Army and on manoeuvres and training resulted in very little more participation by junior members, and the conference closed with a plea by Count Gleichen for greater reticence on confidential matters.[63]

Gleichen's exhortations were best directed at himself; as Assistant DMO he had, not long before, gone home for the weekend leaving his office safe open. This alarming oversight was discovered later that evening by a patrolling policeman who patiently stood guard over the safe until Gleichen's return to work on Monday morning. As it happened, Gleichen had not put the nation's military secrets at risk since at that moment his safe contained nothing more valuable than a spare pair of trousers.

Gleichen's concern with security reflected a concurrent but little publicized development within the General Staff, that of the Secret Service section. This had begun life as H section during the first days of the Boer War but had gone into rapid decline in 1906 with the departure from it of Colonel F. J. Davies. Retitled MO5, it was put in the charge of Lieutenant-Colonel (later Sir James) Edmonds and commenced work on the investigation of cases of espionage in England and the indexing of information on known spies. At the same time lectures in intelligence work were given to units and commands by Count Gleichen and others.[64] As a result of the deliberations of a subcommittee of the CID on foreign espionage which reported in July 1909, Edmonds was empowered to form a counter-espionage section proper. He secured as its head Sir Vernon Kell, an exceptionally gifted linguist who spoke fluent Chinese and Russian as well as four major European languages. Kell was to stay in counter-espionage until 1940.[65]

Kell, who from the commencement of his duties believed that a war with Germany was inevitable, investigated his first case alone. His section grew rapidly thereafter to include a legal adviser, other investigating officers, and a number of female secretaries to run the ever-expanding system of card indexes. In the meantime Edmonds was replaced as head of MO5 by Colonel G. M. W. Macdonogh and it was he who devised what defence regulations and measures for the control of aliens existed in August 1914. As a former subordinate of Macdonogh's afterwards wrote:[66]

Full credit belongs . . . to MacD. and Edmonds for their revolutionary pre-vision in the inception of the above measures [i.e. Defence Regulations], but when we come to the actual work of spy-catching and making it difficult for enemy agents to ply their trade as spies or as saboteurs, from 1900 onwards the credit must be given to K[ell] and his staff.

While the Military Operations Directorate was working industriously on the problems of counter-espionage and the DMT on the structure of the Territorial Force, Haig was trying to accustom the army to the idea of Staff Rides to deal with tactical problems. In doing so he was working against time for by mid-April 1909 he knew that there was a strong possibility of his going to India as Chief of Staff to the new commander, Sir O'Moore Creagh. Thus two cavalry Staff Rides were held under his direction in the space of four months; in each case participating officers were presented with certain tactical problems, such as the approach and deployment of cavalry in the face of an enemy force, to which solutions had to be evolved. This was an invaluable advance in training technique but it did reveal an ominous faith in the effectiveness of cavalry attack on the part of the participating and directing staff. The general tenor of the doctrine was clear:[67]

> Cavalry, of itself, cannot produce this state of moral and physical decadence in the enemy in a general engagement. It must, therefore, keep close to *the other arms who attack the hostile infantry and prepare the way for a decisive action of the Cavalry*.

Thus a valuable technical innovation served to cement into strategic thought an outmoded doctrine.

Haig left the War Office for India on 7 October 1909 and was replaced by his assistant Kiggell. This move severed Esher's last personal link with the higher levels of the General Staff and King Edward's death the following year made this severance complete. None the less Esher was far from unhappy about the controlling hand for his opinion of Nicholson had undergone a change. He wrote to Lord Knollys that he had a high opinion of the CIGS as a quiet but hard worker—'an underrated man'. Much was owed to him for his hard work, patience and good sense in administering the army and far from being a self-advertiser he was a quiet, sensible man.[68] Nicholson had certainly supported Haig in his attempts to reform the General Staff and to institute common discussion and consideration of the higher problems of war, but there was still a long way to go before the British General Staff could compete with its German rival. Reporting on the Imperial

Manoeuvres of 1909, Sir Ian Hamilton remarked upon the seriousness with which the Germans viewed their conferences with fewer speakers and lasting much longer than the British equivalents. Partly as a result of this German staff work was infinitely superior to British and orders were issued more rapidly and more clearly.[69] Haig's contribution was to attempt in some measure to narrow the gap between the two professional bodies before they became locked in conflict. In this he was certainly successful.

In 1910 Ewart left and was replaced as Director of Military Operations by Sir Henry Wilson. That the latter's first act was to hang an immense map of the frontiers of France, Belgium and Germany on the wall of his room at the War Office was symptomatic of the changed attitude towards the General Staff in this period. Structural development and change gave way to a more single-minded preparation for war with Germany. From this time onwards what changes took place in the General Staff tended to come from within the structure as it had then come to exist. The resulting near stultification, for such it was, meant that there was no follow-up to the experiments introduced by Haig and others.

So it was with the Staff Conference of 1910, which followed the pattern laid down by Haig. Again, each day was devoted to the discussion of a series of questions of a strategic or tactical nature. There was one remarkable change and that was in the personal role played by Nicholson. The CIGS now summed up on the following morning each day's findings and indicated where his views diverged from those of the main speakers and what action would be taken. The general atmosphere in which the conferences took place, in strong contrast to the German pattern, was not one of unremitting effort: the conference met for only three and a quarter hours each morning and no formal work was done in the afternoons or evenings. There was also a growing tendency to narrow the spectrum of the discussions which did not escape Haig, far off in India: 'I already see from your discussions at the Staff Coll. Confer. a tendency to split hairs, and a desire for *precise* rules to guide officers in every conceivable situation in war. This wants watching.'[70] Nicholson even felt it necessary to remind officers in positions of importance to keep notes on the performance of their duties so that they could be discussed the following year. As yet this form of running record only existed in the DMO's department.[71]

The death of King Edward VII and the growth of the crisis over the House of Lords during the latter half of 1910 occupied the attention of most people in the political arena, so that Esher could write to Haig that 'military questions have got into a very sleepy state'.[72] However, Wilson's advent galvanized the General Staff into an intense if limited activity—that of preparing plans for war with Germany. By October of that year planning based on Holland as the possible future theatre of war was sufficiently far advanced for the General Staff to request the co-operation of the Admiralty in the detailed arrangements to be made for the conveyance of an Expeditionary Force to France or Holland.[73]

In other areas of the General Staff besides that concerned with strategic planning there were signs of development which corresponded to the supposed needs of war. During the same year Sir Edward Ward, Permanent Under Secretary of the War Office, chaired a committee on departmental structure during war. It concluded that the duties of the CIGS would undergo 'considerable change' with consequent modifications to organization: the main grouping would be around MO5. On the outbreak of war a War Section would be formed which would require a staff of only five; its duties were envisaged as being the compilation of a journal of the war, the recording and distribution of war experiences, preparing plans of campaign as directed by the CIGS and serving as the channel of communication between the Imperial General Staff and the General Staff in the field.[74] This paradigm of General Staff activities in war bore an ominous importance since it reflected the widespread and largely unquestioned presumption that such a war would be comparatively short.

Stimulated by a decision of the Committee of Imperial Defence of 26 January 1911 that some consideration of the question of co-ordination of departmental action in war was necessary, the steps towards preparation for war hastened. A standing sub-committee produced a draft, partly the work of Macdonogh, which suggested that in peacetime action be taken to prepare the majority of communications necessary in a period of strained diplomatic relations or of war. Activities to be undertaken during the 'Precautionary Period' and after were devised, chiefly relating to the provision and protection of transport and communications. Underlining the paucity of recognized procedures in the event of possible war, the committee noted that 'there are many instances in which the responsibility for taking the requisite action has not yet been definitely allotted to individuals or sections'.[75]

Thus there were already strong pressures in existence within the War Office and the General Staff which helped to bring into existence one of the most important buttresses to the edifice as a whole before Sir Maurice Hankey took a hand in the preparation of the *War Book*. The first edition of the *War Book* appeared in 1912 and the second the following year; an annual revision was envisaged as essential. Though painstaking in its solution of the tasks facing the War Office, it revealed a machine for use in a war of limited scope only. For example, copies of every message or telegram received at the War Office were to go at once to the Minister's private secretary, each of the members of the Army Council, the Permanent Under Secretary, the Assistant Under Secretary to the Board of Directors, MO1 and MO5 with paraphrases to the King and such Cabinet Ministers as directed. With the reduced staff which was envisaged during a war this would have strained the resources of the War Office to their utmost.

The idea of a War Section of the General Staff was thought to be too disruptive by Hankey and his colleagues and was discarded. The Military Operation Directorate was given detailed tasks to perform with a slightly reduced staff, the emphasis being on the receipt and circulation of information. There was no recognition of the need to continue planning activities during war other than in theatres where the Expeditionary Force was not operating. As a further example of the lack of vision of the planners, it was envisaged that on the outbreak of war MO4c, which was charged with the compilation and preparation of all maps, would go out of existence.[76] There was likewise a similar though greater lapsing of work in the Staff Duties branch and in the Directorate of Military Training, except where the latter was engaged in training the Territorial Force. All in all, pressure during wartime would relax as 'the branch will be relieved of a good deal of work in connection with discussions on general staff principles'.[77]

However expert the General Staff might be within the confines of Whitehall they still lacked the expertise which the German army displayed in the field. Therefore the provision of some guidelines for the performance of staff work in the field was at least as important as the concoction of complex regulations for the administration of the War Office during wartime. At the moment when the *War Book* was being drafted a committee under the chairmanship of Colonel J. Adye reported on the proposals for a draft *Staff Manual (War)*. Sir John French, who had succeeded Nicholson as CIGS on 15 March 1912, endorsed the urgent necessity for a work of this sort and a proof copy appeared later that same year, drafted by a former member of the Military Operations Directorate, Colonel Adrian Grant Duff.

At the outset the *Staff Manual (War)* emphasized that it was the duty of the staff officer in the field to help the troops by all possible means to carry out the tasks allotted to them and to aim solely at the efficient performance of their duties. Therefore it was made quite clear that it was a staff officer's duty to offer advice to his commander if it appeared likely to be of use, though it was rather easier to suggest this novel practice than to legislate for its acceptance. A fairly straightforward division of activities into 'Operations' and 'Intelligence' was devised, and emphasis was again placed on the responsibility of the individual General Staff officer for ensuring that the machine was functioning correctly. Heavy stress was laid on the need at all levels for information as to what was going on in the different branches of the staff.

The draft manual pointed to all the defects with which the General Staff in wartime was later to be charged. None the less without some testing at manoeuvres the book remained a series of aspirations rather than a coherent and practical guide through the complexities of war. At Haig's suggestion copies of the manual were issued to all officers who had passed through Staff College and arrangements were made to collect impressions after the army exercises in the autumn of 1913.

A test exercise held at Sandhurst in January 1913 first revealed the weaknesses in the manual. Among major defects noted were failure to inform the General Staff of movements, the danger of insufficient co-ordination between Operations and Intelligence and the plethora of subsections at GHQ with unnecessarily complicated index letters. All these points were confirmed by observers present at the autumn manoeuvres. Captain Ommaney of the General Staff, who had been attached to Operations during the exercises, reported an insufficient knowledge of points of detail and interior organization at GHQ and a tendency to hold on to too many papers. The poor system of registering documents made it almost impossible to determine who had read what. The signals procedure was inefficient and provisions for the movement and feeding of Headquarters were rudimentary.[78]

Ommaney's critique was confirmed by other officers who commented adversely on the general confusion about registration and communication of despatches and the complex system of receipts. Lieutenant-Colonel Bird included a barbed comment on Sir John French's direction of the exercise:[79]

> I think that although we learnt a great deal the experience was rather short and that in a day or two more definite conclusions could have been made. This points to the desirability of repeating the exercise next year, but with C.I.G.S. as director and not as director and commander. The fact that he worked this year in the dual capacity seemed to me to be prejudicial to practice of staff duties in service conditions.

A start had been made on these very real problems, late though it was. The General Staff was not to have the opportunity of further exercises to perfect what was clearly a deficient technique before it was faced with the test of war.

While the General Staff was thus engaged in the production of manuals and regulations its headship had passed from Nicholson. There were signs towards the end of his period of office that he was growing to resemble Lyttelton in his attitude. The Staff Tour and Conference was run entirely by Murray and Kiggell, respectively DMT and DSD, the CIGS only appearing on the last afternoon. French's subsequent judgment that it was in capable hands under Murray cannot be fully substantiated.[80] Henry Wilson's continued plaints about his chief's lack of interest in the preparation of the Expeditionary Force also bear witness to a certain inactivity on the part of the CIGS.[81]

Nicholson did achieve one notable success, late in his period of office, when a journal was established to disseminate throughout the army the General Staff view of various subjects. Any kind of publication by serving officers had been anathema to King Edward VII, who had opposed an Army Journal of the British Empire in 1904; his son was more prepared to sanction such activity.[82] Nicholson was now able to establish such a public forum, whose aims he delineated as disseminating the latest information on military subjects, inculcating the lessons of history and encouraging the formulation and expression of individual ideas on matters open to discussion. The continental armies had had the

benefit of a number of such journals for some years; belatedly
England was now to have one also. Its chief role was envisaged as
amplifying and elucidating the strategic principles which were
then in the process of formulation:[83]

> It is . . . hoped that the discussion of matters of military
> interest . . . may . . . conduce to the unity of doctrine and the
> intelligent application of the principles laid down by a
> superior authority, which are essential to systematic training
> in peace and successful action in the field.

The editor chosen to direct the fortunes of the new venture was
the military correspondent of *The Times*, Colonel Repington.
This was in some ways an unfortunate choice for Henry Wilson
refused utterly to have anything to do with him as a result of a
scandal over Repington's amours some years earlier. The journal
was therefore excluded from the purlieus of one of the most
important branches of the General Staff. How far Repington's
heart was really in the venture was problematical since he told
Northcliffe that he had accepted the editorship solely for the
money.[84]

Sir John French used the *Army Review* as a platform from
which to state his policy on acceding to the post of CIGS in 1912.
He spoke in vague terms of the need to hold firmly to general
principles but to retain the ability to accept new ideas where they
were sound and useful. He also gave an interesting insight into
his political philosophy:[85]

> Politics are not matters for soldiers to dabble in, and with
> this side of our public life officers should have nothing what-
> ever to do. . . . Our sole duty is to make the best of our mili-
> tary resources, and not to trench upon ground reserved for
> the Government and the Legislature.

These non-committal utterances reflect the tenor of French's
period of office when he seems to have been content to let the
General Staff go its own way.

Throughout the developments of the General Staff from the
publication of the 'Special Army Order' in 1906 Haldane had been
at the War Office. On 12 June 1912 Colonel J. E. B. Seely
succeeded him. The precise manner of his selection is not clear,
though it may have owed something to Harcourt and Crewe who

both had his interest at heart.[86] Certainly Seely never betrayed the same interest in the General Staff as his predecessor had done, so that Henry Wilson was subsequently moved to enquire of Bonar Law whether Seely was 'playing the game by the General Staff' since he was acting without their knowledge in many matters.[87] This was a question which Seely might well have levelled against Wilson in 1914 over Ulster. Law's opinion of Seely was not very high and Repington believed that the efficiency of the War Office had declined by 50 per cent with the departure of Haldane, Nicholson and Murray.[88] The concurrence of French and Seely in the two offices of greatest importance for the development of the General Staff can only be counted unfortunate for that institution.

Aside from certain events connected with the Imperial side of the General Staff, Seely's only contribution in any field relating to the staff was the passing of a stringent Official Secrets Act and an increase in the secret service fund.[89] Sir Maurice Hankey subsequently paid tribute to the former as one of many 'solid achievements' but since he recorded this sentiment on the occasion of Seely's resignation it seems probable that his admiration was tinged with other emotions.[90] Haig certainly noticed the failure of General Staff educational policy at this time to promote the skill and ability necessary to apply the principles embodied in Field Service Regulations. He was deeply critical of the failure to encourage and develop what Clausewitz had called 'skill in sagacious calculation', and suggested new and broader-based educational policies to overcome what was likely to be a factor of very serious consequence in the field.[91]

The most notorious event affecting Seely was the so-called Curragh mutiny in April 1914. As a body the General Staff had little or nothing to do with the machinations surrounding that event although its course does reveal both Henry Wilson's idiosyncratic interpretation of the political responsibilities of a DMO and Sir John French's political naïvety in signing what was in fact a guarantee binding on the government.[92] The Curragh incident was of the greatest importance for the army because, five months before the outbreak of war, both the Secretary of State for War and the CIGS resigned; as an officer elsewhere in the War Office afterwards remarked, 'It is not good to lose your Chief of the General Staff on the eve of war.'[93] The immediate result was that Asquith himself temporarily took over the seals of the War

Office and Sir Charles Douglas, formerly Adjutant-General, was appointed to replace French.

In view of Douglas's earlier stance on the formation and structure of a General Staff there was good reason to suppose that he was not greatly in sympathy with it as it then was. Sir William Robertson afterwards acknowledged two of Douglas's outstanding qualities, his unique knowledge of the details of army matters and his propensity to overwork, which was to cause his death within two months of the start of the war.[94] Henry Wilson certainly quickly sensed the vulnerability of the new CIGS and immediately sought to gain control over Home Defence—which had hitherto been a part of the Directorate of Military Training—and the Movements section of the Quartermaster-General's office. For his part, Douglas was forced to rely heavily on his Directing staff for advice and agreed to accept submissions from them about recasting the General Staff; he also inveighed against the creation of a Sub-Chief of the General Staff, which in view of later events was unfortunate.

Despite his apparent pedestrianism Douglas was well aware that the Curragh incident had left scars on the body of the army and that some measures were necessary to restore its confidence in the Army Council. Accordingly, soon after he came into office, he began to devise secret proposals to bring back the personal element which he felt Esher had destroyed by establishing the post of Inspector-General. Douglas thought that the best way for the Army Council to get back into touch with the army would be by the abolition of that post and: 'the substitution of personal touch of the C.I.G.S. with the superior commanders and staffs, the regimental officers and the rank and file. He should be frequently with the troops.'[95] Douglas believed that this had been the intention of the late Secretary of State and that in proposing such a measure he was merely carrying out that intention. Seely had intended to merge the posts of Inspector-General of Home Forces and of Oversea Forces to create a new position of Inspector-General of the Imperial Forces. This officer was to be the Sub-Chief of the General Staff and the post was designed for Sir Ian Hamilton.[96] The complex cross-postings necessary to create the vacancy were defeated because they depended on Sir Charles Douglas himself vacating the post of IGHF and taking over the Malta Command, but his wife's health would not permit it. After that Seely had abandoned the idea.

Douglas had no intention of creating an Inspectorate of Imperial Forces in order to place an additional block between himself and the army. Instead, he simply suggested abolishing the Inspector-General of Oversea Forces and sending out a General Officer whenever the colonies wished an inspection. On the issue of a Sub-Chief Douglas preferred to let the matter stand over for six months until he had had some experience of the working of the office. He also remarked on the duplication of work at the General Staff and the gulf which resulted from the CIGS issuing orders and regulations for training but seldom seeing how they were put into effect. There was one possible drawback to his proposed amalgamation, of which he was well aware:[97]

> It may be said that my proposals would tend to raise the position of the C.I.G.S. to that of a Commander-in-Chief. It should not have this result; he would not command (except at manoeuvres) but inspect, and action would be taken by the Army Council.

His main aim was to re-establish the relationship between the governing body of the army and the fighting soldier.

It is difficult to assess the probable results of Douglas's scheme had it come into operation. It might well have led to greater contact between the General Staff and the bulk of the army, so that Haig could never have reached the position of almost complete isolation which he did during the war. However, the scheme certainly needed time in which to embed itself in the practice of the army as well as a change of outlook on the part of some General Staff officers. As it was, Douglas had little time to effect any changes before he found himself in the midst of war. He was then hindered in the performance of his duties by Asquith's lack of detailed knowledge of the *War Book* and absence in the Cabinet. The General Staff were thus to go to war under the direction of a novice so far as knowledge of their functioning was concerned. They also had but slender experience of the performance of their duties in wartime conditions, and the manuals which played a vital part in the preparation of the army had not been thoroughly revised or refined. That the General Staff existed at all, and that it had developed some techniques of direction in war, was the work of a few. Esher, Haldane, Ellison, Haig and Wilson had all played major parts.

Yet they must be held responsible also for the development of an ethos which was to make it acceptable that on the outbreak of war the General Staff should be disastrously denuded of experienced officers. This lacuna was to have unfortunate effects with the advent to the War Office of Lord Kitchener.

Notes

1 Sir J. W. Fortescue, *A History of the British Army*, vol. XIII, London, 1930, p. 570.
2 C. à C. Repington, *Vestigia*, London, 1919, pp. 259–60.
3 M. V. Brett and Viscount Esher, *Journals and Letters of Reginald Viscount Esher*, vol. 2, London, 1934–8, p. 126.
4 L. S. Amery, *My Political Life*, vol. 1, London, 1953, p. 212.
5 Esher Papers. Haldane to Esher, 19 December 1905. 'War Office Reconstitution Committee 1903–1905'.
6 Marker Papers. Repington to Marker, 15 December 1905. B.M. Add. MSS. 52277.
7 B. Collier, *Brasshat: A Biography of Field Marshal Sir Henry Wilson*, London, 1961, p. 96; Sir A. Haldane, *A Soldier's Saga*, Edinburgh, 1948, p. 206.
8 Roberts Papers. Nicholson to Roberts, 14 December 1905. Box 20926, file N2.
9 Ewart Diary, 13 December 1905.
10 R. B. Haldane Papers. Haldane to Esher, 5 January 1906. N.L.S. MS. 5907.
11 Wilkinson Papers. Haldane to Wilkinson, 6 January 1906. O.T.P. 13/32.
12 The General Staff, n.d. (marked 'Copies sent to Esher 29–1–06, Haldane 1–2–06'), B.M. Add. MSS. 50836.
13 R. B. Haldane Papers. Haldane to Esher, 4 and 14 February 1906. N.L.S. MS. 5907.
14 Royal Archives. Esher to Edward VII, 16 February 1906. RA W40/5.
15 Brett and Esher, *Journals and Letters*, vol. 2, pp. 144–5.
16 Esher Papers. Clarke to Esher, 18 February 1906. 'Sir George Clarke 1906, Vol. 6'.
17 Ewart Diary, 28 February 1906.
18 Haig Papers. Esher to Haig, 2 March 1906. N.L.S. H.334.E.
19 R. B. Haldane, *An Autobiography*, London, 1929, p. 199.
20 Royal Archives. Esher to Edward VII, 15 March 1906. RA W40/17.
21 Marker Papers. Repington to Marker, 15 March 1906. B.M. Add. MSS. 52277.
22 Hansard, 4th series, vol. CLIII, 8 March 1906, col. 672; vol. CLIV, 19 March 1906, cols 127–8.
23 Esher Papers. Clarke to Esher, 4 April 1906. 'Sir George Clarke 1906 Vol. 6'.

24 Ellison Papers. Clarke to Haldane, 5 April 1906.
25 Esher Papers. Esher to Knollys, 27 April 1906. 'Letters and Memoranda Vol. 1'.
26 Minutes of Proceedings and Precis prepared for the Army Council, 1906. Precis No. 299, The Need of a Trained Administrative Staff, 8 February 1906, p. 138. W.O. 163/11.
27 Esher Papers. Ponsonby to Esher, 19 August 1906. 'Army Letters Vol. 4'.
28 Haig Papers. Diary, 22 December 1906 and 27 January 1907. N.L.S. H.2.G., H.2.H.
29 Wilson Diary, 9 June 1906.
30 Royal Archives. Esher to Knollys, 6 August 1906. RA W40/43.
31 R. B. Haldane Papers. Knollys to Haldane, 9 August 1906. N.L.S. MS. 5907.
32 Royal Archives. Esher to Edward VII, 16 August 1906. RA W40/46.
33 Haldane, *An Autobiography*, p. 199.
34 Ellison Papers. A copy of the memorandum bears the inscription in Ellison's hand: 'Original draft of memo. accompanying A.O. constituting G. S. Written by me Sept. 1906.' For confirmation, *see* Wilson Diary, 12 September 1906.
35 Ellison Papers. Memorandum, p. 4.
36 *Ibid.*, p. 7.
37 M. E. Howard, *Studies in War and Peace*, London, 1971, p. 90.
38 Minute by Nicholson, 22 March 1906. W.O. 32/526/79/288.
39 Royal Archives. Memorandum by Haldane for H.M. the King on his trip to Berlin, 2 September 1906. RA W49/100.
40 A.O. 233, Organization of the General Staff, 12 September 1906, para. 2. W.O. 123/48.
41 *Ibid.*, para. 11.
42 Esher Papers. Haldane to Esher, 8 September 1906. 'Army Letters Vol. 4'.
43 General Report on the Japanese system of Military Education and Training, 1906. W.O. 33/407.
44 Haig Papers. Haig to Ellison, 11 September 1906. N.L.S. H.40.G.
45 Esher Papers. Haig to Esher, 17 October 1906. 'Army Letters Vol. 4'.
46 Esher Papers. Clarke to Esher, 8 October 1906. 'Sir George Clarke 1906 Vol. 7'.
47 Minute by Rawlinson, 26 January 1906. W.O. 32/3094.
48 Wilson Diary, 21 January 1907.
49 Sir J. Adye, *Soldiers and Others I Have Known*, London, 1925, p. 226.
50 Lord Edward Gleichen, *A Guardsman's Memories*, Edinburgh, 1932, p. 313; W. H. H. Waters, *Secret and Confidential*, London, 1926, p. 298; Sir T. Bridges, *Alarms and Excursions: Reminiscences of a Soldier*, London, 1938, p. 55.
51 Marker Papers. Kitchener to Marker, 21 March 1907. B.M. Add. MSS. 52276B.
52 Royal Archives. Esher to Knollys, 5 May 1907. RA W40/111.
53 Hansard, 4th series, vol. CLXIX, 25 February 1907, cols 1289–90.

54 R. B. Haldane Papers. Haldane to Esher, 6 September 1907. N.L.S. MS. 5907.
55 Haig Papers. Diary, 8 November 1907. N.L.S. H.2.G.
56 J. A. L. Haldane Papers. Diary, 14 November 1907. N.L.S. Accession 2070, box 1.
57 Haig Papers. Diary, 23 and 31 August 1908. N.L.S. H.2.H.
58 H. T. Baker, 'Lord Haldane', *Army Quarterly*, vol. XVII, 1928–9, p. 16.
59 Haig Papers. Report on a Staff Tour held by the Chief of the General Staff 26 to 30 October 1908. N.L.S. H.77. General Sir W. G. Nicholson had succeeded Lyttelton as CGS on 2 April 1908.
60 Haig Papers. Report of a Conference of General Staff Officers at the Staff College 7 to 10 January 1908, pp. 15, 16. N.L.S. H.81.
61 *Ibid.*, p. 37.
62 *Ibid.*, p. 48.
63 Haig Papers. Report of a Conference of General Staff Officers at the Staff College 18th to 21st January 1909, *passim*, N.L.S. H.81.
64 Edmonds Papers. Lecture on Intelligence Duties in the Field, 15 March 1908. Lecture on Intelligence in European Warfare, January 1908. K.C.L.
65 Lady Constance Kell, 'Secret Well Kept: The Life of Sir Vernon Kell', unpublished MSS., n.d., p. 119.
66 Edmonds Papers. Sir Eric Holt-Wilson to (?) 17 July 1942. K.C.L.
67 Haig Papers. Report on a Cavalry Staff Ride held by the Director of Staff Duties 1st to 6th March 1909, p. 29. N.L.S. H.78.
68 Royal Archives. Esher to Knollys, 31 December 1909. RA W41/103.
69 Royal Archives. Report on the Manoeuvres held in Saxony, September 1909 (Sir I. S. M. Hamilton). RA W28/109.
70 Kiggell Papers. Haig to Kiggell, 14 July 1910. K.C.L.
71 Haig Papers. Report on a Conference of General Staff Officers at the Staff College 17th to 20th January 1910, *passim*. N.L.S. H.81.
72 Brett and Esher, *Journals and Letters*, vol. 3, p. 44.
73 M.O.1 to Secretary, CID, October 1910. W.O. 106/47/E.1/4.
74 Report of a Committee on Arrangements for Departments of the War Office in the Event of War, 1910, pp. 3, 13. W.O. 32/5964.
75 Co-ordination of Departmental Action on the Outbreak of War, 28 April 1911. W.O. 32/5965.
76 *War Book*, 1913 ed., p. 54. W.O. 32/642.
77 *Ibid.*, p. 70.
78 Memorandum, 22 October 1913. W.O. 106/51/W.D.2.
79 Notes by Lt-Col. Bird and Maj. Evans on the working of Ob during the Army Exercise 1913, 3 October 1913. W.O. 32/4731.
80 French to Esher, 21 January 1912. Quo. E. G. French, ed., *Some War Diaries, Addresses and Correspondence of Field Marshal the Right Honble. The Earl of Ypres*, London, 1937, p. 131.
81 Wilson Diary, 4 January, 21 April, 6 September, 29 December 1911; 8 January 1912.
82 Royal Archives. Edward VII to Knollys, 27 July 1904. RA W25/100.
83 *Army Review*, vol. 1, no. 1, July 1911, p. 5.

84 Roberts Papers. Repington to Northcliffe, 6 July 1911. Box X20927, file R1.
85 *Army Review*, vol. 2, no. 2, April 1912, p. ix.
86 Asquith Papers. Harcourt to Asquith, 26 January 1910. Crewe to Asquith, 22 October 1910. Bodl. MS. Asquith 12.
87 Bonar Law Papers. Wilson to Bonar Law, 20 April 1913. Beav. Lib. B.L. 29/3/22.
88 Haldane Papers. Repington to Haldane, 27 November 1911. N.L.S. MS. 5910.
89 J. E. B. Seely, *Adventure*, London, 1930, pp. 144–6.
90 Seely Papers. Hankey to Seely, 31 March 1914. Box 141.
91 Howell Papers. Memorandum, 16(?) December 1913. Howell 1A 3/3.
92 Varying accounts of the Curragh Incident exist in Seely, *op. cit.*, pp. 160–70; Sir C. E. Callwell, *Field Marshal Sir Henry Wilson: His Life and Diaries*, vol. 1, London, 1927, pp. 136–45; R. Blake, *The Unknown Prime Minister*, London, 1955, ch. XI.
93 Sir G. Macmunn, *Behind the Scenes in Many Wars*, London, 1930, p. 113.
94 Sir W. R. Robertson, *From Private to Field Marshal*, London, 1921, p. 195.
95 Royal Archives. Memorandum, 19 April 1914, p. 1. RA Geo. V. F.809/2.
96 Royal Archives. Seely to George V, 21 November 1913. RA Geo. V. F.621/1.
97 Royal Archives. Memorandum, 19 April 1914, p. 3. RA Geo. V. F.809/2.

5
The Imperial Design

The problems of Imperial defence had exercised theorists throughout the nineteenth century and had introduced to the public such names as Dilke, Wilkinson, Clarke and the brothers Colomb. For a variety of reasons consideration had been chiefly from a naval viewpoint: seapower was traditionally Britain's greatest strength, commercial links with the colonies were of necessity naval and stood exposed in a war to a *guerre-de-course* strategy, and this was also the arena of debate on the probability of an invasion of England itself. The publication of A. T. Mahan's *Influence of Sea Power on History 1660–1783* (London, 1890) gave naval imperialists a theoretician who could rival Clausewitz and was moreover rather easier to comprehend, though as has been remarked this exposition occurred just when technology was beginning to erode its basis.[1] No such doctrines existed within the military spectrum, so that when the General Staff became concerned to spread its influence overseas it lacked any theoretical justifications on which to call. As a result the process by which it sought to transform itself into an organization with influence throughout the Empire had always to fall back on nebulous concepts such as the value of common institutions and patterns in the event of some future and unspecified contest of arms. In the prevailing temper of colonial relations this was to prove something of a vain endeavour.

As it had affected the military establishment in England, so the Boer War also served to soften attitudes towards Imperial co-operation. It led the Colonial Conference of 1902 to discuss both a proposal for a pool of troops for Imperial purposes and an Imperial supervisory body. Significantly it was over the latter issue that the conference came to grief. Colonial representatives feared that they might through such an organization find themselves automatically committed if Britain went into an unpopular war. This unwillingness to participate in co-operative control of defence was reinforced by a contraction of the Imperial idea which resulted particularly from the 'Chinese labour' issue.[2] The conference thus saw a move away from the possibility of realistic colonial military co-operation, although the idea of a conference system was firmly established.

The need for Imperial resources to be brought within the reach of British strategists had been emphasized the previous year by Altham, who held that in a war with one or more European powers the Empire would stand or fall as a whole. Reminding the colonies of their responsibilities, he also stressed the need for the controlling authority to know the size of contingents available for service in any part of the world, a theme which was to be repeated thereafter.[3] The following June the secretary of the Colonial Defence Committee reiterated Altham's view and emphasized that the military forces of the Empire should be used against a common foe 'in conformity with one general plan, and . . . the supreme military control of those forces should be vested in one central authority'.[4] There was now, however, little prospect of such compliance by the colonies and dominions and a growing feeling that colonial governments were intransigent when it came to the expenditure of revenue on defence. Lord Wolseley typified this attitude when he wrote:[5]

in many ways, Colonists are difficult people to deal with. They generally can find money to build monuments to one another, but when asked to put their hands in their pockets to support Military Institutions they do not feel so anxious to spend their money liberally.

In the event it was not until 1906, when the problems inherent in the formation of a General Staff had been resolved, that the idea of expanding this organization to embrace the colonies and dominions first arose.

Haldane's interest in Imperial organization had begun long before he took formal responsibility for military affairs; in June 1903 he had expressed dissatisfaction with the methods of advising the Crown on Imperial affairs and suggested a 'Cabinet of Empire' on the lines of the new CID.[6] He also had a close acquaintance with the Canadian Prime Minister, Sir Wilfred Laurier, on which to build.[7] And he had as a foundation of military policy a paper by Grierson which considered five possible major wars and five small wars. Of the former, combat with the United States was considered the most improbable and war against Germany and in alliance with France well within the bounds of possibility. No direct threat was envisaged to Canada, Australia or South Africa, with the exception of a Basuto uprising.[8]

Haldane began his consideration of the organization of Imperial defence soon after his advent to office, recording a dinner in October 1906 at which he entertained Sir Frederick Borden, Canadian Minister of Militia, Sir Edward Grey, Lyttelton and Sir Edward Ward, Permanent Under Secretary at the War Office: 'We discussed Imperial War affairs all the evening.'[9] Shortly afterwards the War Office forwarded to the Colonial Office a list of seven subjects that they wished to have discussed at the forthcoming Colonial Conference. They were permitted to raise four but not to discuss interchange of units and officers, problems of relative rank or military education. Elgin's reason was to give precedence to subjects suggested by the colonies, and their over-riding concern was with an Imperial Council and Secretariat.

There was at this time some disagreement about the consultative role of the colonies in matters of Imperial defence, notably expressed by Sir George Clarke. He felt it would be 'open to many grave objections' to admit colonial representatives to the deliberations of the CID other than when a 'purely Colonial question' was raised by a colony.[10] Clarke also attempted to put before the forthcoming conference a resolution which would make it plainly apparent that colonial military aid was being sought mainly for a continental conflict. He proposed that the members of the conference formally recognize their obligation to afford 'such military support to the national cause as their circumstances may permit . . . in the event of a war involving vital Imperial interests'. If, however, the war were of such a nature that colonial territories were threatened, 'it is understood that an adequate force must be retained for the self-defence of those territories'. Haldane expressed his sympathy with this proposal but thought it wiser to put one resolution only, relating to an Imperial General Staff system.[11] The motion duly placed before the conference emphasized the value of such a body in fostering the study of military science, collecting and disseminating intelligence, planning schemes of defence on common principles and advising the respective governments on the training, education and war organization of their respective forces. This cautious phraseology, which made no mention of the prospect of offensive operations, seems to have emanated not from Haldane but from his military secretary, Ellison.[12]

When the conference met to discuss military questions on 20 April 1907 it had before it four papers embodying the views of the General Staff on some of the major questions. The most important was an appreciation by the CGS of strategical perspectives which revealed the growing preoccupation with a continental war. The first principle of supremacy at sea was admitted, but it was emphasized that the Empire was confronted with dangers which the navy could not avert.[13] Lyttelton also emphasized the chief lesson of the Russo-Japanese War, which was that the military planners must know in advance the strength and organization of the forces which could be put into the field. Such knowledge meant that one started with 'an incalculable advantage over an opponent who does not enjoy the same position'. The General Staff also warned against the supposed lesson of the South African War that irregulars could stand against trained troops—in offensive campaigns they were useless. They then emphasized the value of an Imperial General Staff as forming a bond of union in regard to military thought across the Empire.

The remaining three papers presented for the consideration of the conference also carried the implication of the use of colonial troops in a continental war, if carefully scrutinized. Lyttelton argued strongly for homogeneous war organization in all Imperial forces in view of the 'probability that the colonies will take an ever-increasing part in future wars in which the welfare of the Empire is at stake'.[14] Other papers dealt with the necessity for common patterns in rifles, machine guns and ammunition, and with the desirability that colonial governments should order their ordnance stores through the War Office. Although emphasizing the reciprocal relationship envisaged between the War Office and colonial military forces, these papers did reveal that the General Staff was not actuated chiefly by fear of war on the borders of the colonies.

From the outset of the conference it was apparent that South Africa and New Zealand were prepared to be more co-operative than either Canada or Australia. One military participant recorded that the Canadians 'seemed especially nervous of committing themselves to anything definite;-? Is Laurier a humbug or an Imperialist.'[15] Haldane set himself to overcome what was in part at least a justifiable colonial caution in his opening speech to the conference. He sketched in for his audience the lesson of the South African War—that preparation for war was the most important element in peacetime military affairs—and the principles behind the Esher report and the establishment of the General Staff. This he suggested might profitably be adopted within broad limits by the Empire. A common purpose or end, he informed his audience, 'may be very potent in furthering military organization'.[16] The fact that his and their conceptions of this purpose would probably differ markedly Haldane carefully refrained from revealing.

To work on a common pattern necessitated a common conception; Haldane therefore suggested that 'the General Staff which we have created at home . . . should receive as far as possible an Imperial character'. The aim was for General Staff officers, trained in a common school and common principles, to be available to advise colonial governments according to those principles; their advice could be accepted or rejected, as was thought fit. Such an interchange would do much, Haldane suggested, to bring about that uniformity in matters military which was 'to some extent essential if there is to be effective co-operation in a great war'.[17] Shortly afterwards, he placed the draft resolution recommending the formation of an Imperial General Staff before the conference for discussion.

The Canadian Prime Minister, Sir Wilfred Laurier, was at this conference to display great sensitivity towards suggestions of Imperial centralization.[18] His attitude was duplicated in this section of the conference by his Minister for Militia, Sir Frederick Borden, who emphasized the limitations upon any Canadian aid in matters of defence and questioned whether the central General Staff would have independent authority throughout Empire and dominions. Haldane repeatedly stressed that the Imperial General Staff would have no authority but would be purely an advisory body, and his efforts led Borden to a hesitant acceptance of the proposals in outline.

Deakin, the Australian Prime Minister, was more ready to express adherence to the principles as well as the policies outlined by Haldane and anticipated 'nothing but great advantage' from such an association. Only Sir Joseph Ward, accepting on behalf of New Zealand the suggestions made by the Secretary of State for War, fully recognized the implication of the papers presented with them. He remarked on the importance of common patterns of arms and ammunition when colonial contingents would be sent 'to another country for the purpose of common defence to fight an enemy'.[19]

Deakin, Ward and others now began to press for publication of Haldane's opening statement but Botha hung back. A final draft was agreed on 23 April, though without quite the degree of unanimity that has been suggested.[20] Apparently trifling debates over the exact phraseology of the resolution revealed a desire held in common by Deakin, Laurier and Borden to avoid definite commitment to any action and especially to any immediate action. Opposing them, Jameson and Smartt of Cape Colony felt that too little was being pledged. Haldane steered between both factions with his customary skill, reminding them that as this was a deliberating conference agreement on the broad principle was the important point. The final resolution, recognizing and affirming the need for an Imperial General Staff 'without wishing to commit any of the Governments represented', reflected the attitude of the dominion representatives that, whatever might be the case in terms of fleets, they were wholly unwilling to put either their countries or their own majorities at risk by overtly sanctioning a centralized military control for the Empire in any form.[21]

Behind the scenes of the formal conference the War Office betrayed an anxiety to influence the structure of military control in Canada, which was rapidly becoming the most advanced of all the Imperial possessions in such matters. An informal conference was held on 30 April at which the only non-British members were Sir Frederick Borden and Major-General P. H. N. Lake, Chief of the Canadian General Staff. The main topic of debate was the nature of the General Staff in Canada. According to A.O. 233, two of the five General Staff posts allotted to the Dominion were to go to professors at the Royal Military College, Kingston. The Canadians, seeking to establish a better qualified staff of their own, successfully had these switched to an Assistant Director of Military Operations and Staff Duties and an Assistant Quarter-master-General. In exchange the British secured adherence to the rule that, except in very special circumstances, the same qualifications would be required to fill local General Staff posts in Canada as in England. Since Canada possessed very few officers so qualified, this meant that she would have frequently to apply for a General Staff officer from England. It was through this loophole that influence was to be exercised over the development of military affairs in Canada. As a subsidiary concession it was agreed to accept two Canadian officers for the Staff College each year, providing they passed the usual entrance examination.[22]

Haldane had made his proposals without first discussing them with the King, a course of action which had strained relations between the Crown and several of his predecessors. However, when the content was made known to the King he approved particularly of the Imperial General Staff—'an admirable ground-work to start on'—and the means of eventual continuity in military policy. He was shrewd enough to add the suggestion that Haldane draw up the essential conditions under which such forces must operate 'and without which it would be useless when acting in co-operation with us'.[23]

Cautious and qualified though the recommendations were, Haldane was to be congratulated for achieving the best result possible in the atmosphere of the times. Laurier had made plain his view of military policy to the Canadian House of Commons on 27 March 1907, just prior to departing for the conference: 'I must adhere to the view I expressed five years ago that for no consideration would Canada be induced to be drawn into the vortex of European militarism.'[24] The diffuseness of the belief present at the conference in the value of closer Imperial links found other expression in the acceptance of an Imperial Secretariat in preference to an Imperial Council endowed with legislative and executive powers. As in the case of the War Office, certain elements in the Colonial Office were desirous of a re-organization to enable them more firmly to embrace colonial affairs.[25]

As Director of Staff Duties, Haig had the chief responsibility for working out the details of the new military organization for the Empire. In the early months of 1908 he was occupied with plans for the establishment of 'war schools', which never came to anything, but on 1 August recorded in his diary: 'Gave C.G.S. memo. on Impl. Genl. Staff'. A further meeting took place on 4 November, after which the CGS agreed to have the paper printed and sent to the colonial premiers.[26] The War Office did not intend to fall into the trap of presenting the colonies and dominions with proposals which did not offer a good chance of acceptance, so the draft was discussed with Sir Frederick Borden and General

Hoad of the Australian army on 15 December. The following day Haig made final corrections to the proofs with Nicholson and two days later he recorded posting his missive to Australia and New Zealand. The view of those involved in strategic planning was encapsulated in the comment of the DMO on reading it: 'We are, I hope, moving in the direction of Imperial Cooperation for defence, in which lies all our hope for the future.'[27]

The memorandum, which appeared over Nicholson's signature, was a cleverly constructed polemic designed both to quiet the fears of the dominions and colonies about the use to be made of their military forces and to ensure that local General Staffs did not slip from the control of Whitehall. Thus the concept of 'Imperial defence' was divided into two categories, of which local defence was the first. In the second category, the general defence of the Empire, it was emphasized that organization not designed for offensive action was inadequate. As far as the location of such offensive action went, the probability was that troops would be required to 'come to the assistance of, and act in combination with, the forces maintained for local defence in some particular portion of the Empire'.[28] In terms of strategy then being planned this statement was somewhat misleading.

With regard to the establishment of an Imperial General Staff, it was emphasized that unity of thought was the essential preliminary to successful united action. Hence what was required was a central body to formulate broad principles of defence, to prepare detailed plans and to collect and disseminate information; also local branches were necessary to study local needs, possibilities and applications. But the Imperial General Staff must be an entity, therefore 'these local branches must form parts of one whole, springing from the central body'.[29] To ensure this desirable uniformity of method and purpose there must be a single head, the CGS in London.

The tender spot was clearly going to be the relationship between the titular head of the new body and its representative overseas. The formula devised was that within the local sections, 'more or less' under the direct supervision of the CGS, each Chief would be the adviser of his own government and head of all General Staff officers. They would receive information from him on the correct principles of strategy and advise their government on the local application of those principles; where they were not accepted, it was their duty to carry out the orders of their respective governments. The loophole in this scheme of de-centralization was the appointment as chiefs of sections of officers from London. In addition it was recognized that if a common standard of military knowledge was to obtain personnel for the staffs would have to come from Camberley and Quetta. Thus an educational stranglehold would be exerted by the Staff Colleges, except upon Canada which possessed the Royal Military College at Kingston on which to build.

Despite the small numbers of trained officers in the dominions the paper made it clear that in London the matter was viewed with some urgency:[30]

> It is so important that the military forces of the Empire should not be allowed to develop on divergent and in-dependent lines, but on common and approved principles, as regards organisation and training, that an attempt should be made to start the General Staff organisation now with the means available.

The basic spirit in which the organization was conceived was one of 'loyalty to the Empire and to one another, at all times and in all places'.

There were two separate spurs to a formalization of the relations between London and the Empire from a military standpoint which dictated rapid action at this time. On the one hand there were fears that in the event of a sudden war and military expedition to Europe all regular British troops would be rapidly used up with no absolute guarantee of dominion assistance, a risky eventuality.[31] On the other, the Military Operations department was aware of anxieties on the part of 'our friends abroad'—presumably the French—as to Britain's ability to render effective aid at the most useful point. Bluntly put, doubts were being felt abroad about the value of an alliance with England, doubts which might in a few years result in Britain's again experiencing a period of isolation and one this time not voluntarily induced. 'Isolation might well mean an hostile naval combination against us which would render our dream of Imperial federation for defence for ever in vain.'[32] Hence the need was to make an Imperial General Staff a reality in order to work out an acceptable scheme of mutual defence, when 'we' would be rendered almost unassailable and 'our alliance coveted by all'.

The reception by the colonies and dominions of Haig's

proposals was mixed, and was affected most by the requirement of autonomy which was becoming a watchword throughout most of the Empire. The South African colonies forebore to make any pronouncement at all on the grounds that this would be a subject which would concern the central government in the event of unification. Canada remarked that precise definitions were required in certain matters, particularly where the autonomy of the Canadian government was at stake. Hence Borden laid down the need for all communication of a non-routine nature between the Canadian Chief and the Chief of the Imperial General Staff to be submitted to the Minister of Militia for his concurrence before despatch. Canada also announced her intention not to lay down any definite standard of qualification for service on the General Staff, thereby evading the necessity to send officers to Camberley.[33]

A note of extreme caution was also adopted by the Australian government, which stressed the principle of full local control. It demanded the power to terminate the appointment of an Australian officer to the Imperial General Staff, that all communications not on matters of routine be made via the Minister of Defence and that its approval be necessary for the appointment of an Australian to the Imperial General Staff and any officer to the Australian section. A shrewd insight was also displayed into the probable motives behind Britain's approaches:[34]

> The Commonwealth Government desires to state specifically that its assent to the general principles mentioned above is not to be considered as binding it to raise or equip any force or designate any existing troops for employment outside the Commonwealth or territories under the control of the Commonwealth.

Without any sign of collusion there was a remarkable degree of unanimity amongst the dominions and colonies about how much, or how little, they were prepared to subscribe to any common and centralized military organization.

The Colonial Conference of 1909 was called primarily to consider the naval implications of Imperial defence as a result of increased German naval power. There was also a hope that the conference might reach agreement on military matters, something which it always found more difficult. The Director of Military Operations remarked in his diary that 'it is high time that the Colonies realized that unless they hurry up, they will be too late to help the Mother Country in her hour of need'.[35]

Haldane duly placed before the conference a paper containing proposals for so organizing the forces of the Empire as to ensure their effective co-operation in time of war. Prefaced by remarks similar to those he had made two years before, the paper contained the major points of the earlier memoranda. However, in an attempt to secure a more positive result, the CGS spelled out his fears of a European war more overtly:[36]

> in proportion as danger threatens the heart of the Empire and compels the Mother Country to concentrate her naval and military forces, the responsibility for the safety of the outlying portions of the Empire must tend to be delegated to her daughter nations.

The War Office still clearly expected to make heavy use of the loan system for senior posts for some time to come due to lack of educational facilities. However, Nicholson diplomatically supported the principle of full local control, asking only that the CGS be kept informed.

Military defence was discussed at the second meeting of the conference on 29 July at the War Office, at least one of the latter's representatives feeling that the increased activity might actually precipitate war 'for Germany may realize that she had better lose no time if she really means to go for us'.[37] At the main meeting the principle was accepted that each part of the Empire would make its preparations on lines which would enable it, should it so wish, to take its share in the general defence of the Empire. The military section agreed to all recommendations put before it for homogeneity of forces and recommended that all General Staff officers throughout the Empire should be members of an Imperial General Staff, whilst remaining under the control of their own governments.[38] On a more pedestrian but equally important level, detailed financial arrangements were for the first time worked out for the interchange of staff officers.

Edward VII regarded the conclusions reached by the conference as admirable and helping to bring into closer touch 'in the most practical manner' Mother Country and colonies.[39] Certainly it did represent a success for the proponents of the Imperial General Staff, albeit that they had been forced to accept that in dominions where there were insufficient qualified staff the local section would be formed and its duties performed by the same officers as at present.[40] The opportunity now existed, through the loans system, to guide and direct Imperial military development. However, it remained to establish the fact of such co-operation, which in the face of repeated affirmations of dominion control might prove exceedingly difficult. It was to furnish the dominions with a necessary example, rather than solely to extricate the government from embarrassment, that Haldane offered Kitchener the newly-created Mediterranean command.[41]

One consequence of the conference was that, by Army Order 314 of 1909, Sir William Nicholson adopted the title Chief of the Imperial General Staff, something of an anticipatory action. Twelve months later, speaking in the Commons to the army Estimates, Haldane had to restrict his horizons in referring to the advances being made in Imperial defence: 'A great deal of work . . . is going on, and there is no doubt that foundations have been laid—I do not say more—on which progress may be hoped for.'[42] The War Office certainly knew the direction in which it wanted that progress to travel. Nicholson unequivocally envisaged the use of colonial contingents 'for Imperial purposes' outside the dominions as the main motive for changes in military organization and Ewart felt a similar sense of purpose and urgency.[43]

The creation of a CIGS did not meet with universal approbation. Esher was called upon to provide King Edward with memoranda on the proposal and two days later Haldane received a note from the King's private secretary:[44]

> The King desires me to say that he does not much like the word 'Imperial' and that he thinks there is a little too much talk these days of 'Imperial' and 'Empire'. He does not understand what is meant by 'local section'. Is India in future to be a 'local section'. If not, the word 'Imperial' he thinks would be a misnomer.

It may have been these sentiments which caused the King's idea of a Royal Essay competition for the Imperial General Staff to lapse, something which can only be counted unfortunate.[45] On this occasion Haldane succeeded in assuaging the King's doubts and the title was approved. It rang more hollowly in the dominions than it did in London.

During 1910 pressure for closer Imperial co-operation grew as the Round Table movement, and particularly its parliamentary spokesman Leopold Amery, pressed for an Imperial Secretariat and a Dominions Department separate from the Colonial Office.[46] Haldane was himself sufficiently satisfied with the progress of the Imperial General Staff to use it as an example to support his belief that the solution to the problem of Imperial relations was a form of unwritten confederation: 'The developments which have taken place in the Imperial General Staff organization . . . show how much is possible with very slight machinery.'[47] Others were both less satisfied with the situation and more anxious to inform the forthcoming 1911 conference of the true state of affairs.

Esher, a member of the sub-committee appointed in 1910 to formulate naval and military questions to be discussed by the forthcoming conference, remarked caustically on the 'pious aspirations and somewhat vague generalities' which had been the outcome of its predecessor. He also commented on the absence of any kind of combined General Staff and on the fact that the Empire was 'as far as ever' from the solution of the problems of co-operation against hostile powers.[48] Sir Arthur Nicolson, Permanent Under Secretary at the Foreign Office, was concerned to make the fundamental point that in the event of war no component part of the Empire would be considered as neutral by a belligerent, an argument designed to force the hand of the dominions but which would probably have produced a renewed wave of 'Little Imperialism' if overtly stated. Nicolson also raised the question of whether it would be wise to communicate to dominion governments confidential details of the measures to be taken upon the outbreak of war unless they were prepared to share the resulting responsibilities.[49]

The necessity to improve the machinery in existence for Imperial co-operation with regard to military and naval defence was now clearly recognized at Cabinet level.[50] It was even more strongly recognized at the War Office. A paper by the CIGS on invasion stressed the need for superiority at sea in order to transport land forces rapidly 'to any point outside the Empire where our vital interests may be threatened' and held that the first duty of land forces was to 'influence contests which may take place outside the Empire in such a manner that our vital interests are safeguarded'.[51] This was a far cry from Australian concern about the dangers they faced should the Anglo-Japanese alliance ever be terminated, in which event the scale of probable attack by any other major power would certainly have to be revised.[52]

During the preparations for the conference the Director of Staff Duties, Kiggell, was privately warned that Australia would ask what contingencies were likely to arise before the next conference was due to meet in 1915 and what obligations would be entailed by Australia agreeing to the principle of mutual support. A paper was duly put up for the CIGS about such contingencies but in the accompanying minute Henry Wilson reported that precise definition was impossible and in any case of limited value: 'the real truth of the matter is, that in order to get full value out of such assistance as the Dominions may elect to give us, their troops should be placed under the orders of the CIGS and made available for service in any part of the world.'[53] The paper was slanted at the help which could be given to Great Britain by the dominions rather than *vice versa*: reference was made to the four great dominions to which 'the Mother Country will naturally turn in time of emergency' and operations in North West Europe specifically mentioned. Such sentiments were far too forthright for Haldane and Nicholson had twice to water them down before the final paper was printed for the CID. By that time the accent had changed from mutual help outside the dominions to help within them. As an example, 'The four great Dominions to which the Mother Country will naturally turn in time of emergency' became in the final draft 'The four great Dominions which *will* turn to the Mother Country or to which the Mother Country *may* turn for help in time of emergency.' All details were prudently omitted as more properly the responsibility of the Imperial General Staff.[54]

The conference also had before it a paper which showed that loans and attachments to dominion forces since January 1909 had totalled 47 in the case of Canada, 31 for Australia, 28 for New Zealand and 6 for South Africa. These figures masked a situation which was less than satisfactory from the viewpoint of the dominions, for since 1903 only 7 Canadians, 4 Australians, 2 New Zealanders and 2 officers from Natal had received Staff College educations.[55] Unless there was an expansion in the capacity of the Staff Colleges the dominions would either have to accept a number of senior officers from England or lower their own educational standards. Canada particularly was to choose the latter course to avoid domination from Whitehall.

At the military sub-committee which met on 14 and 17 June Haldane's earlier caution was well justified. G. F. Pearce, Australian Minister of Defence, did indeed ask for the views of the Imperial General Staff on Australia's 'natural sphere of operations' and Sir Frederick Borden repeated several times that it was of greater importance to develop local forces so that the 'Imperial Central Army' could assist them and not *vice versa*.[56] Realizing the importance of staff college education for their own troops, the dominions agreed without demur to contribute £200 a year for each officer sent to Camberley.

At the second meeting of the committee Pearce and Borden came close to open conflict and at the same time revealed that the attitude of the various colonies and dominions to the problems of Imperial defence was far from homogeneous. Pearce said that although New Zealand was not allowed by law to send her forces overseas many would volunteer, and pressed local sections to prepare mobilization schemes. Borden was extremely reluctant to go further than the vague generalizations of 1909 about assisting the Empire 'in a real emergency'. Concluding a somewhat fruitless discussion, Nicholson admitted that England did have a scheme for the deployment of dominion forces overseas but refused to go into any detail, reminding his audience of the Persian proverb that 'What two ears only hear, God himself does not know.'[57] He did add that he could see no reason why the dominions should not themselves formulate plans for assistance in a general war.

After 1911 the principle of selected dominion representatives attending the Committee of Imperial Defence by invitation when topics concerning them were under discussion weakened the idea of the Imperial General Staff as the forum for such debate. It also resulted in the demise of the four yearly conferences as the main instrument for such debates. The dominions in general favoured the new formula, although on one occasion Laurier did remark that the Dominion section of the Imperial General Staff was the organ upon which Canada was most desirous of being represented.[58] From this point discussion switched to the nature and degree of dominion representation on the CID.[59] A letter from Hankey reveals that there was at this time a certain bankruptcy of ideas about military defence over which discussion might profitably ensue: 'Apart from the Naval Question the only other subject which I am at present able to suggest for discussion with the Canadian representatives at the C.I.D. is the Treatment of Neutral and Enemy Merchant Ships in Time of War.'[60] The absence of the dominion representatives at the War Council and its successors during the opening months of the war prevented them having any influence on the development of Imperial strategy, and the fact that Asquith could remark on the novelty of Borden's playing an active part in Cabinet deliberations in mid-1915 underlines the lack of influence of the dominions at this level when war did occur.[61]

If the Empire failed to make its presence felt in matters of defence at Whitehall, there were yet the local sections of the General Staff upon which some participation might have been built. Here inherent difficulties were exacerbated by the fact that precise areas of responsibility of the War Office and Colonial Office were never clearly defined. Also the successive Secretaries of State at the Colonial Office involved (the Earl of Elgin, Lord Crewe and Sir Lewis Harcourt) were uninterested in military affairs. The latter has been aptly described as 'a man generally unsympathetic to the aspirations of the self-governing Empire', which fact acted as a further barrier to the development of integrated planning organizations.[62]

The South African case is the easiest to comprehend. The Union Defence Force was not established until 1912 with the passing of the South African Defence Act Number 13. It had, however, possessed a Brigadier-General, General Staff since 1908 in the person of Sir George Aston. This post did not reflect advanced strategic designs on the part of any of the Union's constituent states, for the post was created at the express request of the British Commander-in-Chief in South Africa.[63] Until the Union Aston's task was limited to training the British army and advising local governments on raising defence forces. Such was the lack of adequate machinery even for collating military information in the area that the administration in Northern Rhodesia had to be informed from London that the detachment of King's African Rifles in Western Nyasaland had been withdrawn some time previously.[64]

In 1912 also the South African Staff Corps came into being when a course was begun at Bloemfontein for 100 future officers in the Union Defence Force. After five weeks Aston could report that 'all has gone excellently so far', feeling that the instruction given on the course would spread good feeling.[65] The first full training year did not, however, begin until 1 July 1913, so that there was little opportunity to assess progress before the war broke out. Aston was replaced in 1913 by a South African, General F. C. Beyers, and from then on relations between the South African section and the Imperial General Staff seem to have been non-existent. This was due in part to the adoption by the War Office of an attitude at once too direct and too impolitic, and to a failure to take account of Smuts's sensitivity on matters of internal administration.[66] Its late formation and small size help to explain why the South African General Staff did little to participate in strategic counsels.[67]

In the case of New Zealand the Defence Act of 1906 substituted for a Commandant a Council of Defence headed by the Defence Minister. There was considerable anxiety to obtain the services of an Imperial officer on this new body as chief military member and Chief of the General Staff, at a salary of £550 a year.[68] The Army Council felt unable to recommend a British officer as the salary proposed was too little to attract a first-class man. This avenue of development then closed until 1910, when the introduction of compulsory training offered another opening. The Governor General suggested that the Defence Council, which had been a failure, would be replaced by a British officer; however, he also feared that Sir Joseph Ward 'will still be influenced by political pressure, and will keep the real power in his own hands—with disastrous results to military efficiency'.[69] Plunket had gauged the situation correctly and in June a request was made to secure the services of Major-General P. H. N. Lake, Chief of the Canadian General Staff, in the new post. The War Office refused to release him on flimsy grounds and instead Major-General A. J. Godley was appointed on 7 October 1910, combining the functions of Commander and Chief of the local section of the Imperial General Staff.

Godley's appointment was a good one. Three months later the Governor could report that he was making excellent progress appointing Imperial officers to districts and, what was more important, getting on well with Ward.[70] New Zealand, however, played no great role in developing the central Imperial General Staff because Godley's first and over-riding concern was to produce qualified and experienced staff officers for the New Zealand forces. His sympathies plainly lay with those at White-hall, for he informed Henry Wilson that he was working out the details of an expeditionary force 'which this country will clamour to send at once if war broke out'.[71] Progress was interrupted in April 1912 when a change of government led to Mackenzie replacing Ward as Premier. The defence issue now began to turn predominantly on naval matters, with a major debate over what form New Zealand's contribution to 'naval responsibility' should take. At the same time the administration began to display signs of jealousy towards Canada, demanding that New Zealand be admitted to closer confidence with England. This affected the military greatly since the political argument ran that no commitment could be made to assist in time of war unless there was adequate preparation beforehand.[72]

Harcourt's reaction was not calculated to mollify New Zealand's tender feelings. He did not object in principle to the dominion's proposal for more frequent meetings, but refused to hold them anywhere else save in London and made it apparent that he favoured meetings with separate ministers rather than the 'set pieces' New Zealand wanted.[73] Such was the dominating nature of this dispute that the Army Council had to remind New Zealand that the agreement whereby four of her officers served in England for an aggregate of four years was due to lapse in September 1913, and ask whether they wished to enter into a further agreement. No answer to this query was ever received.

As Inspector General of Oversea Forces, Sir Ian Hamilton visited New Zealand in the spring of 1914. He reported that the great concentration of responsibility upon the Commandant led to his being preoccupied with financial questions.[74] On the eve of the war the government were considering a scheme to give the CGS more freedom by handing over financial responsibility to the Quartermaster-General. When war did break out New Zealand responded promptly. An expeditionary force left on 16 December and further reinforcements followed soon after. The attitude of the Colonial Office and the War Office was not, however, one which encouraged co-operation on any wider strategic front in the direction of the war. This was summed up when Harcourt informed Liverpool in a curt note that the time for any discussion with the dominion premiers would be when it came to peace terms and not before.[75] Godley, who commanded the New Zealand division at the Dardanelles with great gallantry, would probably have been better admitted to the strategic counsels of Whitehall, such as they were. Unfortunately there was not the fund of experience necessary even to attempt to shake Kitchener from his rigid and independent mould.

Canada always offered the example of the most independent of the dominions over matters of defence, an attitude seen as early as 1902 when objections were voiced to the then Commanding Officer of the Canadian Militia, General Hutton, on the grounds that he occupied a standpoint too Imperial in tone.[76] This post, in many ways a hapless one, then went to Lord Dundonald, who held it from July 1902 to June 1904. At the same time Sir Frederick Borden was invited to London to discuss radical amendments to the Canadian Militia Act designed to remove any British hegemony, which involved removal of the restriction preventing a Canadian militia officer being appointed General Officer Commanding the Militia and deletion of the clause which gave British officers seniority over Canadian Militia officers of equal rank regardless of dates of promotion.

Canadian resolve was stiffened when the Governor General, Lord Minto, failed to comprehend that a quasi-independent GOC was incompatible with complete ministerial responsibility. He recommended that a Canadian GOC should not be permitted and offered the opinion that in the last resort Canada would appeal to Great Britain to 'maintain the integrity of the Dominion'. Minto also remarked that there might well be a recrudescence of racial feeling if a French Canadian were appointed.[77] His solution was to 'Imperialise' senior Canadian officers by conferring a brigade on selected officers, who could then be nominated for the appointment from Whitehall.

When Borden introduced his Militia Bill in March 1904, he made no reference to the Esher report, although he had probably learned of it during his visit to London the previous winter.[78] However, in April he informed Lord Minto that he intended to adopt the organization of the Esher report *mutatis mutandis* and that the Canadian CGS should 'for some time to come' be a Regular officer given a commission in the militia.[79] By thus adopting and adapting the organization already in operation in England, Borden was in effect insuring Canada against interference from Great Britain on the grounds that her military institutions did not correspond with the template for Imperial ones.

Borden was greatly aided in his task by the 'Dundonald affair'. Dundonald appears to have been a brusque man who resented anything smacking of political interference, and he spoke out

against various ministers in this vein during 1904. His final
outburst came when Fisher, Minister of Agriculture, displayed
great interest in a proposal to raise a new regiment in the eastern
townships of Quebec whereupon Dundonald accused him of trying
to select officers on political grounds. The Canadian Privy Council
found Fisher's interest perfectly legitimate and in the light of
Dundonald's subsequent correspondence with a member of the
Opposition recommended his dismissal.[80] This gave Borden his
chance to establish the new office in place of the old, and to ask
for Colonel P. H. N. Lake as its first incumbent. Arnold Forster
was at first reluctant to appoint Lake since he would have to be
appointed substantive Major-General and would thus be jumped
over the heads of 287 other colonels; instead he tried to free
himself of his own *bête noir*, Wolfe Murray. Lake was seconded
for six months on 1 November 1904 after renewed requests from
Borden but at least in part as a result of the threat from
America.[81] Lake was to prove sympathetic to Canadian aspirations.
On the same day the new Militia Act was put into force vesting
responsibility for the development of a Canadian General Staff
in the Governor in Council.

One of the most effective agents resulting from the Act was the
advisory Militia Council which now came into being, and which
proved an efficient forum for the discussion of military problems;
it brought the minister into close contact with his advisers and,
what was more important, removed questions of military policy
from the public prominence they had come to occupy during the
Dundonald era. Moreover the new appointee was eloquently
praised by Earl Grey, who had succeeded Minto as Governor
General: 'I do not think it possible to find anyone who could fill
so efficiently an extremely difficult and important position: he
has great ability, exceptional tact and can persuade Canadians to
accept his advice.'[82] So great was local appreciation of Lake's
abilities that Borden exerted scarcely veiled pressure on Grey to
retain them, warning the Governor that were the Army Council
not to confirm Lake in his post:[83]

it may become a matter for grave consideration by Your
Excellency's Council whether it would be altogether ex-
pedient to recommend Your Excellency to apply for the
services of another Imperial officer, in whose experience and
tact the same confidence could not, perhaps, be placed.

Under the weight of this pressure the Army Council gave way and Lake was retained—a symbol of Canada's determination to control her own military affairs.

The period following Lake's appointment was largely occupied with the resolution of problems of military precedence and officer exchange though the Canadian General Staff did take it upon itself to open up unofficial communications with the Australian General Staff at the same time.[84] The cool reception given by Canadian representatives to the proposal mooted at the 1907 Imperial Conference to establish an Imperial General Staff has already been noted; Canada's intention to develop its own strategic planning and controlling organ independent of any Imperial body was made more plain at the meeting of the Militia Council held on 13 June 1907 when the minister ruled that selection of officers for posts in the Canadian General Staff would not necessarily be limited to officers qualified to serve on the British General Staff.[85] The aim of this ruling was to secure for Canadian officers ample opportunity to learn staff duties and become qualified for service in staff positions inside the dominion without having to rely upon, or be subservient to, the requirements of Whitehall.

One factor adding to dominion 'separatism' on military matters was the failure to employ Canadian officers in England. Since the subject had been raised in 1907 nothing had been done, and in reminding the British government of this Borden displayed signs of irritation:[86]

> The Minister further observes that it is perhaps desirable to add that the principle of reciprocity is fully accepted by Your Excellency's Government. Indeed the Canadian Government may be said to have already done more than its share in this respect.

What irked the minister was that many Canadian posts were already held by British officers, either in a permanent or a temporary capacity. This feeling was doubtless exacerbated by the brusque refusal of the Army Council to allow officers of the Canadian Militia and Volunteers to compete for entry into the Staff College; the tenor of the letter was that Camberley was a privilege extended only to the select few.[87]

The debate over the degree of dominion military independence from London was at this point considerably affected by the departure of Lake from the post of Chief of the General Staff. Lake possessed a remarkable sensitivity to the Canadian political scene and a very real sympathy with demands of ministerial responsibility.[88] Yet he had also managed to prevent the dominion from anything approaching a military declaration of independence, which was in itself a considerable achievement. What could happen when the local CGS was out of step with the dominion or with London was to be amply displayed by his two successors.

The general reception of the War Office memorandum on the organization of an Imperial General Staff of December 1908 has been described. Borden examined its contents closely and advised the Governor General that the government might safely assent to the general principles but should precisely define certain points. The official reply could assent to the general principles 'the more cordially in . . . that . . . the great principle of local control . . . is fully safeguarded'.[89] The idea of a separate Canadian Staff College was rejected in favour of free interchange of officers between various branches of the Imperial General Staff despite possible financial burdens. It is instructive to note that, unlike their British counterpart, the Canadian House of Commons was sufficiently exercised by the implications of an Imperial General Staff to move on 23 February 1909 that copies of all papers bearing on the subject be laid before it.

Otter revealed his determination that Canada should make its own way in terms of military organization soon after his appointment as CGS, pleading successfully that it was 'out of the question' to confine appointments to the permanent General Staff to officers on permanent staff, although these were the only officers allowed to pass through the Staff College.[90] His opportunity came when the CIGS remarked, in reply to a letter from the Inspector-General, that he expected Canada to make the next move 'for in laying before you the general principles which you have so cordially accepted, we recognised that these would have to be applied in accordance with local conditions'.[91] In the light of this pronouncement Otter rapidly prepared a paper on the organization of the Canadian General Staff which was approved by Lake on 17 May 1909 and by the Militia Council the following day.

In a covering letter to Otter's memorandum the Deputy Minister of Militia explained that it was Canada's intention to organize its own General Staff and gradually evolve from it a Canadian section of the Imperial General Staff to include only four officers.[92] The memorandum itself formulated three reasons for the creation of a Canadian General Staff: to provide the Militia Council with specialist advice in the formulation of military policy, to secure uniformity and continuity in the execution of that policy, and lastly to advance the formation of an Imperial General Staff as recommended at the 1907 conference. The proposed construction of the staff was to be more varied than the British model, containing both headquarters and district staff as well as personnel at RMC Kingston, and the point was reiterated that no definite standard of qualification was to be laid down for officers on the Canadian section.[93] Shortly afterwards Otter won a distinct victory in persuading the Army Council to agree to alternative questions in Military Law for Canadian officers under examination and to permit the Militia Council to examine on certain subjects.[94]

The War Office did not reply to Otter's memorandum until after the 1909 Imperial Conference and when it did so it endeavoured to persuade Canada to create a section of the Imperial General Staff at once instead of organizing Otter's Canadian General Staff. Such a section could fulfil at least two of the tasks for which the Canadian General Staff was designed and was, moreover, more in keeping with the resolution agreed to by the military sub-committee of the Imperial Conference that all officers performing General Staff duties throughout the Empire should be members of one body, the Imperial General Staff.[95] To reinforce this recommendation Army Order 263 was published on 20 September 1909, designating as General Staff posts six Canadian positions and including Lake as chief military adviser but excluding Otter.

Lake was sufficiently sensible of the purpose of this order to write personally to the CIGS asking whether 'it would not be well' for Otter to appear on the list also. He further endeavoured to have more Canadians added to the list.[96] This overture receiving no reply, Otter tried again to form his Canadian General Staff in June 1910, asking whether the government would decide between a section and an independent body. This submission was withdrawn before it came to the attention of the Militia Council and soon afterwards a complicated manoeuvre took place as a result of Lake's impending retirement on

1 November 1910: Otter was switched to Inspector General and a British officer, Major-General C. J. Mackenzie, was appointed CGS in his stead at Borden's direct request. Clearly Otter had aroused some antagonism within the government, and the request for a British officer to replace him appeared to betoken a new era in the relationship between dominion and 'Mother Country'.

In 1911 the administration of Sir Wilfred Laurier went out of office and was replaced by that of Sir Robert Borden, who chose Colonel Sam Hughes as his Minister of Militia. Mackenzie soon came into conflict with Hughes over a number of issues the chief of which, in his own mind, was Hughes's advocacy of the adoption of a new service rifle, the Ross rifle. This was considered an excellent target rifle, but Mackenzie opposed it on the grounds that it had no bolt action and a tendency to jam.[97] It was this which was to lead to the 'Mackenzie affair', and as a by-product to reveal the reserves of tact and intelligence Lake had possessed.

Relations between Mackenzie and Hughes became so unpleasant that on 7 April 1913 the former tendered his statutory six months' notice, whereupon he was told by Hughes to go at once. Mackenzie immediately informed Sir John French of his impression that Hughes wanted to sever all connection with the War Office as soon as possible and might not appoint another CGS.[98] The CIGS drew the matter to the attention of the Secretary of State, and made no secret of his views on the merits of the two:[99]

> I have known for some time that matters were not working smoothly in Canada, due I think entirely to the distorted view which the Minister of Militia takes of the role he has to fulfil and of his own personal military capabilities.
>
> I have repeatedly urged upon General Mackenzie the necessity for exercising the utmost tact and forebearance, and he has acted up to these demands in a manner which shows him to be possessed of the highest qualities necessary to such a position as he fills. I know of no other officer who could have behaved better in so difficult a position.

Hughes attempted to take advantage of the blurred line of demarcation between the War Office and the Colonial Office by enlisting Harcourt's support in the dispute. Accordingly he wrote an eleven-page memorandum supporting his own stance which was remarkable chiefly for the pettiness of character it revealed. Hughes complained of Mackenzie's failure to take advantage of his offers to consult him at any time when everyone else 'fully recognised his duty in the premises, and took advantage of the invitation'. He accused Mackenzie of 'antagonism and negation' towards the cadet movement, military training, conferences, advisory committees and a multitude of other things, but repeatedly stressed that he did not hate Mackenzie for failing to make him a Brigadier General. Finally he castigated the mobilization and training plans prepared under Mackenzie's supervision as 'absolutely devoid of merit'.[100] Harcourt's reception of this farago was contained in his note to the then Governor General of Canada, the Duke of Connaught, that having read it 'I thought that it was not a document that should be seen by the Colonial Office or placed on any official file.'[101]

The Hughes–Mackenzie dispute certainly marked a retrograde step in the relations between Canada and London. A conscientious and, by general approbation, efficient officer was lost to Canada and was replaced within a year of the war by one who had little time to remedy the situation. The ramifications spread farther than the dominion: not only did Hughes rid himself of Mackenzie but pressure from the Colonial Office, concerned not to offend Canada, deprived that officer of the succession to Kiggell's post of Director of Staff Duties in London.[102] The military situation in Canada was allowed to deteriorate to such a degree that Lord Arthur had to report six months before the war broke out 'an alarming shortage both of personnel and of war material' and record that at 75,000 the peacetime military establishment was 21,000 under strength.[103] A special parliamentary session between 18 and 24 August 1914 did go some way towards remedying this situation by authorizing an extraordinary expenditure of $50,000,000 but Arthur still had to report in September that the standard of training of the militia was considerably below that of the territorials. From the commencement of the 'Mackenzie affair' Canada had lost ground, so that when the war broke out her military resources were nowhere near the state they might have been in under Lake and her entrenched strategic separatism—Otter's legacy—offered no base from which to penetrate the wartime fastnesses of Whitehall.

In the case of Australia, it has been remarked that the achievement of its own federation drained away some of the enthusiasm and effort which might have gone into the imperial cause.[104] As with Canada, the arrival of Esher's report did much to awaken the dominion to the dilemma of military organization and resulted in the formation of a small committee, including Lieutenant-Colonel W. T. Bridges, to examine the formulation of defence policy. This it criticized strongly as changing whenever the General Officer Commanding changed rather than when circumstances dictated, recommending instead a Defence Council 'to collect and discuss all information necessary to enable the Government to decide upon questions of policy' and a Military Board to administer the military forces. The duties of the latter's First Member corresponded closely to those of his opposite number on the Army Council but no mention was made of the term Chief of the General Staff.[105]

As with Canada, much time was subsequently expended on the problems of exchanging officers and little was done to develop the functions of an Australian General Staff. However, Australia did participate in minor strategical planning at a much earlier stage than any of her fellow members of the Empire, sending an officer to London in 1906 to assist in the preparation of a general scheme of defence for Australian ports. Equally Australia showed much greater readiness than Canada to implement the resolution of the 1907 conference; Colonel J. C. Hoad was ordered to Whitehall in the summer of the following year in order to make 'an immediate beginning' in carrying out the General Staff resolution.[106] Such was Australia's eagerness that formalities were ignored and it was arranged between the Australian Agent in London and Haldane that Hoad should place himself in personal communication with the General Staff. Crewe only learned of the arrangement on 15 September 1908, the day of Hoad's arrival, and it took a personal letter from the Premier, Fisher, to mollify him.

Hoad was in England from September 1908 until the following February, during which time he had talks with almost every important senior officer at the War Office and was 'fully consulted' on the Haig memorandum of 15 December 1908. He also attended the Staff Conference in January 1909, during the course of which a draft paper on his own proposals for the creation of an Australian section of the Imperial General Staff was 'fully discussed and considered at a special Conference'.[107]

From the outset Hoad's proposals differed entirely from

Canadian conceptions. Hoad accepted as patently obvious the advantages of having an Australian General Staff included as part of the Imperial General Staff and recognized that local Australian forces had a role to play both in home defence and in Imperial co-operation. His proposals fell in with the cautious tone adopted by Whitehall about the nature of appointments in the Dominions bearing in mind the lack of fully qualified staff; appointees would have to be specially qualified and would be provisional only. It was also requested that an officer be always attached to the 'Central Staff' in London. Hoad was clearly committed to the view adopted at the War Office and even proposed a system of triennial conferences of the Imperial General Staff in London to assess the results of the system.[108] This latter was a suggestion which did not apparently meet with Nicholson's approbation.

Hoad's ideas were much closer in spirit to those of the General Staff than either Lake's or Otter's, and were accepted by his own government and Nicholson. Five years previously the latter had assessed Hoad as 'an officer of inferior education and small military capacity'; his apparent change of heart and Hoad's later success may be explained by reference to the same letter: 'On the other hand, he is personally pleasant, good tempered and obliging; and . . . he possesses tact and knows how to keep in touch with the leaders of political parties in his own country.'[109] Hoad clearly enjoyed the complete trust of the Australian government for, on enquiring whether the proposals outlined in Nicholson's letter of 15 December were acceptable, Crewe was requested to solicit Hoad's views.

The Australian government accepted the proposed arrangements but emphasized their own local control and Hoad was duly selected as Chief of the Commonwealth section of the Imperial General Staff with Colonel W. T. Bridges as the London representative. That the latter would have no *de jure* place in the counsels of the General Staff was clear in his government's request that it 'would be glad if he could be consulted in the selection of Imperial Officers for employment in the Commonwealth'.[110] Bridges arrived on 22 August 1909, so rapidly after his selection that the status and work of dominion representatives had not been considered at Whitehall. He therefore advised the War Office about his own post, though it gradually became clear that he was insufficiently informed of events and attitudes in

Australia to be able to make much impression in London. He wrote afterwards:[111]

> My experience in the appointment has convinced me that if the Commonwealth is to derive the full benefit from maintaining an Officer on the Central Section . . . he must not only be kept acquainted with what takes place in the Commonwealth, but also with the opinions formed regarding proposals submitted from England.

For himself, he did receive all printed material except Intelligence Diaries from Australia but got little response to his own enquiries and suggestions.

Hoad clearly occupied a much more influential position. In theory he was controlled and directed by the Council of Defence, roughly equivalent to the Committee of Imperial Defence but not containing the Prime Minister, which decided general defence policy and then referred its decisions to the Board of Military Administration, of which Hoad was also a member, for execution. However, for some years prior to Hoad's appointment the former body had never met with the result that the latter carried out its functions and 'practically settle[d] all matters relating to the defence of the Commonwealth'.[112] Reporting in the autumn of 1910, Hoad confirmed that no meetings of the Council of Defence had been held and that much of his time was involved in organizing the division of duties and framing a Defence Bill, though he also managed to complete defence and mobilization schemes and carry out a number of local staff tours.[113] The report of the Inspector-General of Forces the following year none the less thought that not enough attention had been given to plans for concentration and troop movements and suggested more officers be sent to Camberley or Quetta to fill the gaps in the ranks of trained staff officers.[114] Hoad probably would have been able to remedy these deficiencies, and his growing friendship with Haig in India might subsequently have been capitalized upon, had he not unfortunately died in 1911.

Despite an appeal from the War Office, Australia sent no officer to fill Bridges's place when he was recalled in 1910 and her posture during the 1911 conference did little to alter the belief current in Whitehall that she was no longer interested in the dominion section. *A propos* of this Henry Wilson wrote to Godley: 'I must say that nothing I saw or heard in the conference makes me optimistic.'[115] The General Staff took the initiative when Kiggell wrote informing Hoad that accommodation was available for a representative at the War Office and suggesting that the government might make formal enquiries as to whether one could be received—a move of unaccustomed eagerness on the part of the War Office.[116] The acting Australian CGS, Colonel H. Wilson, felt it highly desirable that the vacancy be filled and recommended a Lieutenant-Colonel Legge.

Australia was undoubtedly stimulated in this belated move by news that Canada had at last appointed a representative, Major P. K. Packer, and Legge was appointed on 25 January 1912. He was to be less circumscribed by his terms of appointment than by the usage he got in London. It was emphasized to him that: 'the Dominion representative clearly remains the subordinate of the Chief of the local section, and such duties as the Chief of the Imperial General Staff may require of him he may be deputed to perform on behalf of the local section.'[117] His task was again primarily one of observation of methods and techniques whilst procuring advice from the CIGS where desirable, and he could only assist in the construction of defence schemes for Australia or the Empire when deputed to do so by his own Chief.

On 22 July Legge took up his duties. He arrived to find that he had been equally circumscribed by Whitehall, being restricted to studying methods of education, training and staff duties in vogue 'under the eyes of the Chief of the Imperial General Staff' and giving advice when requested. He had no statutory place on strategic counsels and was situated in the Staff Duties branch while MO1 continued to deal separately with matters relating to the dominions. Also he was not authorized to empower the despatch of any letters to Australia independently.[118]

Legge did send sporadically for information on technical matters with which to assuage Whitehall but made only one incursion into the devising of strategic plans. At a meeting of the Overseas Defence Committee shortly after he arrived he was asked what Australian public feeling was likely to be about how and where Australian volunteer troops should be employed outside the Commonwealth in the event of an emergency. His reply was that the Australian public 'were not likely to hold any decided views on the question, provided that the troops volunteering for such service were employed for active and not passive operations'.[119] Sir Henry Wilson was present when this opinion was solicited, and it seems to have provided all the advice he ever needed from Australia in his own strategic lucubrations.

Thus, as far as colonial and dominion participation in the strategic planning of the General Staff went, there was on the outbreak of the war little to see. Some never sent representatives to London at all; others so hemmed their officers round with rigid instructions that they had little opportunity to exploit their position. In either case, Whitehall was never really interested in using to the full what willingness there was to participate. It is therefore hardly surprising that by the eve of the war the term 'Imperial' in the title of Chief of the Imperial General Staff signified little and served only to 'assuage the Imperialism in Australian sentiment'.[120] The events of the first eighteen months of the war were to show that the Imperial design came in practice to nothing.

Notes

1 G. S. Graham, *The Politics of Naval Supremacy*, Cambridge, 1965, p. 124.
2 A. P. Thornton, *The Imperial Idea and its Enemies*, London, 1959, pp. 108–10.
3 The Organization of Colonial Troops for Imperial Service, 25 November 1901. Cab. 8/3/293.
4 Colonial Troops for Imperial Service in War, 13 June 1902, p. 2. Cab. 8/3/293.
5 Hutton Papers. Wolseley to Hutton, 5 June 1902. B.M. Add. MSS. 50085.
6 J. E. Kendle, *The Colonial and Imperial Conferences 1887–1911: A Study in Imperial Organization*, London, 1967, pp. 58–9.
7 Cf. Haldane Papers. Laurier to Haldane, 12 July 1902. N.L.S. MS. 5905.
8 Robertson Papers. Memorandum upon the Military Forces required for Oversea Warfare, 4 January 1906. K.C.L. Robertson 1/2.
9 Haldane Papers. Haldane to Mrs Mary Haldane, 12 October 1906. N.L.S. MS. 5976.
10 Clarke to Campbell-Bannerman, 24 January 1907. B.M. Add. MSS. 41213.
11 Ellison to Clarke, 19 April 1907, enc. both resolutions. Cab. 17/77.
12 The copy of the resolution in Ellison's papers, in his hand, bears the following note by him: 'My original draft proposing an Imperial Gen. Staff, laid before Conference of Premiers 20.4.07 and substantially agreed to by all.'
13 Cd 3524, Papers laid before the Colonial Conference 1907. The

Strategical Conditions of the Empire from the Military Point of View, 14 April 1907, p. 18.
14 Cd 3524. The Possibility of Assimilating War Organisation throughout the Empire, 14 April 1907, p. 24.
15 Ewart Diary, 19 April 1907.
16 Cd 3523, Minutes of Proceedings of the Colonial Conference 1907. Fourth day, 20 April 1907, p. 95.
17 *Ibid.*, p. 97.
18 Kendle, *op. cit.*, p. 91.
19 Cd 3523, p. 109.
20 E.g. R. A. Preston, *Canada and 'Imperial Defense'*, Durham, N.C., 1967, pp. 360, 361.
21 Cd 3523, pp. v, vi.
22 Notes of an Informal Conference held by the Chief of the General Staff at 3.45 p.m. on Tuesday 30 April 1907. C.O. 42/917.
23 Haldane Papers. Ponsonby to Haldane, 28 April 1907. N.L.S. MS. 5907.
24 Quo. H. Borden (ed.), *Robert Laird Borden: His Memoirs*, London, 1938, p. 185.
25 Kendle, *op. cit.*, pp. 94–108.
26 Haig Papers. Diary 5 November 1908. N.L.S. H.2.h.
27 Ewart Diary, 18 December 1908.
28 Cd 4475, Correspondence relating to the Proposed Formation of an Imperial General Staff. War Office to Colonial Office, 15 December 1908, p. 8.
29 *Ibid.*, p. 9.
30 *Ibid.*, p. 13.
31 Haig Papers. Unheaded memorandum, 8 March 1909. N.L.S. H.89.E.
32 The Value to a Foreign Power of an Alliance with the British Empire, March 1909, p. 9. W.O. 106/45/E1/1.
33 Further Correspondence relating to the Proposed Formation of an Imperial General Staff, no. 14, 8 June 1909, pp. 14, 15. C.O. 886/2/14.
34 *Ibid.*, no. 10, 8 April 1909, p. 11.
35 Ewart Diary, 5 May 1909.
36 Proposals for so Organising the Military Forces of the Empire as to Ensure their effective Co-operation in the event of War, 7 July 1909. W.O. 106/43/Imp. C.10.
37 Ewart Diary, 9 June 1909.
38 Cd 4948, Correspondence and Papers relating to a Conference with Representatives of the Self-Governing Dominions on the Naval and Military Defence of the Empire 1909, p. 29.
39 Royal Archives. Note by Edward VII, 26 August 1909. RA X 10/28.
40 Seely Papers. Sub-conference on Military Defence 29th July and 4th August 1909. Box 139.
41 Haldane to Kitchener, 8 July 1909. B.M. Add. MSS. 49724.
42 Hansard, 5th series, vol. XVIII, 27 June 1910, col. 708.
43 Haldane Papers. Nicholson to Haldane, 23 August 1909. N.L.S. MS. 5908. Ewart Diary, 19 August 1909.

44 Haldane Papers. Knollys to Haldane, 10 October 1909. N.L.S. MS. 5908.
45 Royal Archives. Memorandum by Haldane, 3 February 1909. RA W 28/74.
46 Kendle, *op. cit.*, pp. 136–53.
47 Memorandum on a possible solution of the question as to the relation of the Dominions to the Home Government, 12 January 1911, p. 2. Bodl. MS. Asquith 24.
48 Note by Lord Esher, 10 January 1911. Cab. 17/79.
49 Minute by Sir A. Nicolson, 24 February 1911. Cab. 17/79.
50 Imperial Conference 1911, 12 May 1911. Cab. 37/106/58.
51 Home Defence: Memorandum on the principles governing the Defence of the United Kingdom, 23 April 1911, pp. 3, 4. W.O. 33/515.
52 Australia: Scale of Attack under existing Conditions, 24 February 1911, p. 3 (J.R. Chancellor). Cab. 8/5/429.
53 Minute by D.M.O., 10 April 1911. W.O. 106/43/Imp. C.10.
54 The desirability of such a general uniformity of organisation throughout the military forces of the Empire as may facilitate their rendering mutual support and assistance, 12 May 1911. Cab. 5/2/2/8OC. Author's italics.
55 Progress of the Imperial General Staff and the development of its functions, 19 May 1911. Cab. 5/2/2/84C.
56 Proceedings of the Defence (Military) Committee of the Imperial Conference 1911, pp. 3, 12, 13. W.O. 106/43/Imp. C.10.
57 *Ibid.*, p. 22.
58 113th meeting of C.I.D., 30 May 1911. Cab. 2/2/2.
59 F. A. Johnson, *Defence by Committee*, London, 1960, pp. 123–41.
60 Hankey to Harcourt, 3 July 1912. Cab. 17/101.
61 Asquith to George V, 15 July 1915. Cab. 37/131/17.
62 Kendle, *op. cit.*, p. 155.
63 Minutes of Directors' Meetings, 27 March 1907. D.R.O., M.O.D.
64 Under Secretary War Office to Under Secretary Colonial Office, 20 April 1912. C.O. 417/578.
65 Harcourt Papers. Aston to Harcourt, 5 August 1912. Series C.O. 1910–1915, box 6, file 'Official Correspondence Vol. I'.
66 Harcourt Papers. Gladstone to Harcourt, 23 April 1913. Series C.O. 1910–1915, box 2, file 'Lord Gladstone'.
67 *See* G. Tylden, *The Armed Forces of South Africa*, Johannesburg, 1954, p. 179.
68 Plunket to Elgin, 11 and 15 November 1906. C.O. 209/269.
69 Plunket to Crewe, 2 February 1910. C.O. 209/271.
70 Harcourt Papers. Islington to Harcourt, 6 January 1911. Series C.O. 1910–1915, box 1, file 'Lord Islington: NZ'.
71 Godley to Wilson, 6 September 1911. W.O. 106/59.
72 Harcourt Papers. Liverpool to Harcourt, 11 December 1912. Series C.O. 1910–1915, box 1, file 'Lord Liverpool: NZ'.
73 Harcourt Papers. Harcourt to Liverpool, 8 March 1913. Series C.O. 1910–1915, box 1, file 'Lord Liverpool: NZ'.

74 Report by the Inspector General of Oversea Forces on the Military Forces of New Zealand, 1914, pp. 11, 46. W.O. 32/4819.

75 Harcourt Papers. Harcourt to Liverpool, 21 April 1915. Series C.O. 1910–1915, box 1, file 'Lord Liverpool: NZ'.

76 D. C. Gordon, *The Dominion Partnership in Imperial Defence 1870–1914*, Baltimore, 1965, p. 154.

77 Minto to Nicholson, 25 November 1903. C.O. 42/896.

78 L. R. Cameron, 'Constitution of the Army and Militia Councils and the Creation of the Imperial and Canadian General Staffs', p. 1, unpublished MS., Department of National Defence.

79 Borden to Minto, 15 April 1904. C.O. 42/896.

80 Extract from Report of the Committee of the Canadian Privy Council, 14 June 1904. C.O. 42/896.

81 Preston, *op. cit.*, p. 351. Lake was CGS November 1904–March 1908, when he became Inspector-General and was succeeded by a Canadian, Brigadier-General W. D. Otter. He in turn was succeeded in October 1910 by Major-General C. J. Mackenzie.

82 Grey to Lyttelton, 6 January 1905. C.O. 42/900.

83 Grey to Lyttelton, 10 February 1905, enclosure. C.O. 42/900.

84 Preston, *op. cit.*, p. 354.

85 Cameron, *op. cit.*, p. 8.

86 Grey to Elgin, 24 December 1907, enclosure, C.O. 42/914.

87 War Office to Colonial Office, 20 June 1908. P.A.C., H.Q. 6890–1.

88 *See* Lake to Aston, 20 October 1908. C.O. 42/929.

89 Minister of Militia to Governor General in Council, 9 February 1909. P.A.C. H.Q. 6890–1.

90 Memorandum by Otter, 19 November 1908. P.A.C., H.Q. 6890–2.

91 Nicholson to Lake, 30 April 1909. P.A.C. H.Q. 6890–1.

92 Deputy Minister of Militia to Governor General, 28 May 1909. P.A.C., H.Q. 6890–1.

93 Draft accompanying Minister of Militia to Governor General, 28 May 1909. P.A.C., H.Q. 6890–1.

94 War Office to Colonial Office, 14 October 1909. C.O. 42/936.

95 War Office to Colonial Office, 27 September 1909. P.A.C., H.Q. 6890–1.

96 Lake to Nicholson, 8 November 1909. P.A.C., H.Q. 6890–1.

97 Colin Mackenzie to the author, 19 August 1968.

98 Seely Papers. Mackenzie to French, 21 April 1913. Box 141.

99 Seely Papers. Memorandum by French, 2 May 1913. Box 141.

100 Harcourt Papers. Memorandum re General Mackenzie, August 1913. Series C.O. 1910–1915, box 6, file 'Official Correspondence Vol. 2'.

101 Harcourt Papers. Harcourt to Connaught, 7 January 1914. Series C.O. 1910–1915, box 3, file 'Duke of Connaught'.

102 French to Roberts, 15 January 1914. Quo. E. G. French (ed.), *Some War Diaries, Addresses and Correspondence of Field Marshal the Right Honble. The Earl of Ypres*, London, 1937, p. 139.

103 Arthur to Harcourt, 19 February 1914. C.O. 42/970.

104 Gordon, *op. cit.*, p. 188.
105 Defence forces of the Commonwealth, 18 November 1904. C.O. 418/36.
106 Memorandum by Department of Defence, 3 August 1908. C.A.O., MP 84, series 1, file 1894/6/104.
107 Hoad to Secretary, Department of Defence, 22 April 1909, C.A.O., MP 84, series 1, file 1894/6/104.
108 Major-General Hoad's proposals with regard to an Australian section of the Imperial General Staff, 1909. C.A.O., MP 84, series 1, file 1894/5/19.
109 Nicholson to British Ambassador at Tokyo, 24 September 1904. C.O. 418/42. *See* Preston, *op. cit.*, pp. 405–6.
110 C. 11969 (Australia) Defence: Imperial General Staff—Correspondence relating to proposed formation, no. 17, 22 June 1909.
111 Report by Bridges, 20 June 1910. C.A.O., MP 84, series 1, file 1897/2/11.
112 Military Forces: Commonwealth of Australia, A. J. A. Hore-Ruthven, 29 September 1909. C.O. 418/71.
113 Memorandum by the Chief of the General Staff and of the Commonwealth Section of the Imperial General Staff, 8 July 1910, p. 7. C.A.O., MP 84, series 1, file 1894/5/43.
114 Annual Report by Major-General G. M. Kirkpatrick, 30 May 1911, pp. 3, 4. C.O. 418/80.
115 Wilson to Godley, 29 June 1911. W.O. 106/59.
116 Kiggell to Hoad, 25 August 1911. C.A.O., MP 84, series 1, file 1894/5/63.
117 Memorandum by Acting C.G.S., Australia, 8 May 1912. C.A.O., MP 84, series 1, file 1894/5/83.
118 Formation of a Dominion Section of the General Staff, 4 April 1912. W.O. 33/Gen. No./407.
119 Minutes of Oversea Defence Committee, 229th meeting, 10 December 1912. Cab. 7/8.
120 Preston, *op. cit.*, p. 406.

6
Strategic Reorientation

The South African War exposed the weaknesses in Britain's traditional diplomatic prophylactic—misleadingly cast as 'Splendid Isolation'—and it was succeeded by a period of some half dozen years of unprecedented diplomatic activity. By the time that Britain had passed through this *bouleversement* diplomacy seemed to have solved her major strategic problems. But such a fortunate outcome was a bonus in negotiations which were not primarily directed towards providing for the security of British interests across the world. Balfour's recognition that because of the Boer War 'we were for all practical purposes at the present moment only a third rate Power' was the appreciation of a politician who was aware to a unique degree of military factors.[1] Few appreciated the impotence of the strategic planners, and calculated diplomacy upon it.

It has recently been remarked that 'British diplomacy between 1902 and 1907 was able to reduce the task of British military planners to a manageable size.'[2] Other factors, however, contributed at least equally to this new and welcome state of affairs. One was the acceptance by the army of the naval doctrine of command of the sea, which was to have important corollaries for military strategy. Another was the internal evolution of strategy within the War Office which, while it owed something to naval policy, was yet sufficiently important to rank as a major independent influence.

Although unaware of it, the Admiralty had helped to initiate the transition of military strategy as early as 1896. Utterly convinced of the thesis of Admiral Mahan that command of the sea was the decisive factor in naval affairs and that this was achieved by the possession of large battle fleets designed to offer combat to opposing navies, it accepted the responsibility of defending all overseas territory from seaborne invasion as part of the corpus of sea supremacy.[3] This strategy—giving up localized operations in favour of over-all command of the sea—worked well in a context of Imperially-orientated isolation. It was less suited to a situation of foreign alignments, which offered the prospect of enemies as well as friends, and was much less efficacious in the case of continental or sub-continental military engagements. This was something the navy itself was slow to realize. The War Office did, however, come gradually to accept it, to change its own attitude to localized operations and to move ahead to the problems of military activity on continental land masses.

The naval doctrine of command of the sea had its first effect, appropriately enough, on the most immediate strategic problem, that of an invasion of the United Kingdom. The putative foe in such an event was France. The reconstituted Committee of Imperial Defence[4] began its first enquiry into invasion on 18 February 1903, taking as a reference point the conditions operative three years earlier which seemed to suggest invasion by a lightly equipped force as the most probable occurrence. By the time that Balfour produced a digest of the conclusions of the enquiry in the autumn only one member, Sir William Nicholson, remained convinced of the dangers of such an attack.[5] It was Balfour's estimation that the minimum force for invasion proper was 70,000 men requiring 200 boats and a twenty-hour crossing, which would give ample time for interference by the Royal Navy. Under ideal conditions the minimum time necessary for disembarkation was forty-eight hours. So great were the difficulties attendant upon such an operation, concluded the Prime Minister, that it would not succeed.[6] The impact of this conclusion was reinforced by a speech he made shortly afterwards identifying the invasionist stance with Campbell-Bannerman and the Liberal party; Britain's greatest difficulty, he emphasized, lay not in home defence but in action overseas.[7] From this time onwards acceptance by the army of the doctrine of command of the sea as it affected overseas bases and garrisons, as well as the home island, gradually increased.

The concomitants to Mahan's doctrine first became apparent in the retraction, during Balfour's premiership, of British commitments in the western hemisphere and more particularly with regard to the defence of Canada. Economy certainly played a part in this retreat, as did the burden of needs elsewhere. It was not, however, the case that the War Office used the threat of a war with America in order to resist reductions in the size of the army and that they further sought, by drawing attention to British responsibilities in Canada, to force additional commitments on the navy.[8] There were many more potent arguments for a larger army if they were needed, chief amongst them the threats posed to Indian security. More particularly, the army had no interest in expanding the obligations of the navy; rather it sought during these discussions to display the military significance of the doctrine of command of the sea in order to ease its own task in Canada and elsewhere.

As far as the calculation of military strategy went the implications of naval doctrine were straightforward. If the doctrine of command of the sea was genuinely as effective an instrument as the navy claimed then there was no need to garrison any overseas possession with large bodies of troops. This was recognized by the newly appointed navalist secretary of the Committee of Imperial Defence, Sir George Clarke, who realized the implications of the doctrine not only in the Canadian but also in the Imperial context. Just as there was no need to garrison Esquimault and Halifax, so there was no need either to lock up large garrisons in Malta and Gibraltar.[9]

As the question of the defence of Canada was discussed the role of naval doctrine in military planning became clearer. As far as the War Office was concerned, if Canada was to be defended at all then control of the Great Lakes was crucial.[10] The navy realized that there was, at the moment, nothing they could do to prevent the American navy gaining command of those lakes.[11] A meeting of the Committee of Imperial Defence on 13 July 1905 formally concluded that the navy could not themselves undertake the defence of the lakes, or recommend any measures by which Canada might do so herself. This was a conclusion which, as Hankey afterwards remarked, 'vitiates any measures of military defence'.[12]

Here was a contingency in which diplomacy was the only way to solve a strategic dilemma; as long as relations between Britain and America remained amicable the inability of the former to provide for the defence of Canada was unimportant. The lessons for military planning were quickly grasped, chief among them the hopelessness of relying on the Committee of Imperial Defence to resolve strategic problems. After two important meetings of that body on 5 and 12 April 1905, the Intelligence Department reviewed progress thus: 'For all practical purposes the questions brought forward as to the defence of Canada remain unanswered. The fundamental principles governing the defence of the

Dominion have still to be fixed.'[13] After the meeting in July the War Office recognized also that they could hope for little in the way of co-operation from the navy, and indeed must continue their strategic deliberations with the same expectation: 'The discussion has made it clear that the military must take their own action afloat as well as ashore.'[14]

The defence of Canada was a microcosm of the role of diplomacy in resolving otherwise intractable military problems. But the immediate stimulus to Britain's emergence from her island splendour came as a result of the diplomatic miasma raised by the South African War. The clash of Britain and France at Fashoda in 1898 had made Britain aware of the vital importance of alliances; if hostilities between the two powers should break out then in all probability France would not find herself alone, but would be supported morally and materially by Russia.[15] This apprehension was seized upon by the German Foreign Office early in 1899, when it began stirring up fear of England in the mind of France. Having created a situation of tension, Germany capitalized upon it at the moment when Great Britain was at the nadir of her strength and had exhausted her reserves to provide troops for the Boer campaign. In April 1901 Baron Eckardstein, First Secretary at the German Embassy, intimated to Lord Lansdowne that Germany was willing to consider a defensive alliance with Britain against France and Russia.[16]

The immediate German approach came to nothing, chiefly because the only attraction of such an alignment for Britain was to gain international support for Japan against Russia, which was not Germany's object. It did, however, prompt Lord Salisbury to spell out the strategic objections to such an alignment: the liability of having to defend the German frontier against Russia he felt to be much heavier than that of defending Great Britain against France. Also he felt unable to commit the government to a course of which the electorate might not approve: 'If the Government promised to declare war for an object which did not commend itself to public opinion, the promise would be re-pudiated, and the Government would be turned out.'[17] This sensitivity in matters of strategic diplomacy was to affect the Liberal as well as the Conservative party, and was a sentiment from which probably only Balfour of all pre-war Premiers was in any sense free.

Lansdowne set himself to temper the Prime Minister's

instinctive isolationist feeling. Admitting the point that until now Britain had fared well in spite of her isolation, the Foreign Secretary remarked on the danger of pushing too far the argument that 'because we have in the past survived in spite of our isolation, we need have no misgivings as to the effect of that isolation in the future'.[18] In the place of general agreements such as that proposed by Germany, which offered the risk of alienating France and Russia, he proposed the consideration of international understandings about particular aspects of policy. Such a course, while it conflicted with German notions of international agreements, conformed with French approaches made earlier in the year to resolve minor international problems concerning the two powers.[19]

The modest proposals made by Lord Lansdowne prompted the consideration of a hitherto unforeseen military dilemma which touched the War Office and the Foreign Office in equal measure. In an aura of increasing, if latent, international hostility what action was to be taken in regard to the small powers to whom Britain had obligations? In the cases of Belgium, Norway, Sweden and Portugal there were formal obligations going back as far as 1703; towards Holland Britain had no such formal obligations but something more than a by-stander's interest. In formulating his answer to this problem Lansdowne revealed what he considered the scope of future conflict might be. Single-power wars he thought most unlikely: 'If there is a European war, the Powers will almost certainly be ranged against one another in groups, with the result that the theatre of war will virtually extend all over the world.'[20] This diplomatic prognostication made allies a military necessity; it also had corollaries for strategic policy which Lansdowne recognized. The best means of helping an ally in this situation, he felt, would not be to waste force by sending small expeditions to assist his defence but by waging war on his assailants wherever their weak points could be ascertained. In saying this, Lansdowne was adding a further dimension to the doctrine of command of the sea and encouraging the War Office to consider the development of offensive plans.

The role of diplomacy in widening strategic horizons first became apparent after the conclusion of the Anglo-Japanese alliance in 1902. In purely diplomatic terms, Lansdowne had become alarmed at the signs of growing reconciliation between Russians and Japanese in July 1901 and had determined to seek an agreement rather than risk isolation in the Far East.[21] To this motive was added the powerful stimulus of naval economy. At a moment when rivalry with France, Germany and the USA was making onerous demands upon the navy, the prospect of Russian superiority in the Far East became 'an important element in the conclusion of the alliance'.[22] In order to avoid the danger of facing war solely in order to support the Japanese against Russia, Lansdowne negotiated on the basis of an attack by two hostile powers activating the alliance.

Consideration of the military implications of an alliance between Britain and Japan did not arise until after the treaty had been signed, and then the first overtures were made by the Japanese themselves. On 7 April 1902, the Japanese military attaché called on Sir William Robertson at the Intelligence Branch to suggest some definite agreement in case of war; his visit was avowedly unofficial but Robertson's impression was that he had been instructed to undertake the mission. Robertson's colleague, Lieutenant-Colonel E. A. Altham, concurred in his feeling that this advance should be followed up. If war were to break out, all military plans in any way involving Japan would be hypothetical and a considerable delay would ensue before any effective co-operation could take place. Altham also had one eye on what was happening on the continent; Paris and St Petersburg would have reached some such agreement and if England did not do likewise she would be 'at a serious disadvantage'.[23]

Anglo-Japanese military co-operation was given a further impetus as a result of a naval conference between the two powers which took place at the naval dockyard at Yokosuka early in May 1902. The two powers discussed matters of mutual interest in the naval sphere, among them a mutual signalling system, reciprocal coaling arrangements and docking facilities and the interchange of intelligence. As a result of these discussions the Japanese approached the Indian Commander-in-Chief and informed him that arrangements for the exchange of intelligence information had been made. The War Office was forced to sanction such exchanges lest the Japanese think the alliance lukewarm.

Altham was therefore set the task of working out the strategic implications of a military partnership between the two powers prior to a military conference. His assessment began by emphasizing that the secret of success in modern war was preparation in peacetime, and that such preparation must be based on a clear understanding both of the general scope of operations to be undertaken and the general plan to be adopted when carrying them out. It was clear that specific plans of campaign could not be drawn up, but Altham urged that this should not be regarded as a bar to any sort of planning:[24]

> this proviso should not hinder the allied Governments permitting their naval and military staffs consulting together and after consultation and exchange of confidences elaborating plans of action which, when the time comes, can be given effect to on the outbreak of war.

This philosophy was to open the way to the deeper commitments made to France under Campbell-Bannerman's regimen.

The most probable contingency activating the alliance was a war between Britain and Japan on the one hand and France and Russia on the other. It was believed at the War Office that one of the main objects of Russian policy was to undermine Britain's position in Asia, and therefore it appeared that the most likely theatre of operations would be the Indian frontier. Here the extent to which military plans hinged on the use to be made of sea power began to become apparent: sea command could paralyse the enemy's armies by picking off his overseas possessions. In this context France was far more vulnerable than Russia, and Altham offered as possible objectives Bizerta, Dakar, Martinique, Diego Suarez and Saigon. In passing, he urged the formation of five army corps for such overseas operations and not three as Brodrick was currently suggesting.

As an ally, Japan appeared to have considerable qualities. Her field army available for overseas operations numbered 182,000 men and was characterized by courage, discipline and good leadership which made it the match of any European troops. She also possessed excellent supply and support services. About her strategy, though, Altham was rather more dubious. Her objectives in a war with Russia would probably be Port Arthur and Manchuria, and to pursue them she would require sea transport from Great Britain in order to invest Port Arthur and Vladivostok and to advance northwards towards Harbin. The Japanese favoured winter activity because then the roads would be firmer, but this would increase the hardship on the troops; also they would be entirely dependent on a 600-mile railway line from

Port Arthur to Harbin which in the light of British experience in South Africa would be very vulnerable. To pursue her strategy Altham assumed that Japan required assistance in two areas: the securing and maintenance of sea command and the provision of sea transport. In return Japan indicated that she might consider aiding Britain against France in Indo-China.

Altham felt that under existing conditions Japan's strategy was a suitable one. It only demanded what England was able to give, and most importantly made no demands upon her slender troop reserves. What was required now was some statement on the necessary command structures which were, in his opinion, British control of the combined naval units and Japanese control of the Manchurian theatre.

It was clear that further discussions were essential, and a joint military conference duly met at Winchester House on 7 July 1902, immediately after a combined naval and military conference.[25] The latter had agreed in principle to a concentration of the combined fleets and to the production of a common plan, and had then gone on to discuss the issues raised at the Yokosuka conference. The soldiers, by contrast, at once plunged deep into the problem of strategy. A conflict of interests immediately appeared over how best to distribute Britain's available force of 120,000 men. Britain felt the North-west Frontier to be especially vulnerable since Russia would shortly have two railways in the area, and also expected trouble with France in either Siam or Burma. The Japanese representatives clearly wanted British troops in Manchuria alongside their own—Major-General Fukushima openly requested one British army corps in Manchuria as soon as command of the sea had been gained. Sir William Nicholson prevaricated over this, raising the question of Indian defence, and as a result was asked whether England would definitely be on the offensive there. He could only reply that this depended entirely on the attitude of Afghanistan; if it were neutral or hostile, any offensive would be greatly delayed.

The conclusions reached by the conference, although not startling, represented a significant commitment to military co-operation. As far as England was concerned, Japan's request for British troops was 'noted', with the proviso that meeting it must depend upon current circumstances. In the meantime maps and handbooks of Manchuria and Korea were to be prepared jointly and the military conference was to meet periodically. Japanese pressure for military assistance in Manchuria was in fact very much secondary to her desire for naval aid; as he signed the agreement, Fukushima remarked that the size of the British contingent was immaterial. Altham read into this the primacy of political over military considerations—'I gather therefore that for political reasons the Japanese consider it important that some British troops should be detached to cooperate with them.'[26]

These negotiations represented for Great Britain the first step along the road to external military commitments, and by taking that step she had for the first time begun to grapple with the problems of alliance strategy. The conclusions of the conference were duly put to the government, which sanctioned them and suggested that measures be taken to implement them.[27] Cautious moves were then made to explore the extent of military co-operation between the two powers. Altham recommended that the Japanese advise on what form they would require a British contingent to take, on the basis that such assistance might be forthcoming after the start of a Russo-Japanese war.[28] In doing so, he was undoubtedly influenced by a report on the Japanese army which had remarked that the deficiencies in the Russian forces were over-estimated and prognosticated a Japanese defeat unless their troops were stiffened by a British contingent.[29] The Foreign Office expressed no opposition to further measures of collusion between the military authorities as long as it was made clear that they did not represent any change of attitude in the non-committal nature of the link.[30] In the face of this cool directive, the Commander-in-Chief and the Secretary of State for War between them decided to take no further action.

As this decision was being reached, the probability of hostilities between Russia and Japan was increasing. During July 1903 the British military attaché reported from Peking that far from ending her occupation of Manchuria, Russia was building up her forces there. To support his belief that a quarrel between the two powers was likely by late autumn or winter he cited barrack construction, the collection of stores and coal, and the fact that the Chinese bakeries were employed in making biscuits in huge quantities for the Russians.[31] The prospect somewhat alarmed the War Office, which offered the opinion that if Japan fought alone she might suffer a disastrous defeat and even if she won no great damage would be inflicted on Russia.[32]

The government was not, however, to be panicked into extending its tenuous strategic commitments to Japan. Balfour pointed out that although naval disparity meant that Japan might not defeat Russia, yet she would not herself be crushed as a military power. From every point of view other than that of trade, he argued, it was in Britain's interests that Russia should become embroiled in Korea and be forced to deploy a large part of her military and naval forces there.[33] He therefore suggested that Britain neither encourage Japan to war nor request her to abate her demands. Lansdowne, viewing strategy very much in the light of diplomatic expediency, recommended that Britain act as a friendly mediator.[34]

As far as the Intelligence Department was concerned the prognostication made by Balfour about the course of a Russo-Japanese war was too simplistic. Recognizing that the land campaign would be determined by the contest to gain command of the sea, they foresaw three separate possibilities. If Japan gained sea command a large-scale land action in Manchuria would follow which, even if it lasted for some months, would see the Japanese securely ensconced in southern Manchuria. Should sea supremacy pass to Russia, Korea would become the scene of land operations and the final result would probably be that the northern portion would come under Russian domination. However, if Russia sought to avoid a general naval action then Britain's stance might become crucial since a Japanese expedition to Manchuria would be a hazardous undertaking while the Russian fleet lay unharmed at Vladivostock. In this event, Japan could not and should not risk such an expedition unless sure of naval support from her ally.[35]

It was Balfour who combined the military and the diplomatic in a masterly outline of British policy on this difficult strategic issue. He worked from the basis that if Britain were morally bound to defend Japan when she was liable to be defeated by Russia, then the alliance was not guaranteeing peace but endangering it. Since France was bound to aid Russia 'the Government at Tokio would be the arbiters of peace and war for half the civilised world!'[36] It was in Britain's interests that Japan should not be crushed by Russia, but of this there appeared no chance; the worst that could happen would be Russian command of the sea. Britain was not in any case bound by the alliance in the event of a single-handed war, and it was in her interests to have Russia weakened in a war in the Far East. Balfour remarked particularly on the consequent reduction in the dangers facing India and Persia. This lead the Prime Minister to hazard by way of conclusion that if Russia did undertake a war against Japan 'her whole diplomacy, from the Black Sea to the Oxus might be weakened into something resembling sweet reasonableness'.[37]

The War Office was not prepared to see strategic considerations displaced by diplomacy in so cavalier a manner. A new military appreciation of the situation several days later raised fresh strategic considerations. The Intelligence Department considered it unlikely that either France or China would support Russia and thereby precipitate British action through the terms of the treaty, though it added that the improbability of such a contingency did not mean that its strategic consequences could be ignored. As a by-product of the assessment of the military preparedness of Japan, Russia, France and China serious deficiencies were revealed in the two army corps available in England for service overseas. The conclusion drawn from this, and from the improbability of any material assistance from the Empire, was a gloomy one:[38]

> the military forces at our disposal for over-sea service are greatly below the strength which was needed in the South African War, and are probably considerably less than would be required to bring to a satisfactory termination a struggle in which Great Britain was engaged single handed against one or more of the Great Powers.

The military logic of the situation was therefore precisely the reverse of that contained in Balfour's diplomatic formula: Britain could hardly afford not to assist her ally when reciprocal aid in the event of a Russian attack on India would be sorely needed.

In the event of a war against Russia the War Office could afford only one brigade for Manchuria after meeting India's requirements, to do which would entail stripping South Africa of most of its garrison. Two major problems then remained to be solved. One was whether the 63,000 troops which India would require at the end of six months of war should first be loaned to the Manchurian theatre, a course which might result in their being weakened and Japan becoming hostile when they were withdrawn in a short space of time. The other was the question of the route by which the troops should be transmitted. The journey to the Far East took forty-seven days via the Cape but only thirty-five days via Vancouver and the Canadian Pacific Railway.[39] The army favoured the Canadian route, especially as the force would have to begin embarkation before it was clear what action France intended to take. The Admiralty objected to it on the grounds of lack of protection in crossing the Pacific, lack of available transport, the need to avoid the China Seas and coaling difficulties. As a way out of this *impasse* seemed far from obvious, the War Office could only suggest further negotiations with the Admiralty.

The extent to which the army depended on the navy's successfully putting into practice its own doctrine of command of the sea was revealed in a second scheme which assumed France to be hostile. In this case troops from South Africa would have to go to India, preparations would have to be made for the capture of Dakar and 'the disposal of the residue of troops available for oversea action must depend on the strategical situation in India and Manchuria when sea command is attained'.[40] What was clearly needed was further exploration of the possibilities, and the War Office recommended that certain preparatory steps be taken such as ascertaining what Japanese transport might be available 'without committing His Majesty's Government' and tackling the Admiralty about transport to India and Manchuria.

Politically the army was prepared for involvement with Japan on the grounds that if Britain held aloof it might damage her prestige, her material interests and the future safety of the Empire. On the other hand, they reasoned, if Russia were notified before a breach occurred that Britain was likely to side with Japan in such an event then war would be less likely. In the event, war between Russia and Japan broke out in February 1904 and Britain held aloof along Balfour's lines. When the question of the Japanese alliance was raised again a year later, its complexion had been somewhat altered.

In the case of the Anglo-Japanese alliance diplomacy had revealed unforeseen strategic implications which were considered on an *ad hoc* basis. However, before the alliance had been constructed the War Office had begun a series of major strategic reviews which were also to widen its strategic outlook. In

October 1901 Altham had written the first such paper, examining the implications of a war against what then seemed the most hostile combination, that of Russia and France. Since this antedated the CID's decision on the improbability of invasion, Altham still had to take as first priority the question of the defence of the United Kingdom. Even so, he suggested that the proportion of troops allotted to home defence was too great and that a proportion of garrison troops could be safely released for service overseas when command of the sea was gained.[41] In suggesting this course of action Altham was initiating the army's acceptance of the primacy of sea command; as he pointed out, if it were lost then England could be starved into surrender without the need for invasion at all. Of 700,000 troops of all types, 594,000 were currently employed on home defence; Altham suggested the total need be no larger than 350,000.

On the defence of the British colonies and protectorates Altham felt War Office and Admiralty to be in accord. The War Office accepted the principle of command of the sea and the consequent naval responsibility for protection against organized invasion, with the concomitant that ships could be put wherever the Admiralty thought best. The exception to this was Malta, over the defence of which there was to be some debate. The only point of danger on land, provided America remained neutral, was West Africa where France could field a force of 13,850 but the West African Frontier Force of 8,250 was thought adequate to cope with this. South Africa appeared likely to remain a weak point for some years to come, requiring enough troops to guard against a general rebellion. In all, colonial defence absorbed 55,988 British troops and need absorb no more in existing circumstances.

In terms of defence commitments there remained Egypt and India. In the case of the former, it was not known whether the Admiralty could guarantee Egypt against a full expeditionary force in the event of a war against France or Russia. The British garrison amounted to 4,259 and the Egyptian army to 13,000, but doubts existed about the loyalty of the latter in the event of an attack. Without a clear Admiralty assurance on the matter Altham felt the garrison to be inadequate and to need augmenting by at least 3,771 British troops. Altham used this instance to demonstrate more clearly the relationship between military strategy and command of the sea:[42]

In this, as in all parts of our system of Imperial Defence, sea supremacy is the basis of the whole matter. Any doubt as to the sufficiency of the Navy to ensure sea supremacy at once vitiates all our plans, and involves a situation in which, even with a very great increase in our land forces, it would be difficult and almost impracticable to prepare any really sound scheme for the defence of the Empire as a whole.

Looming large over the problems of defence lay the question of India, at once the most vulnerable and the most prestigious of Imperial possessions. Here politics and strategy alike seemed to dictate an advance into southern Afghanistan as the minimum action in the event of war with Russia. Yet the native Indian army was insufficient for its own needs, and left 91,000 British and native troops to face an invader and possibly 100,000 Afghans as well. Since the Commander-in-Chief and the Government of India both agreed that it would be impossible not to oppose a Russian advance into Afghanistan, various solutions were posed to free sufficient troops to face a hostile force which might amount to 300,000, particularly the creation of a force of 10,000 white police which would free 30,000 troops of the 'obligatory garrisons'. However, this was no substitute for the government facing up to the strategic problem, which Altham urged it must now do:[43]

> Unless . . . we are prepared to accept the loss of India, as an inevitable result of a war between this country and France and Russia, it is manifest that drastic measures are necessary to place this portion of our general scheme of Imperial defence on a safe footing.

Altham therefore suggested an immediate reinforcement of 30,000 men for India in the event of war, together with the organization of Imperial forces in such a way as to provide another 60,000 troops as soon as command of the sea had been obtained.

The prospect of offensive action offered more speculative realms into which to venture. Of one thing Altham was sure: dependent as it was upon trade for prosperity, the Empire must terminate a war quickly. A long war would enhance the cost of living and lessen the demand for labour; as a result the labouring and artisan classes would become discontented and force the government to make peace.[44] The military planners also felt themselves to labour under a second domestic burden, that of democracy:

'Governments, in shaping their military policy, must necessarily have regard to political conditions, and there can be little doubt that democratic institutions are unfavourable to the continuance of prolonged wars, in which national existence is not directly at stake.'[45] Altham clearly perceived the basic strategic problem, which as yet eluded the Admiralty: that in the case of offensive operations against a major continental power sea power alone was incapable of inflicting a decisive blow. Even defeat at sea meant much less for such a nation, as Trafalgar had revealed. But sea power did offer the opportunity to attack the overseas possessions of an enemy.

Russia appeared to be vulnerable to such action in four areas. She could be attacked in Central Asia through India, but such a move was conceived of as being primarily defensive due to the difficulties confronting it. In the Far East, Vladivostok and Port Arthur might be engaged, but the former was now thought impregnable and the latter would not be a loss of sufficient magnitude to force Russia to end the war. The third possible objective, hitherto considered the most appropriate, lay in the Caucasus; such an operation depended on Turkish support which was unlikley to be forthcoming, and in any case Russian communications with India lay to the north of the area and so would not be vulnerable. The improbability of Turkish support also rendered any plan to destroy Russian commerce in the Black Sea nugatory. The inevitable conclusion was that, so far as Russia was concerned, the Far East was the only area in which attack was possible. For this there was one prerequisite: a Japanese alliance.[46]

The prospects for successful action against France appeared much brighter. Unlike Russia she had extensive overseas possessions, the capture of which would badly dent her national pride and would provide valuable hostages for peace. It was believed that, with the exception of Martinique, the French colonial possessions all contained huge and discontented national populations which made them especially vulnerable. The loss of such colonies might well make an excitable French democracy declare for peace by overthrowing the government. Immediate action was therefore to be directed against the naval bases of Bizerta, Dakar, Martinique, Diego Suarez, Saigon and Noumea in time of war. Such a strategy was particularly attractive because of the economic use it made of manpower: British expeditions against the five first-named bases would require only 115,000 men in all.

Manpower was always one of the chief constraints upon strategy. Taking account of this, Altham estimated that the cost of his over-all strategy was not insupportable. Home defence would require 350,000 men, colonial defence 71,036, Egypt 8,010, India a normal garrison of 102,159 together with 72,518 reinforcements in time of war and overseas raid strategy 115,800 men. The total came to rather less than the 798,015 men to be provided by the Estimates of 1901–2 and allowed an ample margin for the creation of a reserve.[47] But the picture was not as unclouded as it seemed, for though Altham's strategic design did not involve a physical enlargement of the army it did require important changes in its structure. Chief amongst them was the recommendation that all 124 battalions of militia be made liable for service overseas, which currently they were not. Without such a measure there was a deficiency of seventy-five battalions of infantry against the number required overseas. Objections to such a measure based on constitutional or financial grounds or on the lack of training and efficiency of the militia Altham brushed aside as unimportant.

Altham's conclusion was a powerful plea for England to break out of her shell. For too long British defence policy had been insular in tone. The South African War had provided a cheap object lesson of the dangers of such an approach, and one which might have been more costly had it occurred at the time of the Venezuela incident in 1896 or of Fashoda. Were such a situation to occur again, the proposed strategy could deal with it. It would also have benefits in the diplomatic field by adding value to Britain as an ally in war: her sea power would enable her to choose a point at which to launch a force of 200,000 men. 'Even by Germany, aid of this description could not be despised, and would tend to make it more reasonable that she should support Great Britain in a war with France and Russia.'[48]

In putting his final emphasis on the value of diplomatic engagements to those entrusted with the task of devising military strategy, Altham was voicing the opinion of a growing number of soldiers. Sir William Nicholson, head of his department, had noted on hearing that the Foreign Office had rejected overtures from both Germany and Japan a few months previously that 'our policy of isolation is very expensive'.[49] In the course of the steady, if intermittent, stream of general strategic analyses which followed Altham's epoch-making paper, strategic perceptions of Britain's vulnerability and diplomatic perceptions of the relative threats posed by Germany, Russia and France were to modify Altham's original proposals quite considerably.

In a paper written late in 1902 and arising out of the sensitive position of British interests on the Persian Gulf, Sir William Robertson pointed out that it was fallacious to suggest that the way out of Britain's strategic problems was an alliance with Germany, a suggestion which had apparently been made by Altham. Colonial ambitions made that power one of Britain's strongest rivals, and added to the commercial, naval and popular rivalries which already existed between the two powers. From a purely strategical point of view, Robertson was sure that Germany would wish to widen any alliance so that Britain would have to assist her against France. The result would be to involve Britain in a costly war against France provoked for purely German reasons. Robertson was not yet wholly anti-German, for he did admit that it might be in Britain's interests to preserve Germany against France and Russia, but he followed Lord Salisbury's diplomatic paradigm in believing that the best way to do so was to preserve a free hand.[50]

Robertson pointed out that a Germany in alliance would be no help in securing the defence of the most sensitive portion of the Empire, the Indian frontier. To hold aloof from Germany might, however, make Russia more amenable in her dealings with Great Britain. The hinge of Robertson's position was his rejection of the belief that the Indian problem made Britain a continental power which needed a continental means of defence in the form of an alliance with a European power. His conclusion was that 'instead of regarding Germany as a possible ally we should recognise her as our most persistent, deliberate and formidable rival'. Nicholson concurred in this unfavourable view of Germany, and went so far as to recommend that the paper be sent semi-officially to the Foreign Office.

The explanation of Robertson's rejection of a continental role for Britain lay in a memorandum he had written earlier in the same year on the likely strategy of a war between Britain and Russia. The scene of such a confrontation was certain to be India, and Robertson had no doubts about the significance of such a fray. 'In fighting for India, England will be fighting for her Imperial existence, and a clear recognition of this fact is essential to the proper treatment of the question.'[51] Russia could field an army of 65,000 men in Turkestan one month after mobilization and could add to it at the rate of 20,000 a month thereafter; her only problem was transport, which would depend on the rate of railway building she could achieve.

A survey of the state of Russia's coastal defences from the Black Sea to Port Arthur brought Robertson to much the same conclusion as that reached by Altham—that Russia offered little in the way of targets for offensive operations. Nor was she as vulnerable to blows at her seaborne trade as in the past since the advent of railways and her increased volume of trade with the west had changed her focus towards Europe.

As to her strategy, Robertson felt Russia had three main aims: the occupation of Constantinople, the undermining of British power in Asia and the reduction of British trade with China. The first seemed also the foremost, and Russia had so prepared her theatre of war as to be able to bring pressure on Britain via the Northwest Frontier. In the event of hostilities she would probably move to occupy Herat and Mazar-i-Sharif, thereafter creating unrest within India and among the frontier tribes whilst awaiting a British advance. For her part, Britain had little hope of remaining on the defensive since this would satisfy neither the Amir of Afghanistan nor the frontier tribes and might shake the loyalty of the Indian army. 'In fact, England's position might conceivably become so intolerable as to render anything short of a vigorous offensive absolutely impossible.'[52] Were Britain to fail to make such an advance, peace by negotiation would result which would merely afford Russia time for the 'next and final move'.

As Russia appeared to offer an increasingly dangerous threat, so that presented by France was seen to be declining. In a paper written in 1901 Robertson had considered that to the French an invasion of the United Kingdom was both attractive and feasible, and that such a strategy was her ultimate goal.[53] Balfour's conclusions on invasion helped to change this view; so too did a reassessment of the prospects of offensive action against French possessions. By 1903 Robertson had come to doubt the feasibility of attacking French colonial bases by way of retaliation. The efficiency of French native troops had been increased, and those in Senegal, Dahomey, Guinea and the Ivory Coast had been put under a single commander responsible to the Governor General.

Also the defences of many of the naval bases mentioned in the paper on 'Military Needs of the Empire' had been strengthened.[54] The growing impregnability of French naval bases had been remarked upon elsewhere in the Intelligence Branch; at about this time, Nicholson gave it as his opinion that due to the strong fortification of Bizerta any amphibious operation against it 'would present great difficulties'.[55]

By 1905 Robertson's interpretation of the strategy to be pursued in the event of war against a Franco-Russian alliance had become an orthodoxy, so much so indeed that it could be suggested that Britain must be prepared to accept the loss of prestige which would result from the probable seizure of her own West African colonies by the French.[56] The strategic argument about the probable domestic effects of loss of overseas territory earlier applied to France had now been completely reversed. Moreover, this had occurred in a vacuum so far as co-operation from the Admiralty was concerned. The War Office had had to work out their own transport routes independently, being prepared to have to send unconvoyed transports to India. It was believed by them that the Admiralty would be unable to pursue its policy of concentration of the fleet at the opening of hostilities because of the obligation to protect some 900 large sea-going vessels which would be on the shipping lanes when war broke out; the War Office hoped to take advantage of the necessary patrolling in the passage of their own transports.

So far had the War Office moved that it was now forced to construct its own naval strategy to fit in with its military plans. It was proposed to send the convoys via the Cape, hopefully being able to slip past Dakar since the French would not be expecting an unconvoyed expedition and would not therefore be keeping watch. There were considerable dangers involved in such an action, particularly if the French established advanced bases at Diego Garcia, Reunion or the Seychelles, but the War Office concluded that such risks as there were must be accepted.[57] To carry out this exercise they were prepared, if the navy should prove unwilling to loan its fast auxiliary cruisers, to subsidize their own vessels and if necessary to enlarge the Transport Department in order to select them.

The heavy expense to which the War Office might be put in effecting such an action, which included earmarking escort vessels for their convoy, was held to be justified by the Admiralty's insistence on command of the sea. It was remarked that if the enemy elected to remain in a defended port it was difficult to see how he could be obliged to come out and fight. If command of the sea were not to be considered as attained until 'every ship, torpedo boat and submarine of the enemy has been burnt, captured or destroyed', an expedition under naval convoy might have to wait months before it set out. Naval strategy might be based on such a principle; the pressure of time ensured that military strategy could not. 'Such a delay as this might be fatal to our Indian Empire, it would certainly be fatal to our prestige, sacrifices must be made and risks must be run to avoid such a disastrous contingency.'[58]

The restricted nature of the *entente* between France and England had not absolved the strategists from examining the contingency of a war against France in combination with Russia. At the same time, strategic appreciations were constructed for hostilities against other combinations of powers. A Russo-German combination was held to be analogous with that of France and Russia, and it was thought that the same provisions should apply.[59] A Franco-German combination was considered so utopian that it scarcely merited discussion; in a sense this was unfortunate, for it would relieve the War Office of its most difficult task, the reinforcement of India. Were it to come about, operations on the west coast of Africa would be essential since Togo would no longer act as a buffer against France. With this exception, 'there would be no pressing need for military action and oversea operations might well wait until our navy had established at least a superiority at sea'.[60] The worst possible combination was that of Germany, France and Russia. Here the problem was so huge as to make the strategic solution simple.[61]

> There would be a large choice of oversea operations the sequence of which would depend on the course of events but, beyond despatching the first reinforcements to India and carrying out . . . cable cutting operations . . . there is nothing to be done until supremacy at sea has been attained.

As strategic assessments of warfare against the major continental powers, either singly or in combination, went ahead so the War Office began to abandon strategic ideas of the raid type which went with peripheral operations. Prior to the Boer War, such plans had been adumbrated to deal with what seemed the most pressing danger—that of a war with France.[62] In 1902 the War Office had turned its attention to the possibility of a war with Germany and had discovered that of all the European powers she was the least likely to be affected by the loss of overseas possessions.[63] Here was one case where the fate of colonies would be decided by a continental strategy; outside Europe, Germany could only be affected by blows at her seaborne commerce.

The interpretation put by the Admiralty upon its own doctrines served as a spur in this development as it did in others. In reply to Altham's paper the Director of Naval Intelligence, Admiral Battenburg, pointed out that the bases singled out were all strongly held except for Martinique. In any case, it was thought that there was no need to earmark troops for such oversea expeditions: 'By the time they become possible, the army for home defence should be able to provide all that is needful.'[64] The question of the availability of manpower was, however, largely irrelevant, since the navy doubted whether such operations were strategically feasible anyway. When, early in 1904, the First Lord of the Admiralty was thinking of combined operations against the coast of Russia, he was informed that the navy had no option but to do what it could against its Russian counterpart in the North Sea. 'If we find it so difficult to find vulnerable points with France who possesses colonies, how much more so with Russia who possesses none, and makes her home ports into first class fortresses.'[65]

The rejection by the War Office of a raid strategy flowed naturally from the problems of prosecuting a war against France and Russia. It followed also from concurrent examinations of the problems of defending vulnerable parts of the Empire, and particularly Malta. Ever since February 1901 Lord Grenfell, Commander-in-Chief at Malta, had been complaining that his garrison was too small to resist an assault, which he envisaged in the shape of a fleet attack and a landing by 33,000 men. The Admiralty anticipated no difficulty in so distributing the fleet that such an attempt against the island would not be possible without a general combination of maritime powers ranged against Britain. Should such a situation arise, 'their Lordships are of opinion that the island must in time be captured and that no addition to the garrison could possibly do more than delay its inevitable fall'.[66] In other words, it was the fleet and not Malta that guarded the Mediterranean and Egypt. If the fleet lost its superiority nothing could save the island; if it did not, then the island was safe anyway.

Both Grenfell and Nicholson dissented strongly from this point of view. The latter pointed out that the French, from whom the chief threat to the island seemed to come, might well attempt the transport of troops overseas before command of the sea was attained. Malta possessed fourteen miles of assailable coastline and only 5,900 troops to defend it, together with artillery which was inadequate in numbers and calibre. The military standpoint was based in part upon an instinctive dislike of the navalist thesis and in part upon the desire to get more resources for what was regarded as a woefully inadequate force. None the less, the navy's view was upheld by the Joint Naval and Military Council, which concluded that 'an attack without effective naval interference on our side is extremely improbable'. The present garrison would suffice, it was thought, to defend the island for such a time as would allow of naval interference and relief.[67]

Whilst the War Office thought that large garrisons were necessary to defend its own bases, the practicability of its undertaking similar action against enemy bases seemed less apparent. In the case of a war against France alone the suggestion had been made that the Indian government might find troops to attack Diego Suarez. The necessary numbers were now thought to be of the order of 24,000 and the India Office was told that 'the prospect of our being in a position to undertake such an operation is very improbable'.[68] Schemes were concurrently being drawn up for the seizure of islands off Algeria, Tunisia and Madagascar as torpedo bases on the attractive grounds that they would require almost no troops, being largely naval enterprises.[69] Practical evidence of the infeasibility of raids came from the manoeuvres held at Clacton in the summer of 1904 as part of the invasion enquiries. Sir Neville Lyttelton, Chief of the General Staff, remarked that as a result of this experience it was 'very questionable whether in these days of improved firearms a descent on a coastline could be carried out in the teeth of resolute opposition'.[70]

Evidence of the extent to which the General Staff's attitude to raids had undergone a transformation was the refusal to replace Gibraltar's 9.2-inch guns with the new 12-inch gun; since the new guns were in relatively short supply they had to be carefully allocated, and it was simply not worthwhile allotting any to the island.[71] None the less Malta appeared peculiarly susceptible to expeditions of the raid type and in August 1905 the General Staff suggested that a force of 10,000 infantry with some howitzers and portable guns landing on the island might succeed in breaking its defences. The 7,000 infantry now available to defend it were totally inadequate.[72] This prompted Balfour to comment somewhat caustically on one of the features of 'raid strategy': that completely different standards of what was possible were adopted when considering possible enemy activities than when dealing with possible British action overseas.[73] Grierson was forced in reply to propound the theory that the size of the target determined the amount of risk which would be taken to get it, and also that the danger increased with the possibility of protracted rather than short operations. In both cases, Malta was more vulnerable to France than either Dakar or Saigon were to Britain.

The logical conclusion of this argument, which had some merit when applied to specific instances, was that Britain herself offered the supreme target to France, or indeed to Germany, yet the War Office had accepted the findings of the invasion enquiry of 1904 as freeing them to look overseas. Their increasing awareness of the flaws in a 'raid strategy', particularly in the light of the navy's confident assertions about command of the seas, was coupled with a growing recognition that the army need concern itself in the future less with perimeter operations than with a major land campaign, probably in India. At this moment, the question of renewal of the Anglo-Japanese alliance gave the War Office a critical insight into the problems of diplomatic commitment, in itself closely inter-related to continental strategy.

The first sign that Japan wished to renew the existing alliance came when the Japanese Ambassador, Viscount Hayashi, sounded out Lord Lansdowne late in March 1905. In particular, he hinted that some eminent Japanese soldiers were in favour of an arrangement whereby in return for certain concessions Japanese troops might be employed in India.[74] The military and naval authorities at once took this up on the grounds that a reciprocal arrangement would greatly simplify the problem of the defence of India. England would find herself provided with 'the services of a large and thoroughly efficient field army' which could arrive in India much more quickly than an army of equivalent size from England, 'even if a numerically equal army was forthcoming at all, which is quite open to question'.[75]

On 12 April 1905 the Committee of Imperial Defence discussed the future of the alliance at the Cabinet's request. It was emphasized that any renewal or extension of the treaty should not menace powers assumed to be friendly, such as France or the United States, nor be regarded as 'an Anglo-Japanese Alliance against Europe'.[76] It was agreed that the treaty should be extended to cover attack on either party by a third power alone, and that in return for naval help Great Britain should require military assistance in defending India. Two concerns had, however, to be kept in mind: the views of the Indian government on employing Asiatic troops in co-operation with native troops, and the difficulty of defining a *casus foederis* in the case of India. The latter difficulty was met by making the agreement operative only when the contracting parties were in full agreement; thus Afghanistan or Persia could not provoke Russia into war and then afterwards call the alliance into operation. In answer to the first reservation, the Secretary of the Committee of Imperial Defence pointed out that a precedent already existed: fifty years before, Great Britain had allied with Turkey.[77]

Lansdowne was prepared to open negotiations on a purely political basis. He believed that if Japan won the war against Russia, then Russia would make it her task as soon as she could to 'renew her attack upon Japan in such strength as to crush her completely out of existence'.[78] This view was controverted by the signs that Russia was growing increasingly concerned about Germany's threatening attitude in Europe;[79] Lansdowne may have feared that Russia might seek alliance with Japan herself. Certainly it had been made clear to him by Hayashi that Japan would not accept military obligations beyond the Far East, of which she did not regard India as a part.

In June the General Staff were requested to give their observations on the proposed Anglo-Japanese agreement. Sir James Grierson remarked that Japan would gain rather more advantage from it than Great Britain, and that even in the case of an attack by Russia 'the value of Japanese assistance is somewhat problematical'.[80] The memorandum spelled out the War Office's doubts more overtly: it was not thought to be prudent to place 'too much reliance on Japan coming to our assistance in the event of our becoming involved in war in defence of our special interests in

India'.[81] In the event of war against Russia alone it was thought that action by the Japanese in the Far East would not necessarily relieve the pressure on India. If France or Germany were hostile, then the main weight of the attack would be in the west and would fall on Britain. If America were the hostile power, then Japan could act against her in the Philippines and assist in the defence of Canada. Lansdowne and the General Staff concurred in thinking it undesirable to define the character of assistance or the territorial limits to be set upon it in any of the suggested eventualities. Their motives were antipathetical, Lansdowne feeling that mutually acceptable definitions would be impossible and the War Office that if a treaty were to be made at all they needed a loophole.[82]

On 12 August 1905 the treaty was signed with the precise military obligations still undefined. Lansdowne was willing to leave matters there since there were signs of a growing accord between Great Britain and Russia, though the military were probably not aware of this.[83] Esher was quite correct, though not entirely for the right reasons, when he informed Kitchener that 'the defeat of Russia by Japan and the new treaty between Japan and Great Britain very much alters the character of the Indian problem'.[84]

There were no further discussions of the military significance of the agreement with Japan until November, when the General Staff reviewed its strategic implications. By this time they had clarified in their own minds the nature of the military action which should be pursued by the two contracting parties. Russia was vulnerable to pressure only in the Far East, hence the Japanese would meet their obligations by a vigorous offensive in that theatre. All available British manpower would be concentrated in India, with the possible exception of two brigades of cavalry and one of horse artillery which could be sent to Japan if required. Their presence would have a political rather than a military significance. There was no question, however, of a reciprocal Japanese presence in India and indeed Britain should not ask for troops:[85]

Such a request on our part would, in fact, be interpreted, and not without reason, as a clear proof of our national decadence, and would be highly detrimental, if not absolutely fatal, to our prestige throughout the Asiatic continent.

In the event of war with either France or Germany, Japan's contribution would then be to attack their respective possessions in Indo-China and at Kiao Chao.

The effect of the agreement on the construction of naval and of military strategy was remarkably different. The Admiralty began to devise plans based on the possibility of attack by France, Russia and Germany against the alliance. The long-term aim was for the two partners to maintain between them a three-power standard of superiority.[86] The navy also suggested that, while they maintained the earlier arrangements over cyphers, the exchange of intelligence, docking and repairing facilities and the transmission of up-to-date information about transport requirements, plans for land operations should be prepared by the military authorities and kept up to date. They were unaware that the alliance had done little to remedy the strategic problems facing the General Staff, foremost among them the question of the defence of India. The military position was the worse in that the government refused to take the next logical step and construct an agreement with Russia.[87]

The departure of Balfour's administration from office in December 1905 coincided with two major changes in military strategy. Planners had begun to think in continental terms, and they had seen that agreements concluded along diplomatic lines alone were likely not to provide the assurances of safety they needed, indeed might provide none. The Japanese experience was fresh in their minds when the conversations with the French began some few weeks later.

When France made the first informal approaches to England about military assistance in the event of a war with Germany, they were channelled through a cabal led by Esher and representing the Committee of Imperial Defence; the General Staff were not formally brought in until mid-January. Thus by the time that Grierson became involved in detailed discussions the Committee of Imperial Defence had already discarded one strategy, that of action against the North German coast, and had come to favour either action in defence of Belgium or directly assisting France to defend her eastern frontier. Grierson had already learned from his experiences of the Japanese negotiations that politicians might well conclude agreements which took little or no account of strategic possibilities, and might equally call on the military to perform tasks for which they had not been forewarned. There was evidence that both attitudes of mind persisted, though Grierson himself probably did not know of it. The Foreign Secretary was prepared to support the idea of conversations on the grounds that a situation might arise 'in which popular feeling might compel the Government to go to the help of France', thus practically admitting that the determination of policy could lie in realms outside his control.[88] Also the political dimensions of the issue were at that time limited to helping France against Germany, and made no mention of Belgium.[89]

Grierson's contribution to the development of the Anglo-French understanding was therefore to press for immediate conversations between the respective General Staffs, so that the experts could devise a sound strategic plan without being pre-empted in any way by politicians or by the Committee of Imperial Defence.[90] He also extended the theatre of operations to include Belgium.[91] Though the formal discussions died away after the Moroccan crisis diminished in importance, they were succeeded by a continued interest in planning to assist France in a war against Germany which confirmed the continental tendencies already apparent within the General Staff.

The semi-formal liaison between France and England had occurred solely as a result of the stimulus afforded to France by the Moroccan crisis to find military support elsewhere than in Russia. While its importance was to grow in succeeding years, it was at the time an aberration; the formal arrangement between Britain and Japan seemed to offer the surest pattern for the future course of military co-operation with other powers. As yet, however, no specific military agreements had been concluded and prior to them the attitude of the Government of India over the employment of Japanese troops there and of Indian troops in the Far East had to be ascertained. Kitchener informed the Committee of Imperial Defence that he thought it inadvisable at present to employ Japanese troops in India, and Sir John French gave it as his opinion that the artillery and cavalry earmarked to support Japan could neither be found nor improvised.[92] At a stroke the military aspect of the agreement seemed to have disappeared, and the only firm agreement was that a military conference might meet alongside the naval one which was deemed essential. This was subsequently postponed by the Japanese until the following year, when 'the numerous changes consequent upon the war have been settled'.[93]

When, early in 1907, the General Staff began to consider the forthcoming conference their attitude was formed chiefly by the signs of growing tension between Japan and America which had become apparent. Although American aggression in China was unlikely, if it did occur then the Japanese might wish to call the alliance into operation and that would prove an embarrassment to England. The General Staff therefore determined that they would enter conversations negatively; no troops would be offered to assist the Japanese in Manchuria and no Japanese troops requested for India. As far as strategy was concerned, discussions would centre on exhausting the Russians in each power's respective theatre.[94]

This attitude changed somewhat after the Committee of Imperial Defence suggested in April that the question of Japanese troops operating in India should after all be discussed. Kitchener wrote from India arguing that it was doubtful 'either on military or political grounds' whether they should be so employed, the political grounds being those of prestige and the military related to the shortage of communications facilities.[95] None the less the General Staff did suggest detailed proposals for discussion between the powers based on the assumption that Japan might support India if British troops could not get there, and went so far as to suggest the line Karachi-Quetta-Kandahar as best suited for their operations. This strategy received support from the representative of the Indian government, Sir O'Moore Creagh, who felt that local assistance from Japan in the circumstances outlined would be vital 'notwithstanding all the grave and undoubted drawbacks to such a course'.[96]

The Japanese had no intentions of aiding Britain anywhere outside the Far East, and this was soon made clear. A memorandum by their chief negotiator, General Baron Nishi, informed the conference that the alliance was thought to be directed against Russia, and that since she possessed superior numbers the allies should not divide their own forces but should act in their respective theatres. In order to make a successful diversion, the Japanese would have to move quickly against Manchuria, hence Nishi argued they would need a large amount of transport from England.[97] Thus the detailed proposals of the British General Staff were rejected, the Japanese making it clear that they did not expect British reinforcements in the Far East and that they in their turn did not want to endanger their own position by releasing troops for India. Clarke, one of the British team, commented after the first day that his impression was 'that the Japanese want ships and railway plant and nothing more, and that they don't take us very seriously'.[98] Even Esher noticed the clear slant of Japanese policy, informing the King that while they looked upon Korea, Manchuria, Formosa and the Chinese coast opposite it as their own special interests the Japanese did not regard Persia as being a special interest for Britain.[99]

The General Staff might still have salvaged something from the conference, had not two factors gravely weakened their case. One was the admission by Nicholson that it was in any case difficult to operate in Afghanistan against the Russians whatever the situation of India, which weakened the case for Japanese support there. The other was a sudden transformation on the part of the Admiralty over the provision of 140,000 tons of shipping for Japan in the event of war. An initial attitude of *non possumus*, which could have been used as a lever, was subsequently and inexplicably reversed. The agreement eventually reached therefore required each power 'operating as far as circumstances admit in their respective theatres of war' to seek to create a diversion on behalf of their ally. The question of aggression by powers other than Russia, or by Russia in alliance with other powers, was to be left for consideration if and when it arose. Finally both parties agreed to establish liaison between their General Staffs and to keep one another informed of their material requirements.[100]

In the aftermath of the conference Clarke was justified in thinking that 'the Japanese have got all they wished, and we have got practically nothing'.[101] The venture contributed nothing to the easing of the strategic tasks of the General Staff, though it did provide a strong stimulus to keep military conversations from being merely an adjunct to political agreements. It was not until the conclusion of the agreement with Russia in 1907 that the problems of the Far East were overcome, and within five years Japan was to become a menace rather than a welcome ally *vis-à-vis* Australia and New Zealand.[102] The experience was valuable within the context of the seven-year period from the start of the twentieth century, however, since it confirmed the General Staff in their new-found habit of thinking in terms of continental strategies, and also highlighted the problems attendant on strategic requirements being tied to purely diplomatic or naval policies. The insignificance of the agreement itself was reflected in the discovery by the War Office in 1912 that they had lost it.

Notes

1 Hamilton to Curzon, 4 July 1901. Quo. G. E. Monger, *The End of Isolation: British Foreign Policy 1900–1907*, London, 1963, p. 13.
2 M. E. Howard, *The Continental Commitment*, London, 1972, p. 29.
3 *Ibid.*, p. 23.
4 For the history of the creation of the CID, *see* J. Ehrman, *Cabinet Government and War 1890–1940*, Cambridge, 1958; N. Gibbs, *The Origins of Imperial Defence*, Oxford, 1955; F. A. Johnson, *Defence by Committee*, London, 1960.
5 H. R. Moon, 'The Invasion of the United Kingdom: Public Controversy and Official Planning 1888–1918', vol. 1, Ph.D. thesis, London, 1968, p. 231.
6 Draft Report on the possibility of serious invasion: Home Defence, 11 November 1903. Cab. 3/1/18A.
7 Moon, *op. cit.*, vol. 1, p. 244.
8 S. F. Wells, 'The British strategic withdrawal from the Western Hemisphere 1904–1906', *Canadian Historical Review*, vol. XLIX, no. 4, December 1968, pp. 348, 352.
9 Indian Defence No. 1, 9 July 1904. B.M. Add. MSS. 50836.
10 Minute, Callwell to Grierson, 3 October 1904. W.O. 106/40/B1/3.
11 Minute, C. L. Ottley, 23 June 1905 attached to Notes on the Naval Defence of the Canadian Frontier. Cab. 17/47.
12 Hankey to Asquith, 10 July 1912. Cab. 17/100.
13 Minute, Grierson to Lyttelton, 25 May 1905. W.O. 106/40/B1/4.
14 Minute, Grierson to Lyttelton, 12 August 1905. W.O. 106/40/B1/4.
15 Sir E. Monson to Salisbury, 27 October 1898. *B.D.* I, no. 218.
16 Lansdowne to Sir F. Lascelles, 18 March 1901. *B.D.* II, no. 77.
17 Memoir by Lord Salisbury, 29 May 1901. *B.D.* II, no. 86.
18 Memorandum by Lord Lansdowne, 11 November 1901. *B.D.* II, no. 92.
19 Monger, *op. cit.*, pp. 38, 39.
20 Minute by Lansdowne, 17 March 1902. W.O. 106/44/E1/6.
21 Monger, *op. cit.*, p. 47.
22 A. J. Marder, *The Anatomy of British Sea Power*, Hamden, Connecticut, 1964, p. 428.
23 Altham to Nicholson, 8 April 1902. W.O. 106/48/G3/3.
24 Memorandum on the proposed conference between Naval and Military Representatives of Great Britain and Japan as to joint action in event of war, 2 June 1902. W.O. 106/48/G3/1.
25 Report of a conference between Military Representatives, Great Britain and Japan at Winchester House, W.O., 8.7.1902 to discuss concerted military action in war. W.O. 106/48/G3/2.

26 Minute, Altham to Nicholson, 22 July 1902. W.O. 106/48/G3/2.

27 Minute, Brodrick, 18 September 1902. W.O. 106/48/G3/2.

28 Minute, Altham, 12 June 1903. W.O. 106/48/G3/4.

29 Report by Colonel Churchill on the Japanese Army, 27 April 1903. W.O. 106/48/G3/4.

30 Foreign Office to Director General of Military Intelligence, 18 June 1903. W.O. 106/48/G3/4.

31 Report by the British Military Attache at Peking, regarding warlike preparations by Russia in the Far East, 1 July 1903. Cab. 4/1/8B.

32 Communication from the War Office, 29 July 1903. B.D. II, no. 241.

33 (Military Observations in case of a war between Japan and Russia) 22 December 1903. Cab. 37/67/92.

34 (Observations on no. 92), 24 December(?) 1903. Cab. 37/67/93.

35 Forecast of the first phase of a war between Russia and Japan, 28 December 1903. Cab. 4/1/12B.

36 (Position in the Far East), 29 December 1903, p. 2. Cab. 4/1/11B.

37 Ibid., p. 5.

38 British Intervention in the Far East, 31 December 1903, p. 5. Cab. 4/1/13B.

39 Ibid., pp. 16, 17.

40 Ibid., p. 8.

41 The Military Needs of the Empire in a war with France and Russia, 10 August 1901, p. 16. Cab. 3/1/1A.

42 Ibid., p. 24.

43 Ibid., p. 28.

44 Ibid., p. 30.

45 Ibid., p. 31.

46 Ibid., p. 33.

47 Ibid., p. 40.

48 Ibid., p. 49.

49 Roberts Papers. Nicholson to Roberts, 24 April 1901. Box X 20926, file N2.

50 Robertson Papers. Possible German English Alliance with special regard to Turkey and the Persian Gulf Area, 10 November 1902. WRR 2/4.

51 Resources of Russia and their probable employment in a war with the British Empire, 27 January 1902, p. 1. W.O. 106/48/E3/1.

52 Ibid., para 21.

53 The military resources of France, and probable method of their employment in a war between France and England, 27 December 1901. Cab. 3/1/4A.

54 Robertson Papers. Note added to Military Resources of France, and their probable employment in a war between France and England, 17 February 1903. WRR 2/3.

55 Note by Nicholson, 16 January 1903. W.O. 106/48/E3/2.

56 War with France and Russia combined, Germany neutral, 1905, p. 38. W.O. 106/48/E3/3.

57 *Ibid.*, p. 68.
58 *Ibid.*, p. 87.
59 War with Germany and Russia combined, France neutral, 8 February 1905. W.O. 106/48/E3/6.
60 War with France and Germany combined, Russia neutral, 8 February 1905, p. 96. W.O. 106/48/E3/6.
61 War with France, Germany and Russia combined, 8 February 1905, p. 98. W.O. 106/48/E3/6.
62 *Vid.* Plan for attack on Brest in the event of war with France, 12 August 1898. P.R.O. 30/40/2.
63 The Military Resources of Germany and their eventual method of employment in a war between Germany and England, 18 January 1902. W.O. 106/46/E2/4.
64 Memorandum on oversea expeditions with reference to Paper 1A, 1 July 1903. Cab. 3/1/14A.
65 Kerr to Selborne, 2 April 1904. B.M. Add. MSS. 49707.
66 Admiralty to War Office, 4 October 1901. Cab. 5/1/4C.
67 Joint Naval and Military Committee Report No. XL, 22 September 1903. Cab. 18/22A.
68 (Impossibility of attack from India on Diego Suarez), 10 March 1904, p. 1. Cab. 4/1/18B.
69 Schemes for occupying Halibas, Galita and Minnow Islands, May 1904. W.O. 106/40/A3/1.
70 Army Manoeuvres 1904, 19 September 1904. B.M. Add. MSS. 49722.
71 Royal Archives. Grierson to Knollys, 13 May 1904. RA W25/72.
72 Estimate of the minimum strength of an expeditionary force which could attack Malta with a reasonable prospect of success, 12 August 1905. Cab. 5/1/35C.
73 Balfour to Arnold Forster, 12 August 1905. W.O. 106/41/C2/6.
74 Lansdowne to Sir C. MacDonald, 24 March 1905. *B.D.* IV, no. 111.
75 The Future of the Anglo-Japanese Alliance, 8 April 1905, p. 9. Cab. 17/67.
76 70th meeting of C.I.D., 12 April 1905. Cab. 2/1.
77 Esher Papers. Clarke to Esher, 20 April 1905. 'Sir George Clarke Vol. 3'.
78 Lansdowne to Sir C. MacDonald, 17 May 1905. *B.D.* IV, no. 115.
79 Spring Rice to Lansdowne, 7 May 1905. *B.D.* IV, no. 69.
80 Grierson to Sir T. H. Sanderson, 16 June 1905. *B.D.* IV, no. 127.
81 Observations by the General Staff, War Office, on the Proposed Japanese Agreement, n.d. *B.D.* IV, enclosure to no. 127.
82 This would answer the problem raised by Marder of why specific military stipulations were excluded from the renewed treaty. *See* his *Anatomy of British Sea Power*, p. 452, n. 14.
83 *See B.D.* IV, nos 185, 188.
84 Esher Papers. Esher to Kitchener, 26 July 1905. 'Army Letters Vol. 2'.
85 Anglo-Japanese Agreement of August 12, 1905: Proposals for concerted action, 4 November 1905, p. 2. Cab. 4/1/68B.

86 Anglo-Japanese Agreement of August 12, 1905: Proposals for concerted action, 7 December 1905, p. 2. Cab. 4/2/70B.

87 Sanderson to Clarke, 10 November 1905. Cab. 17/60.

88 Haldane Papers. Grey to Haldane, 8 January 1906. N.L.S. MS. 5907.

89 Grey to Sir F. Bertie, 10 January 1906. *B.D.* III, no. 210 (a).

90 Grierson to Lord Sanderson, 11 January 1906. *B.D.* III, no. 211.

91 *See* below, p. 282.

92 84th meeting of CID, 15 February 1906. Cab. 2/2/1.

93 86th meeting of CID, 25 May 1906. Cab. 2/2/1.

94 Anglo-Japanese negotiations arising out of the treaty of August 12, 1905: Memorandum by the General Staff, 15 March 1907. Cab. 4/3/1/101B.

95 Memorandum by Kitchener, encl. with Clarke to Ewart, 25 April 1907. W.O. 106/48/G3/12.

96 Creagh to Lyttelton, 1 June 1907. *Ibid.*

97 Memorandum by Baron Nishi, 2 May 1907. *Ibid.*

98 Esher Papers. Clarke to Esher, 29 May 1907. 'Sir G. Clarke 1906–1907 Vol. 8'.

99 Royal Archives. Esher to Edward VII, 31 May 1907. RA W40/117.

100 Conclusions of a Conference held at 2, Whitehall Gardens on May 29, June 1 and 6 (1907), between the military reps. of Great Britain and Japan in accordance with Article VII of the Agreet. between the United Kingdom and Japan, 12–8–1905. W.O. 106/48/G3/12.

101 Esher Papers. Clarke to Esher, 6 June 1907. 'Sir G. Clarke 1906–7 Vol. 8'.

102 Australia and New Zealand: Strategic situation in the event of the Anglo-Japanese Alliance being determined, 3 May 1911. Cab. 5/2/2/78C.

7
India

For several decades before the outbreak of the Boer War, India had offered to the Victorians an unequalled opportunity to experience the 'small wars' which passed as the only substitute for European experience on the battlefields of Sadowa and Sedan. But the jewel of Empire displayed a serious, possibly fatal, flaw: the delicate strategic situation occupied by Afghanistan. Here, if anywhere, the Empire might suffer its first defeat, a concept of such enormity as to transfix the imagination of most of those concerned with the problems of the sub-continent. Afghanistan had long been an area of concern, particularly as far as a possible Russian move towards India was concerned.[1] It was not, however, until England had become embroiled in another Imperial struggle in South Africa, that the first moves were made which awakened all the latent alarums in both Delhi and London.

In February 1900, Russia conveyed a memorandum to the Foreign Office stating her intention to establish relations with Afghanistan in order to discuss what were termed frontier matters.[2] The inference of a forward move by Russia seemed to be confirmed by War Office intelligence that in the previous two months up to 150,000 Russian troops had been moving on Kushk. The author of this report regarded such action as an 'act of insolence' which resulted directly from the parlous position the Empire now found itself in, and 'to remedy which should now engross the whole of our attention'.[3] The mathematics were incorrect, since the true figures for Russian troop movements would appear to have been 4,000; and in any case there was little prospect of military aid being diverted to India at that moment.

The dangers apparently threatening India from Afghanistan took little hold in the War Office at that time: St John Brodrick felt that if Russia were prepared for war anywhere, it was more likely to be in Persia than in Afghanistan.[4] This attitude was somewhat shaken when, in October 1901, the Amir of Afghanistan suddenly died. Curzon, then Viceroy in India, had been reasonably confident of Abdur Rahman's loyalty to the Crown; the attitude of his successor was less clear. Coincidentally the first major examination of the question of Indian defence was then being undertaken by the War Office.

As a result of the alarming news prevalent in the spring of 1900, the Indian administration had been requested to prepare a scheme of defence in the event of a Russian attack upon Afghanistan. In the resultant document, India postulated a forward policy of moving into Afghanistan to occupy a line stretching from Kabul to Kandahar. India also requested 30,000 immediate reinforcements from England on the outbreak of such a war, with 70,000 more to follow, figures which were subsequently to become a focus for heated debate. In reply to subsequent queries from Brodrick it became apparent that the Indian military authorities felt a defensive stance would be of little effectiveness and would require more troops than an offensive posture, that the numbers they had requested were irreducible *minima* which they might well wish to increase, and that in the event of no reinforcements from England being forthcoming India would move to Kandahar anyway should Russia occupy Herat, and possibly even to Kabul.[5] At this point Brodrick handed over the problem to a small committee, headed by Sir William Nicholson.

In considering the problems raised, the committee first pointed out that the obligatory garrisons stationed throughout India could not be safely reduced. The attitude of the native populace during the Boer War had been reassuring, but it was thought that any check or long pause after offensive action might result in internal disturbances. Thus the attitude which had resulted from the mutiny was built into strategic calculations from the outset. India could therefore field an effective force of 31,700 British troops, 42,000 natives and 240 guns. Cautiously it was observed that more English troops might be necessary.

Examination of Russia's position revealed that there were two basic routes through Afghanistan which offered potential: Kushk to Herat to Kandahar and Samarkand to Mazar-i-Sharif to Kabul. A common feature of both was that Russia would have to pause and make good her position before moving on the Indian frontier, either at Herat or Kabul. 'The longer the pause, the greater would be the strength of Russia for the next move.'[6] But because of the possible internal difficulties, such a pause without some form of counter was precisely what India could not afford.

By the end of the second month's campaigning Russia could have in the theatre a total of 124,000 troops and 248 guns. Cold numerical calculation was telling against India, and the construction of the Orenburg–Tashkent railway would greatly facilitate supply to these troops, which in the meantime would have to rely on the extant Trans-Caspian line.

The attitude of Afghanistan was clearly going to be crucial and no one knew what that was likely to be. The notion of attacking Russia elsewhere was rejected in favour of sending available reinforcements out to India, though this was not the occasion of the final abandonment of such theories.[7] The strategy finally advocated by London required India to be self-sufficient for at least nine and possibly twelve months. It was suggested that the main force should remain on the Indian frontier, since this would avoid taxing the army beyond its powers, would minimize complications with Afghanistan and would at the same time test the temper of that country. Among the measures which India must take were the construction of the Kabul River railway as far as Dakka on the frontier and the extension of the Quetta railway to Nushki and on towards Seistan. At the same time it was acknowledged that some addition to the European garrison seemed necessary.

The Indian response to what was an alarming rejection of their own strategic theories was to shun almost every part of it. India refused to pay for the extra 18,500 troops suggested, but held that without a larger field army 'the interests not of India so much as of the Empire might be placed in jeopardy'.[8] If such additions were necessary, it was chiefly because the British government could not guarantee command of the sea for nine months, something which in any case they thought unduly pessimistic. The Kabul River railway had been rejected in 1899 as liable to alarm the frontier tribes, and the Quetta-Nushki railway was already under construction. If, as India thought, a Russian advance so sudden and so menacing as to require at an early stage the attention of a large part of the Indian army was unlikely, then she would rather continue as she was since an extra 18,500 men would make no appreciable difference. If, on the other hand, the home government thought the danger more acute then they must pay for the necessary additions to Indian defence capability. For, as the Indian Army argued, a war with Russia in Afghanistan would be an Imperial war 'since it cannot be doubted that not

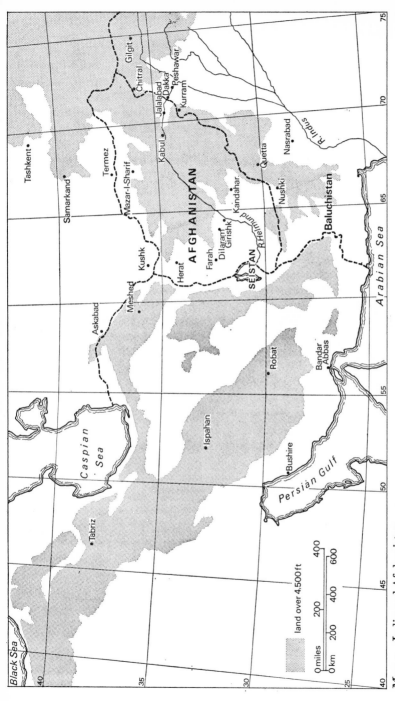

Map 1   India and Afghanistan

merely the credit but the very existence of the British Empire would be at stake'.[9]

At the first meeting of the reconstituted Committee of Imperial Defence on 18 December 1902 Sir William Nicholson requested that the first strategic examination which that body should undertake be into this very issue.[10] This was coupled with the growing importance of Anglo-Russian relations in the eyes of the Foreign Office, so that Indian strategy became a part of the wider canvas of diplomacy and was evolved in the CID and not by the service departments alone.

A further War Office committee soon scotched any notions India might have of relying on troops from South Africa or Australia by confirming the Admiralty's *diktat* about the time necessary to secure command of the sea. India was informed that 45,000 British troops were considered necessary for a scheme involving a preliminary advance to Kandahar and Jalalabad, and since 30,000 were already available the figure of additions arrived at was 15,000. However, thoughts of an Anglo-Russian conflict were themselves beginning to alter the opinion of the War Office. In particular, the Orenburg–Tashkent railway was due for completion in 1905, when it would add immensely to the danger India was in. Growing anxiety found expression in the theorem now propounded that the ultimate issue of such a war 'depends largely upon the relative readiness of the two Powers to undertake the preliminary operations which would precede an actual conflict'.[11] It was upon this emotion that India was increasingly to play.

The defence of India was beginning to assume alarming proportions, and to reveal a distinct cleavage of opinion between the two sets of authorities. In order to establish more precisely the dimensions of the problem, and possibly also in the hope that a more efficient use of available manpower might result, the Committee of Imperial Defence called for a report on the possibilities of an offensive-defensive defence with the aid of railway building. In opening up the vast question of the use of railways this was to produce bitter controversy, and at the same time to reveal that the British military had no clear concepts of what railways could or could not do.

The War Office pointed out that with her present track Russia could supply 150–200,000 men in the Afghan theatre by the end of the fifth month of a war; when the Orenburg–

Tashkent railway was completed, that figure would swell to 500,000.[12] Under the existing conditions, 104,000 troops would be needed to defend the line Kabul–Kandahar which meant adding 42,000 troops as well as the long-term reinforcement of 70,000. These figures were way beyond the resources of Britain, but a prospect of hope did beckon. If a railway were to be constructed to Kandahar and Jalalabad, then the time necessary to concentrate British troops on the forward line would be cut from eighty-four days to forty-five days. In such a case, and particularly if Britain had been in Afghanistan long enough to connect the ends of her position with a railway, the large reinforcements might not be necessary.

The War Office was now in fundamental agreement with India about where a strategic posture should be made; 'all the best authorities, with few or no exceptions, now agree that it would be a far more difficult task to defend India from its existing frontier than from a line beyond it', they held. The explanation of this apparent *volte-face* was that the War Office had realized that unless such a strategy were adopted, and the necessary railroads provided, the bill which India could legitimately present in manpower terms would rise higher still. If Russia were allowed to advance into Afghanistan unchecked, 500,000 troops would be necessary as well as an unspecified increase in the size of the obligatory garrisons.[13]

Two lines of development now began to occur simultaneously. On the one hand, Nicholson pressed for a railway to Seistan in order to deny it to the Russians. On the other, Lord Roberts, the Commander-in-Chief, remarked on the need to control the 200,000 tribesmen in Afghanistan: 'With the tribesmen on our side we could meet the Russians in Afghanistan on fairly equal terms.'[14] The Committee of Imperial Defence could see no advantage in the course proposed by Nicholson so long as the Russo-Persian convention of 1900 remained operative, whereby Persia bound herself not to construct any railways nor allow any foreign power to do so.[15] Thus the problem became one of whether political or military solutions were to solve the dilemma of Indian vulnerability.

The War Office produced further studies which supported the notion of a forward strategy in Afghanistan during the following months. It was pointed out that, even assuming the completion of the Orenburg–Tashkent railway, Britain could outnumber

Russia in Afghanistan until the fifth month of a campaign. In the hypothetical timetable they evolved, the War Office expected the first clash in the war to occur at Farah on 12 June, assuming the war to have begun on 1 January. They also remarked that the course of a campaign was difficult to predict not only because of variations produced by the actions of the enemy but because of the 'many others which may be introduced by our allies the Afghans'.[16] This was aside to the main argument, but it indicated a switch in the nature of the strategic debate as it came to be realized that a forward defence required rather more consideration of the Afghans themselves, and of policy towards them.

It was Balfour who first saw the importance of this facet of the problem. The Prime Minister remarked that Afghanistan would be nothing more than a drawback to Russia but only as long as the present conditions of transport and supply prevailed. Its value to England was as a buffer state and one which, if India was to be unassailable, must remain un-Russianized. In the event of a Russian incursion, therefore, British forces must themselves advance to occupy the line Kabul–Kandahar; resting on secure flanks, this position offered a good opportunity to limit the Russian freedom of action with an attractive economy of force. Equally pertinent was the fact that if Russia possessed this line then: 'she could perfect at leisure schemes of further advance, and, established at our very gates, would find herself in a situation equally convenient for military aggression or political intrigue.'[17] Relations with the Afghans were complicated since they were far from being a homogeneous nation, and their value as an ally was poor; Balfour suggested that the only way to diminish the political dangers was by successful diplomacy to quiet Afghan suspicion of Great Britain and prevent Russian intervention in the country. His reaction to the issue was cooler since he saw it in the context of a world-wide war; other participants in the debate increasingly viewed it in isolation.

At the CID meeting which discussed Balfour's paper early in May its author revealed that the fundamental strategic proposition behind it was that the Kabul to Kandahar line could not be crossed at any point by a hostile force advancing from the northwest on India. Some discussion then arose about what action should be taken if Britain did not concentrate at Kabul, but occupied a line from Jalalabad to Kandahar instead. The call went out for a paper on his new strategic prospect.[18] The War

Office duly replied that there were three routes across the Kabul to Kandahar line, all of which offered great difficulties to an invading force. It also opined that, were the Kandahar to Jalalabad line to be occupied, the intervening passes could not be effectively blocked by fortifications as they could be turned.[19] Britain might have been able to supply money where, without conscription, she could not supply men; now this avenue seemed closed to her.

At the end of May, Balfour produced the second portion of his evaluation of Afghanistan's strategic role, a paper considering the vulnerability of either end of the Kabul–Kandahar line. To the northeast there was no danger since British garrisons at Chitral and Gilgit barred the way to the Indian heartlands. The picture was not so sanguine at the southwestern end, for Seistan offered the ideal point from which Russia could threaten or attack Kandahar. Were Russia to seek permission for a railway line connecting the area with Askabad, she would then possess an advanced base of great natural resources. Were Britain to seek authority from the Amir to extend the line from Nushki to Seistan, then Russia would probably also seek and get permission to build a line from Askabad to Meshed to Nasrabad. The spectacle such development offered was horrific: a through railway line from St Petersburg to Calcutta, its only impediment being the gauge break at the Indian frontier. Such a railway would be difficult to destroy since there were no important bridges and no tunnels north of Nushki; nor would the gauge break offer much of an obstruction, since Russia could relay the track or adapt her own rolling stock. The conclusion to be drawn from this sober survey was that Seistan was an acute embarrassment to British strategy. In wartime it could not be held without dangerously weakening the Kabul–Kandahar force; in peacetime, to anglicize it by constructing a railway line would only prompt Russia to do the same. Diplomacy offered the best way out: an agreement with Russia to defer all railway building in Eastern Persia.[20]

The two sides in this strategic debate began to drift further apart as the War Office became more and more immersed in calculations as to the carrying capacity of railways in the area. Were Russia to extend her rail network to Farah during the second six months of an offensive campaign, it now seemed possible that she could support 300,000 troops in Afghanistan.

Additional British troops would be necessary to cover this increase, to absorb a high level of wastage and because without an eventual offensive defeat would be inevitable 'as the history of every campaign shows'.[21] Even with the addition of 25,000 extra British troops, the margin of superiority would still only be slight, so that the prospect loomed up of a third reinforcement for India in addition to the first two of 30,000 and 70,000.

The Committee of Imperial Defence were anxious to hear the views of the men on the spot before committing themselves to any firm pronouncements about Indian defence, and accordingly Balfour wrote to Curzon and Kitchener early in July soliciting their views on his two papers. At the same time he informed them that the CID had provisionally accepted the notion that an immediate reinforcement of 30,000 and a subsequent one of 70,000 would be necessary should Russia invade Afghanistan, having completed the Orenburg–Tashkent railway.[22] Curzon's reaction to the papers was that they were essentially an academic statement of the position about which he had no recommendations to make. Only two points called for comment: the strategical importance of Seistan to both sides, and the desirability of extending the Quetta–Nushki railway to Seistan.[23] For his part, Kitchener was reluctant to say anything at all, in order to avoid tying his own hands.

In the face of a direct request from Curzon and Balfour even Kitchener could not maintain his unfettered attitude, and a joint memorandum from the Viceroy and Commander-in-Chief was laid before the CID early in August. It began by denying that India had ever framed her military calculations on the basis of the completion of the Orenburg–Tashkent railway, or that the Government of India had ever officially committed itself to the figures of 30,000 and 70,000 which had been the subject of so much discussion. The authors then challenged all British calculations of the carrying capacity of Russian railways as being far too low. A vivid picture was painted of the attractions to Russia of an advance into Seistan, from which point she could reach for a base on the Persian Gulf and threaten Baluchistan. The goal of India's strategy was then revealed as being no less than the development of Persian Seistan. A lease was to be obtained on the southern bank of the Helmund river which could help develop the immense irrigational prospects of the area and produce a revenue of £330,000 a year. Such a scheme, Curzon and Kitchener felt, would 'revolutionise the entire Central Asian question in its Afghan and Persian aspects', as well as killing all Russian ambitions in the area south of Khorassan.[24] It was not proposed that the line be extended from Nushki to Seistan right away; rather that, since Great Britain could win a railway-building race there, the line should be begun the moment that Russia laid a single mile of track in Khorassan.

Reception of Curzon's and Kitchener's thunderbolt caused a note of tangible acerbity to enter into the paper debate. Nicholson regarded their product as 'very poor' and reported surprise that Kitchener should have signed such a document.[25] The Intelligence Department refuted the assertion that the Government of India had never committed itself to any figures for reinforcements, providing chapter and verse from several communications and remarking that it seemed 'difficult to understand why . . . India should on three different occasions have allowed to pass unchallenged the statement . . . if they did not concur in that statement'.[26] The assertion that Great Britain could build a Seistan railway faster than Russia was queried, and so was the concept inherent in the Seistan plan that just because that area was under British protection Russian ambitions in that direction would be killed. Balfour's own reply stressed the political arguments against a forward policy comprehending Seistan, chief among them being the fact that a scheme such as that posed by Curzon and Kitchener would make the region an even more attractive jumping-off point for Russia. He also remarked that Russia already possessed two lines of advance; to create a fertile Seistan would offer a third when the defending power could scarcely muster enough strength to cover the first two.[27]

The tension between the notion of some form of absorption of Afghanistan, possibly through railway construction, and that of diplomatic activity directed at gaining the political support of the Afghans now began to increase. Balfour suggested that Curzon be informed that the government considered that nothing could be gained by endeavouring to extort from the Amir concessions for the construction of roads or railways in Afghanistan, no matter how important they might be for the defence of India. The Amir's fidelity was seen to depend upon the belief that Great Britain would respect his independence; any different impression would destroy all British influence.[28] Brodrick duly conveyed this view *verbatim* to the Viceroy as the expression of Cabinet policy should the Amir accept his invitation to meet him at Peshawar.[29] Lord Roberts, representing a lifetime of Indian military experience, pressed for as much extension of the railway system as could be brought about, totally lacking faith in the brand of argument put forward by Balfour.[30] It was now up to Kitchener to prove his case, and at the same time make the definite pronouncement about the strength which India could field which he had long intimated would be forthcoming.

The reason why India had been so intransigent about the 100,000 man reinforcement became plain early in the new year, when Curzon informed Brodrick that India assumed she would get these figures even before the Orenburg–Tashkent railway was completed.[31] This was quite contradictory to the view held by the CID that it was only that railway which would make the figure necessary. Lord Roberts was privately informed of India's intentions by Kitchener with such clarity that he could be left in no doubt as to the voraciousness of India's appetite for reserves: 'Our memo was so worded as only not to tie ourselves down absolutely to these figures. We may want more.'[32] At this point the CID sought to impose its answer to the Orenburg–Tashkent railway upon India by asking the Prime Minister to urge on the Government of India the importance of proceeding with the construction of a railway up the Kabul river.[33] This would increase the speed of the Empire's arrival in Afghanistan and thus decrease the need for additional numbers.

Indian reaction, when it came, was of an unexpected ferocity and laid itself open to accusations of *lèse-majesté*. Carefully focusing on the sensitive Persian area, the Government of India totally rejected any notion of the solution of the problem by diplomatic means. An alliance with Germany was strongly deprecated since her interests were likely to clash with the Empire's, and there was even less sympathy for an agreement with Russia. In the view of Calcutta, Russia would never fight in strength in Persia since she had so many other frontiers to guard, and there was equally little to fear from an international combination blocking a forward move by Britain. The strategic policy suggested therefore was to make it quite clear to Russia that any attempt on her part to advance on Tabriz or Meshed would at once be followed by a British move on the gulf ports of Bushire and Bandar Abbas, and possibly even the occupation of Ispahan in the heart of Persia.[34] Such a view revealed little sympathy with the problems of diplomats feeling for the niceties of any foreign relationship, and was utterly different in its conception of likely international reaction from that which the Foreign Office would have put forward.

The War Office now came into open conflict with India's civil administration and with Foreign Office opinion. Sir William Robertson had examined the question of a Persian entanglement in 1902 and had reached the conclusion that the Empire should at all costs try to keep out of it. 100,000 men would be necessary to control the area and there was at the same time the threat of more Russian troops in Afghanistan when the railways were complete. More men would then be necessary for the Northwest Frontier, and Robertson had no doubt which was the more important priority: 'The provision of these additional men should be our first and immediate care'.[35] Altham put the dilemma even more plainly in a minute on Robertson's appreciation: 'There is in fact no sound solution of the Persian question if we adhere to our present lines of military organisation and to our present policy of isolation from all European alliances.'[36] The farthest the Empire should go, in the opinion of the War Office, was the occupation of Seistan.

The Foreign Office representative in Tehran, Sir A. Hardinge, informed Lord Lansdowne that he would go farther than the military and occupy Ispahan should Russia enter Tabriz and Meshed.[37] Subsequently he again sought to bring the Foreign Secretary around to the view that the military policy proposed was tantamount to an abdication of the British position in Persia. His fear was that Russia would enter the country, create a Russian Egypt and then withdraw, forcing Britain simultaneously to withdraw from her tiny enclaves of Seistan and Bandar Abbas.[38] The dispute had not at that time been resolved but India had now resuscitated it and with it the possibility of a deep cleavage of opinion.

Viewed from the Indian end, the problem of defending the sub-continent had become immensely involved as it spread to include consideration of Afghanistan and of Persia, as well as of the technicalities of railway building and railway capacity. In March 1904, therefore, the military authorities changed their approach to it. They now began to put forward two arguments against providing the vast numbers India seemed to require, both of which were closely related: that the nature of the military organization meant the numbers simply were not forthcoming and that in any case they ought not to be provided. These arguments arose in part as a justification of another, and distinct problem, whether or not Britain should follow most major military powers and introduce conscription.

Lord Roberts, a fervent believer in the danger of invasion despite the *ex cathedra* pronouncements of the navy, suggested that the prime task must be to calculate the numbers necessary for home defence. This done, he believed that a first reinforcement would be limited to 14,677 and the second to 53,000, of which some might perforce be militia. According to his calculations, this left at home 85,000 troops 'which would not, I think, be one too many under the conditions we are considering'.[39] The aim of the Commander-in-Chief, which he felt he had now achieved, was by this approach to make Balfour aware of 'the real state of the army' and of the impossibility of undertaking a war against a European power under existing conditions.[40]

Support for Roberts's view came from the newly-appointed Director of Military Operations, Sir James Grierson, who admitted that he, too, believed in compulsory service. Grierson pointed out that in theory Britain could if she used all her resources send overseas rather more than the 100,000 requested; however, if she did so then the units remaining would be so weak as to be unfit to take the field. He felt that the Volunteers were quite incapable of providing for the defence of the United Kingdom, and this no doubt accounted in large part for his belief that 'from the point of view of Imperial defence, it is more important to have good troops in the so-called expeditionary force than in the reinforcements to be sent to India'.[41] Grierson was expressing the view which came increasingly into predominance as the General Staff developed, that its responsibilities were widespread and that even an object of such importance as the defence of India could not necessarily be held to be its sole, chief, or even immediate responsibility.

During the previous month the Prime Minister had been unwell, so that the CID had not considered the Indian question for some time. When, during March, it did so, it came to two decisions. Despite the eloquent arguments of Roberts and Grierson, it agreed to transmit an immediate reinforcement of 30,000 on the outbreak of war provided two conditions were fulfilled: that naval conditions allowed it and that South Africa remained quiet. It further agreed to a second reinforcement after six months consisting of 50,000 Regulars and 19,000 Militia.[42] In addition, it emphasized its faith in the policy of railway construction by requesting that the Government of India be told to push on railway construction up to the Afghan frontier.[43] The response from India was to admit that the extension of the Kabul river railway to Dakka was feasible, but to hold off from attempting it until the autumn in order to try to reach an agreement with the Amir about its outlet.

In all the tangled discussions about railway capacity and possible Russian plans, there was some danger that the importance of Afghan intentions might be lost to view. However, even Lord Selborne, the First Lord of the Admiralty, who held firmly to an offensive war if Russia should ever cross the Afghan frontier, admitted that all hung on the attitude of the Amir and his tribesmen 'in respect of which we are as much in the dark now as we were 20 years ago'.[44] The Prime Minister certainly believed that the dangers faced on the Indian frontier could only be fully met by diplomatic means, and the Committee of Imperial Defence noted both that this was the case and that there was little that they or the home government could do about it since this was a question of Indian diplomacy.[45]

To rest policy on the belief that diplomacy both should and would afford a solution to the Indian dilemma was a luxury beyond the means of the War Office. To the Commander-in-Chief in India such a luxury was positively sinful. Kitchener responded to previous War Office memoranda on 15 April with a paper which revealed more clearly than anything hitherto his mystical qualities. It began with the proposition—rather more an article of faith to its author—that Russia possessed not only leisure and unlimited manpower with which to prepare for a campaign, but also a screen which British intelligence sources could never penetrate. Thus schemes such as those put forward by the War Office, based on seemingly mechanistic assumptions about the probable notice of declarations of war and the like, were of a 'certain academic interest but they cannot be regarded as serious contributions to the solution of this problem'.[46]

Kitchener's basic recommendations were that the Empire should increase its force levels in India and at the same time make a clear declaration of intent to Russia. He assumed completion of the Termez to Samarkand section of the Orenburg–Tashkent railway, which would take one year and which the War Office had ignored; he also made several criticisms of the estimates of carrying capacity generally, remarking that were Russia to couple two engines to a train instead of one it could pull up to fifty wagons. The basis of his criticisms was that in the War Office memoranda the Russians were made to move too slowly and the Imperial forces too quickly.

The Director of Military Operations, called upon to comment on Kitchener's interpretation, remarked that it was unduly pessimistic in its assumptions about Russia's being able to collect vast bodies of troops behind an impenetrable screen. He also added a new dimension to the battle over transportation by pointing out that to the General Staff the chief difficulty facing Russia was the movement and feeding of troops beyond the railheads. Grierson was able to point out in the course of his rebuttal that some of the figures which Kitchener disputed, notably the speed with which a British force could advance, were based on those of the Indian Mobilization Branch. He also pointed out that in order to arrive at definite conclusions about defending the frontier of India it was necessary in the first place that the Indian authorities prepare a comprehensive scheme and submit it to the CID for consideration: 'no scheme properly so-called . . . has yet been received and, as far as is known, none has been prepared.'[47]

Early in May, Grierson was commenting for the CID on just such a scheme as the one he had said was lacking: the results of a war game played by Kitchener and his staff in Simla the previous autumn. The scenario had envisaged the completion of the Orenburg–Tashkent railway as far as Termez and the Afghan frontier and an attack by 300,000 Russian troops on an augmented Indian Field Army of nine divisions. Chiefly owing to the effective development of the Russian railway network into Afghanistan, a series of remorseless victories had put 74,000 Russians on a line from Quetta to Jalalabad by January 1904. It was precisely this facet of Kitchener's calculations which came under the most severe attack by Grierson. He pointed out that in the Far East Japan was currently constructing railways at a maximum rate of less than two-thirds of a mile a day, in an ideal situation as regarded labour, facilities and terrain. Kitchener had the Russians building in an infinitely less favourable environment at a rate of 152 miles in 152 days.[48] Grierson also criticized Kitchener's *Kriegspiel* for assuming that Russia would be allied with France while England was isolated, and that the Russians could collect the 200,000 camels necessary to supply their troops in front of the railheads.

As the strategic discussions were reaching new levels of complexity, with accusations and counter-assertions about the capacities of railways being marshalled by both sides, two vital influences were being ignored. The Russo-Japanese War had begun in February 1904, and it was beginning to seem possible that Russian military power was going to suffer a setback in Manchuria. This had little effect in the minds of most of those engaged in the controversy. The most extreme exemplar of this school, Lord Kitchener, gave it as his view that 'we shall have some time thanks to the Japs', but added that 'at the end of the present war there may be a critical moment between us and Russia'.[49] It was to be left to a new participant in the debate to explode this supposition. At the same time, Sir Charles Hardinge was obeying instructions from Lansdowne to follow up earlier expressions of good intent made by Benckendorff, the Russian Ambassador. Lansdowne was concerned to get some form of general agreement from Russia rather than a particular one, so that diplomacy here offered no immediate prospect of solving the Indian dilemma, and his hopes were being skilfully fostered with assertions that other questions besides that of Tibet might be solved in an agreeable and friendly manner.[50]

In an attempt to clear away at least one part of the problem, the CID now turned its attentions specifically to the question of Seistan. Curzon's views were put before it afresh in the form of yet another paper from him, though it was little more than an expansion of his earlier ones. The crux of his argument now was that Seistan was a much easier place to defend than Balfour made it out to be, and that if Russia were to be allowed into it unmolested the natural resources of the area would be of invaluable benefit to her.[51] Since it was the firm belief of the General Staff that Russia would concentrate her efforts in the north, against Kabul, there was a fundamental difference of opinion to be overcome.

On 9 June there took place at the CID what Roberts subsequently termed 'a great discussion' on Seistan.[52] The idea was postulated that a small force at Robat, in British territory, might check the growth of Russian influence and prestige in the area, though in war it might not be possible to safeguard it. The conclusion reached by the committee was that Kitchener should be telegraphed to give his opinion about the desirability of such a project and whether he would advocate occupying Seistan as part of the defence of India.[53] This was something of a sop to Curzon, but before it was reached he had come in for some rough handling. Lord Roberts, generally to be regarded as India's watchdog on the committee, came out against Seistan as a theatre of operations, and Curzon and Lansdowne had a sharp difference of opinion over whether the British Ambassador in Persia had done all that might be done to safeguard British interests there.[54] The general sense of the meeting was strongly against the Curzon line on Seistan.

July brought attacks on Curzon's Indian strategy from all directions. Kitchener himself had now come to think that pushing a railway forward to Seistan would be a mistake.[55] In London, Grierson considered the prospect of a Russian advance from Seistan on Nushki, and found that it would be possible only after a good rainy season; even then the state of the roads, lack of supplies and need for transport would fix the maximum size of such a force at 10,000 men. Though possible, such an advance was improbable; the most that he expected was a raiding party some 4,000 strong.[56] And from the recently appointed secretary to the CID, Sir George Clarke, came the first of a long series of salvoes in which he stated categorically that there was no probability of a development of Russian strength on the Afghan frontier for some years in view of the international situation. Wild projects of aggression against India, remarked Clarke, 'if they exist outside the brains of ambitious Russian military officers, will be quite beyond chance of realisation'.[57] Clarke's words would be echoed later in the year in the remark of Hartwig, Russian Minister of Foreign Affairs, to Sir Charles Hardinge that any ambitions to invade Afghanistan were 'only to be found in the most shallow brains of the military classes'.[58]

None the less, the estimates from India mounted remorselessly. In August the CID received a defence scheme based on the *Kriegspiel* figures which calculated that by the end of the twelfth month of a campaign 189,581 troops would be needed to face 160,000 Russians. Because of the estimated effect of the Termez railway, the entire Indian Field Army would be committed within four months of a declaration of war, and heavy reinforcements would be needed from England, to the tune of 113,694 men in one year. Moreover, the warning was issued that this figure was 'the minimum by which we may be able to obtain moderate security'. Kitchener, believing the wastage allowance too low and that there would be a need for subsidiary expeditions, raised the figure to 135,614, remarking that in any case he considered the figures for available camels and rates of railway construction too low: 'The Russians could doubtless do more.'[59]

The cost of defending India was becoming astronomical, and there was no hope of meeting it even should circumstances allow of such a course. As the actual strength of the army stood early in August, a reinforcement of 91,000 would use up the whole of the Regular army and Reserves and leave behind in England twenty line battalions for which there were insufficient troops to make mobilization a feasible proposition.[60] The question now seemed more pressing than ever because Balfour was anxious lest the neutral powers be called on to settle the points at issue between Russia and Japan, when there was a strong possibility of trouble on the Northwest Frontier.[61] This danger soon diminished, but was to be followed by other spurs to action.

Lord Roberts launched the first challenge against the most recent Indian estimates, motivated by his own favourite design which was to build railways right up to the Afghan frontier regardless of the feelings of the Amir. It was because the Viceroy had wasted money on a Quetta–Nushki line rather than on lines to Dakka and Kurram that he levelled the charge that 'Three valuable years have been lost since Curzon became Viceroy.'[62] It was this which lay behind his taking up an unremarked point in the India calculations: the number of camels necessary to supply troops ahead of their railheads. To feed the proposed five divisions in Kabul, thirty-one days' journey from their railhead, would require a minimum of 234,794 camels, excluding any allowance for animal fodder.[63] Hence, Roberts argued, the solution to this logistics problem was to extend the railways forward.

At this moment, the forward policy began to receive strong attack *au fond*. It came from a new angle, and one revealed by the Viceroy himself before the CID: what should the policy be towards Afghanistan and her army? Curzon thought it better from the Imperial point of view that the Afghan army remain a disorganized and ineffective rabble; however, he was forced to add that his own military authorities favoured using British officers to train it to a higher state of efficiency. Curzon's own solution was to supply the Amir with arms to the extent of one third of the amounts he requested.[64] Such a policy risked alienating the Amir, and also carried the concomitant that it would be India which would first be facing such well-armed foes. Sir George Clarke began battering the Prime Minister with memoranda arguing that Afghanistan should be left quite alone except for trade questions, that the role of aggressor should be left to Russia and that in such an event Afghanistan would turn to the Empire for help anyway.[65] In this sense Clarke's arguments were running counter to both Kitchener's and Curzon's for he was questioning whether a forward policy was necessary at all where they and the General Staff, as participants in the debate, swapped largely unsupported assertions about transport in an endeavour to modify their policy whilst ignoring its fundamental validity.

To the broad question of whether a forward policy should be put into operation at all, Clarke's answer was that it was time enough to wait for the construction of the Termez spur of the Orenburg–Tashkent railway. This would offer a good pretext and satisfy Afghan opinion.[66] On the more precise question of India's mathematical calculations, he offered the opinion that the data which formed their basis were 'absolutely fallacious' and suggested that the scheme be returned to India for reconsideration by the railway experts there.[67]

Further activity in the intellectual sphere was interrupted when, on the night of 21–22 October, the Russian Baltic Fleet on its way to the Far East inadvertently bombarded British trawlers on the Dogger Bank in the mistaken belief that they were torpedo boats. There was never any question of Russia permitting this to escalate into a full-scale war with Britain, and all the resources of diplomacy were used to mend the breach in relations between the two powers.[68] None the less, the War Office spent a hectic week going over its mobilization plans. The whole issue of the Northwest Frontier might well have come more to the fore, and the forward school had its way in strategic debate, had the Tsar not refused to allow an experiment involving the movement of a full Russian division to Turkestan by way of the Orenburg–Tashkent railway some seven days prior to the North Sea clash.[69]

Clarke's criticism of the Simla *Kriegspiel* made its mark on Balfour and early in November the Secretary of State for India wrote to Kitchener informing him of the Prime Minister's suggestion that he consult his railway authorities afresh.[70] Balfour had had a long talk with Curzon on the evening of 9 November, in which he totally failed to shake the Viceroy in his conviction that the main Russian advance on India would be by way of Seistan. To his argument that it would be a combination of financial, military and naval developments that would force peace on one side or another in the event of a war between the two powers, Curzon could only respond lamely that at least his own plan saved Seistan.[71] His amanuensis tried to put across a similar view to Kitchener in India. Writing a little over a week after Balfour's meeting with Curzon, Clarke forcefully put the view that an agreement with the Amir should omit anything which might be interpreted as a *casus belli*, binding upon Britain. Clarke's view was based on the conviction that there were 'so many possibilities arising on the European chessboard' that Britain could not be sure of concentrating her whole military resources upon that corner of the Empire.[72]

The question of the volume of Imperial resources which India could absorb, of which Clarke was all too conscious, appeared in a heightened form early in the same month; a telegram from the Viceroy on 5 November put the latest estimate in the event of an Anglo-Russian war at 143,686 officers and men within nine months of the outbreak. Balfour reported the new demand, which he inexplicably gave as 158,000, to the CID together with the opinion of the Adjutant-General that if they were met to the extent even of 100,000 men 'there will be no troops left for any other Imperial purpose'.[73]

Pressure now began to mount against the notion that India could or should in any sense dictate to the Cabinet in London. At a CID meeting late in November Austen Chamberlain urged the committee to stick to its earlier decision of 100,000 as the maximum to be committed to India.[74] At the same time, Clarke privately warned Balfour that compliance with Kitchener's demands 'will have the effect of making India the predominant partner in Imperial defence'. This was in itself undesirable; and it was the more so since the basis of India's demands was the *Kriegspiel*, which Clarke regarded as puerile:[75]

The great factors of war—supply and communications— are either ignored or absolutely miscalculated. Great masses of men are moved across the most difficult country in the world as if they were pawns on a chess board. Railways are assumed to be made at prarie speed over routes which in some parts prohibit railway construction except as an engineering feat requiring a long time, a great supply of labour, and freedom from all interruption. In other parts, it is even doubtful whether a railway could be made at all.

It was, Clarke reminded the Prime Minister, for the Cabinet at home to decide when the occasion arose whether it was desirable to commit the whole of the country's military resources to India, not for the Government of India to do so. The more men were allowed to India, the more ambitious would her plans become. He suggested operating the procedure in reverse; Britain should determine the numbers she could afford to commit—say 50,000— and Indian strategy should be devised on the basis of that figure.

The homily delivered by Clarke had its effect upon Balfour, for early in December he wrote himself to Kitchener to inform him that he was 'profoundly disturbed' by relations between the two countries. They were, he felt, more like allied states than parts of a single Empire, the Indian part of which was growing in independence and thereby making common action difficult. It was just this division which Balfour hoped, wrongly as it turned out, that the nascent General Staff would bridge. He also gave the Indian Commander-in-Chief a sharp reminder of his own political responsibilities as Prime Minister; were India successfully invaded, the moral and material losses would be great 'but the burden of British taxation would undergo a most notable diminution'.[76] There were growing signs that India had finally demanded too much.

Coincidentally this phase in the strategic debate over India occurred at a time when Esher and Clarke, with Balfour's connivance, were attempting to prevent Arnold Forster from wreaking havoc on the British army. The Secretary of State had proposed an army split into three parts: a long service segment, serving nine years with the colours and designed for colonial service, a short service segment serving one and three-quarter years with the colours for home defence, and a Militia liable for foreign service. Such a structure, which three members of the Army Council bitterly opposed and most interested parties viewed with acute suspicion, would provide troops for India.

Indeed Arnold Forster was using the Indian problem as one of his main planks. At all costs it was felt that the Aldershot Command must be kept out of Arnold Forster's clutches, since it represented the only autonomous, fully trained and fully equipped striking force in the country. Thus Esher now put forward the notion that the Aldershot divisions would never be sent to India whatever the situation, and further that they might possibly have to fight on the continent.[77] This argument was further fuel for the opponents of Kitchener's and Curzon's grandiose schemes.

1905 brought two fresh factors into the calculations of future Russian strategy towards India: the fall of Port Arthur and the first Russian Revolution. The former swayed opinion in London toward the view that Russia was now too crippled to attempt any immediate incursion into Afghanistan after the war in Manchuria was over. The latter seems to have made its mark only in the mind of Sir George Clarke. There was yet another setback for Curzon's *quondam* policy of controlling the Persian Gulf when the navy questioned his policy of hoisting British flagstaffs as fruitless and unlikely to deny harbours to an enemy.[78] The Viceroy was none the less working assiduously to bring his policy towards the Helmund valley into fruition; he reported to Balfour late in January that the Amir had received his suggestion about renting a portion of the area favourably, and had even suggested it himself.[79] However, debate hung fire during the first month of the new year awaiting the results of a reworking of the *Kriegspiel* figures by the General Staff.

Clarke got the first sight of the paper late in January, and was somewhat depressed by what he found. It was, he contended, more carefully worked out than the previous General Staff memoranda, but it was still too sanguine about the proposed rate of railway construction that Russia could achieve. He could conceive of nothing, he informed the Prime Minister, 'more difficult than railway making in a hill country occupied by well-armed tribesmen'.[80] The memorandum itself bore out much of Clarke's criticism. It was based, at Balfour's behest, on the postulates that Russian assembly would not be secret, that the Termez railway would be completed, and that a slower rate of bridge construction was possible than Kitchener had made out. Much closer analysis than hitherto had been given to rates of railway building in Manchuria, and this showed in a more complex calculation of the number of trains per day that a given length of line could accommodate.[81]

Assuming that the railways to the Hindu Kush and to Farah took fifteen months to build, the General Staff had no doubts that Russia could in that time amass a force of 400,000 and that the Central Asian Railway and Orenburg–Tashkent railway between them could support such a force. The physical difficulties facing the southern prong of an advance into Afghanistan were rather greater than those in the north; accordingly it was estimated that while there might be 40,000 Russians in Kabul by the end of the sixth month of war, it would be the sixteenth month before 100,000 Russians would be at Dilaram and in striking distance of Kandahar. Judged by these criteria, the Indian army alone could cope with both fronts until the end of the fourth month of war when Great Britain would then have to supply the needs on the Kabul front; but since there would be no increase in Russian troops there for a further four months, the first British reinforcements need not arrive until the eighth month. The figures calculated as necessary amounted to 211,824 between the eighth and fifteenth months of war, of which 98,224 would be required between the fifteenth and sixteenth months.[82]

Though the General Staff had done as the Prime Minister wished, they were manifestly in disagreement with the figures which resulted. A coda pointed out that the railway rate might well be too low and that no account had been taken of hostile Afghan tribesmen; equally no provision had been made for Russian moves against the Chitral or Seistan. Moreover, the scenario envisaged neither side having any allies, an increasingly unlikely occurrence, when not much could be done to Russia elsewhere. Again, it was Clarke who was most alive to the latter point. In mid-February he urged Balfour to take the wider view of Indian defence, remarking that he was himself 'more than ever sure that the best first line of defence of the Indian frontier is to be found in the Foreign Office'.[83] However, there was little that Clarke's exhortations could do against Lansdowne's determination to secure a general agreement with Russia rather than deal in specific issues.

It was perhaps the complexity of the issues involved which caused the subject to drift in the following month. Clarke pleaded for some clear policy over the Persian Gulf as a necessary preliminary to solving the Afghan problem, since the Indian

Government wanted an extension of Imperial influence while the Foreign Office wanted to sustain the *status quo*.[84] It was he who took the General Staff's logic a step further in asserting that if the Afghans were not hostile to Russia, the assumption made in the General Staff's paper, then they would be hostile to Imperial forces, in which case any question of advancing to the Kabul–Kandahar line must be abandoned anyway. In any case, he challenged the assumption that Russia would make straight for Kabul and Kandahar; in his opinion she would occupy Herat and Afghan Turkestan, from which it would be very difficult to evict her. Clarke was endeavouring to gain acceptance for the belief that an invasion of the type forecast in the Simla *Kriegspiel* was 'out of the question for twenty years'.[85] What had first to be determined was whether Britain would consider a Russian occupation of Herat and Afghan Turkestan a *casus belli*, and what action she would take as a result.

That Clarke's mind moved too quickly and too hypothetically for the Committee of Imperial Defence was revealed in mid-April, when Grierson remarked that he had asked for full information about pack animals in preparing his paper but that India had not sent it. The question was of some importance since it would take two and a half years to complete the Peshawar–Dakka line, and even then it would be 140 miles from Kabul. As a consequence of this intervention, Balfour requested that Lord Roberts put to the Government of India 'certain specific questions' about how they intended to keep in the field the vast numbers of reinforcements they had requested.[86]

The strategic debates over numbers had hitherto been chiefly, if not exclusively, occupied with the question of rail transport and its potentiality. Now in turn the various proponents came to realize that the issue of transportation beyond the railheads was as important as that of the railheads themselves and perhaps more so. Roberts opened the new phase with a paper calculating that 234,794 camels would be needed to maintain five divisions at Kabul; and since only 57,348 appeared to be available in India, such a venture was strewn with obstacles.[87] The General Staff worked on calculations which demonstrated to their own satisfaction that Kabul and Kandahar theatres together would require 441,170 camels, of which 180,000 were available—Lord Roberts was informed that he had misread the telegram on which his figures were based. Astute use of bullock carts could reduce the figure to 211,694 camels. Their argument was somewhat weakened, and the stringency of their calculations cast into doubt, when they admitted that their underwriting of Kitchener's reinforcements was based partly on the conviction that with his vast experience of transport he would never contemplate employing a large force unless he was satisfied that enough transport was available.[88]

At a meeting of the CID on 17 May the question of animal transport was raised for the first time. Brodrick pressed for India's figures on transport needed to mobilize and keep in the field the units she had requested, whereupon Roberts offered his doubts as to the feasibility of the operation, based on his own paper.[89] Grierson reported that the resources around Kabul would support two divisions for one year, which would relieve the strains upon transport resources, a statement with which Roberts publicly disagreed. It was left for the two to look further into the matter. In the same month, the General Staff also made a plaintive attempt to remind the CID that the very arrival of reinforcements in India at all was a matter of conjecture. No decision about the transportation of troops had been made since the navy had reported in June 1903 that convoys could not be provided with escorts. How far, the committee was asked, should the protection of trade outweigh the protection of transports? And was there no middle course between a big convoy and single transports?[90] As it happened the camel question assumed a predominance over this vital issue.

At this juncture, Sir George Clarke abandoned his oblique attacks upon Kitchener and his fellow-believers in Russian aggression, perhaps recognizing that the subtleties of diplomatic assessment were failing to move them, and turned his attentions to the camel question. To resolve the issue once and for all he called into service the hitherto untried tool of calculus. Basing his figures on a requirement of 1,600 camel loads to feed one Indian division for one day, Clarke computed that according to the distance from their bases (7–15 marches) and the local provision of fodder, to supply five Indian divisions for one year would require between 302,000 and 3,056,000 camels. As he later remarked to Kitchener, the result of his mathematics was 'rather startling'.[91] The conclusion Clarke drew from this exercise was that, even with railways to the Afghan frontiers, it would be as impossible for the Empire to maintain five divisions in Afghan Turkestan as for Russia to occupy Kabul with an equal force:[92]

The working of huge numbers of animals backwards and forwards on these mountain routes, of which all except one are closed for at least four months during the year, and where in many places camels cannot pass each other, is impracticable.

Clarke's attempt to introduce a new rigour into examinations of the Indian problem had to overcome profound sentiments of the importance of prestige in maintaining the Empire. Such sentiments were the basis of Kitchener's suggestions as to future policy which were founded on the twin beliefs that Russia had not been crippled for a generation by the set-backs she had met with in Manchuria, and that she had a policy of establishing herself in Afghanistan in order to recover the prestige she had lost in the Far East. His own forecast now placed direct invasion as secondary to a policy of gradual encroachment which, no matter what its scale, should be regarded as 'an act of war which we must resist with all means at the disposal of the Empire'.[93] His policy was one of controlling the tribes in the regions of the Kabul and Kurram rivers and co-operating with the Amir. The same concern with prestige impelled the General Staff's recommendation that if Russia occupied Herat and Afghan Turkestan then Britain should advance to the Kabul–Kandahar line, and further if necessary, in order to meet and defeat the Russians.[94] It was hard to combat such intangible beliefs, amounting in some cases to dogma, with numerical calculation; and in any case, Clarke himself was not entirely free of them. He confided only to Esher one strong reason why he opposed Kitchener's strategic redistribution of the army: that he felt 'great aggregations of native troops . . . to be a mistake and a danger', and that concentration towards the frontier would make it difficult to suppress a rising.[95]

August was a month of defeat, admitted and implied, in resolving the growing number of problems relating to the defence of India. In reply to the General Staff's demands for special precautions to provide 'reasonable security' for troop transports before command of the sea might be won, Sir John Fisher adopted his customary stand of stone-walling. Such considerations were, he informed the CID, part of a general plan for the protection of mercantile shipping in time of war, and he therefore requested that consideration of this question be postponed until the new scheme had been finally approved.[96] Meanwhile the Prime Minister was admitting that his government had failed to find and get adopted an army organization which had the necessary powers of expansion to reinforce India to the tune of over 100,000 men.[97] His unspoken implication was that there was little chance that it would ever do so. Clarke set the General Staff examining the problem posed by Belgium's position in a Franco-German war partly in the hope that they might be rather more successful than they had been in dealing with the Indian problem.[98]

The autumn saw Balfour's administration travel through its last few months of office, the Prime Minister himself being too involved in the difficulties posed by the situation to give his customary attention to matters of Indian defence. He did admit to Clarke that he thought Kitchener's forward policy foolish since it risked a rupture with Afghanistan whilst at the same time aiming at keeping the frontier tribes innocuous.[99] Clarke for his part felt that the Indian Commander-in-Chief was deliberately raising a scare in order to justify an additional expenditure of £2,500,000 which his reorganization scheme would throw onto the Indian budget.[100] This was probably an unjust accusation, since the tenor of Kitchener's strategic pronouncements fitted too well with his narrow mental outlook to be the product of special pleading.

Balfour betrayed a growing irritation with the Indian authorities in the dying months of his premiership. He agreed emphatically with Clarke that the time was propitious for a general agreement with Russia encompassing Central Asia, Afghanistan and Persia.[101] Unfortunately such a concept ran counter to the methods of his Foreign Secretary, and even Lansdowne's successor was to hold off for two and a half years before applying this remedy. Had he continued in office, Balfour's determination to enforce on India the admission that she was the junior partner might have resulted in a victory of views of the Clarke variety.

As it was, the sole contributions to the problem were the printing by the CID of a paper written by Balfour nineteen months previously which pointed to the dangers of Russian encroachment into Persia and tacitly admitted that there was no effective action Britain could take without at the same time taking on commitments she could not possibly fulfil, and a further piece of calculus from Clarke. This was based on a revision of the amounts of forage needed for transport animals and now demonstrated that to keep 155,000 Russians poised before Kabul and Kandahar would require 2,521,846 camels for a short period and 5,043,692 for a long one.[102] A realistic estimate of the troops Russia could supply in Kabul was 6,000 in summer and only 1,500 in winter when two of the four available passes would be closed.

During the winter of 1905–6 the Indian question settled into the background of strategic concerns. In part this was due to the multiplicity of factors surrounding the Moroccan crisis and the beginnings of Anglo-French military conversations; so serious was the crisis that supplies of the new field gun destined for India were held back in England in case they should be needed nearer to home. Clarke probably spoke for all when he justified this decision to Kitchener by expressing the belief that for the moment 'the danger is in Europe and not in India'.[103] But of equal importance was the drastic change of heart suffered by Kitchener. Once Curzon had ceased to be Viceroy, his attitude towards excursions into Seistan and Persia changed completely. Of the former he informed Clarke that 'You are quite right I am opposed to the wild projects that have been put forward with regard to Seistan.'[104] With regard to Persia, he was convinced that India could undertake no fresh responsibilities with her present resources; realizing that she was unlikely to increase those resources, he therefore opposed any action likely to precipitate matters there.[105] This *volte-face* culminated in his asking Clarke to dispel any impressions that he believed in the Russian bogey: 'I do believe in a possibility but recent events have for the time placed it far away in the background of probabilities.'[106]

Kitchener's conversion was certainly not occasioned by Clarke's mathematical calculations, for he remained resolutely unconvinced by the figures. None the less, his response encouraged Clarke to try to bury the Seistan project permanently. A bitter critique of Indian strategists as victims of a self-imposed cult of strategic speculation provided his starting point for pulverizing Curzon's scheme of the previous summer. Seistan was totally unsuitable as a concentration area for an army, he informed the CID; its total annual export of 18,000 tons would feed an army of 200,000 men and 40,000 horses for only forty days. The region was valueless without a railway, and if it came to a race to build one in wartime India could easily win it by reason of the terrain between her and Seistan. The burden of these arguments was that every possible measure should be taken to avoid provoking Russia; the reason was that otherwise such rash action would 'effectually destroy the possibility of an arrangement to the permanent advantage of both nations'.[107]

Clarke's was not the only mind veering towards the prospects of some kind of diplomatic solution to the Indian problem, a course which by his sanction of the informal military conversations with France Grey might seem to favour. At a meeting of the CID in March, Haldane asked the Foreign Secretary how the Russo-Japanese War and the Anglo-French *entente* had affected the probabilities of Russian aggression, in connection with his scheme to re-organize the structure of the army. Grey replied that in his opinion Russia was for some years to come incapable of undertaking a serious campaign against India. He then added that relations between the two powers were becoming more friendly than of late, and informed his audience that in the last fortnight Russia had expressed a wish to open negotiations along the lines of the Anglo-French *entente*.[108]

Grey was in the event to follow the path set by Lansdowne, holding off negotiations but hoping for some sort of general agreement. Thus it was not for some eighteen months that diplomacy would provide the resolution of the Indian problem. To extrapolate from the Anglo-French conversations that Grey was prepared to use diplomacy to solve strategic problems would have been an error: they were an experiment, which he sanctioned only in the belief that there would be no war.[109] Grey also had to guide him an appreciation of the strategic factors involved in an Anglo-Russian *entente* which began by emphasizing the need to abstain from suspicious action, and concluded by recommending the building of railway extensions up to Dakka and Peiwar Kotal while Russia was still in a crippled state.[110] This somewhat contradictory advice was reached via the conclusion that the Central Asian railways were the most dangerous threat to India, but that it was difficult to request Russia to desist with strategic lines since this meant distinguishing them from the commercially necessary lines. Moreover the author, Sir William Robertson, argued that such a mutual embargo would work more against Britain than Russia, since the latter had not to cross difficult and turbulent country before reaching the Afghan frontier.

The Indian question assumed a decreasing importance as the spring and summer wore on; in Clarke's words, 'nothing is less probable than Russian aggression of the nature of a move towards India for some years'.[111] Yet this was only a passing substitute for a decision, and a poor one at that. Clarke endeavoured to produce the decision he favoured by yet more mathematics, this time demonstrating that in perfect conditions a railway taking eighteen trains per day could supply 375,000 troops, and in the face of scanty water supplies such as obtained in Afghanistan and allowing four hours intermission in twenty-four for maintenance, that number shrank to 90,000.[112] No decision would therefore be reached on the Afghan frontier inside some two and a half years. The 'Bolt from the Blue' applied as little to India as to an invasion of the United Kingdom.

At the CID meeting on 25 May, Clarke unjustly informed members that Balfour had been unwilling to give a decision about the number of troops to be earmarked for India, seeking to encourage the Liberal party to do what the Conservatives had failed to do. Haldane held out against any definite undertaking, and thereby clashed with Morley who was under the illusion that the question had been decided and urged emotionally that a pledge should be made to India in general terms. Grey turned the scales with his report that the military weakness of Russia had absolutely changed the situation and that any operation on the Indian frontier by her was now out of the question. As a result, the committee concluded that no definite undertaking should be given to supply a specified number of troops to India.[113] The CID would not discuss the Indian question again during the year.

Perhaps the clearest indication that Kitchener would never get the troops he so stoutly demanded came from Esher, himself a dedicated believer in the necessity to provide India with a strong defence. After confidentially informing Kitchener that the CID would support further railway building 'whatever you may hear of Sir George Clarke's opinions', Esher then informed him that it would be dangerous to rely on the supports and reinforcements discussed the preceding year, since Haldane's calculations had shown that they did not exist. He concluded by suggesting that Kitchener might reopen the previous discussions with Balfour on the Russian menace '(say 6 or 7 years hence)'.[114]

Esher was perhaps over-hasty in thus dismissing Clarke's soundly based pleas for a halt in railway-building up to the Afghan frontier. It was Clarke's contention that a halt in railway construction was a prerequisite of negotiations with the Amir, which together with an agreement with Russia were the essential bases for ensuring the security of India. Clarke was firmly convinced of the need for the Cabinet to be in full control of such negotiations, and was also clear in his own mind that the Afghan problem should now properly be treated as a diplomatic one, free from 'schemes of meeting vast Russian armies in that inhospitable country'.[115] In arguing for such a policy, Clarke was in line with the attitudes of both Foreign Office and India Office. On 7 September 1906, Grey authorized an approach to Russia based on her recognizing that Afghanistan lay outside her sphere of influence, though it was to take some six months and more before this came to any sort of fruition.[116] Some few weeks later Morley informed the new Viceroy in India, Lord Minto, that he must not offer or invite proposals from the Amir on his own responsibility, and that His Majesty's Government must know of and sanction all plans or demands made to him.[117] The chief participants in the debate over Indian strategy for the past six years were being replaced, and with new men came new attitudes.

Before the diplomats resolved the problem, the CID was persuaded to set up a special sub-committee to examine the problem of Indian defence and to make authoritative recommendations upon it. This was the outcome of some persuasive talking by Esher, who got Campbell-Bannerman to agree to taking up the problem where Balfour had left it.[118] In securing this sub-committee, Esher was motivated largely by a conviction that Haldane's proposals for the reorganization of the army were gravely inadequate, since they did not relate to war requirements but to the need for economy. His aim was to ensure that the needs of India became the datum line for the reconstruction of the army; 'India is the key' he argued, and to be prepared for a war there was to be prepared for a war anywhere.[119] He was also activated by a temperamental dislike of diplomatic solutions to imperial problems, terming dependence on foreign alliances 'a fatal trap'.[120] When both Haldane and Morley, members of the sub-committee, pressed during its preliminary deliberations that the most realistic and immediate problem was not a Russian invasion but the troops necessary should the frontier become restless, it was Esher who coined the formula that the greater peril encompassed the lesser and thereby ensured that Indian fears were not pushed into the background. The whole tenor of the report was to reflect his conviction that Kitchener was correct in his views of the dangers facing the sub-continent.

The habitual Indian perspective was put to the sub-committee at its first meeting on 22 January 1907 by Sir Beauchamp Duff, Chief of the Indian General Staff and shortly to succeed Kitchener as Commander-in-Chief. India, he informed the committee, could not be defended against Russian aggression with the forces available within it; Persia represented a dangerously open flank, best guarded by a declaration that crossing a geographically defined north-south axis by Russia would mean war.[121] Duff was subsequently 'led' by Esher to formulate the most embarrassing strategic situation, that of Russian absorption of Herat and Afghan Turkestan and then a pause for consolidation.

Duff was to be recalled before the committee on 25 February, when he flatly disagreed with all the railway construction estimates that did not correspond with those computed in India. The solution he then posed to the food problem, which he thought greatly over-rated, was to push forward food from India 'to create great depots of supplies'.[122] At this point Clarke could restrain himself no longer, and dissected Duff's views in a short but harsh passage of cross-examination. He drew from the Indian officer the astonishing opinion that it was harder to supply the current needs of 30,000 civilians in Quetta than it would be to supply all the requirements of 30,000 troops in the field. Clarke also demonstrated beyond all doubt that Duff had no under-standing whatever of the geometric ratio involved in supplying a given number of troops at varying distances from their base.[123]

Abundant evidence was produced to demonstrate the weak-nesses in the Indian case. Duff himself admitted that he had no idea of what forage was in fact available around Kabul for a British force, a vital and integral part of any supply calculations. Sir William Nicholson and Sir Ian Hamilton both drew heavily on their experiences as observers with the Japanese armies in Manchuria to emphasize the immense problems which supply posed in modern war even in more favourable surroundings than Afghanistan, and Nicholson said flatly that it was impossible to maintain five divisions at Kabul and four at Girishk until railway communications had reached those places.[124] Ewart, the Director of Military Operations and a member of the sub-committee, was in no doubts that 'alarmists have greatly exaggerated the facilities for a Russian advance on India', and came to believe that Russia would take at least a year, possibly two, to cross Afghanistan.[125] He accordingly submitted a paper to the sub-committee recommending that in the light of the length of time Russia would need to build her railways India should be sent 20,000 men when war became imminent, when she could then hold out for at least a year; it evoked no response from the committee.[126]

The proponents of the Kitchener view were not to be overcome by such logic. Roberts appeared to echo Duff's appreciation; Esher found the latter's evidence and papers 'quite excellent', and the Chief of the Indian General Staff was wholeheartedly backed by the new Viceroy, who found that he always wrote 'a most excellent minute' and offered it as his belief that India 'could not have found a better man'.[127] Asquith signed the report as a member without having attended any of its hearings. Clarke was so incensed by its recommendations that he did not sign it at all; his subsequent attribution of his failure to influence Indian defence policy to the inability of the British government to control the Indian, if kind to his colleagues, disguised the fact that the cause of his failure lay nearer home.[128] In at least one case it was suggested that an attempt be made to talk a member of the sub-committee round to a more favourable view of the Indian argument—the victim being Ewart.[129]

Whatever the machinations which ensued, the report when it appeared totally ignored the arguments put forward by Clarke and the support given them by other expert witnesses. Indeed it made as its opening statement the point that the relationship between the three variables in Indian policy—the Amir, the tribes and Russia—was 'uncertain, complicated and obscure', as if to justify the rejection of higher mathematics as one way to lessen the obfuscations surrounding it.[130] Militarily, the most likely strategy Russia would adopt was thought to be one of advance by stages, taking Herat and Afghan Turkestan; the solution should be a slightly modified forward policy. The Oxus, the boundary between Russia and Afghanistan, was taken as being the *de facto* Indian frontier from the point of view of defence.

To fulfil the strategy they advocated, the sub-committee

suggested the continued construction of railways towards the Afghan frontier and Dakka, implicitly agreed to Roberts's suggestion of taking control of the border tribes by admitting 'that partial advances of our administrative frontier may possibly from time to time be imposed upon us by the persistent and defiant misdeeds of an individual tribe' and recommended a military organization in England capable of sending 100,000 men to India in the first year of a war.[131] The importance of manpower was the sole lesson they admitted to having absorbed from the Russo-Japanese War. On the one specific question of how many men England would send to India they made no overt recommendation, but suggested obliquely that she should prepare to receive the numbers suggested by Duff in his memorandum—135,500. This was a victory for Kitchener and a major setback for the General Staff.

Morley's sub-committee had justified its action in presuming to impart a strategy for India on the grounds that 'in the absence of diplomacy and convention, it is our business to examine the course of warlike operations'.[132] Fortunately the Foreign Office was about to provide the best solution of the huge problem of preserving India from violation. At the moment when Morley and his colleagues were preparing to re-examine their voluble witness, General Duff, Grey was informed that the chief stumbling block in the way of an Anglo-Russian understanding was crumbling now that the Russian General Staff were 'ready to accept in principle' the need for an understanding between the two powers.[133] It subsequently became apparent that the Russian Chief of the General Staff, General Palitsin, had been motivated in his hostility to Britain in large measure by the exact counterpart of Kitchener's fear of Russia: that the British might move into Afghanistan and thereby stir up the Mohammedan population in Russian Central Asia.[134] Such a prospect having been convincingly repudiated, and the general diplomatic pressures upon Russia being sufficient to impel her to such an agreement, the convention was signed between the two powers on 31 August 1907, and with it the problem of providing for the defence of India became academic.

Subsequent CID papers in the India series were few, and were concerned almost entirely with the question of Persia and the Persian Gulf which were part of the strategies to be adopted against Turkey and then Germany. From the summer of 1907

India ceased to bulk large, indeed to bulk at all, in the cycles of strategic debate in England. Thus the almost untouched issue on which the Kitchener school might come to grief was never seriously debated, and by many people never realized. For in a paper published just prior to the diplomatic settlement the Admiralty announced that while it might manage to transport troops to India when engaged in a single-handed war against Russia, such transport probably could not be convoyed should Russia find herself a partner in an alliance, with either Germany or France.[135] The War Office had already experienced the strategic timorousness of the navy, and its fixation with the decisive battle to win command of the sea. The Committee of Imperial Defence would remain largely in ignorance of the poverty of naval strategic planning until August 1911, when revelation of it would decide the strategy of the war against Germany.

Notes

1 For the history of the Afghan question in the preceding years, *see* D. Dilks, *Curzon in India, 1: Achievement*, London, 1969, pp. 162–5.
2 Memorandum communicated by the Russian Embassy, February 6, 1900. *B.D.* 1, no. 376.
3 Russia: Increase in military force in Central Asia during the Boer War, 5 February 1900, p. 199. P.R.O. 30/40/14./2.
4 Brodrick to Kitchener, 5 January 1901. P.R.O. 30/57/22.
5 Report of a Committee appointed to consider the Military Defence of India, 24 December 1901, pp. 2–4. Cab. 6/1/1D.
6 *Ibid.*, p. 8.
7 *Contra* Dilks, *op. cit.*, p. 183. *See* above, pp. 182, 185.
8 Reply of Indian Government to the Report of the Committee . . . to consider the military defence of India, 21 August 1902, p. 2. Cab. 6/1/2D.
9 *Ibid.*, p. 10.
10 1st meeting of C.I.D. 18 December 1902. Cab. 2/1.
11 Second Report of a Committee appointed to consider the Military Defence of India, 21 August 1902, p. 6. Cab. 6/1/3D.
12 Memorandum on the Defence of India, 10 March 1903, pp. 5, 6. Cab. 6/1/6D.
13 *Ibid.*, pp. 12, 14.
14 Roberts to Kitchener, 27 March 1903. P.R.O. 30/57/28.
15 8th meeting of C.I.D., 26 March 1903. Cab. 2/1.

16 Diary of movements of Russian and British forces in Afghanistan, 7 April 1903, p. 7. Cab. 6/1/11D.

17 Defence of India: Relations with Afghanistan, 30 April 1903, p. 4. Cab. 6/1/12D.

18 12th meeting of C.I.D., 7 May 1903. Cab. 2/1.

19 Defence of India: Replies to questions raised by the Prime Minister at the Meeting of the Committee of Imperial Defence on 7th May 1903, 9 May 1903. Cab. 6/1/14D.

20 (Second Instalment of Draft Conclusions on Indian Defence by Mr Balfour, dealing chiefly with Seistan), 20 May 1903. Cab. 6/1/19D.

21 Defence of India: (1) Estimated maximum force which Russia could assemble in the vicinity of Kabul and Kandahar within one year; (2) Additional British troops required . . . in order that Russia may be opposed in slightly superior strength, 13 June 1903, p. 4. Cab. 6/1/22D.

22 Memorandum to be sent to Lord Curzon and Lord Kitchener with the first two instalments of the memorandum on Indian Defence, 3 July 1903. Cab. 6/1/28D.

23 Curzon to Kitchener, 20 July 1903. P.R.O. 30/57/26.

24 Memorandum . . . on the Provisional Report of the Defence Committee on Indian Defence, 7 August 1903, p. 6. Cab. 6/1/30D.

25 Roberts Papers. Nicholson to Roberts, 24 November 1903. Box X20926, file N2.

26 Defence of India: Observations on the Memorandum dated 7th August 1903 (Paper No. 30D), 11 November 1903, p. 3. Cab. 6/1/31D.

27 Defence of India: Draft reply to memorandum by Lord Curzon and Lord Kitchener, 24 November 1903. Cab. 6/1/32D.

28 Balfour to Brodrick, 17 December 1903. B.M. Add. MSS. 49720.

29 Brodrick to Curzon, 22 December 1903. Cab. 37/67/89.

30 Roberts to Kitchener, 21 May 1903. P.R.O. 30/57/28.

31 (Despatch of Reinforcements and supplies to India in the event of war). Viceroy to Secretary of State for India, 8 January 1904, p. 3. Cab. 6/1/37D.

32 Roberts Papers. Kitchener to Roberts, 28 January 1904. Box X20930, file K.4.

33 30th meeting of C.I.D., 27 January 1904. Cab. 2/1.

34 (British Policy in Persia). Government of India to Secretary of State for India, 4 February 1904. Cab. 6/1/38D.

35 *Ibid.* Attached document No. III: Strategical relations between England and Russia with regard to Persia, 4 October 1902. p. 3.

36 *Ibid.* Minute, 14 October 1902. p. 7.

37 *Ibid.* Attached document No. VI: Hardinge to Lansdowne, 3 January 1903.

38 *Ibid.* Attached document No. VII: Hardinge to Lansdowne, 17 June 1903.

39 What number of troops could be spared for India, 23 March 1904, p. 3. Cab. 6/1/41D.

40 Roberts to Kitchener, 30 March 1904. P.R.O. 30/57/28.
41 Replies to questions as to the existing strength and efficiency of the military forces of the Crown having regard to Indian and Home Defence requirements, 12 March 1904, p. 4. Cab. 6/1/40D.
42 36th meeting of C.I.D. 24 March 1904. Cab. 2/1.
43 34th meeting of C.I.D. 10 March 1904. Cab. 2/1.
44 Roberts Papers. Selborne to Roberts, 3 April 1904. Box X20926, file M. 3.
45 Balfour to Selborne, 6 April 1904. B.M. Add. MSS. 49707. 38th meeting of C.I.D., 15 April 1904. Cab. 2/1.
46 Defence of India: (1) Comments by the Commander-in-Chief in India, dated February 15, 1904, on the War Office Memoranda on the Defence of India, p. 4. Cab. 6/1/45D.
47 Defence of India: Observations on the comments of the Commander-in-Chief in India, dated February 15, 1904, on the War Office memoranda regarding the Defence of India, 18 April 1904, p. 19. Cab. 6/1/45D.
48 Defence of India. Observations on the records of a War Game played at Simla, 1903, 5 May 1904, pp. 9, 10. Cab. 6/1/50D.
49 Kitchener to Roberts, 16 June 1904. P.R.O. 30/57/29.
50 Hardinge to Lansdowne, 18 May and 8 June 1904. B.D. IV, nos. 185, 188.
51 Memoranda supplied by Lord Curzon in regard to the question of Seistan, 2 June 1904, esp. pp. 9–17. Cab. 6/2/52D.
52 Roberts to Kitchener, 10 June 1904. P.R.O. 30/57/28.
53 45th meeting of C.I.D., 9 June 1904. Cab. 2/1.
54 Brodrick to Kitchener, 9 June 1904. P.R.O. 30/57/22.
55 Kitchener to Roberts, 30 June 1904. B.M. Add. MSS. 49725.
56 Defence of India: Information regarding the feasibility of a Russian advance from Seistan via Nushki towards India, 1 July 1904. Cab. 6/2/61D.
57 Indian Defence Number 1, 9 July 1904, p. 1. B.M. Add. MSS. 50836.
58 Hardinge to Lansdowne, 25 September 1904. B.D. IV, no. 192.
59 Defence of India: Estimate of Forces required for the Defence of India during the First Year of a War with Russia, by Colonel H. Mullaly, R. E., with comments by Viscount Kitchener, 30 June 1904, pp. 10, 12. Cab. 6/2/64D.
60 54th meeting of C.I.D., 15 August 1904. Cab. 2/1.
61 Roberts to Kitchener, 11 August 1904. P.R.O. 30/57/28.
62 Roberts to Kitchener, 18 August 1904. P.R.O. 30/57/28.
63 Supplies in Afghanistan: Memorandum by Earl Roberts, 26 August 1904. Cab. 6/2/69D.
64 52nd meeting of C.I.D., 3rd August 1904. Cab. 2/1.
65 Indian Defence Numbers 3 and 4, 2 and 4 August 1904. B.M. Add. MSS. 50836.
66 Clarke to Balfour, 9 August 1904. B.M. Add. MSS. 49700.
67 Clarke to Balfour, 23 September 1904. B.M. Add. MSS. 49700.
68 See B.D. IV, nos. 5–31 for the diplomacy of the incident.

69 Hardinge to Lansdowne, 31 October 1904. *B.D.* IV, No. 24.
70 Brodrick to Kitchener, 11 November 1904. P.R.O. 30/57/22.
71 Balfour to Brodrick, 10 November 1904. B.M. Add. MSS. 49721.
72 Clarke to Kitchener, 18 November 1904. P.R.O. 30/57/34.
73 57th meeting of C.I.D., 16 November 1904. Cab. 2/1. *Vid.*
   Cavalry, Artillery and Infantry Reinforcements for India, 15
   November 1904, p. 2. Cab. 6/2/73D.
74 58th meeting of C.I.D., 22 November 1904. Cab. 2/1.
75 Indian Defence Number 9, 'Sent to A. J. B. 24.11.1904'. B.M.
   Add. MSS. 50836.
76 Balfour to Kitchener, 3 December 1904. B.M. Add. MSS. 49725.
77 Memorandum by Esher on correspondence between the King and
   Mr Arnold Forster, 3 December 1904. B.M. Add. MSS. 49718.
78 Erection of Flagstaffs in the Persian Gulf, 25 January 1905. Cab.
   6/2/76D.
79 Clarke to Balfour, 26 January 1905. B.M. Add. MSS. 49732.
80 Clarke to Balfour, 18 January 1905. B.M. Add. MSS. 49701.
81 Memorandum by the General Staff on the strength in which
   Russia can advance towards India—and the reinforcements
   required by India—based on assumptions laid down by the Prime
   Minister, 16 February 1905, pp. 3, 12–13. Cab. 6/3/77D.
82 *Ibid.*, p. 10.
83 Clarke to Balfour, 16 February 1905. B.M. Add. MSS. 49701.
84 Indian Defence Number 18, 'Sent to A. J. B. 30 March 1905'. B.M.
   Add. MSS. 50836.
85 The Afghan Problem, 20 March 1905, p. 5. Cab. 18/24.
86 71st meeting of C.I.D., 19 April 1905. Cab. 2/1.
87 Transport resources of India, 6 May 1905. Cab. 6/3/79D.
88 Transport resources of India and supplies in Afghanistan, 15 May
   1905. Cab. 6/3/80D.
89 72nd meeting of C.I.D., 17 May 1905. Cab. 2/1.
90 Protection of Reinforcements from the United Kingdom to India,
   27 May 1905. Cab. 6/3/81D.
91 Clarke to Kitchener, 7 July 1905. P.R.O. 30/57/34.
92 Suggestions as to a basis for the calculation of the required transport of an Army operating in Afghanistan, 7 June 1905, p. 3. Cab.
   6/3/83D.
93 A Note on the Military Policy of India, 18 July 1905, p. 13. P.R.O.
   30/57/30.
94 Action to be taken in the event of a Russian occupation of Herat
   and Afghan Turkestan, 13 July 1905. Cab. 6/3/82D.
95 Esher Papers. Clarke to Esher, 13 June 1905. 'Sir G. Clarke 1905
   Vol. 4'.
96 76th meeting of C.I.D., 20 July 1905. Cab. 2/1.
97 Roberts Papers. Balfour to Roberts, 12 August 1905. Box X20931,
   file B1.
98 Clarke to Balfour, 17 August 1905. B.M. Add. MSS. 49702.
99 Balfour to Clarke, 27 September 1905. B.M. Add. MSS. 49702.
100 Clarke to Chirol, 2 September 1905. B.M. Add. MSS. 50832.

101 Balfour to Clarke, 11 October 1905. B.M. Add. MSS. 49702.
102 Suggestions as to basis for the calculations of the required transport of an Army operating in Afghanistan, 20 November 1905, p. 9. Cab. 6/3/89D.
103 Clarke to Kitchener, 5 January 1906. P.R.O. 30/57/34.
104 Kitchener to Clarke, 11 January 1906. B.M. Add. MSS. 50835.
105 Kitchener to Clarke, 18 January 1906. Cab. 17/53.
106 Kitchener to Clarke, 23 January 1906. B.M. Add. MSS. 50835.
107 The question of Seistan, 26 March 1906, p. 5. Cab. 17/53.
108 85th meeting of C.I.D., 9 March 1906. Cab. 2/2.
109 Grey to Bertie, 15 January 1906. *B.D.* III, no. 216.
110 Military considerations involved with regard to an entente cordiale between Great Britain and Russia, 20 March 1906. F.O. 800/102.
111 Clarke to Balfour, 20 May 1906. B.M. Add. MSS. 49702.
112 Number of troops that can be maintained by a single line of railway, 20 May 1906. Cab. 6/3/93D.
113 88th meeting of C.I.D., 25 May 1906. Cab. 2/2/1.
114 Esher to Kitchener, 16 August 1906. P.R.O. 30/57/33.
115 Anglo-Russian relations as affecting the situation in India, 16 July 1906. British Policy in relation to Afghanistan, 1 October 1906, pp. 4, 5. Cab. 18/24.
116 Nicholson to Grey, 23 February 1907. *B.D.* IV, no. 472.
117 Roberts Papers. Morley to Roberts, 3 November 1906. Box X20926, file M1.
118 Esher to Balfour, 7 January 1907. B.M. Add. MSS. 49719.
119 M. V. Brett and Viscount Esher, *Journals and Letters of Reginald Viscount Esher*, vol. 2, London, 1934–8, pp. 210–11, 218.
120 *Ibid.*, p. 191.
121 Report and minutes of evidence of a Sub-Committee of the Committee of Imperial Defence appointed by the Prime Minister to consider the Military Requirements of the Empire as affected by the Defence of India, 1907, p. 15. Cab. 16/2.
122 *Ibid.*, p. 169.
123 *Ibid.*, pp. 175–6.
124 *Ibid.*, pp. 47, 49, 55, 57; 185–6, 188–90.
125 Ewart Diary, 1–3 February 1907.
126 Report and minutes of evidence of a Sub-Committee . . . to consider . . . the Defence of India, Appendix IV: The Defence of the North West Frontier of India, 12 February 1907, pp. 228–34.
127 Esher to Kitchener, 15 February 1907. P.R.O. 30/57/33. Roberts Papers. Minto to Roberts, 7 March 1907. Box X20926, file M1.
128 Sir G. S. Clarke (as Baron Sydenham), *My Working Life*, London, 1927, p. 200.
129 Kitchener to Marker, 28 February 1907. B.M. Add. MSS. 52276B.
130 Report of a Sub-Committee on the Military Requirements of the Empire: India, 1 May 1907, p. 2. Cab. 6/3/98D.
131 *Ibid.*, pp. 8–10.
132 *Ibid.*, p. 6.
133 Nicholson to Grey, 10 February 1907. *B.D.* IV, no. 150.

134 Napier to Nicholson, 27 April 1907. *B.D.* IV, no. 476 encl.
135 Transport of Reinforcements from the United Kingdom to India: Memorandum by the Admiralty, 17 July 1907. Cab. 6/3/99D.

8
Egypt

Egypt had become a part of the British Empire more recently than had India, and Britain's position there was rather more precarious than elsewhere. It had been occupied in 1882, not as the outcome of a conscious Mediterranean strategy nor of a 'purposeful new imperialism' but in order to quell internal opposition to a decaying regime.[1] As Gladstone was replaced by Salisbury, so the occupation was transformed into a state of semi-permanence by the assumption that Cairo might replace Constantinople as the bulwark against Russia. Whilst the Sultan of Turkey remained suzerain, real power in Egypt lay in the hands of the British Consul-General, a post occupied from 1883 until 1907 by the redoubtable Lord Cromer. The complexity of Britain's political presence was matched by the varied nature of the military problems confronting the authorities: the maintenance of internal security, the prevention of foreign incursions into the country and the sensitive position of the area in the event of a war between Great Britain and one or more of the major powers. The latter issue meant that fluctuations in the international balance of power could quickly throw the theatre into the forefront of strategic considerations.

One of the earliest military appreciations of the dangers facing Egypt came some seven years after its occupation, as a result of the threatening posture taken up in the Mediterranean by France in 1888–9.[2] A war with France and Russia seemed within the bounds of possibility, and the likely outcome for Egypt was thought to be an attack by a flying squadron with a small military force. A more dangerous prospect was the establishment of a force of 20,000 enemy troops in the country, when a reinforcement of 7,000 men from India would be necessary in addition to the six battalions stationed in Egypt in time of war. In any event chief reliance was placed on naval command of the Mediterranean, which would enable Britain to double the peacetime garrison of three battalions and would result in the enemy fleets being brought to battle or blockaded.[3] The question of offensive action against a Franco-Russian combination also led to an early consideration of the forcing of the Dardanelles and to the conclusion that a naval exercise alone would be both dangerous and ineffective and that an army corps would be required in a combined action if the element of surprise were lost.[4] These themes were to be displayed and expanded after 1900, but until then they were largely left unremarked.

The first thorough-going examination of the problem of defending Egypt resulted from the attempt to build up a general scheme for the defence of the Empire in the contingency of a war with France and Russia which had been adumbrated by Altham in August 1901.[5] It was now assumed that England would not have command of the sea until an indeterminate period had elapsed. Since England could not therefore provide reinforcements and India could not spare them, this made the question of the size of the peacetime garrison crucial. In its turn, this depended upon the probable nature of hostilities. A major seaborne invasion by 33,000 French and Russian troops was considered unlikely since its supply lines would be severed when England regained command of the Mediterranean; this left the possibilities of land attack from the west or from the east.

An expedition from Algiers or Tunis was dismissed as highly impracticable since the force involved would have to cross 1,400 miles of country which was mostly desert and waterless. A sizeable attack launched from Syria was equally unlikely since it would have to move along the coastal strip and would therefore be vulnerable to naval attack; what was much more likely, and more dangerous, was a small raid which could inflict damage on Alexandria, Port Said or the Suez Canal. The latter move was thought 'not only feasible, but one which would very likely be attempted'.[6] To meet this danger stood a British garrison of 4,050 combatant troops and an Egyptian army of 13,000.

The suggestion of employing the Egyptian army raised two issues which were to be of continuing importance in strategic discussions. The international status of the Suez Canal under the terms of the Suez Canal Convention of 1888 meant that native troops could legitimately be used only if it was assumed that the defence of the Canal and the defence of Egypt were inseparable. The War Office considered that they were, but the point was at the least a debatable one. From a practical point of view, the reliability of the *fellaheen* without a considerable British 'stiffening' was doubtful. In January 1900, a serious mutiny had broken out at Omdurman which had revealed the existence of a secret society within the army dedicated to the expulsion of the British. Despite this the native army had to be used in any defence scheme because there were too few British troops available, and also because they were even more dangerous if isolated in the rear of any action.

In the event of the large-scale attack, it was calculated that Egypt could rely on four days respite between the outbreak of war and the arrival of the invading force; her tactics must then be to hold on to Alexandria as long as possible and then retire on Cairo. To meet the small raid, plans for patrolling the Canal had to be devised by the local commanding officer. A permanent addition of three infantry battalions was recommended to meet such a raid, but the report concluded that one vital ingredient was lacking in the formulation of any satisfactory plan: 'beyond all, and before all, a satisfactory arrangement with the Admiralty and a frank statement of the amount of co-operation we may expect from the Navy, must precede any authorized scheme for the defence of Egypt.'[7]

The diplomatic difficulties involved in defending the Suez Canal from attack had occurred to both the Admiralty and Lord Cromer. The navy's solution was easy; since Her Majesty's Government had decided strictly to respect the neutrality of the Canal in the event of a maritime war, 'at such a time none of His Majesty's ships shall be stationed either in the Canal or within 3 nautical miles of Suez or Port Said'.[8] The Consul-General saw the issue as one half of the twin problems of using British troops for local requirements and for external defence. In the former case, he made it clear that no decisions ought to be made until the GOC had consulted him; in the latter, he pointed out that while Britain could not afford to leave the defence of the Canal to native troops, nor could she withstand the difficulties of mobilizing on the Canal but being debarred by international laws from taking any action.[9]

The War Office reacted strongly to the first part of Cromer's letter, alive to the dangers of the civilian adviser being in a position to impose his will upon a trained soldier. They were prepared to allow consultation with the Consul-General over political matters connected with the employment of native forces and over the preservation of internal order; 'local requirements'

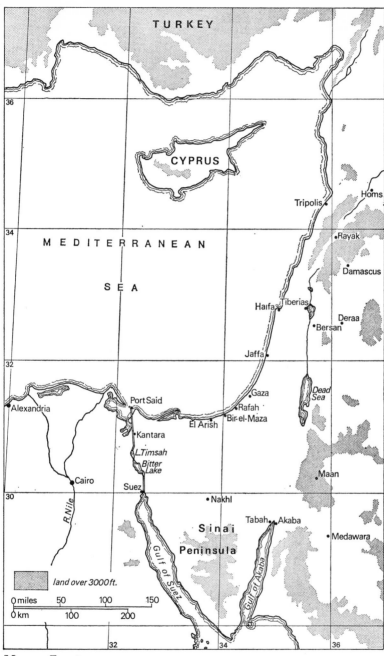

Map 2 Egypt

went thus far and no farther.[10] This somewhat hostile attitude was modified as the issue was passed up to the Secretary of State for War, so that the War Office finally concurred in Cromer's solution to the relationship between Consul-General and General Officer Commanding; but it was emphasized that such a situation would obtain only as long as Cromer remained in Egypt.[11]

With regard to the second part of Cromer's letter, the War Office replied to the Foreign Office—whence a copy had come—outlining the substance of their plan. It was also pointed out that it was quite possible that French or Russian troop transports might enter the Canal under false guise, disclaim the Convention and land at Ismailia; in such case it would be 'unfair' to leave the military commander without guidance. If the Consul-General agreed with the GOC that it appeared that troops were being passed through the Canal with the intention of obtaining military possession of it or of operating against Egypt, it was suggested that the GOC might take steps at his own discretion to frustrate the enemy.[12]

General Talbot, GOC Egypt, when invited to prepare a defence scheme suggested throwing up expensive fortifications particularly at Alexandria. Such a reconstruction was considered politically impossible, and he was instructed to revise his scheme accordingly and also consider the problem of control of local native insurgents as well as of full-scale external attack.[13] Talbot replied that his demands, particularly for new quick-firing guns, were based on the assumption that they might be desirable in a domestic as well as an external context. In making such demands, which the War Office viewed somewhat dubiously, he was undoubtedly motivated in part by Cromer's optimistic notions about the maintenance of internal tranquillity without increasing the nucleus of British troops.[14] In the following three years Cromer was successfully to press for the reduction of the garrison to little more than 3,000 men, contrary to the suggestions of both Talbot and the War Office.[15]

The Foreign Office assented to the provisional instruction given to Talbot by the War Office that the appearance of any attempt by an enemy to use the Canal for military occupation or for operations against Egypt should be resisted, which enabled the War Office to press ahead with a general scheme of defence.[16] They duly suggested that Cromer set up a small local committee, consisting of himself, Talbot, the Sirdar of the Egyptian Army and a naval representative, to work out a local scheme for defence. It was to consider both forms of attack envisaged by the War Office, and to form its conclusions on the basis of France and Russia being the hostile powers. The coincidence of all three major participants, Cromer, Talbot and Wingate (the Sirdar) being due for leave in England in the summer of 1902 held up the formation of the committee. In lieu of its deliberations, Cromer sent his own appreciation of the situation.

The basic assumption from which the Consul General worked was that the problem of defence was a purely military one only if the attitude of the populace was friendly and complete reliance could be placed on the Egyptian army. These were hazardous assumptions to make. Whilst the majority of Egypt's 10,000,000 native inhabitants were satisfied with British rule, and would probably prefer it to Turkish or French occupation, they were subject to pan-Islamic agitation which might blind them to the disadvantage of losing the British administration and its attendant benefits. The Khedive, a devout Moslem, had little energy or ability, and his friendship would be suspect in war. As far as the native army was concerned, its attitude depended on his own and any scheme of defence 'based on the fidelity of the Army to its British officers, will be quite valueless'.[17] Cromer offered three alternative courses of action in the event of war: complete withdrawal of the garrison for use elsewhere, reinforcement to enable it to resist a raid and preserve internal order or leaving it at its present strength. In the latter case, the army was of sufficient size to maintain order unless the Egyptian army mutinied but would in all probability be powerless against a French or Russian attack.

Cromer's political assessment shook the War Office. He had suggested leaving the final course of action to the dictates of circumstance; since it was envisaged that in the earlier stages of such a war Britain would not have sea command, circumstances would dictate that the garrison could neither be withdrawn nor reinforced. Unless, therefore, the peacetime garrison was substantially increased 'we are placing Egypt at the mercy of a comparatively small Russian or French raid'.[18] Reconquest would be possible, but at the cost of damaged prestige, a reduction in the offensive force generally available and a grave interference with the large reinforcements India was currently claiming. Altham recommended, and Brodrick concurred, that an informal conference be held in London while Cromer, Talbot and Wingate were on the spot, to determine the additions to the standing force necessary in the light of these considerations. At the conference Kitchener suggested that instead of adding a British battalion to the garrison, four Sudanese battalions be raised under British officers as with the native Indian army. The cost he estimated to be £85,000, to be borne from Imperial funds.[19] With such augmentation, the Egyptian garrison could deal with a raid of 5,000 if there were no general uprising and no army mutiny. Even so, it would take eleven days for the native brigade to reach Alexandria from Khartoum, whereas the Russians could land a force from the Black Sea in four days. The alternatives which were raised were to add three battalions and two batteries of artillery from the Regular troops in England or to raise battalions from Cyprus—a course to which Kitchener was strongly opposed.

Kitchener was not without an ulterior motive in making his suggestion. He would have preferred an increase in the British garrison, which could be used to reinforce India if necessary; otherwise he favoured the Sudanese battalions which could ensure that the line to India remained open in the event of an attack by a larger force.[20] Wingate was prepared to concur in this scheme provided that it did not mean any consequent reduction in the strength of the native army which had reached 'the irreducible minimum' in size. He did, however, foresee considerable difficulty in recruiting them since there was already a high demand for native Sudanese labour. Talbot too was prepared to accept this solution, and felt sanguine that with such an addition, and taking into account his ability to control railways and canals and cut off water supplies to Port Said, he could 'render an invasion a difficult operation even when opposed by an inferior force'.[21]

The War Office had suggested that the additional cost of the Sudanese or Cypriot troops might be met by reductions in the size of the Egyptian army. Cromer now made it plain that he would not countenance any increase under such terms. He could conceive nothing more impolitic, or 'more calculated to create local difficulties in Egypt, than the sudden transfer to half-pay or pension of a large number of native officers of the Egyptian army'.[22] He would have preferred to see the Egyptian army reduced to the figure of 3,500 at which the Egyptian contribution had been agreed rather than raise the financial question again. Indeed he argued that the situation be left quite alone since Egypt had 'with infinite trouble, and after many years of patient labour, got matters into a fairly satisfactory condition in Egypt'.

Reviewing the various proposals, Cromer opposed adding 4,000 to the British garrison because it would attract foreign attention, entail the expense of constructing additional barracks, contradict the policy of sending reinforcements to India, and in any case might not be sufficient in the event of any native rising. He was prepared to run the risk of a Russian or French attack since the outcome of such a war would in the end be decided by the power which won maritime supremacy. That power could then reconquer Egypt. It was this attitude which lay at the basis of the later belief that the security of Britain in Egypt depended less on her military presence than on Cromer's own prestige.[23]

These views together brought the question to a head. Altham did not view the possible loss of Egypt with the same equanimity as did the Consul-General, since command of the sea *per se* would not regain Egypt; rather he felt that its possession by an enemy power until the end of a war would make its recovery extremely doubtful. There was some force in this view, since Altham was better able to place such a contingency as the loss of Egypt within a much broader strategical framework than Cromer could. In such a light, the prospect of having to reconquer that country was far from attractive:[24]

> A task of this nature would be a most serious drain on the very limited force which, under our present military organization, would be available for over-sea service in war, and would render that force incapable of fully supplying the reinforcements required by India.

Overall, Altham saw more advantages in the addition of a British brigade than in a Sudanese one. He also remarked that much depended on the Admiralty's view of the probability of a raid.

There was good ground for discovering the latter point since changes were currently going on in the composition of the Mediterranean fleet which might be thought to affect the naval balance of power there. The Admiralty certainly felt that they would, and replied to a War Office enquiry that as a result 'the chances of a successful raid as indicated will in their Lordships' opinion be still more remote'.[25] From other correspondence with the Admiralty the War Office learned that such vague Admiralty formulae did not mean any guarantee against oversea attack, and Altham rightly pointed out that the assurance given was meaningless unless the navy were prepared to station a force on watch at the Dardanelles; their current station at Gibraltar would not ensure the safety of Egypt against a raid from the Black Sea.

The two proposals and the discussion surrounding them were now embodied in a memorandum for the consideration of the CID. This was strongly slanted towards the value of having potential reinforcements for India available in Egypt in view of the navy's reluctance to guarantee passage for them in the first stages of a war. The initial cost of the British scheme would be greater; the Sudanese scheme would add 4,000 troops to Imperial forces.[26] The subject came up at the meeting of 25 June 1903 as part of a general consideration of Altham's paper written in October 1901 on the military needs of the Empire in a war with France and Russia. Although the problem of Egypt came fourth in the order of priorities (behind the United Kingdom, the colonies and India), the committee dealt with it first. So great was the impact of that paper upon them that they decided to adopt both the proposed solutions, and increase the garrison by four British and four Sudanese battalions.[27]

These proposals fell into abeyance as the preliminary negotiations began which were to lead to the conclusion of the Anglo-French *entente*. Nicholson crossed swords with the Admiralty representatives in the CID over the proposed agreement, arguing that while it weakened Britain's strategical position in the Mediterranean 'no corresponding strategical advantages would accrue to this country in Egypt'.[28] His point was over-borne by the navy, which felt that the disadvantages were not such as to outweigh the general advantages which would result from the agreement as a whole. His concern at the military position of Egypt was also unsupported by Cromer, who wanted a free hand in Egypt for purely political reasons.[29]

In January of the new year, the War Office raised the question of the strength of the Egyptian garrison once more. The proposed army Establishments for the year required that the mountain battery in Egypt be brought home and replaced by a field battery; if, as seemed the case, the CID inclined to Cromer's view that the present garrison should be kept in a state of maximum efficiency rather than altered, then the mountain battery should be retained. On balance, the War Office favoured this course. However, if the CID agreed to its retention, and if they further agreed to new artillery for the army of occupation, even so the garrison of Egypt would not in their opinion suffice to protect that country from a raid 5,000 strong.[30]

The matter was further complicated by the issue of the neutrality of the Suez Canal as affected by the proposed Anglo-French *entente*. The War Office pressed that, since it had been recognized in 1901 that the army of occupation was not strong enough to ensure the safety of the Canal and since it was far from clear whether the powers regarded the 1888 convention as operative, France and Britain should make a mutual declaration of adherence to it.[31] Even so, diplomatic protection was not felt to be sufficient on its own, and Grierson pressed to be allowed to increase the artillery strength in Egypt from one battery of field artillery to three.[32]

At the subsequent meeting of the CID the proposal to increase the strength of Egypt's field artillery was accepted, but the suggestion to raise the four Sudanese battalions was turned down. In reaching this decision the CID explicitly agreed with Cromer's earlier argument that the garrison could never be made strong enough to resist an invasion by 5,000 men, and that therefore its scope 'should be limited to the maintenance of internal order and security in Egypt'.[33] These views were embodied by Balfour into a memorandum for the Foreign Office which demonstrated how Cromer's influence and the Prime Minister's own navalist attitude combined to overbear the real fears of the War Office. His opening words contained two startling observations: 'Egypt has for us no strategic importance. An oversea invasion of Egypt, say by 5,000 or 10,000 men, is not probable, in view of the superiority of our naval force in the Mediterranean.'[34] In March of the next year, the first sentence was deleted from this paper.

Balfour's remarks elicited a strong response from two separate quarters. Cromer wrote from Egypt that the army of occupation fulfilled a vital role in ensuring that no other power occupied the country; if Britain held aloof in the event of internal disturbance then France would probably step in. Whether or not an Imperial purpose such as this could be described as 'strategic' was a matter of opinion and, he implied, a distinction that was at most academic.[35] He also pressed for the abandonment of the proposal for extra field artillery. The War Office responded that Balfour's overall strategic view was acceptable only if two preconditions were met. One was that in a maritime war the seizure of Egypt would be of no material disadvantage to England, and the other that the navy could guarantee Egypt against a raid in the first phase of such a war. The former was unlikely since public opinion at home and prestige abroad would both be affected by such an occurrence, and the latter inoperative since there was no such guarantee and without it Egypt had only troops sufficient for internal purposes. To emphasize the difficulties facing the War Office, it was remarked that India was demanding large numbers of British troops as reinforcements in the event of such a war.[36]

In attempting to put its strategic ideas into effect, or even to ensure that they received a proper airing in strategic counsels, the General Staff had to combat powerful, though not united, opposing views. To those of Cromer and the Admiralty was added, at this time, the voice of the secretary of the CID. Sir George Clarke was trying to establish in Balfour's mind, and elsewhere, the principle that the British force in Egypt existed solely to preserve internal order, 'protection against over-sea aggression being the province of the Navy'.[37] In this light, and in the light of Cromer's affirmation that the Anglo-French agreement modified Britain's earlier position and justified a reduction in the garrison, the CID shortly afterwards reaffirmed the principle that the garrison existed solely to maintain internal order.[38] Cromer put forward a scale of 3,000 infantry, one company of garrison artillery and 120 mounted military police as appropriate, and agreed to accept an increase in Egypt's contribution from £87,000 to £100,000 per year.

The solution thus arrived at with regard to the strategic problem posed by the defence of Egypt interlocked with the diplomatic climate of Franco-British accord. It did not, however, take account of the prospect of a strategic threat other than that posed by France and Russia in conjunction. Although such an alternative was some time off, Clarke mentioned one possible hostile combination late in the year, if only to dismiss it. He considered that a Russo-Turkish alliance for hostile purposes was difficult to conceive, and that in any case 'nature had ordained a defence of the Eastern side of the Canal, which is and will remain an absolute barrier to the movement of even moderately large forces'.[39] This barrier—the Sinai Peninsula—was later to be the subject of much strategic debate. Moreover, the Foreign Office finally gave a considered opinion that 'we may consider Egypt as associated with us in any war in which we may be involved', a declaration of vulnerability to which Lansdowne subscribed.[40]

Egyptian strategy was tested in a way in which no other strategy was tested early in 1906, when Turkish troops occupied the port of Tabah at the head of the Gulf of Akaba on the eastern side of the Sinai Peninsula. According to the terms of an agreement between the Khedive and the Sultan in 1892 it lay under Egyptian jurisdiction. That agreement had drawn the frontier on a line Tabah–Rafah; as the crisis developed the Sultan claimed control over territory up to the line Tabah–Suez, which at a stroke deprived Egypt of the Sinai Peninsula and transformed the problem of defence from being primarily naval to being primarily military. Its general effect was to increase British suspicions of Germany's intentions.[41]

It was the War Office which awoke first to the dangers posed by this new move, and in February Grierson examined the dangers posed by the loss of the Sinai Peninsula as a barrier to Egypt. The area was, he pointed out, a true desert across which the best route was along the coast via El Arish, though following it had cost Napoleon 5,000 troops in 1799. War Office thinking on the value of a naval defence of the area had undergone something of a change, for Grierson now concluded that since the coast route was the only practical one 'our naval supremacy in the Mediterranean and in the Gulf of Akaba secures the Egyptian–Turkish frontier'.[42]

The first reaction of Grey and of the Cabinet was to regard the incident as not being serious; they were particularly anxious to avoid a situation where ineffective action by the fleet would then require seizure of Turkish territory to back it up.[43] Cromer however grew increasingly anxious that the incident would arouse Moslem feeling, which he felt to be already at a dangerous pitch.[44] Accordingly Grey informed him on 26 April that reinforcements were being sent from Crete, Malta and when the transport was ready from England also.[45]

The reinforcement of the garrison in Egypt temporarily resolved the sensitive position there, but it did not provide any permanent solution to the problem of defending Egypt; nor did it offer any possibility of coercing Turkey into giving way. The War Office now turned its attention to both these aspects of the problem. A more thorough examination of the Sinai Peninsula resulted in the opinion that any invasion of Egypt was 'not an enterprise to be lightly undertaken'. There were only two routes across the area, and of the old *haj* route from Akaba to Suez via Nakhl little was known save that it was thought to be waterless. The coast road from Gaza via Rafah and El Arish to Kantara on the Canal had supplies of water at only two points, and could be bombarded from the sea between Rafah and Bir-el-Maza. Nevertheless, Egypt stood in a position of some danger. Though an invasion by 10,000 troops would require preparations which would give the intention away, it was not out of the question that a small force might seize bridgeheads on the canal under the cover of a diversion, improve the water facilities en route and turn Nakhl into a base. From a wider viewpoint, were the Turks in a position to extend the projected Medawara–Akaba railway to Suez, this would prove, 'a ready solution to the main difficulty of invasion'.[46]

Sir William Robertson considered the problem of active operations against the Sultan, which he felt must do one of three things: damage his pocket, weaken his prestige as Caliph or endanger him personally. Possible support by other powers ruled out any demonstration against Basra, the coasts of Syria, Asia Minor, or European Turkey, or Tripolis. The most favourable prospect seemed to be the seizure of the customs of the island of Mytilene, whose trade was worth £700,000 a year, and if necessary occupying the neighbouring islands of Lemnos, Tenedos and Imbros. There was a precedent for such action for in 1901 the French had seized the Mytilene customs without international objection. A second, and less desirable course of action, would be to seize the ports of Jeddah and Hodeida; the danger inherent in such a course of action was that if the Arab tribes freed themselves from Turkish rule insurrection might spread and unsettle tribes under British influence. Robertson added the *caveat* that if, as seemed the case, Turkey was being supported by Germany, then only extensive and severe coercion would force her to back down.[47]

Grey at first followed the War Office line that an invasion of Egypt was sufficiently improbable for it to be unnecessary to prepare plans for active operations in the Sinai Peninsula.[48]

Cromer for his part had now been awakened to the vulnerability of his charge to something other than native insurrection, and telegraphed back requesting consideration of the stationing of native vessels in the Canal and on Lake Timsah, the fortification of the Canal banks, and of some means of reinforcing Egypt from England or India.[49] Grey was sufficiently affected by Cromer's telegram to write to the Prime Minister suggesting that the questions of the military defence of Egypt and of a naval demonstration against Turkey be discussed at the CID. As far as Egypt herself was concerned, the Admiralty had suggested that the Canal could in the last resort be turned into a line of floating forts.[50] The crisis had grown sufficiently serious for the War Office to be considering a partial mobilization in the six days which elapsed between Grey's note and the meeting of the CID.[51]

At the same time as he pressed for greater defensive capability Cromer had turned his attention to the problem of an offensive strategy. His suggestion was to interdict Turkish reinforcements directed to the Yemen; he opposed any direct action against ports there however, on the grounds that the Egyptian populace might construe such a move as a threat to the Mahommedan holy places at Mecca and Medina.[52] Meanwhile, in London, the Admiralty adopted the strategy suggested by Robertson of occupying the islands and seizing the customs, from which position they would then be in a good position to stop all Turkish transports. The question of action against the Dardanelles was also raised at this time, Lord Tweedmouth reporting to the Foreign Secretary that the Admiralty view 'is to leave the Dardanelles and its forts severely alone'.[53]

The strategic options open to the government were now rapidly narrowing. The War Office independently examined the prospect of direct action in the Gulf of Akaba, and rejected it. At least 12,000 men would be required to drive the Turks into the desert; their mobilization could not escape attention. Furthermore successes on the coast could not be followed up, partly because the hot season was about to commence and partly because there was a considerable deficiency in intelligence about the area.[54] Grey was prepared to agree that direct action was impracticable but clearly anticipated that the proposed naval demonstration might not work, for he warned Lyttelton of the need to bring pressure elsewhere if it failed.[55]

Grey dealt with the strategic crisis alone, apparently secure in Fisher's assertion that the Mediterranean fleet could defend Egypt.[56] He was prepared to order the naval demonstration against Mytilene and Lemnos on Monday 14 May if the Sultan had not responded to diplomatic overtures.[57] However, in drawing the Prime Minister's attention to the need to examine the issues, Grey inadvertently initiated a process which transferred general consideration of the question from the Foreign Office to the CID.

At the request of the Prime Minister, the staff of the Secretariat now examined the questions raised in Grey's letter of 5 May. A working paper by an assistant secretary, Sir John Chancellor, demonstrated that the Yemen was one of Turkey's most vulnerable points, since the mere cessation of reinforcements would result in a steady depreciation in the size of the Turkish garrison at the rate of some 2,500 a year. This course was the more attractive in that a purely naval demonstration would not cause European complications.[58] The main paper however came from Clarke. He commenced by surveying the possible motives of the Sultan in precipitating the crisis, which he presumed must be aimed at an extension of the Maan–Akaba railway line to Suez. Egypt herself was in little danger, since he came to the same conclusions about the two possible lines of advance as had the General Staff.

Turning to the problem of a coercive strategy against Turkey, Clarke concurred in the occupation of Lemnos and Mytilene and suggested similar action against Tenedos, Imbros, Samothraki and possibly Chios and Rhodes also. Where he diverged radically from previous strategic notions was in his proposals for action should these measures fail. Severing Turkish communications with the Yemen and occupying the western shore of the Persian Gulf and Basra might be effective; what would probably be most effective would be the appearance of British warships before Constantinople: 'There is little doubt that the threat to open fire on Yildiz Kiosk would bring the Sultan immediately to terms, but certain risks would have to be run.'[59]

Chief amongst such risks was the problem of by-passing the Turkish shore defences on either side of the Dardanelles passage. Clarke reviewed the numbers and calibre of the guns *in situ* and pointed out that most were of a comparatively old type, their gunners 'doubtless inexpert'. Likewise, he did not think the minefields would be effective. Thus it was suggested that two or three armoured cruisers or a battleship might pass through the Straits by night with little danger, though their return passage would involve considerable losses. The venture might be justified 'only if the results were certain', and in any case the possibility of inflaming Mahommedan fanaticism should be taken into account. Clarke concluded by recommending that diplomacy and the measures necessary to support it continue *pari passu*.

The CID met on 11 May to decide a course of action. Grey reported that the Sultan had agreed to withdraw from Tabah but not to participate in a joint delimitation of the frontier. In these circumstances the committee agreed to some form of coercion, only Morley opposing this course on grounds of cost. Tweedmouth reported that the Admiralty had already put into operation certain measures suggested by Clarke, stationing ships at Port Said and Suez, patrolling the coast between Rafah and El Arish and planning patrols of the Canal. The committee therefore accepted a proposal to occupy Lemnos and Mytilene if necessary, Campbell-Bannerman being instrumental in the exclusion of any of the other islands from the scheme. If this did not work, Turkish transports for the Yemen were to be intercepted, customs posts on the Persian Gulf seized and trading vessels on the Tigris seized. Fisher concurred in Grey's opinion that the forcing of the Dardanelles must be reserved for some more serious occasion.[60] None of these measures proved necessary for on 13 May the Sultan agreed to withdraw Turkish troops from the Sinai Peninsula and to accept an accurate delimitation of the Egyptian–Turkish frontier.

The crisis had the effect of revealing two grave deficiencies in the General Staff's strategic deliberations: it had no plans to counter an invasion across the Sinai Peninsula and neither could it offer an offensive strategy for use against Turkey. By 15 May a plan had been drawn up for the occupation of Haifa, in the course of which the interest of the General Staff turned to the Dardanelles scheme. Callwell offered the opinion that the Tabah incident had revealed that the navy could do little against Turkey since it was neither a naval nor a mercantile power. In the recent affair the navy had declined the only effective action, and had been reduced to 'pinpricks': a 'conjunct undertaking against the Dardanelles if successful strikes a vital blow'.[61] Such a venture would mean an opposed landing, therefore Callwell offered as second best the Haifa scheme. He was overruled by the DMO who felt such an action should be subsidiary to 'our main object of attack, which should be the Gallipoli Peninsula'.[62]

News of the new direction in military strategy quickly reached the ears of Repington, who remarked caustically that if the General Staff attempted to force the Dardanelles they would get eaten up by Turkish opposition.[63] There was, however, influential support for the idea of a more searching consideration of the prospects offered by an attempt to force the Dardanelles: Cromer wrote from Egypt urging that the question be thoroughly studied by competent naval and military authorities. It was desirable to know whether the venture was possible 'in the not improbable case of decisive action sooner or later being necessary against the Sultan'.[64]

The War Office worked away at the idea independently during July. It concluded that the measures proposed by the CID on 11 May were acts which might have led to serious consequences, among them the seizure of up to 170 British ships in the Black Sea and Turkish waters and the severance of an important part of Britain's food supplies. At the same time the Turks might send raiding parties of up to 2,000 men across the Sinai Peninsula to excite Moslem fanaticism in many British possessions, especially India. The Aegean islands could not be permanently held, and since their population was chiefly Greek the revenues were already hypothecated.[65]

An effective strategy was not easy to find, particularly since the nature of the Turkish empire meant that British naval preponderance could not be brought to bear on any vital point 'unless the fleet is prepared to take the risk of attempting to force the Dardanelles'. An invasion of Turkey was out of the question because of the relative size of the two armies, therefore it was desirable to choose a location where naval co-operation and local conditions would mean that an invading force would en-counter only a portion of the Turkish army. The Dardanelles was the obvious target for such an operation: it would suit the nature of Britain's forces, it would be a short operation and if successful it would be immediately decisive.

At this juncture, the question of Egyptian defence was inserted into the concurrent debate over Haldane's proposals to reorganize the regular army into a striking force of six infantry divisions and one cavalry division. Feelings ran high at the CID meeting on 6 June, when French cited the case of Egypt to show the inadequacy of the proposed arrangements. Both Grey and Lyttelton rejected French's proposition that within ten years an army of 150,000 might be needed to protect that country from internal and external assault, arguing that such a situation could only occur if Britain stood alone in the civilized world.[66] Esher, who agreed with French, noted the latter's response to Lyttelton's suggestion that any land attack across the Sinai Peninsula could be repulsed by ships in the Canal: 'He [French] became scarlet in the face, and speechless!'[67]

To support his contention, French produced a lengthy strategic appreciation of the Egyptian situation. Allowing for a close relationship between Germany and Turkey, which he suggested might even amount to a secret alliance, the likelihood that neither France nor Russia would intervene in a dispute and that Austria and Italy would cancel one another out, it was highly probable that the two powers might oppose England in a three-handed war. Though at the commencement of such a war 'the hand will be the hand of Turkey, the voice will be the voice of Germany'.[68] The logic of such a situation, as French quite rightly argued, led to the conclusion that if passage of the Dardanelles were feasible the Germans would never permit the defences to remain in an obsolete condition. If such a situation pertained, 150,000 men would be required to defend Egypt.

Turning to a closer examination of the problems of defending Egypt, French rejected the notion of the Sinai Peninsula as being waterless which lay at the basis of the General Staff's assumptions about its impregnability. The Arabs were, he argued, adept at concealing cisterns. Also modern transport developments, particularly railways, would allow water to be brought forward and stored. The conclusion French reached was that it was within Turkey's capacity to place 100,000 men within twenty miles of the Canal and to maintain them there. Nor was it likely that the transmission of Turkish troops could be interrupted since they would in all probability follow inland routes rather than moving along the Mediterranean coast. He concluded that by the time the Turks were established within striking distance of the Canal, which might take six or seven months, diplomatic complications would enable Germany to give her partner active support.

Before the CID met to consider French's paper, support had appeared for some of his strategic contentions. Major General

Bullock had to admit that hitherto unknown water sources had been discovered, particularly on the El Arish–Kantara road. However, the northern route could support a force no larger than 3,000 men to operate against Suez and the Bitter Lakes. A passive stance would enable Turkey to build up her forces, so Bullock suggested the establishment of a small military base at Nakhl and remarked on the attraction of a British operation at Haifa designed to cut the Hedjaz railway. He concluded that there was a danger of a rapid raid of some 3,000 men which might ignite a local rising, but that 'an invasion on a large scale of Egypt from the East could only take place if England was paralysed by disaster elsewhere; or was incredibly supine'.[69]

Cromer addressed himself to French's diplomatic assumptions, pointing out that the General had ignored the difficulties confronting Turkey in the Balkans and particularly from Bulgaria in the event of a war elsewhere. Any attempt by Germany to use Turkey as a cat's-paw would face the acute internal disorganization and weakness which afflicted her supposed ally and especially 'the remarkable capacity of the Turks for missing all their opportunities, and for doing the wrong thing at the wrong time'.[70] An advance by 100,000 men upon Egypt he therefore considered improbable. Two points did deserve more seaching consideration however: resistance to a small Turkish raid and the means by which the Sultan might be coerced. This last was a problem which had greatly concerned Cromer during the Tabah incident and he now raised once more the question of whether or not the Dardanelles could be forced. He no longer put much faith in seizure of the islands as an effective measure of coercion, but saw this area as one of crucial importance; if nothing could be done there, then 'our diplomacy will have to be suited to the naval and military possibilities when the voice of diplomacy has ceased to exercise any effect'.[71]

The following day French's patron sought to answer his *protégé*'s critics. Esher began by commenting somewhat tartly on Cromer's philosophy which he understood to require that only problems which were likely to be soon translated into fact should be examined by the CID. Given French's basic assumptions, the logic of his paper appeared to Esher unassailable, though he made no observation about the validity of those assumptions. Fleet action was excluded, therefore at least 100,000 men would be required to engage the Turkish army in Egypt or Syria. Esher concluded by urging that the problem of Egyptian defence be considered not from the point of view of an island defensible by sea power, but as 'possessing a land frontier, which, under certain circumstances, may be crossed by a hostile force'.[72] His concern was as much to point out the deficiencies in Haldane's proposals as it was to resolve the problems facing Egypt.

When it met on 26 July to discuss the issues related to the defence of Egypt, the CID paid little attention to the points raised by French. Grey pressed the view that the defence of Egypt could only be discussed once a decision had been reached on whether or not the Dardanelles could be forced.[73] The importance attached by the Foreign Office to a means of coercing Turkey was emphasized by its new Permanent Under Secretary, Sir Charles Hardinge, who felt that it was feasible to force the Straits by landing a force to take the forts from the rear. If it could indeed be shown that such an operation could be carried out it would 'present the most effective means of defending Egypt from Turkish attack'.[74]

The navy's attitude to the venture had apparently changed since May, for Tweedmouth informed the committee that it had no doubt it could force the passage alone; however, it would be a costly undertaking. His Director of Naval Intelligence, Ottley, at once qualified this remark by pointing out that experience during the Russo-Japanese War suggested that forts had a great advantage over ships. Supported by Cromer, the Foreign Office view won the day when the CID reached the conclusion that circumstances might arise in which the forcing of the Dardanelles, with or without the co-operation of an expeditionary force, might be the most certain way of bringing a war with Turkey to a conclusion. In that case the operation might have to be undertaken 'even if it entailed considerable losses'.[75] Following a suggestion made by Campbell-Bannerman, it was agreed to set up a joint committee of military and naval experts to examine the possibility of landings on the Gallipoli Peninsula and at Haifa.

With regard to the defence of Egypt proper, Cromer was reassured by Grierson that two battalions from Malta could be there within seven days and two more could be transported from Great Britain to Malta in fourteen days. Thus Egypt could be reinforced to the extent of a full brigade within twenty-one days. The CID concluded its brief discussion of this topic by recommending that Cromer take measures for the defence of the Suez Canal against a raid.

Despite the doubts expressed earlier in the year by Callwell the decision by the CID ensured that the schemes for landings at Haifa and at the Dardanelles progressed simultaneously at the War Office. By the end of August the schemes were in a sufficient advanced state for it to be suggested that they should be sent to the Director of Naval Intelligence. They were never sent because the DNI was found to be on leave until October and because Robertson felt that the spirit of the decision of 26 July required that piecemeal schemes should be subordinated to a general plan.[76] Here Robertson illuminated one of the major defects in the planning of Britain for a war against Turkey, for it was always looked upon as essentially a conflict of one power against the other and no account was taken of international complications.

The propensity of the CID to concentrate upon offensive rather than defensive strategy when considering the defence of Egypt was reinforced when, in October, Clarke produced a paper designed to refute French's. In part this resulted from Clarke's conviction that invasion across the Sinai Peninsula was physically impossible; in part, also, it reflected his view of strategic priorities. As he wrote to Esher, 'the importance of the Dardanelles question is greatest, and . . . it should be most carefully studied'.[77] To this end, Clarke once again employed the method of detailed analysis of the ground to be covered as well as mathematical calculation of the camel transport required for a force of some 22,000 troops. Somewhat less exhaustive than his earlier Afghanistan memorandum, Clarke's paper concluded that 45,995 camels would be required to transport a force 19,000 strong across the Sinai Peninsula and provide bridging materials for use when it reached the Suez Canal.[78] Such transport, he was convinced, was unavailable.

Clarke's conclusions were that a Turkish invasion was impossible without the construction of a railway to support it, and that otherwise the only feasible course was a small raid designed to foment internal risings. If a line were to be started it would take at least a year to complete, during which time the defence of the Canal could be organized. Clarke also pointed out that Turkey would be exceptionally foolish to start a war in Egypt while she still had to deal with disturbances in the Yemen, and that if she did there was a strong probability that Bulgaria would seize the opportunity to take the offensive against her.

Two things weakened Clarke's otherwise convincing case. One was that it relied heavily on extant British intelligence to the effect that water was scarce in the Sinai Peninsula, which was to be proved incorrect. The other was that it took for granted the inefficiency of units of the Turkish army. This view was not a unanimous one. The military attaché at Constantinople, Colonel H. C. Surtees, accurately remarked on the Turks' 'extra-ordinary talent for improvisation; and their capacity for enduring privations of all kinds without losing courage'.[79] It was Surtees's opinion, moreover that the desert represented a serious but not insurmountable problem to Turkey.

Clarke partially achieved his aims, for the CID met to consider the Dardanelles venture in the context of Egyptian defence in mid-November. By this time, however, the War Office had changed its mind about the potential of a combined operation. Haldane reported the belief that if troops were landed on the Gallipoli Peninsula 'there would be grave risk of a reverse, which might have a serious effect on the Mohammedan world'.[80] Such might equally be the result of ships being lost in the attempt to force the Narrows. Haldane therefore returned to the earlier suggestion that Aegean islands be seized should it become necessary to coerce Turkey. The prospect of the international friction which might result from such action caused Campbell-Bannerman to reject it outright. Fisher expressed the hope that no attack on the Dardanelles would ever be undertaken 'in any form', and as a result of the general discussion Esher succeeded in having the paragraph about an expedition contained in the minutes for 26 July expunged, and also in changing Cromer's terms of reference so that he was asked merely to advise on measures for Egyptian defence.

The General Staff worked feverishly on the problem of offensive action against Turkey during November and December, Robertson going on a two-week trip to Constantinople in the process in order to gather information. Ewart conferred with Clarke, Ottley and Callwell, and the resulting paper, though modified in some respects by the DMO, represented a return to Callwell's earlier scepticism.[81] In the light of this re-examination, the General Staff now accepted that a purely naval operation was unlikely to be effective in coercing the Sultan, since he could easily withdraw from Constantinople and 'a defenceless and undefended town, however otherwise important, offers no objective to ships of war'.[82] Should such an expedition meet with a reverse the effects on the Empire might be catastrophic. If ever an attempt were made to force the Dardanelles, then it must be by means of a combined operation, a move which the General Staff believed offered many positive advantages. Chief amongst them was the fact that a complete military occupation of the Gallipoli Peninsula would sever Asiatic from European Turkey, when the Sultan could only return to Constantinople as a suppliant for peace. On the other hand, failure could quite possibly result in a general uprising against British authority throughout the East, so that any government playing for 'the high stakes represented by a successful occupation of the Gallipoli Peninsula' must be concerned to weigh the great military risks involved before reaching any decision.

Was a landing possible at all in the face of modern armaments? The General Staff thought not, unless the supporting naval force could guarantee landing an invading force unmolested on an area free from enemy fire which was of sufficient size to enable it to form up for battle. The General Staff expressed doubts as to 'whether the co-operating fleet would be able to give this absolute guarantee'.[83] For one thing it was highly unlikely that the Sultan would fail to avail himself of the chance offered by a period of growing tension between the two powers to fortify the high ground behind the Dardanelles forts. Since there was no discretion in choosing a landing place in the event of hostilities, an expeditionary force must be prepared to face up to 100,000 defenders when it reached the peninsula. So great were the risks attendant upon a combined operation against the Gallipoli Peninsula that, despite the consequences should it succeed, the General Staff were not prepared to recommend its being attempted.

There was also pessimism about a suggestion made by Campbell-Bannerman for a *coup-de-main*. Even if a small force succeeded in getting ashore and paralysing the defence sufficiently to permit the passage of the navy, the ability of that force to hold on until reinforced or to extricate itself was highly doubtful. In any case, a singlehanded war was improbable and if Turkey were being supported by a major power it was questionable whether a fleet and a striking force could be sent to the Mediterranean at all.

A search for alternative objectives proved equally dismal. To attack Smyrna would be to challenge the Osmanlis, who were firm supporters of the Sultan, whilst a venture against Salonica would greatly alarm Austria. Operations on the Red Sea littoral were dismissed, since they might appear to threaten the Mohammedan Holy Cities, and, surprisingly, so was the proposal for a landing at Haifa. Such an operation would require a large expeditionary force including a powerful contingent of artillery and cavalry and yet offered no decisive object. In the opinion of the General Staff, 'it hardly seems wise to try a fall with a great Military Power in attempting an operation which, even if successful, would be little better than a pin-prick to the Turkish Empire'.[84]

Such findings were not too disheartening to the General Staff, since they felt that the defence of Egypt presented little in the way of serious difficulties. Command of the sea would enable Britain to transport the troops necessary to secure internal tranquillity and to ensure the safety of the Suez Canal 'which should be our main line of defence'. Until the Turks could build a railway up to the Canal, Egypt was in no danger. Whilst thus secure from the point of view of defence, the only strategy the General Staff could suggest in the context of offence, apart from political pressure, was naval blockade or seizure of the islands.

In a note appended to the General Staff memorandum, Ottley supported its contentions save for the question of the efficacy of naval support in a landing against enemy opposition. Japanese experience at Kinchow during the Russo-Japanese War led him to believe that naval gunfire in support of a landing might be more effective than the army made out. He also made the point that an operation of this sort might be forced upon Britain by 'arrogance or outrage on the part of the Ottoman Government', in which case there was no reason to despair of success 'though at the expense, in all likelihood, of heavy sacrifice'.[85]

In propounding the notion that the Canal could be defended, the General Staff were more vulnerable than they at first realized. For the Foreign Office had now clarified its own attitude to the neutrality of the Canal in the light of a declaration made in connection with the Anglo-French *entente*. In the event of Britain being a belligerent, no warships could be kept at Port Said or Suez; none could in any case be kept in the Canal.[86] This weakened Clarke's argument and, less obviously, that of the General Staff.

The growing tension in the Mediterranean during the latter part of 1906 prompted the creation of a new command to co-ordinate defence measures there. Esher had proposed a Commander-in-Chief, Mediterranean, in August on the grounds that the state of both Malta and Egypt was 'far from satisfactory'.[87] He suggested that the Duke of Connaught might fill the post. During the winter, Haldane received information that the Turks were strengthening their forts and garrisons in the Sea of Marmora 'and may be difficult to deal with on the occasion of the next trouble'. He formally proposed the creation of the new command on 7 December, precisely because of the sensitive position Egypt now found herself in.[88]

At the CID meeting which took place on 28 February 1907 it was agreed that an operation against the Dardanelles should be undertaken only if no other course were open. Grey suggested that this decision be transmitted to the Foreign Office so that in dealing with Turkey they should be aware of the limitations on Britain's powers of coercion. Esher secured the formation of a sub-committee which was to examine possible means of bringing military force to bear on Turkey other than via the Dardanelles.[89] As a result of this decision, all copies of the memoranda by the General Staff and Naval Intelligence Department were recalled shortly afterwards, and were thus not available to the War Council when the decision was made to attempt the forcing of the Dardanelles in 1915.

Esher's sub-committee, formed under the chairmanship of Lord Morley, took oral evidence between June and November 1907, though it did not produce a signed report until sixteen months after its last witness had been examined. In the event, the discovery of other means to coerce Turkey was to take second place to the problems of defending Egypt and preventing any popular insurgence in Sudan and the Delta.[90]

In the view of the Egyptian military authorities, as purveyed by Bullock, the great danger lay in the appearance on the frontier of a force, no matter how small, of a foreign power. In that event 'there is little doubt that a very large conflagration would be started'.[91] He calculated that a force of some 3,000 men could be on the Canal in seventy-two hours, and that the Canal itself was the obvious defensive line. Bullock was all too well aware that the force he had at his disposal was pitifully small to maintain internal order and oppose such a raid; indeed, manoeuvres had demonstrated that he could only spare 900 men and two guns for active operations against the enemy. His position was the more difficult since he put no faith in the naval view that cruisers could be stationed in the Canal; they could not turn there, and if stationary could be rendered harmless by floating burning oil down on them.[92]

Bullock's preferred strategy was to split his available forces into small detachments which would be parcelled out along the length of the Canal, reinforced by naval landing parties and troops from Malta. He also suggested the formation of a camel corps of 300 British troops which would move forward to occupy Nakhl in the event of any disturbance.[93] This was not, however, a unanimous view of the Egyptian authorities, for Bullock's Intelligence Officer submitted a paper in which he strongly deprecated splitting up the already small defence force, which must be held back to concentrate quickly against a crossing point. He also made the point that Egypt was so weak militarily that successful defence against a raid hinged on whether or not reinforcements arrived in time.[94]

The General Staff's view was that a serious Turkish raid was the last on an order of serious probabilities of which the first, and most important, was a disturbance in Egypt in which the Egyptian army stood neutral. A small Turkish raid could be repulsed if the garrison were reinforced by two battalions from Malta and two from Britain. A major invasion across the Sinai Peninsula was thought to be wholly impracticable without railways; if the Turks were misguided enough to launch one, 'almost every advantage would be on our side'.[95] Passive defence would require the addition of two divisions and two cavalry brigades to the garrison; active operations would be best directed at Syria. The latter, however, would be a vast undertaking since it could not be attempted without 'a complete mobilization of the Regular Army, and without the despatch of at least four divisions to the theatre of war in addition to the reinforcements to Egypt'.[96] A war on this scale might justify raising the Arab tribes against the Turks, to destroy the Hedjaz railway and harass the Turks in the Yemen and southern Syria, though the General Staff emphasized that such a desperate measure should not be undertaken merely to coerce the Sultan.

Both the Duke of Connaught, Inspector General of Forces, and the Sirdar, Sir Reginald Wingate, recommended an attack on Syria in the event of a serious invasion of Egypt being launched by Turkey. Ewart expressed no clear opinion one way or the other in his cross-examination of Connaught, but contented himself with remarking that such an action 'would mean a great military effort, and would bring the whole Turkish army down upon us'.[97] French proved much more sceptical, pointing out to Wingate that the Hedjaz railway lay some way inland from the Syrian coast and that to get to it an attacking force would have to cross the range of mountains which lay close to the sea.[98]

The committee were becoming alive to the fact that Egypt was severely short of manpower with which to resist even a small raid, as well as to the difficulties posed by finding an alternative to the Dardanelles for hostile operations. Even Clarke lost something of his former certainty about the safety of Egypt, being unwilling to risk life and property there: 'If we were caught unprepared, all Europe could point the finger of scorn.' He was also less happy with the talents and qualities of Cromer's successor: 'Lord C. was a man, and he never lost the soldier's instinct. His successor *is* not the first and *has* not the second.'[99] There was small comfort to be offered by the navy for the local commander, Sir Hedworth Lambton, displayed little knowledge of the Sinai Peninsula or the fact that from Kantara to Lake Timsah on the Canal the bank was too high to be commanded by ships' guns. His own role in a defensive operation he saw with complete simplicity: 'I should just wait until they got pretty close, and mop up the lot.'[100] Esher, who was keeping the King *au fait* with the progress of the sub-committee, informed his royal master after this examination that it was clear both that the force available to defend Egypt was inadequate and that the navy had no plan for such defence at all.[101]

Early in July, the General Staff expanded their views on both Egypt's defence and the prospects of an attack against Turkey elsewhere. As far as defence went, they admitted that during the eighteen or nineteen days it would take to despatch a division from England, Egypt would be heavily reliant on the Royal Navy to intercept any striking force. Since a purely defensive stance would destroy Britain's prestige in the east she would have to move onto the offensive, and here the Syrian seaboard offered an attractive target for raids designed to cut the rail link between a force operating in Arabia and its home bases. However, even allowing for Bulgarian and Macedonian hostility and the threat of a British attack on the Dardanelles, such an operation would still require five of the six divisions which composed the striking force and its one cavalry brigade.

As to the actual plan of such a venture, the General Staff suggested a series of diversionary feints at Ayas, Tripolis and Jaffa as well as at the Dardanelles, to be followed by a landing at Haifa. The force should then advance inland to a position over-looking Tiberias and link up with the warlike Druses to destroy the Hedjaz railway at or near Deraa. Such a move, though full of risk, offered the certain result of Turkey recalling any invading army from Egypt, as well as of a possible uprising:[102]

> The risks to Great Britain of such an expedition would necessarily be great, but the consequences to Turkey would be so disastrous if it were successful, that the mere threat of it would probably bring the Sultan to his knees before it became actually necessary to effect a landing.

A full reconnaissance of southern Syria had just been completed, and the General Staff was now ready to work out the details of the campaign.

The delay between the sub-committee's hearing its last witness on 19 November 1907 and producing its report on 11 March 1909 was due chiefly to the attitude of that last witness, Lord Cromer. He was adamant that Egypt need never worry about invasion; the greater danger facing her was that of internal disturbance. He was equally opposed to any suggestion of occupying and fortifying Nakhl, since this would greatly antago-nize the Sultan.[103] There was some support for this stance from the Foreign Office, and Gorst, his successor, succeeded in vetoing a proposal to build a motor road from the Canal to Nakhl for this reason.[104]

When the sub-committee did make its report the influence of Cromer's views could clearly be gauged. It was reported that a serious invasion would face difficulties which, though very great, would not be insuperable. The General Staff recommendations about a strike against Haifa were accepted, the report faithfully echoing their anxieties about the scale of potential opposition and the need to devote a large force to it—a minimum of four divisions. In the event of a raid the strategy recommended was to guard what portions of the Canal lent themselves to it with ships and the rest with a mobile force, together with the continuous occupation of Nakhl, to which a motor road should be built. Of equal importance with such prophylactic measures was 'a good system of intelligence and rapid communication with the eastern portion of the Peninsula, whereby early warning of a raid could be received in Cairo'.[105]

So far as the physical strength of the garrison in Egypt was concerned, the committee elected to follow the advice of both Gorst and Cromer that any increase in peacetime would be misunderstood by the Khedival government and bring about unrest. Reorganization was more important than numerical expansion. In the event of disturbances, two battalions could be sent from Malta.

Encouraged by the earlier reactions of the sub-committee, the General Staff pressed ahead with its planning for an attack on Haifa and by the middle of the following year had a draft printed. Their ideas had undergone a considerable expansion, for the main aim of such an expedition was now envisaged as the capture of Damascus. This was considered a desirable target for doctrinal rather than tactical reasons: 'Its capture would . . . strike a decisive blow at Turkish dominion, and tend to bring about the submission of the entire country.'[106] Advance towards Deraa and the destruction of the Hedjaz railway were seen as secondary objectives. In the month which would elapse whilst an expeditionary force was mobilized at Malta it was envisaged that action might be necessary as a reprisal in the event of a massacre of Christians in Syria. Four operations were suggested for consideration in this eventuality: the bombardment of Acre, a naval landing at Beirut, a feint at Tripolis to distract the Turks from Haifa and a landing in the Gulf of Alexandretta to prevent troops in northern Syria reinforcing those in Damascus.

By 1910 the General Staff had forged a link between its defensive and offensive plans for Egypt. It was now thought that a Turkish advance by way of Maan and Akaba was less likely than an attack via Gaza which was served by two railway lines from Damascus to Bersan and Haifa and thence by roads to Gaza itself. Ideally the line from Aleppo serving these two branches ought to be cut as far north as possible; two things prevented anything other than an attack in the south, namely the location of the friendly tribes and the fact that almost throughout the

Turkish communications were protected by a line of mountains some 10,000 feet high. Only opposite Haifa were they exposed.[107] Four roads crossed the chain of mountains and offered four targets. Of these, neither Alexandretta nor Tripolis were thought feasible operations. Beirut offered an excellent target forty miles inland in the railway repair shops at Rayak, but the Turks could bring up troops by road to oppose an invading force. Operations against Acre and Haifa, however, had none of the disadvantages associated with the other three areas and would put a force astride one line of Turkish communications and in striking distance of the other, the Hedjaz railway. As far as the organization of the attacking force was concerned, the War Office suggested that since 200 ships would be required to transport the four infantry divisions and two cavalry divisions the force might be split in two. This would economize on shipping, but no thought was given to the indication it would provide of British intentions. It was necessary because the Admiralty offered no hope of collecting the requisite transports in a short space of time.

During 1910 Fisher proved increasingly hostile to the Committee of Imperial Defence, and withdrew from its deliberations. In an effort to ensure its continued existence Esher suggested the formation of sub-committees to look at various specific questions. This was a notion that was particularly attractive to the General Staff, and one such enquiry was charged with further examination of the landing places proposed by the General Staff in the event of war against Turkey in the Middle East.

The sub-committee found that the prospect of a full-scale raid upon Egypt, which would initiate the General Staff's planned action in Syria, was improbable and therefore recommended that 'no considerable expenditure should be incurred in anticipation of a landing in Syria or indeed elsewhere in the Middle East'.[108] From a naval point of view Beirut and Tripolis were preferred as landing places since bad weather could disrupt operations more easily at Haifa. None the less, the sub-committee found the arguments put up by the War Office in favour of Haifa to outweigh the 'purely hydrographical point of view'. They did suggest that the General Staff devote more time to an examination of Beirut as an objective before arriving at a final decision, and adjured both War Office and Admiralty to keep up-to-date intelligence on the area in view of projected railway developments in Syria.

While the General Staff pressed ahead with plans for offensive action against Turkey the problem of defending Egypt and the Suez Canal against Turkey had not been lost sight of, and in June the CID reported on the findings of a sub-committee which had examined the relative responsibility of army and navy in this sphere. Since the view of the Foreign Office was that isolated action by Britain in the event of a Turkish attack on the Canal would be a violation of the 1888 Convention, the sub-committee found naval action 'inexpedient' and suggested it should not be resorted to 'except in cases of extreme urgency'.[109] It followed from this that the military authorities were to be held solely responsible for defence of the line of the Suez Canal against attack overland. This decision represented a complete reversal of the conclusions of Morley's committee about the possible role of the navy. Such a position owed much to the opinion now current among the members of the sub-committee that even a raid was a remote contingency.

The General Staff were aware of the current of thought about the naval defence of Egypt, for immediately after the report of the sub-committee was signed a paper was produced which examined the options open in a purely military defence. The available force of 900 rifles was to be split up as a mobile column between three bases, but would need a further four divisions of reinforcements in order to resist a raid by 6,000 Turks. Since this force could not be transported to Egypt from England and Malta in less than eighteen days, some additional means had to be found to hinder an attack. The solution suggested was a forward stance: the occupation of the oases at El Arish and Nakhl on the eastern side of the Canal. As advanced posts they would be of 'inestimable value' since an enemy would be 'compelled either to capture these places or to march round them'.[110]

As with the case of naval defence of the Canal, diplomacy served to negate this suggestion for easing the task of the War Office. Gorton, author of the paper which suggested occupying advanced bases, had remarked that such an operation might well offend the Young Turk regime now in power. The view of the Foreign Office was that since Turkish suspicions of Britain were now dormant nothing should be done which might stir them up. Thus Grey urged Gorst, the Consul-General, to discourage Sir Ian Hamilton from visiting El Arish and Nakhl during his tour of inspection the following winter.[111]

The War Office then sought support from the Colonial Defence Committee and such was the force of their case that very similar recommendations were made by that body to the Committee of Imperial Defence. El Arish and Nakhl should be fortified and garrisoned in peacetime, or else arrangements should be made for their rapid occupation in time of hostility. Should this prove unacceptable, and should it be decided that Egypt must be defended on the line of the Canal, then either the British force in Egypt must be increased or arrangements must be made to accelerate the arrival of reinforcements in time of emergency.[112]

Opposition to such a proposal was manifest so strongly at the meeting of the Committee of Imperial Defence on 24 March 1911, particularly by Sir Arthur Nicolson, that Sir William Nicholson suggested a decision be deferred in order to allow the General Staff to give further consideration to the problem.[113] Wilson, who had succeeded Ewart as DMO the previous year, suggested that since the Foreign Office would never agree to peacetime occupation of the Sinai Peninsula one solution would be to increase the strength of the Egyptian police there. He also recommended a permanent increase of one battalion in the size of the garrison.[114] Not until the following March did the CIGS reply to this adroit suggestion, and then only to inform Wilson that it was too late for him to take up this question.

The question of increasing the strength of the Egyptian garrison highlighted the general problems of an insufficiency of troops to carry out the grandiose offensive plans which the General Staff had devised. In July 1907, five infantry divisions and one cavalry division had been thought necessary for a Syrian expedition, together with another division for internal purposes within Egypt itself. However, by the end of 1907 it had been decided that the 4th and 6th divisions of the striking force would have to be retained in England while the Territorial Army was brought to a state of efficiency. Since it was formally laid down that that force required six months to reach such a state only four divisions at most would be available for operations against a hostile power.[115] Thereafter the General Staff had spoken only of four divisions as being necessary for this operation.

In April 1908 it had been decided that a VIIth Division would be formed for reinforcement of Egypt or India when necessary.[116] Its three infantry brigades were to come from Egypt, the Mediterranean garrisons and South Africa respectively and it was to draw ancillary personnel from Section A of the Army Reserve, which could be called up without the necessity of proclaiming a general mobilization. Sir Ian Hamilton pressed in July 1910 that the position of the VIIth Division be clarified, suggesting that it be 'regarded as a force held available for small wars in any part of the world'.[117] Wilson thereupon pointed out the defects in the proposed VIIth Division, namely that troops taken from Malta and South Africa must immediately be replaced and that this would necessarily mean cutting into troops earmarked for the Expeditionary Force. If the proposed division were to operate anywhere else other than Egypt, the brigade withdrawn from that country would also have to be replaced.[118] In October, the Military Members of the Army Council decided that the VIIth Division was not meant for fighting small wars and that the mobilization of the Expeditionary Force must take precedence over its mobilization. This latter decision meant that only four divisions of the Expeditionary Force would be available for both offensive operations in Syria and the defence of Egypt, should a war break out with Turkey.

There were other grounds besides the demise of the VIIth Division on which the General Staff was led to reject both the proposed Syrian expedition and the forward defence of the Suez Canal. The former notion was thought to be particularly unsound:[119]

To commit such a force with what may be termed a geographical objective in a country devoid of supply or means of manoeuvre, with an enemy on every side would be opposed to all laws of strategy. Although the Turkish communications may be cut there would be sufficient Turkish troops to reach Egypt and stir up insurrection.

Here the General Staff had remarked upon the overriding weakness of the Syrian plan. The Egyptian authorities had always held the view that the appearance of even a small hostile force on the frontier could spark off an internal insurrection, and to a lesser extent so had the General Staff. The essential result of an expedition against Syria must therefore be the total withdrawal of any attacking force; the most the scheme could offer was to halt a movement against Egypt.

Also by 1914 the planners were prepared to make a political assumption that they had hitherto avoided; that a war with

Turkey was most probable in the context of a wider European conflagration. In such a case it might prove impossible to reinforce Egypt through loss of command of the Mediterranean, or undesirable because of the calls made on British forces elsewhere. If Turkey should attack Egypt before a war broke out between Britain and Germany the Expeditionary Force would still have to be retained intact since Germany might become hostile at any moment. The 'main decision' would be fought out in Western Europe 'and it is there that all available army units other than those actually required for home defence should be sent'.[120] It was improbable that Turkey would have the power to attack Egypt in such a situation.

Turkey was in any case thought to have little power of offensive action. An advance across the Sinai Peninsula would require careful preparation, organization and training and it was 'open to doubt whether these qualities can ever be found in the Turkish Army'. This opinion was doubtless the result of Wilson's visit to Constantinople in October 1913, when he recorded in his diary the opinion that 'The Turkish Army is not a serious modern Army . . . no sign of adaption to western thoughts and methods. The Army is ill-commanded, ill-officered and in rags.'[121]

Sir John French was not prepared to subscribe to the General Staff views about the role of Egypt in a major European confrontation, and excised the opinions on it from the finished memorandum. He was prepared to accept the recommendation that Egypt be defended on the line of the Suez Canal, and that no detachments should be pushed forward to El Arish and Nakhl. To the garrison might be added two cavalry brigades and two divisions from England. One way of reinforcing the British presence in Egypt in peacetime, it was suggested, was the stationing of an aeroplane detachment there. In doing this, French overruled Wilson's wish to provide only one division from England and find the other from India. It was expected that 23,000 Turks might arrive at the Egyptian frontier at Kantara and on the Canal by the thirty-seventh day after mobilization; since it took an Indian division forty-four days to arrive, the margin for safety was too narrow.[122]

Just as the prospects of offensive action had undergone a distinct reverse by 1914, so too had the prospects of defence. The proposal made by the Admiralty in 1912 to withdraw from the Mediterranean significantly affected the prospects of defence which hinged on command of the sea.[123] In the event of command of the sea passing into the hands of the Triple Alliance, the General Staff warned, not a man could be spared from the garrison of Egypt to resist external aggression. Reinforcements would only be available from India and would take at least a month to arrive; in that time the Turks could land forces of 10,000 men at Alexandria and east of Port Said, as well having 23,000 men in the Sinai Peninsula a few days march from the Canal. Thus, once command of the Mediterranean was presumed lost, the General Staff reckoned that the Egyptian garrison must be permanently increased to 30,000 'to ensure the safety of Egypt until the arrival of reinforcements from India'.[124]

The new Consul-General in Egypt, Lord Kitchener, was confident that India could supply whatever forces he might need in the event of a war against the Triple Alliance unless in the interim the Government of India let their army run down.[125] The General Staff were much less sure of the security of Egypt. Sir John French offered the opinion that if command of the Mediterranean were abandoned for the first two months of a war, no diversionary operations could be staged in the Mediterranean.[126] At the crucial meeting of the Committee of Defence on 4 July 1912 he added that the increases necessary in the garrison had been underestimated by the General Staff since they had had to prepare their papers in a hurry. He now thought four divisions might be necessary to hold Egypt against Turkey for two months. None the less, the committee concluded that maintenance of a 60 per cent majority in battleships over Germany in the North Sea was the foremost requirement; subject to its being met, a fleet equal to that of the strongest power in the Mediterranean excluding France would be stationed there.[127]

The Committee of Imperial Defence thus demonstrated that they were more susceptible to naval requirements than to military ones in the light of the decreasing probability of a single-handed war against the Triple Alliance. They were also falling into line with Balfour's strategic presumption made eight years earlier, subconsciously echoed by Churchill in the phrase that 'a decisive naval victory would open up a series of situations which would lead to the capitulation of any force landed in Egypt in the interim'.[128] While the General Staff were far from happy at the prospect of losing the command of the Mediterranean or risking it by placing it in the hands of the French, naval agreement resolved the problem of freedom of operation *vis-à-vis* Egypt.

The decision reached subsequently about military operations in and around Egypt, both offensive and defensive, resulted from narrow military calculations and owed much to Wilson's belief that the decisive theatre of operations would be in western Europe. As far as the Committee of Imperial Defence knew, the strategic issue was still whether or not Haifa was a suitable landing place. The decisions reached by Wilson and his colleagues about the defence of Egypt by February 1914 remained unknown to them until four months after war had broken out. Then an enquiry by the Secretariat of the CID elicited the response that no further action had been taken since July 1910 on a Syrian expedition because French, acting on Wilson's advice, 'considered the importance of concentrating all efforts on the continental theatre of war to be so important that the remoter possibility of an attack on Egypt ought not to occupy the time of the General Staff'.[129]

Notes

1 R. Robinson and J. Gallagher, *Africa and the Victorians*, London, 1961, pp. 83, 467.
2 *Ibid.*, pp. 268–73.
3 Brackenbury to Wolseley, 10 May 1889. P.R.O. 30/40/14/2.
4 The Eastern Question in 1896 (Ardagh), October 1896, pp. 32–4. P.R.O. 30/40/14/1.
5 Minute, Altham to Nicholson, 12 July 1901. W.O. 106/41/C3/4b.
6 On the Defence of Egypt, May 1901, p. 7. W.O. 106/41/C3/4b.
7 *Ibid.*, p. 24.
8 Admiralty to Vice-Admiral Sir J. Fisher, May 1901. W.O. 106/41/C3/2a.
9 Cromer to Lansdowne, 14 June 1901. W.O. 106/41/C3/2a.
10 Altham to Nicholson, 9 July 1901. W.O. 106/41/C3/2a.
11 D.G.M.I. to Foreign Office, 25 September 1901. W.O. 106/41/C3/2a.
12 War Office to Foreign Office, 4 November 1901. W.O. 106/41/C3/2c.
13 D.G.M.I. to G.O.C. Egypt, 23 December 1901. W.O. 106/41/C3/4a.
14 Roberts Papers. Nicholson to Roberts, 22 August 1901. Box X 20926, file N.2.

15 Sir C. E. Callwell, *Stray Recollections*, vol. 2, London, 1923, p. 230.
16 Minute, Altham to Nicholson, 12 April 1902. W.O. 106/41/C3/2b.
17 Memorandum on Egyptian Garrison, 3 June 1902. W.O. 106/41/C3/2b.
18 Minute, Altham to Nicholson, 25 June 1902. W.O. 106/41/C3/2b.
19 The Garrison of Egypt (Altham), 2 August 1902. W.O. 106/41/C3/1a.
20 Kitchener to Cromer, 19 November 1902. W.O. 106/41/C3/1b.
21 Memorandum by the Sirdar, 27 November 1902; Memorandum by G.O.C. Egypt, 28 November 1902. W.O. 106/41/C3/1b.
22 Memorandum by the Earl of Cromer, 24 November 1902. W.O. 106/41/C3/1b.
23 Findlay to Hardinge, 24 March 1906. F.O. 800/46.
24 Altham to Nicholson, 12 January 1903. W.O. 106/41/C3/1b.
25 Admiralty to War Office, 28 February 1903. W.O. 106/41/C3/1b.
26 The Garrison of Egypt, 9 April 1903. Cab. 4/1/3B
27 18th Meeting of C.I.D. 25 June 1903. Cab. 2/1.
28 28th Meeting of C.I.D. 14 December 1903. Cab. 2/1.
29 Cromer to Lansdowne, 14 March 1904. *B.D.*, vol. II, no. 400.
30 Composition of the garrison of Egypt, 21 January 1904. Cab. 4/1/14B.
31 Memorandum on Article VIII of Draft Declaration of His Majesty's Government and the French Government respecting Egypt and Morocco, 29 March 1904. W.O. 106/41/C3/2c.
32 (Garrison of Egypt), 18 April 1904. Cab. 4/1/19B.
33 39th meeting of C.I.D. 20 April 1904. Cab. 2/1.
34 The British Garrison in Egypt, 21 April 1904, p. 1. Cab. 4/1/20B.
35 Expenses of the Army of Occupation in Egypt, 13 May 1904. Cab. 4/1/24B.
36 Egypt. Expense of Army of Occupation, 6 June 1904. Cab. 4/1/35B.
37 Clarke to Balfour, 4 August 1904. B.M. Add. MSS. 49700.
38 53rd meeting of C.I.D. 10 August 1904. Cab. 2/1.
39 Esher Papers. Clarke to Esher, 6 December 1904. 'Sir G. Clarke 1904 Vol. 2'.
40 Status of Egypt in a war between Great Britain and other powers (T. H. Sanderson), 5th January 1905. Cab. 17/58.
41 G. E. Monger, *The End of Isolation: British Foreign Policy 1900–1907*, London, 1963, pp. 296–7.
42 The Feasibility of a Turkish Force invading Egypt by Way of the Sinai Peninsula, 23 February 1906. F.O. 800/107.
43 Grey to Cromer, 6 April 1906. F.O. 800/46.
44 Cromer to Grey, 16 April 1906. Cab. 17/70.
45 Grey to Cromer, 26 April 1906. Cab. 17/70.
46 Strategical notes on Sinai Peninsula (Maj. G. M. Franks), 17 April 1906. Cab. 17/70.
47 Coercion of the Sultan of Turkey, 27 April 1906. W.O. 106/41/C3/10.

48 Grey to Cromer, 2 May 1906. Cab. 17/70.
49 Cromer to Grey, 5 May 1906. Cab. 17/70.
50 Grey to Sir Henry Campbell-Bannerman, 5 May 1906. Cab. 17/70.
51 Ewart Diary, 9 May 1906. *See* M. V. Brett and Viscount Esher, *Journals and Letters of Reginald Viscount Esher*, vol. 2, London, 1934–8, pp. 162–3.
52 Cromer to Grey, 17 March 1906. F.O. 800/46. Cromer to Grey, 27 April 1906. Cab. 17/70.
53 Tweedmouth to Grey, 4 May 1906. F.O. 800/87.
54 The question of military action in or near the Sinai Peninsula (Lt Col. A. Grant Duff), 5 May 1906. W.O. 106/42/C3/13b.
55 Grey to Lyttelton, 8 May 1906. W.O. 106/43/C3/13c.
56 Grey to Cromer, 7 May 1906. F.O. 800/46.
57 Grey to Cromer, 10 May 1906. Cab. 17/70.
58 The Akabah Question, 8 May 1906. Cab. 17/70.
59 The Egyptian Frontier Question; Note prepared by direction of the Prime Minister, 8 May 1906, p. 3. Cab. 4/2/74B.
60 87th meeting of the C.I.D. 11 May 1906. Cab. 2/2/1.
61 Minute, Callwell to Grierson, 15 May 1906. W.O. 106/42/C3/14b.
62 Minute, Grierson to Callwell, n.d. W.O. 106/42/C3/14b.
63 Repington to Marker, 1 June 1906. B.M. Add. MSS. 52277.
64 Cromer to Grey, 16 May 1906. F.O. 800/46.
65 Military Policy in a war with Turkey, 11 July 1906. W.O. 106/42/C3/21a.
66 90th meeting of the C.I.D. 6 July 1906. Cab. 2/2/1. A Turco–German Invasion of Egypt; Note by Sir John French, 16 July 1906, p. 1. Cab. 4/2/84B.
67 Brett and Esher, *Journals and Letters*, vol. 2, p. 170.
68 A Turco-German Invasion of Egypt, *op. cit.*, p. 2.
69 *Ibid.* Comments on Sir John French's note, 22 July 1906. Cab. 17/71.
70 *Ibid.* Remarks by Lord Cromer on Sir John French's Memorandum, 23 July 1906. p. 1. Cab. 4/2/86B.
71 *Ibid.*, p. 2.
72 *Ibid.* Memorandum by Lord Esher, 24 July 1906, p. 2. Cab. 4/2/87B.
73 92nd meeting of C.I.D., 26 July 1906. Cab. 2/2/1.
74 Esher Papers. Hardinge to Esher, 26 July 1906. 'Letters 1906'.
75 This conclusion does not appear in the records of the CID, having been expunged the following July. It survives in W.O. 106/42/C3/21b.
76 Minute, Robertson to Grierson, 5 September 1906. W.O. 106/42/C3/21b.
77 Esher Papers. Clarke to Esher, 6 August 1906. 'Sir G. Clarke 1906 Vol. 7'.
78 The Conditions governing an invasion of Egypt from the East, Note by the Secretary, 16 October 1906, p. 7. Cab. 4/2/89B.
79 The Turkish Empire as a military factor (1906). *B.D.* V, no. IVa.
80 93rd meeting of the C.I.D., 13 November 1906. Cab. 2/2/1.

81 The draft was originally prepared by Callwell; *see* Sir C. E. Callwell, *Experiences of a Dug-Out 1914–1918*, London, 1920, pp. 87–8.

82 The Possibility of a Joint Naval and Military Attack upon the Dardanelles, I: Memorandum by the General Staff, 19 December 1906, p. 1. Cab. 4/2/92B.

83 *Ibid.*, p. 2.

84 *Ibid.*, p. 4.

85 *Ibid.*, II: Note by the D.N.I., n.d., p. 5.

86 The Position of the Suez Canal in time of war, 1: Note by the Foreign Office, 23 November 1906. Cab. 4/2/98B.

87 Brett and Esher, *Journals and Letters*, vol. 2, p. 177.

88 Royal Archives. Haldane to Knollys, 10 December 1906. RA W27/51.

89 96th meeting of C.I.D. 28 February 1907. Cab. 2/2/1.

90 Report and Minutes of Evidence of a Sub-Committee of the Committee of Imperial Defence appointed by the Prime Minister to consider: The Military Requirements of the Empire as affected by Egypt and the Sudan, 11 March 1909. Cab. 16/4. The other members of the sub-committee besides Morley were: Grey, Haldane, Asquith, Esher, Lyttelton, Ewart, French and Clarke.

91 *Ibid.* App. IV: Memorandum on the Defence of Egypt; Maj. Gen. G. M. Bullock, Commanding the Forces in Egypt, n.d., p. 178.

92 *Ibid.* Minutes of Evidence, p. 15.

93 *Ibid.*, pp. 4, 12, 13.

94 *Ibid.* App. VIII: Note on the Defence of the Eastern Portion of Egypt by Col. G. J. Cuthbertson, A. A. G. in Egypt, 31 March 1907, pp. 187–8.

95 *Ibid.* App. II: Military Responsibilities in Egypt and the Anglo-Egyptian Sudan, Memo. by the General Staff, 15 April 1907, p. 172.

96 *Ibid.*, p. 173.

97 *Ibid.* Minutes of Evidence, p. 68.

98 *Ibid.*, p. 102.

99 Esher Papers. Clarke to Esher, 15 April 1907. 'Sir G. Clarke 1906–7 Vol. 8'.

100 Report and Minutes of Evidence . . . Egypt and the Sudan, *op. cit.*, Minutes of Evidence, p. 74.

101 Royal Archives. Esher to Edward VII, 3 July 1907. RA W40/122.

102 Operations that might be undertaken in Syria in the event of a Turkish attack on Egypt, 10 July, p. 3. Cab. 1/7/658.

103 Report and Minutes of Evidence . . . Egypt and the Sudan, *op. cit.*, Minutes of Evidence, p. 135.

104 Minute Haldane to Nicholson, 28 October 1909. W.O. 106/42/C3/30.

105 Report of a Sub-Committee of the Committee of Imperial Defence on the Military Requirements of the Empire as affected by Egypt and the Sudan, 11 March 1909, p. iii. Cab. 4/3/107B.

106 General Scheme for the Invasion of Syria, n.d. (printed 13 June 1908), p. 1. W.O. 106/43/C3/29.

107 Scheme for an Attack on Haifa (July 1910?), p. 8. W.O. 106/42/ C3/14b.
108 Standing Sub-Committee of C.I.D: Report regarding Landing Places in the Near East (Secret Series No. 1), 11 July 1910, p. 2. Cab. 17/71.
109 Report and Appendices of an Enquiry by the Standing Sub-Committee of the Committee of Imperial Defence into the responsibility of the Navy and Army respectively for the Defence of the Suez Canal, 2 June 1910, p. 2. Cab. 4/3/115B.
110 Notes on schemes for defence of Suez Canal, 2 June 1910, p. 5. W.O. 106/42/C3/35b.
111 Grey to Gorst, 15 December 1910. F.O. 800/47.
112 Defence of Eastern Frontier (J. R. Chancellor), 20 January 1911. W.O. 106/14/432M.
113 109th meeting of C.I.D. 24 March 1911. Cab. 2/2/2.
114 Minute, D.M.O. to C.I.G.S. 9 May 1911. W.O. 106/42/C3/35c.
115 Notes by MO1a, 1 April 1908. W.O. 106/42/C2/3.
116 Minute by Adye, 6 April 1908. W.O. 106/42/C2/3.
117 Minute by Hamilton, 28 July 1910. W.O. 32/531/79/2167.
118 Minute by Wilson, 19 August 1910. W.O. 106/43/C2/3a.
119 Reinforcements for Egypt (G. M. Harper), 4 February 1914. W.O. 106/43/C3/29.
120 Ibid.
121 Wilson Diary, 18 October 1913.
122 Transport required for Transport of 2 Cavalry Brigades and 2 divisions to Egypt, 23 February 1914. W.O. 106/43/C3/41.
123 On this topic see A. J. Marder, From the Dreadnought to Scapa Flow, I: The Road to War, Oxford, 1961, pp. 287–310; E. W. R. Lumby (ed.), Policy and Operations in the Mediterranean 1912–14, Navy Records Society, 1970; P. Halpern, The Mediterranean Naval Situation 1908–1914, Harvard, Mass., 1971, pp. 86–110.
124 Papers prepared by the General Staff 2: The Defence of Egypt against external aggression, 9 May 1912, p. 8. Cab. 4/4/33/149B.
125 Kitchener to Grey, 19 May 1912. F.O. 800/48.
126 Memorandum by the General Staff on the effect of the loss of sea power in the Mediterranean on British military strategy, 1 July 1912. Cab. 4/4/33/156B.
127 117th meeting of C.I.D. 4 July 1912. Cab. 2/2/3.
128 Roberts Papers. Churchill to Roberts, 12 July 1912. Box. X 20930, file C. 6.
129 Note on Defence of Egypt, 24 November 1914. Cab. 17/71.

9
France and Germany

In dealing with strategic problems relating to Europe, the General Staff had to grapple with a unique combination of two separate realms of operations standing in an uneasy co-existence. The fear of raids and invasions of the United Kingdom continued to activate official enquiries until 1913, whilst from 1906 considerations of active operations in Europe went ahead at a variable pace. The rebarbative effect of an offensive strategy in Europe upon a defensive strategy was reinforced by the hostility between the War Office and the Admiralty deriving from the practical effects of the 'Blue Water' theory, and by the activities of the campaigners for national service who utilized invasion in a political as well as a strategic vein. Thus, when it came to considering the dangers posed by the powers across the Channel, the War Office faced what was politically its most awkward problem.

Fear of a French invasion had initiated positive government action long before Palmerston's construction of a chain of fortifications around southern England in 1859. But by the turn of the century the parameters involved in any discussion of such a probability had widened to include the growing hostility to Germany within certain areas of the War Office and the development of an attitude to strategic problems typified by Nicholson's initiation of the series of general strategic analyses. As the War Office itself began to consider the possibility of overseas operations, so its attitude to home defence underwent something of a change; instead of full-scale invasions, it became prepared to consider home defence as requiring a combination of military and naval forces. In that case a raid was envisaged as the worst possible contingency.[1] Nicholson admitted the force of the Admiralty's argument that if Britain were superior at sea then she had nothing to worry about, whereas if she were not then she could be starved into submission by depriving her of foodstuffs without the need to invade or raid at all. His grounds for fighting the theories of the navalists about invasion were that otherwise a submission to Admiralty doctrine would result in the whittling away of Army Estimates.[2] As time went on Nicholson was to become ever more cantankerous as a result of the revelation of the extent to which Admiralty doctrine affected the War Office's attempts to solve strategic dilemmas overseas.

The first CID enquiry into invasion in 1903 found that even a raid was unlikely to achieve any degree of success. In this it responded chiefly to the views expressed by Balfour, who produced a series of arguments to demonstrate that even if the fleet should be temporarily absent—the line taken by the War Office— modern weapons favoured the defence, there was insufficient French shipping to transport an adequate force across the Channel, and the port space available on which to disembark it was insufficient.[3] For differing reasons both army and navy were prepared to accept the findings of the CID sub-committee: naval doctrine was confirmed by it, whilst the War Office could consider oversea strategy relatively unhampered by a require- ment to retain large numbers of troops for home defence. They were each reassured by a speech delivered by the Prime Minister on 11 May 1905 in which he was careful to emphasize the role of both services in national defence. Even Esher, a staunch advocate of 'Blue Water' theories, was convinced that there was no danger of a reduction in the size of the fleet as a result of the soothing balm administered by Balfour.[4]

Whilst the possibility of an invasion of England was thus being dismissed, the converse possibility of an English raid against the North German coast was being explored. In June 1905 Admiral Sir Arthur Wilson suggested that if Britain became involved in a Franco-German war she should launch amphibious operations against the German coast.[5] In answer to a query from the Admiralty, the War Office examined the prospects of a landing on the Baltic coast and found them unenticing. Objectives there were, chief amongst them the German navy; but defensive arrangements along the coast were too efficient for them to be gained. Moreover there was, at that time, little prospect of French assistance and without it the most attractive target—the Kiel Canal—would be easy to defend against a force of the size feasible.[6]

It was as a result of this experience, which dovetailed absolutely with military doctrine about the prospects for success of an identical operation directed against Great Britain, that the nascent General Staff was led to look more closely at operations in the major theatre in the event of a European war and not on the periphery of it. The playing of a war game in 1905 which envisaged a German violation of Belgian neutrality and British action to defend it reinforced this new direction in strategy. The exercise resulted in a belief that Britain would have both time and space at her disposal: that such a violation would not take place until a war between Germany and France had gone on for some months and that when it did, the German move would be predominantly south of the Meuse. At the conclusion of the game the strength of Germany's position also led to a recognition of the need to speed up the pace at which British troops arrived at the front.[7] The former beliefs were to take some years to eradicate.

The General Staff's conclusions about operations involving the defence of Belgium were spelt out in a paper printed in the autumn of 1905 as an answer to three queries originally raised by Sir George Clarke. In directing the attention of the General Staff to this problem Clarke was not motivated only by a concern about Belgium's position. Such a study, he suggested, was 'just what the G.S. would like, and they might (perhaps) be able to achieve more success than in dealing with the Indian frontier'.[8] The General Staff explained their conclusion about the timing of a German incursion into Belgium, basing their disbelief in an immediate invasion chiefly on the inevitable political complications which would ensue for Germany, expressed doubts about Belgium's power of protracted resistance, and reported that they hoped to have two army corps in position in Antwerp within twenty-three days of the outbreak of war.[9] The danger to Belgium lay, it was felt, in a German attack across the French frontier being checked, when the war game suggested that a move through Belgium might well be successful.

To say that the Moroccan crisis provided the stimulus for the General Staff to shift its perspective from colonial raids and amphibious operations to European involvement would certainly be to over-simplify a complex process.[10] None the less, diplomatic events were soon to reinforce the extrovert rather than the introvert element of Britain's European strategy. Certainly the crisis, coinciding as it did with the resignation of Balfour's administration and the preparations for a general election, offered a unique opportunity to permanent officials of the War

Office and Cabinet to influence the course of strategic policy without regard to the wishes of the government of the day. A preliminary conference consisting of Clarke, Esher, Sir John French and Captain Ottley, the Director of Naval Intelligence, displayed some interest in amphibious operations should war break out between France and Germany and should Belgium not be violated: if it was violated, then direct assistance in some form was recognized as the more desirable course. No one betrayed any doubts that, in some shape, there must be British military intervention in Europe if a war between France and Germany were to take place.[11] At the War Office, Grierson began working independently on his own study of the problem, which concluded that there was no point in capturing German colonies and little chance of success in landing on the North German coast; accordingly if Belgium were violated then there should be a joint Anglo-French attack on her flank, and if she were not Britain must support and reinforce France for reasons of morale.[12]

The shape of Grierson's strategic appreciation lends some weight to the assertion subsequently made by the French military attaché, Colonel Huguet, that he was first approached by the British and that he therefore assumed that the government had authorized the discussions.[13] Certainly when Clarke and the CID group got to hear of them Huguet only envisaged the possibility of British assistance in the event of a violation of Belgium. It was Clarke who urged that they must go beyond that.[14] At the conference held at Whitehall Gardens on 6 January 1906, Clarke's political view was endorsed in strategic terms: it was agreed that British military co-operation at the outset of a war would consist of either an expedition to Belgium or direct participation in the defence of the French frontier. The Admiralty's strategy, which favoured raids launched against the German coast, was thus doomed to decline and indeed military logic meant that it must be. The Admiralty were currently claiming that the fleet could protect England against serious danger from raids much better than could the army, but now sought to argue that the same strategic principles did not apply in the case of a German fleet seeking to prevent a British landing.

There were now two separate strategic options to be explored and assessed, entailing either assistance to the Belgians or direct support for the French. It was at this point that political backing was sought for what were diplomatic as well as strategic initiatives. Sir Edward Grey knew of the unofficial conversations between Huguet and Grierson by 9 January and sanctioned their continuance, though he thought it better not to tell Campbell-Bannerman as yet.[15] He was willing to consider what he termed 'the great question'—the extent and the nature of British support for France—precisely because of the security which the invasion enquiry of 1903 had given him. As he remarked to Bertie in this context, 'We can protect ourselves of course for we are more supreme at sea than we have ever been.'[16] The military, too, could think in European terms for the same reason. However, it was at this moment that the basis of that freedom first began to crumble; for though it would be some years before the fact was openly recognized, with the adoption of a land strategy in Europe the navy had a doctrine but it no longer had a war plan. Ultimately the navy would seek to resolve this conundrum by questioning the validity of its own dogma about invasion.

In large measure the responsibility for this dilemma lay on the shoulders of Sir John Fisher. He remained obdurately wedded to operations against the German coast, refused to guarantee the passage of the Expeditionary Force across the Channel and opposed the use of that force on the European continent. As Repington disconsolately remarked when Fisher withdrew the Admiralty representative from the informal discussions at Whitehall Gardens, 'I thought we had a St. Vincent at Whitehall Gardens but apparently I was mistaken.'[17]

Sanctioned by Campbell-Bannerman in mid-January, staff talks with the French progressed rapidly, so that by May detailed railway timetables were being considered for British troop movement in France.[18] At the same time, exploratory talks were opened up by the British military attaché in Brussels, Lt-Col. Barnardistone, to establish precisely what Belgian strategy was, the better to be able to support it. Barnardistone revealed the Belgian intention to concentrate their field army around Brussels in order to protect Antwerp; the forts of Liège and Namur were thought to be safe from any *coup-de-main*. He also mentioned the possibility of a German move against the Upper Meuse through Mézières and Sedan.[19] This latter suggestion injected the factor of speed into British calculations; if it did occur, then it would be necessary to have British troops on the Meuse between Namur and Dinant by the tenth day after war broke out if they were to be of any value. From this time onwards speed of mobilization became an increasing preoccupation at the War Office. It was reinforced by Grierson's strong opinion that a German attack upon Antwerp would be an 'eccentric operation' and that a move south of the Meuse was far more probable.[20]

By mid-April outline plans existed for British troops to concentrate on the right wing of the Belgian army if it protected Antwerp or if it stood on the Meuse. By that time the Moroccan crisis had diminished in intensity and therefore the need for a choice between the two land strategies was obviated. This was perhaps fortunate, for it enabled Grierson to visit the Belgian army on manoeuvres later in the year and to discover that it had deep and widespread defects:[21]

> The men were unintelligent looking, slack and I should say not well instructed. The infantry were of decidedly inferior physique, the artillery were badly horsed, and the cavalry and engineers only made a good impression. The marching discipline was defective, distances were badly kept, and the pace was a mere crawl. The officers appeared to take little interest in the work, and the staff arrangements were decidedly defective as regards the formation and movement of columns.

The contrast with the French army was absolute; Grierson found them enormously improved in every respect over the past ten years and felt that he had never seen better staff work in any army, in peace or in war. This assessment of the relative merits of the two forces, together with the revelations about the nature of Belgian strategic planning, may have had more than a little to do with the pursual of the French rather than the Belgian strategy in subsequent years.

Throughout the remainder of 1906 and the following year, the General Staff became increasingly convinced that the occasion of their intervention in Europe would be a violation of the Low Countries, and they also came increasingly to favour action in support of France as the best means to counter such an event. Lack of confidence in the Belgian army led to the suggestion that Great Britain must place 100,000 men around Namur or Louvain within ten days of the outbreak of war if they were to be of any use.[22] Any attack on Antwerp was thought to be much less likely than a German turning movement through the Ardennes. The restraining influence upon strategy was always felt to be the lack of government knowledge of how far military arrangements between England and France had progressed and Ewart, who had succeeded Grierson as DMO, would have been much happier with a regular alliance between the two powers for this reason.[23] Ewart's contribution to the strategy of continental involvement had much to do with this feeling, for he was moving towards the idea that the best way to evict the Germans from Belgium would not be by direct support of the Belgians but by co-operation in the field with the French.[24] But by this time diplomacy had taken over the helm once again, and was giving quite the reverse impression from that emanating from the military links between Britain and France. Clemenceau was somewhat taken aback to be told by Campbell-Bannerman that British public opinion would not 'allow of British troops being employed on the Continent of Europe'.[25]

At this moment the issue of whether Britain could afford to neglect her own defences and indulge in what might prove to be costly ventures overseas was once again reopened. From July 1906 the indefatigable Colonel Repington began to work with Lord Roberts to get the invasion enquiry reopened; their object was to bring into existence some form of conscription by awakening the government and the public to the hollowness of the Admiralty's claim that it could protect England. The proposal currently being made by Haldane to create a Territorial Force offered both a target for this group and a model on which could be based something akin to the great European armies for those who saw intervention as inevitable. Together, the two factors won Balfour over to the necessity to reopen the enquiry. The opponents of the 'Blue Water' theories would probably have caused very much less of an impact had not Repington succeeded in recruiting the discontented Admiral Lord Charles Beresford into their ranks; he stayed at his post in the navy and provided important information about the shortage of torpedo boats and light cruisers.[26]

Although Fisher bitterly resented the invasion issue being reopened his fellow-navalist Lord Esher expressed pleasure at this occurrence, since it might alleviate the danger of over-confidence in the senior service.[27] This may well have been a subtle warning to Fisher to remedy the paucity of strategic planning at the Admiralty; if so, it had no appreciable effect. Fisher was saved because, despite being well briefed on the land strategy involved in invasion, Repington was demolished at the hearings of the CID sub-committee by Slade who seized on his failure to consider naval strategy. The end of the 'Bolt from the Blue' school was ensured when Balfour read a paper arguing that invasion would stand a better chance of success after hostilities had broken out rather than immediately that happened.[28] The final report of the sub-committee rejected surprise attack as impossible, and argued for a home army of at least 70,000 men to repel raids and thus to force an enemy to consider invasion only on so large a scale that evasion of the Royal Navy would prove impossible. Until the time that the Territorial Army was fit to take the field, two of the six regular divisions should remain behind in England if the Expeditionary Force was despatched elsewhere.[29] In reaching this latter decision, the sub-committee ignored a forceful and significant argument put by the General Staff in June 1908 that to leave a force of that size at home would devalue Britain's alliance with 'one of the continental Powers'.[30] The proper relationship between navalist and military strategy as regards Europe was perhaps never as clearly defined as in this plea.

In general, the second invasion enquiry had confirmed the line of strategy adopted by the War Office in considering some form of European action in the event of war between France and Germany. However, two government departments significantly failed to operate on the basis of that considered strategic opinion. The navy was working on its own combined operations strategy and by August 1909 had devised war plans for the launching of diversionary land operations against the German coast whilst the navy neutralized its German opposite number. It has been appositely remarked that whilst all pre-war military and naval planning contained elements of fantasy 'the various amphibious schemes propounded by the Admiralty had an excessive share'.[31] In this case, those schemes also contained a massive illogicality. Landings would have to be attempted while the German fleet still existed, even though during the second invasion enquiry Sir Julian Corbett had stressed the difficulty of a landing in the British Isles whilst even a damaged and inferior British fleet stood on the defensive. If Denmark were hostile, the projected landings would take place on the North Sea coast; if she were neutral or allied to England they would have the Schleswig coast as their target.[32] The scanty nature of naval planning, and its internal illogicalities, confirmed the fact that Fisher started such activities chiefly in order to counter criticisms that he had neglected them.

The second area where fear of invasion seems to have had some influence upon policy was in the activities of certain elements in the Foreign Office. Sir Charles Hardinge used it in a defensive light in offering the opinion that England need not feel too alarmed about being confronted by a Franco-Russian coalition since, provided sea supremacy was maintained and defensive forces were put in an efficient condition, there was no danger to national security.[33] Eyre Crowe, minuting a despatch which argued that Germany would make a move against Britain without warning when she thought herself strong enough, and not as many thought after a period of international tension, clearly displayed a belief in surprise invasion.[34] This belief may well have accounted in some part for his opinion that the suggestion by France of 'some closer agreement' deserved 'the most careful consideration', expressed several years later.[35]

The issue of invasion could be utilized in another, and quite different, context: that of the structure of the army. During Balfour's premiership, Clarke had put forward the thesis that although raids were unlikely they were a useful peg on which to hang a reorganization of the Volunteers for purposes of home defence.[36] The Volunteers had been replaced by Haldane's Territorial Army, and the second invasion enquiry had minimized the prospect of incursion from overseas; none the less the invasion issue could still be used in the context of the campaign for compulsory service which lay at the back of Roberts's actions. Esher put the issue most clearly. Although temperamentally in favour of conscription he was, he said, unwilling to go to compulsory service because a force in England able 'beyond all doubt, to hold its own against any probable invading enemy, would gradually but surely lead to the weakening of the Fleet'.[37] Here lay the rationale for keeping the invasion issue alive, and thereby restricting the army's freedom of action.

The War Office was meanwhile working out the strategic options open to it in the event of a war against Germany. If the combatants were limited to Germany and England, then the result was likely to be a stalemate, since operations against the Schleswig coast were ruled out. In the event of a Franco-German war entailing the violation of Belgian neutrality, Britain might intervene directly in either France or Belgium. A vital new departure was, however, made in the case of a Franco-German war which did not entail such a violation; in this case the General Staff still recommended concentrating on the French left, though there were signs of a belief that a large uncommitted force capable of a combined operation might in some way affect German strategy.[38] For a moment, it seemed as though the army might accept a parallel concept to the naval idea of the threat posed by a 'fleet in being'. In the event it did not. But this paper, together with the findings of the second invasion enquiry, led to War Office pressure for a CID sub-committee to determine general government policy on the employment of a military force in Europe so as to enable the General Staff to proceed more efficiently with their plans. The CID concurred in this on 28 October 1908.

The parameters of the enquiry were first set by the Foreign Office, which envisaged a German attack upon Holland, Denmark, Britain or France—with, in this case, one side or the other violating Belgian neutrality—as triggering off such action. They were in turn modified by a General Staff memorandum which refined likely contingencies down to the assistance of France against Germany or attack by Germany on Holland or Denmark.[39] In the event of Belgium not being violated, two alternatives presented themselves. A series of diversionary attacks might be mounted in the Baltic with naval assistance, or the army might be committed to cover the French left wing. The General Staff resisted the former notion, arguing that such operations would produce no decisive effect even if possible at all, and that by then the decisive land battles on the continent might already be lost. If Belgium were violated, the General Staff proposed to concentrate alongside the French.

It was a misfortune that Fisher chose deliberately to starve the sub-committee of information about his own plans.[40] He appears to have done so in an attempt to force a general Cabinet discussion in which to hammer out the relative merits of direct European involvement or of a peripheral strategy of raids and combined operations. Hence it was only in connection with the case of German hostilities towards Denmark that the navy prepared any detailed suggestions; they were for a British blockade of the North Sea and Baltic expeditions to be undertaken by the French. The sub-committee considered this an isolated campaign and thought that in such circumstances an expedition to the Baltic would do little good. As a result, failure to examine Fisher's plans thoroughly meant that the only alternative to the General Staff's strategy was a through-going naval blockade.[41]

The proposal that aid to France should be primarily of a traditional naval variety was put to the sub-committee by Esher, who suggested that the needs of Imperial defence and particularly of India demanded that the first call on land forces should be from outside Europe. He therefore suggested a strategy of blockades and raids, together with the landing of a token force to assist the French. This was opposed by all three military members of the sub-committee, Nicholson, Ewart and Sir John French. They pointed out that a partial mobilization would be difficult and disruptive, and that India now had little to fear from Russia anyway. Also it was doubtful whether a purely naval contribution would have any effect on the land campaign.

Esher made little attempt to defend his thesis against this opposition, especially after Crewe agreed with the CGS about the crucial nature of the first land battles on the French frontier—an indication of the deep-seated belief that the war would be decided quickly once it broke out. The final report therefore strongly favoured the General Staff's idea of a European strategy. A fundamental, and novel, political principle was first adumbrated: that the decision to intervene in a Franco-German struggle must not be left to turn on 'the mere point' of a violation of Belgium.[42] Official recognition was given to the belief that the first battles in France would be decisive and that therefore a blockade strategy was of no importance. Thus it was concluded that, subject always to Cabinet decision at the time, four regular infantry divisions and one cavalry division would be concentrated in reserve on the French left unless needed to cover Antwerp. This decision was ratified by the CID on 24 July 1909.

It is one of the paradoxes of the 'two-way' strategy of offensive and defensive with regard to Europe that the sub-committee reached its conclusions about a land campaign in France at the moment when popular literature about invasion reached its height in the popular press as a result of the German navy *Novelle* of that year and the scare over the construction of the eight dreadnoughts.[43] This was accompanied by an outbreak of spy-fever in the summer of 1909, though thereafter the whole *genre* of invasion literature rapidly declined. The failure of this fear of invasion to affect official policy is explained by the findings of the second invasion enquiry, by the belief shared by Grey, Haldane and Asquith that Britain must uncompromisingly support France against Germany, and by the rejection of invasion as a viable proposition in the minds of key military officials. Ewart confided to his diary the belief that home defence was 'the most poisonous strategic fallacy ever propounded by man' and that the 'only true defence is offence'.[44]

In August 1910 Sir Henry Wilson succeeded Ewart as DMO at the War Office. Wilson's drive, enthusiasm and complete conviction about the necessity to render effective land support to France were to provide the stimulus to move military strategy on from the period of consideration and of deciding between alternatives to that of detailed planning for action. The precise nature of his contribution to the European strategy was revealed early in his tenure of office, when he recorded:[45]

> I am very dis-satisfied with the state of affairs in every respect. No real arrangements for concentration and movements of either Expedy. Force or Territorials. No proper arrangements for horse supply. No arrangements for safeguarding our arsenal at Woolwich.

For the first time a DMO was displaying the tenets of the General Staff mind as it was understood in Germany and as Esher and Clarke had striven to create it. Wilson's considerations of strategy rested on the dual pillars of detailed programmes for Britain's participation on the continent and consideration of what strategy it was feasible for Germany to pursue given the limitations which logistics inevitably imposed upon her.

Until the Agadir crisis in 1911 Wilson worked very much alone in exploring the *minutiae* of his European strategy. In doing so he had not only to combat the hare-brained schemes of the Admiralty: Sir John French proffered one notably fantastic suggestion, loading flat-bottomed boats full of troops and towing them up the Rhine to form what he termed a *point d'appui*.[46] When, as had been the case in the Tabah incident five years previously, ministerial attention was focused on issues of military strategy, the first reaction was the appearance of papers which seemed to controvert the agreement reached in 1909. The Admiralty suggested that it might need troops for small landings, home defence duties and the defence of temporary naval bases and anchorages; it went on to add that, once committed, an expeditionary force would be exceedingly difficult to extricate from Europe. Therefore it recommended a policy of feints against Wilhelmshaven, Bremerhaven, Cuxhaven and the Kiel Canal, any one of which might be taken should favourable circumstances arise.[47] Another contribution to the debate, emanating from Winston Churchill, suggested that immediate intervention was not as crucial as the army made out since the French would not be in a position to strike a decisive blow until the fortieth day of a campaign. By that time the projected German advance would be running into difficulties, requiring a growing proportion of troops to be allotted to the defence of lines of communication. Churchill therefore suggested that the French fall back in the face of a German attack and await British intervention on or about the fortieth day, by which time the addition of colonial troops would have swollen the British contingent to some 290,000 men.[48]

Wilson recognized the significance of the crisis for his continental strategy to the extent of paying an unofficial call on Grey and putting several important points to him, the foremost of which was that all six divisions of the BEF must be sent to France in the event of war. His remarks, he reported, 'were agreed to but with no great heartiness'.[49] The degree to which the issue now rested on professional strategic considerations rather than those of political expediency or of personal strategic preference was made apparent in Wilson's exposition before the CID on 23 August 1911 of the desirable military strategy. Wilson calculated that the main German effort must come in the ninety-mile gap between Verdun and Maubeuge, a region which contained thirteen roads and could therefore support the movement of some forty divisions. Against them France could field between thirty-seven and thirty-nine divisions. These computations resulted in Wilson's pressing the CID to accept three propositions: that Great Britain must mobilize on the same day as France, that she must send all six regular divisions to France and that arrangements had to be made to keep this force up to strength throughout the war.[50]

The Admiralty at first sought to defeat the military strategy on a technicality. The First Sea Lord, Sir Arthur Wilson, informed the CID that the Admiralty could not guarantee the passage of the expeditionary force to the French channel ports if this coincided with a general mobilization of the fleet. He retracted this after being reminded by Asquith of the conclusion of the 1908–9 sub-committee that if military intervention was to be of any value it had to be immediate. The DMO was subjected to a rather closer and more able examination by Churchill and Lloyd George who questioned the assumption behind Wilson's plans that the Germans would not swing north of the Meuse and enter France on a front between Lille and Maubeuge. Wilson's answer was that he thought German forces would not be as adequate to undertake such a task for at least ten years. Opinions differed on the obstacle that the Belgian army would pose, Wilson and Lloyd George feeling that the Germans could not afford to ignore it whilst Churchill and French discounted it. In this instance, Wilson did not follow the line of his partner across the Channel, for Foch reportedly thought Belgian plans for concentration around Antwerp 'useless'.[51] Churchill and Lloyd George also introduced the issue of what would follow a major allied reverse, and in doing so revealed that the General Staff had given no thought to that unpalatable eventuality.

When the meeting reconvened in the afternoon, Sir Arthur Wilson put before it the navy's concept of a European strategy. He revealed a crude plan for close blockade of the German ports and a series of small landings, with the prospect of much more demanding operations against Heligoland, Wilhelmshaven, Danzig and Swinemunde thereafter. Nicholson energetically attacked this ill-conceived strategy, remarking on the increased capacity of the German railway system which would aid powers of concentration, and the fact that naval artillery was of no value in supporting operations of an amphibious nature. In taking this stance he was able to base military offensive strategy on the principles twice adumbrated by the Admiralty and twice accepted by the CID: that the power of the navy could render a successful invasion of the United Kingdom impossible. The unspoken assumption was that what applied in an inward direction must also apply in an outward one. On the eve of the war the navy was to seek to upset this assumption at the cost of their own declarations of infallibility.

Sir Arthur Wilson attempted to use the findings of the second invasion enquiry in his endeavour to defeat the War Office's strategy, citing the decision that had been reached that two divisions of the regular army must remain behind until the

Territorial Force was adequately trained. Counter to this the Director of Military Training, Major-General A. J. Murray, asserted that it was already efficient enough to deal with enemy raids. The relative impact of each of the separate cases could be gauged from the fact that the Prime Minister went so far as to commit himself to the military strategy with the remark that it was for him a question of whether or not to send all six divisions to France.

Despite his victory, the points made by Churchill and Lloyd George about a wider swing by the German army north of the Meuse clearly awakened some doubts in Wilson's mind. By 4 September he was sufficiently convinced of 'the enormous importance to us soldiers of an actively friendly Belgium' to urge Grey to construct an offensive/defensive alliance against Germany, to comprise France, Belgium, Denmark, Russia and England.[52] He also went so far as to argue that once war broke out Belgium could not and should not be allowed to remain neutral, though his hope that she might connive at an Anglo-French violation of her southern borders in order to preserve her heartlands north of the Meuse was somewhat fanciful in the light of earlier reports of pro-German sympathy in Belgium.[53] If the German army crossed into Belgium, then north Belgium would be a secure base from which to attack the German wing. Belgian co-operation had become an essential element in successful Anglo-French action south of the Meuse.[54]

It was as a result of this pressure that in April 1912 Sir John French, newly promoted to CIGS, agreed to reopen the negotiations with the Belgians which had lapsed in 1906. The spur to this was the revelation that the Meuse fortifications offered little in the way of an obstacle to a determined German advance and that the Belgian army was weak in numbers and efficiency.[55] The negotiations were mishandled by the British military attaché, Colonel Tom Bridges, a factor which helped to reinforce the pro-German and anti-British tendencies of the Belgian government at that time. By the autumn it was possible to report to the British ambassador a conversation in which General Michel, the Belgian Minister of War, 'of course refused to give an opinion as to which nation would be likely first to do this [violate Belgian neutrality], though he clearly thought that it would not be Germany'.[56] The resultant planning by Belgium led to her posting one division to guard her coast against a British landing, one on her frontier with Germany and two watching the French frontier in July 1914.[57]

It was a peculiar coincidence that at a time when military commitment to France was growing stronger, naval strategy was beginning to cast doubt upon the invulnerability of the United Kingdom and therefore, by a logical extension of thought, to resuscitate a raid strategy for use in a European context. In January 1912 the War Office formally contacted the Admiralty about provision to ferry the BEF across the Channel; ten months later they received their reply, which was that the navy could not carry out the operation in time for the force to participate in the first decisive battles on the French frontier.[58] This in itself was simply a tiresome display of the attitude of the Admiralty to which the War Office was well accustomed. More alarming, and more significant in the process of conversion, was the result of the naval manoeuvres of 1912, when a 'German' fleet under the command of Admiral Battenburg was adjudged to have evaded detection and landed 28,000 troops in the Humber estuary.[59] This in itself was a worrisome occurrence; it was compounded by the alarm felt by the new First Lord of the Admiralty, Winston Churchill, at the potentiality of the torpedo to nullify the powers of the Grand Fleet. As a result particularly of the latter fact, a third invasion enquiry was instituted the following year.[60]

At least one navalist had no doubts as to why the issue had been reopened, and many in the War Office would have concurred had they known his views. Esher was certain that the Admiralty had deliberately drawn attention to the weakness of what had hitherto been their unshakeable dogma: their object was to keep two divisions of the regular army at home but not to make admissions which would prevent the Admiralty from using those divisions overseas for naval strategic purposes.[61] In other words, the Admiralty were trying to reverse the defeat suffered by Sir Arthur Wilson in August 1911 by creating a chimera sufficiently alarming as to undermine the General Staff's case that the whole of the BEF must go to France immediately war broke out or else be useless.

The degree to which the General Staff was alive to the likely effects if the Admiralty succeeded in proving their case was evinced in the determined opposition they put up and the width of example they drew to counter the notion that regular forces must be retained in England. Other contingencies were cited apart from 'military co-operation with a Continental Power' which might necessitate the employment of the Expeditionary Force overseas, particularly a pan-Islamic movement in the East; a Turkish invasion of Egypt would be one specific manifestation of such a movement. In view of such eventualities it was held that the regular army was no more than adequate to fulfil its obligations and that 'to allot any portion of it to Home Defence might be seriously prejudicial to the safety of the Empire'.[62]

The Admiralty were offered a chance to drive a wedge between the various military officials by the disparity of views which emerged at the hearings of the CID sub-committee appointed to re-examine the issue of invasion. Considerable disagreement soon appeared between Lord Roberts and the General Staff over such basic facts as the number of men available for home defence. Although both agreed on the number left after the despatch of the expeditionary force, Roberts thought there remained 310,000 troops to be found, whereas the General Staff computed the shortage at 116,000. Roberts further argued that a Central Force of 210,000 was needed to meet an invader where the General Staff thought 125,000 quite enough.[63]

There was also a disagreement before the sub-committee between Sir Henry Wilson, who believed in no more serious threat than a 10,000-man raid designed to slow up mobilization, and Sir William Robertson who still believed in invasion as he had done in 1903. It was Robertson who put forward the most sensible concrete proposals to meet this threat, using the 141,000 Territorials to man the coast defences. The divided military opinion was saved by the presence on the sub-committee of Lord Nicholson who repeatedly drew its attention to the major issue, which was the complete reversal of naval opinion after years during which military strategy had been built up on its oft-repeated principles. Hankey recorded:[64]

> a characteristic outburst on the part of Field Marshal Lord Nicholson which made considerable impression on the sub-committee. In trenchant terms he reminded the Sub-Committee of the attitude taken up in the past by the Admiralty with regard to the whole question of Invasion and Raids, and indignantly repudiated any idea that the War Office had failed in their duty. They had, he indicated,

done a good deal more than the Admiralty had ever asked them to.

The report of the third, and last, invasion enquiry was published on 15 April 1914, and differed in few respects from the findings made six years earlier. It was still assumed that the minimum force necessary for a successful attack on the United Kingdom was 70,000 and that the fleet could interrupt an invasion of such a size. However, some consideration was given to the prospects of raids, as this was the first report to consider their putative targets: impeding the Expeditionary Force and the destruction of dockyards and magazines. To meet what dangers did exist, the General Staff were to retain two of the six regular divisions if necessary.[65]

The final demise of the spectre of invasion ensured the dominance of military over naval strategy in a European war in 1914. On all counts Sir Arthur Nicolson was wrong in estimating, some four months before war broke out, that 'should war break out on the continent, the likelihood of our despatching any expeditionary force is extremely remote'.[66] Wilson, supported by the CIGS and DMT, personally pressed his case to send five divisions overseas on Asquith and was successful: 'I spoke openly about it all with result that Asquith settled to allow my present arrangements to stand.'[67] The rapidity with which war followed ensured that General Staff strategy would be followed, though with minor modifications. The only opportunity to resuscitate 'Blue Water' ideas of peripheral operations would be in the event of the failure of military intervention to achieve a decisive result quickly. When that happened Hankey, an avowed navalist in outlook, was to be in a crucial position to foster such a scheme.

Notes

1 The Strength of the Regular Army and Auxiliary Forces, having regard to Peace and War Requirements, 1 May 1904, pp. 1, 2. Cab. 3/1/22A.
2 Roberts Papers. Nicholson to Roberts, 4 September 1901. Box X20926, file N2.
3 Draft Report on the possibility of serious invasion: Home Defence, 11 November 1903. Cab. 3/1/18A.
4 Esher Papers. Esher to Repington, 19 May 1905. 'Army Letters Vol. 2'.

5 **A.** J. Marder, *The Anatomy of British Sea Power* (Archon edition), Hamden, Connecticut, 1964, pp. 504–5.
6 British Military Action on the Baltic Coast in the event of a war between Germany and Great Britain and France in alliance, 9 September 1905. W.O. 106/46/E2/10.
7 Strategic War Game. W.O. 33/364.
8 Clarke to Balfour, 17 August 1905. B.M. Add. MSS. 49702.
9 Violation of the neutrality of Belgium during a Franco-German war, 29 September 1905. Cab. 4/1/65B.
10 S. R. Williamson, *The Politics of Grand Strategy*, Harvard, Mass., 1969, p. 45.
11 Notes on Conference held at 2, Whitehall Gardens, on Dec. 19, 1905, Jan. 6, 1906, Jan. 12, 1906 and Jan 19, 1906. Cab. 18/24.
12 Military forces required for Oversea Warfare, 4 January 1906. W.O. 106/44/E1/7.
13 Esher Papers. Repington to Esher, 18 January 1906. 'Army Letters Vol. 3'.
14 Esher Papers. Clarke to Esher, 2 January 1906. 'Sir George Clarke 1906 Vol. 6'.
15 Esher Papers. Clarke to Esher, 9 January 1906. 'Sir George Clarke 1906 Vol. 6'.
16 Grey to Bertie, 15 January 1906. *B.D.* III, no. 216.
17 Esher Papers. Repington to Esher, 14 January 1906. 'Army Letters Vol. 3'.
18 *See* N. W. Summerton, 'The Development of British Military Planning for a War Against Germany 1904-1914', unpublished Ph.D. thesis, London, 1970, chapter 3.
19 Barnardistone to Grierson, 19 January 1906. *B.D.* III, no. 221 (c) (1).
20 Grierson to Barnardistone, 27 February 1906. *B.D.* III, no. 221 (c) (5).
21 Royal Archives. Grierson to Sir A. Davidson, 10 September 1906. RA W27/36.
22 War with Germany in defence of Belgian Neutrality, 4 January 1907. W.O. 106/46/E2/8.
23 Ewart Diary, 26 and 31 July 1907.
24 Our Position as regards the Low Countries, 8 April 1907. Cab. 18/24.
25 Bertie to Grey, 11 April 1907. *B.D.* VI, no. 9.
26 Roberts Papers. Repington to Roberts, 17 November 1907. Box X20927, file R1.
27 Esher Papers. Esher to Fisher, 1 October 1907. 'Sir John Fisher 1906-8'.
28 *See* H. R. Moon, 'The Invasion of the United Kingdom: Public Controversy and Official Planning 1888–1918', Vol. 1, Ph.D. thesis, London, 1968, pp. 350–74.
29 Invasion: Report of a Sub-Committee . . . to reconsider the question of oversea attack, 22 October 1908. Cab. 3/2/1/44A.
30 Williamson, *op. cit.*, pp. 98–9.
31 *Ibid.*, p. 50.

32 P. K. Kemp (ed.), *The Papers of Admiral Sir John Fisher*, vol. 2, Navy Records Society, 1964, pp. 418f.
33 Memorandum by Sir Charles Hardinge on the Possibility of War (April ? 1909). *B.D.* V, app. III.
34 Trench to Lascelles, 27 April 1908; minute by Crowe, n.d. *B.D.* VI, no. 94 encl.
35 Minute by Crowe, 15 April 1911. *B.D.* VII, no. 207.
36 Clarke to Balfour, 25 March 1905. B.M. Add. MSS. 49701.
37 Roberts Papers. Esher to Roberts, 6 June 1909. Box X20930, file E-G.
38 Military Policy in a war with Germany, 2 July 1908. W.O. 106/46/E2/2.
39 Memorandum by the General Staff, 27 November 1908, pp. 17–19. Cab. 16/5.
40 M. V. Brett and Viscount Esher, *Journals and Letters of Reginald Viscount Esher*, vol. 2, London, 1934–8, p. 375.
41 Summerton, *op. cit.*, chapter 5.
42 Report of the Sub-Committee . . . on the Military Needs of the Empire, 24 July 1909, p. 1. Cab. 4/3/1/109B.
43 *See* A. J. Marder, *From the Dreadnought to Scapa Flow, 1: The Road to War*, Oxford, 1961, pp. 151–85.
44 Ewart Diary, 12 July 1909.
45 Wilson Diary, 25 October 1910.
46 Wilson Diary, 20 March 1911.
47 The Military Aspects of the Continental Problem, 21 August 1911. Cab. 4/3/2/131B.
48 Military Aspects of the Continental Problem, August 1911. Cab. 4/3/2/132B.
49 Wilson Diary, 9 August 1911.
50 114th meeting of CID, 23 August 1911. Cab. 2/2/2.
51 Fairholme to Bertie, 8 April 1911. *B.D.* VI, no. 460 encl.
52 Wilson Diary, 4 September 1911.
53 Lowther to Bertie, 6 February 1909; Chilton to Grey, 25 February 1909. *B.D.* VIII, no. 312 encl., no. 313.
54 Appreciation of the Political and Military Situation in Europe, 20 September 1911. W.O. 106/47/E2/26.
55 Bridges to Villiers, 19 October 1911. *B.D.* VIII, no. 319 encl.
56 Kelly to Villiers, 12 September 1912. *B.D.* VIII, no. 324 encl.
57 J. C. Helmreich, 'Belgian concern over neutrality and British intentions, 1906–1914', *Journal of Modern History*, vol. 36, December 1964, p. 427.
58 Wilson Diary, 18 January and 12 November 1912.
59 A. J. Marder, *The Road to War*, pp. 352–3.
60 Williamson's 'fragmentary evidence' suggesting that Repington initiated the enquiry seems too tenuous to be credible; Williamson, *op. cit.*, pp. 306–7. *See* Moon, *op. cit.*, II, pp. 431–4.
61 Esher to Balfour, 25 June 1913. B.M. Add. MSS. 49719.
62 Seely Papers. Memorandum to Illustrate the necessity for retaining the whole Expeditionary Force solely for service outside the United Kingdom, 4 April 1913. Box 139.

63 Royal Archives. Hankey to Stamfordham, 20 June 1913. RA Geo. V, E.820/4.
64 Royal Archives. Hankey to Stamfordham, 20 November 1913. RA Geo. V, E.820/9.
65 Attack on the British Isles from oversea: Report of Standing Sub-Committee, 15 April 1914. Cab. 3/2/5/62A.
66 Nicolson to Buchanan, 7 April 1914. Quo. Zara Steiner, *The Foreign Office and Foreign Policy 1898–1914*, Cambridge, 1969, p. 130.
67 Wilson Diary, 6 May 1914.

10
Democracy at War

The test of British strategy and of the General Staff organization created to formulate it came in August 1914 and soon revealed deficiencies and weaknesses hitherto unapparent. The departure of most of the experienced General Staff officers to France demonstrated the importance of individual personalities in strategic counsels, and this was to become plainer as the first year of war ground on. Within the War Office chance placed in a close relationship a number of officers who were not fitted to ensure the continued development of the General Staff or even to maintain its position. At their head sat the monolithic figure of Lord Kitchener, pressed by Asquith to assume the office of Secretary of State for War in order to strengthen a very un-militaristic Cabinet. The appointment was a grave mistake—perhaps Asquith's greatest during his wartime period of office. Kitchener never understood the role or functions of a General Staff, a fact which gravely retarded its development, and he lacked the breadth of strategic vision necessary to overcome this shortcoming. There is much truth in Robertson's comment on his assuming the position of Chief of the Imperial General Staff in the winter of 1915—'the War Office General Staff might not have existed'.[1]

The British Expeditionary Force was committed from the outset to fighting in northern France and the conduct of war there soon assumed a pattern which it was to maintain for three and a half years. There was little the General Staff could have done to influence grand strategy in this theatre. Its greatest chance came with the proposition of a new strategic venture at the Dardanelles. The history of this unfortunate venture reveals quite clearly the degree to which the Cabinet depended on responsible professional advice. In its absence, and the absence therefore of any clear blueprint for the operation, the way was clear for the strategic entrepreneurs, within the Cabinet and outside it, to proffer their own grandly conceived solutions. These were usually formulated to resolve political problems, as for example how to persuade Greece or Italy to enter the war on Britain's side, and then sold on their strategic merits. In some cases these merits were non-existent.

Asquith still ran the Cabinet on peacetime lines, and was open to advice from all and sundry; his policy towards the Gallipoli venture was later to be perceptibly influenced by the pessimism of his son Arthur who was serving there.[2] When this coincided with a fount of amateur strategic advice which was not tested against the professional opinion of the War Office the result was hesitation, uncertainty and in the long run disaster.

As the Dardanelles venture proceeded there were perceptible changes in the way the government made up its strategic mind. The arrival of Sir Archibald Murray as CIGS in the autumn of 1915 resulted in the views of the General Staff being put increasingly before the Cabinet, and it was at this time, some months before the arrival in Whitehall of Sir William Robertson, that a 'Western Front' stance came to be adopted. The gradual change of heart on the part of leading members of the Cabinet about how a democracy should wage war led to the establishment of the small War Committee as the directing body; and with the close interest displayed by the House of Commons this helped to ensure a thorough reform of the role and position of the General Staff in December 1915. Sir William Robertson emerged as the only man who possessed the right combination of ability, self-confidence and political support and as CIGS became the sole source of strategic advice in the Cabinet. In just under eighteen months, and chiefly as a result of the mishaps over Gallipoli, the government veered from one extreme to the other. At first relying too little on specialist military advice, it came to rely upon it exclusively. The results were unfortunate, to say the least.

The move towards war in the summer of 1914 was by no means regarded universally as undesirable, and within the army there was a distinct feeling of relief, exemplified by Sir William Birdwood's remark a few months after war had broken out: '*What* a piece of real luck this war has been as regards Ireland—just averted Civil War and when it is over we may all be tired of fighting.'[3] None the less the situation in which the higher echelon of the War Office found itself was far from desirable. The Prime Minister had for the months since the Curragh affair held the seals of Secretary of State for War himself, and proved slow off the mark in declaring the so-called

Precautionary period. Fortunately the provisions written into the *War Book* compensated for this. During the first days of August he clearly betrayed the want of strong professional advice, holding both that Britain was under no obligation, express or implied, to help France and that the immediate despatch of the Expeditionary Force was not contemplated.[4] This may have been the Cabinet's view but it certainly was not that of the General Staff.

For the first five days of August Haldane relieved the Prime Minister of the burden of the War Office, and it was he who pressed Asquith to offer the post to Kitchener. Kitchener accepted the position on 5 August and the general reaction was perhaps best summed up in Esher's observation that 'When Kitchener of Khartoum took control of the War Office . . . there was a sigh of relief, for here was a man in the right place.'[5] Unfortunately, the sigh and the man were both misplaced.

Indications that the government felt no confidence in the strategic advice of the General Staff became apparent at once. The first meeting of the War Council on 5 August 1914 comprised seventeen members of whom twelve were soldiers. This large gathering of military luminaries took place precisely because no confidence was felt in the present CIGS, Sir Charles Douglas, or in his predecessor Sir John French.[6] French outlined the existing plan to concentrate the BEF at Maubeuge and at once proposed departing from it by moving the concentration area to Amiens or landing at Antwerp. After some differences amongst the military had been revealed it was decided to send five divisions to France at once and the sixth when the situation became clear. The following day Asquith informed the War Council that the Cabinet had agreed in principle to send the Expeditionary Force to France as planned, and Kitchener then held out for retaining two Regular divisions in England. This proposal the Prime Minister found attractive since the 'domestic situation might be grave, and colonial troops or territorials could not be called on to aid the civil power'.[7]

Kitchener thus from the outset impeded the working of the General Staff plan. Nor was this an isolated instance. He also completely reversed accepted General Staff policy on meeting an enemy invasion of the United Kingdom, which at that time was to engage the invading forces inland, and returned to the nineteenth-century concept of meeting an assault on the beaches. This greatly contributed to the erosion of his relations with Churchill and the Admiralty during the autumn of 1914.[8] It was also a taste of his future methods.

In attempting to make its views heard, the General Staff was hampered by the loss of all its senior and many junior members to the Expeditionary Force. It was not however, as has been implied, a foregone conclusion that the leading lights of the General Staff would go to France on the outbreak of war.[9] The appointments to the Expeditionary Force were constantly changing, and at one stage it was ordained that Robertson would remain at the War Office as Director of Military Operations. Also at the first meeting of the Military Members of the Army Council it was decided that on mobilization all officers appointed to staff positions were to proceed to places of mobilization except General Staff officers who were to remain at the War Office.[10] This decision was subsequently cancelled but does indicate that there were some qualms about sending off the whole General Staff on the outbreak of war.

The rescinding of this decision cost Whitehall dearly, for the early months of the war saw the death in action of a number of potential General Staff officers of the highest calibre. The loss of Brigadier-General John Gough VC and Major-General Sir Thompson Capper, both acknowledged as first-class minds, was typical of such depletion. At a lower level the death of men such as Grant Duff deprived the General Staff of an invaluable fund of experience and expertise. The loss was magnified by the closure of the Staff College and the total absence during the greater part of the war of any machinery to train new General Staff officers.

To head what remained of the General Staff and attempt to stem the tide of Kitchener's advance stood Sir Charles Douglas, the CIGS. His difficulties were exacerbated by his being the principal victim of Esher's exhortations not to oppose Kitchener's methods. Esher regarded Douglas as a conscientious and unimaginative administrator who was unfitted to head the General Staff.[11] In this view he was perhaps correct; in his assertion that Douglas soon abandoned the attempt to struggle with Kitchener's monolithic attitude he was not. In one of his last papers on strategy Douglas attempted to bring Kitchener's extreme views on the dangers of a raid on the United Kingdom back into line with General Staff appreciations. He concluded:[12]

The decisive point at the present time lies on the Continent and our correct strategy is still to maintain the strongest possible offensive there. In doing so we are not only taking the most effective action to bring the war to a successful conclusion, but we are indirectly protecting England from any serious attempt at invasion.

Douglas had however very little time to persuade Kitchener of the validity of this view of strategy, for within a month he was dead of overwork.

The post of Douglas's successor, not in the circumstances an enviable one, fell to Sir James Wolfe Murray who became CIGS on 25 October 1914. Wolfe Murray—nicknamed 'Sheep' Murray by Winston Churchill—was wholly unfitted by temperament or experience to be CIGS and quite unable to deal with Kitchener. He was notoriously incompetent and his performance bore out the estimate of an earlier Secretary of State for War: 'He is an impossible person to work with, and how on earth he ever got his reputation in the Army passes my understanding. He really sometimes gives the impression of being only half-witted.'[13] In fairness to Wolfe Murray it should be pointed out that he had been lifted precipitately out of the South African Command and now found himself occupying a most senior position, faced with a war of ever-expanding horizons and subject to the overbearing reputation of Lord Kitchener.

Before this massive personality, Wolfe Murray collapsed. When he appeared before the Commission of Enquiry into the Dardanelles in 1917, he was asked whether he ever had enough information in his possession to form an opinion on the Dardanelles. His reply was revealing:[14]

I had not, I could have got it no doubt; but Lord Kitchener was a man who had a very overwhelming personality, we will say, and was a man of very great experience, and it did not appear to me that he, having, so to speak, taken the whole thing in hand and working on it almost entirely himself, to be necessary or desirable that I should interfere.

Wolfe Murray was as good as his word. In meetings of the War Council and Dardanelles Committee he regarded himself as Kitchener's staff officer and had in any case the haziest notion of the performance of those bodies. He never really grasped what their functions were and admitted that he left their meetings without having any idea that a decision had been reached at all. Only once was the CIGS ever directly challenged to say something. At the meeting of the War Council on 16 February 1915 Sir Edward Grey asked him if he had any suggestions to offer on the broad question of the Dardanelles and Russia. The minutes record that he 'replied that he had no suggestions to make'.

Lord Kitchener's defects complemented those of his CIGS. He was constitutionally unable to delegate authority and even acted as his own private secretary. His painstaking concern with administrative detail meant that he also attempted to act as his own Army Council and only the Quartermaster-General, Sir John Cowans, was prepared to oppose him. As soon as Kitchener arrived at the War Office he began throwing the military arrangements into confusion, and this was to be the case for many months thereafter. To gain access to him at all was difficult, and when he saw his professional colleagues he did so individually and alone, thereby making the formation of any common front extremely difficult. His passion for secrecy was overwhelming and he refused in August 1915 to appear before the War Policy Committee on the grounds that such action should be reserved for the Cabinet alone.[15] It subsequently became apparent that what he really objected to was the presence of a shorthand writer.

There is no doubt that Kitchener attempted to perform an impossible burden of tasks. It was doubly unfortunate that he never perceived the assistance which the General Staff might give him, since he had a strong dislike for formulating broad strategic plans which he was never to lose. Pressed by Esher in February 1915 to divulge any such strategic plans as he had to the French in connection with Russia and the East Kitchener replied:[16]

> The point you raise is no doubt of considerable importance, but, owing to the rapid changes that take place on the political horizon in the Balkans and that part of the world, it seems difficult to see how any very fixed plan of action can be determined upon when we are dealing with such unstable factors.

Not only did Kitchener never recognize that the General Staff might be able to help him in what he found such an unpalatable task, but his reluctance to call upon it was reinforced by an over-developed concern for the autonomy of the Commander-in-Chief in the field. Thus when Bonar Law suggested that a general policy might be laid down in broad terms for Sir Ian Hamilton at Gallipoli, as it had been in France, Kitchener replied that 'if it was intended to tie the hands of the General in the field by orders from London he would not support it'.[17]

The reverse of this attitude was also true. When it came to making a strategic judgment Kitchener preferred to request the opinion of his man on the spot rather than call on the General Staff. Early in January 1915 he wrote to Sir John French that the likelihood of a successful French push appeared to be diminishing and that there was a strong feeling that troops might be better employed elsewhere than in Flanders. 'The question of *where* anything effective can be accomplished spans a large field and requires a good deal of study—what are the views of your staff?'[18] French's reply was that it was by no means certain that a decisive stroke could not soon be made in Flanders. Kitchener held to this faith in Sir John French as late as 20 August 1915, when he informed the Dardanelles Committee that he would be glad to get rid of the Dardanelles problem but only after consultation with the General and his staff. He had in the meanwhile been subjected to a hail of partisan advice from French about the policy of future operations, all of which urged him to concentrate on Flanders.[19]

On the specific question of operations at the Dardanelles Kitchener did not use his General Staff at all, despite being pressed by Esher to confide in the CIGS. He was, however, subjected to a barrage of advice from many other interested parties; a typical letter from Rawlinson ran: 'So they have begun the Dardanelles. It must be pushed through to a successful conclusion whatever happens and whatever it may cost us for we cannot afford to fail at a job like that.'[20] Kitchener was the more culpable in that he was receiving from a source close to him excellent and prescient advice. Sir William Birdwood at Cairo was warning him by March 1915 that he had no faith in Admiral Carden's ability to force the Straits and anticipated a landing against fully entrenched positions.[21] It was to Birdwood that Kitchener turned for information as to what combined operations against Gallipoli would involve, and to inquire whether 64,000 troops would be sufficient for operations in Constantinople after the Straits had been forced, when plans prepared by the General Staff already existed.

Kitchener showed most clearly his reluctance to use the machinery at his disposal when, in response to a query from Churchill as to who was responsible for examining the situation at the Dardanelles from a general point of view, he replied 'that it was the work of the General Staff'. Upon being requested to present a memorandum on the possibilities of remaining on the peninsula for the winter, he assented with pleasure but asked for Sir Maurice Hankey to help him. When Asquith agreed Kitchener promised Hankey 'all the staff and assistance he required'.[22] Even contemporaries could be pardoned for thinking that by this time the Secretary to the Cabinet had usurped the position of the General Staff with Kitchener's approbation.

In Kitchener's defence it may be remarked that had he decided to overcome his hostility to his professional colleagues and turn to them for strategic advice, he probably would not have fared very much better than he did .The departments of the Directors of Staff Duties and Military Training, Major-Generals Mackenzie and Heath Caldwell, had both been severely reduced as arranged before the war, and since there were no organized programmes of staff training or manoeuvres their work had in any case ceased to have any importance. Potentially the most influential post was that of Director of Military Operations; unfortunately its occupant, Major-General Callwell, was in many ways another Wolfe Murray.

Kitchener never discussed strategic questions with Callwell, who neither sought nor got an opportunity to put forward his views opposing a naval action at the Dardanelles. Viewing events from a safer vantage point of hindsight, Callwell felt it very unlikely that such an operation would have been undertaken had the Naval War Staff and General Staff discussed such a scheme in concert; but at the time he made no attempt to initiate such discussions. His statement to the Dardanelles Commissioners that 'the real reason why the General Staff practically ceased to exist was because it was not consulted' embodied only a half truth.[23] Hankey has left an interesting account of a General Staff meeting involving both Callwell and Wolfe Murray:[24]

He [Kitchener] sits at the head of the table and talks a lot, and bludgeons everyone into agreeing with him. I was the only one who put up any opposition, the Chief of Staff . . . merely mumbling assent, and Callwell just agreeing.

The War Office certainly did not stand up to the overbearing personality and reputation of Lord Kitchener, and may be criticized for failing to do so. But a greater weight of blame rests with the Prime Minister who invariably took the chair at meetings of the War Cabinet and similar bodies. He had it in his power to require of Kitchener that he produce appreciations and plans by his General Staff, yet he never did so. He clearly displayed his own frame of mind with regard to matters military when closely pressed by the Dardanelles Commission:[25]

> The War Office were very indisposed, perhaps rightly, to discuss, even at the War Council, what I might call tactical questions. Lord Kitchener was, I will not say secretive, but he kept his own counsel and we always forebore secrecy being so very important, and the lay mind not being adapted to fathom those problems to press him on tactical operations.

This reserve extended right through the spectrum of tactical and strategical questions, and should not be thought peculiar to the Prime Minister alone, although it was perhaps his possession of it which was most unfortunate. Churchill described the mixture of awe, respect, sympathy and confidence which he and others felt for Kitchener, and the belief that he had 'plans deeper and wider than any we could see'.[26] However, he did himself less than justice in remarking that 'he (Kitchener) dominated absolutely our counsels at that time'. The marquess of Crewe said afterwards that the political members of the committee did too much of the talking and the experts too little, a judgment in which Curzon concurred. For the purposes of the Dardanelles Committee, Curzon afterwards remarked, the CIGS did not exist in the spring and summer of 1915.[27] The general attitude of the political members at the time was best summed up by Grey: the weight of Kitchener's pronouncement was so great that no one felt the need to ask the CIGS his opinion.

The one man who had the greatest understanding of military issues among the civilians, and who had a fund of experience in the Committee of Imperial Defence to call upon, was Arthur Balfour. A word from him might have brought the experts into greater prominence. He did feel that figures such as the CIGS were present to offer technical professional advice on matters which they could discuss with authority; he also suggested that it was the chairman's obligation to extract an opinion from them. Like many of the opinions already cited this was given *post hoc*, and Balfour himself contributed to the relegation of the experts to a minor role. During a discussion in the War Council on whether to land north of Bulair Line to cut Turkish communications, he read extracts describing Port Baklar from a General Staff appreciation dated 1909.[28] It did not apparently occur to him or to anyone else to question whether there were any more recent appreciations, and if not why not. In fact Balfour, as much as any of the civilian ministers, relished the opportunities afforded by a strategic discussion to try to persuade his colleagues of the unimpeachable logic of his own particular views.

The combination of attitudes and personalities which amalgamated to render the General Staff virtually a vestigial organ contributed greatly to the débâcle at Gallipoli, and by the strength of the reaction which followed it, to the Somme and Passchendaele also. It was not until 1917 and the Report of Enquiry into the Dardanelles that the government met any deep criticism of its relations with its military advisers.[29] But this paled into relative insignificance, then and for far too long afterwards, beside the strictures levelled against Lord Kitchener—who was by that time dead. 'We think', the Commissioners reported:[30]

> that the conditions of a military attack on the Peninsula should have been studied and a general plan prepared by the Chief of the Imperial General Staff . . . special attention being paid to the probable effect of naval gunfire in support of the troops; and that it was the duty of the Secretary of State for War to ensure that this was done.

The picture of government in the first year of the war was a gloomy one, with its groping attempts to discover a viable system by which to direct a war effort and yet which preserved at the same time the fundamentals of Cabinet responsibility. The contrast between patterns of behaviour in peacetime and in war was striking: in the former the military had acquired considerable influence, particularly within the Committee of Imperial Defence, and had forged its own strategy, whilst in the latter the politicians had reclaimed all responsibility. But to fill the lacuna which now existed between government and opinion, between direction and advice, and which was the rightful domain of the General Staff, there stood the influential figure of the secretary to the War Council—and to practically every other government committee—Sir Maurice Hankey.

There is no doubt that during the course of the first year of war Hankey usurped the role of General Staff, though it can be argued that it was perhaps a good thing that the Cabinet had a somewhat irregular source of strategic advice rather than none at all. It is this interpretation that has been generally adopted, and as a result has obscured the fact that Hankey was in a sense permitting the government to live on borrowed time by staving off the realization that the conduct of the war demanded the admission of strategic experts into political counsels on equal terms. There is no evidence that Hankey followed this course deliberately, but his written papers were exceptionally able and distinct and represented precisely the work which the General Staff should have produced. His very ability coupled with the willingness of the politicians to accept his appreciations combined against the development of the General Staff. Hankey certainly enjoyed his personal influence and was perenially alarmed when the possibility of an assistant, and therefore successor, was raised. And it is perhaps not too fanciful to detect a note of pleasure in his protestations of embarrassment at the way Asquith talked as if he and not the Cabinet were in charge of the Dardanelles operation.[31] The Dardanelles venture did in fact demonstrate all too clearly that, without the professional advice of the General Staff functioning through the medium of the government, the result was a haphazard and irresolute selection of objectives which doomed a military operation to disaster.

At the Dardanelles Commission Enquiry in 1917 both the CIGS and DMO disclaimed any chance of introducing plans for the operations at the Dardanelles. Wolfe Murray was emphatic that he never prepared or saw plans connected with the expedition, was never instructed to prepare plans and never thought to suggest to Kitchener that he should do so. Callwell, however, admitted being well acquainted with the question before the war began;[32] and he also afterwards averred that a dissenting military expert in a Cabinet council should speak out and take his chance.[33] He was certain that the General Staff and the whole of the military side at the War Office were opposed to operations elsewhere than in France, at the same time admitting that he felt a military plan would have been desirable and would have helped Sir Ian Hamilton, who never ever got one. His plea was that he had not been asked to produce one. Yet a number of General Staff appreciations existed upon which he could have drawn.

The earliest paper by the General Staff which was strictly relevant to 1914 was an appreciation drawn up as part of the enquiry of 1906 into a war with Turkey. At that time a detailed examination of the problem posed by the Straits had led to the conclusion that only a combined operation could have any real chance of success. The danger was that the Turks might recognize that Gallipoli was a vital spot which if forced would probably end a war; they might then occupy in force, rendering a landing more costly than we could contemplate. Therefore a landing to dismantle the forts was feasible on one condition only:[34]

> To ensure the success of the actual attack on the Gallipoli peninsula, it must be of the nature of a surprise. To secure this every effort must be made to mislead the enemy and our own intelligence must be prompt and accurate or the attempt may result in a severe repulse.

This element of surprise was irretrievably lost when an impetuous Churchill ordered the navy to shell the outer forts on 3 November 1914.

When in September 1914 the possibility of Greek aid in a joint attack on Gallipoli arose, Callwell drew on this and other papers in framing his reply. His memorandum was extremely unclear; he began by adopting a pessimistic view of the chances of success as a result of the recent Turkish fortification of the Straits and stating that it was 'understood that what was then done renders them secure against anything in the nature of a surprise attack'. He concluded that a force of 60,000 attacking in two echelons might well succeed but 'the actual details would of course have to be worked out by the General appointed to command the Expeditionary Force'.[35] Clearly Callwell had, even at this early stage in the war, no intention of pressing his own claims as the source of strategic advice.

In October 1914 the DMO attended a joint conference with Churchill and Fisher which he described as:[36]

> really the only occasion on which the General Staff were afforded anything like a proper opportunity of expressing an opinion as to operations against the Dardanelles until after the country had been engulfed up to the neck in the morass

and was irretrievably committed to an amphibious operation on a great scale in the Gallipoli Peninsula.

According to his own account, he chose the opportunity to point out the dangers of a landing at the Dardanelles. In doing so he was being unduly influenced by a report from the military attaché in Constantinople which he had seen on 9 October and which stated that naval action alone against the Straits would be disastrous and that the British population in Constantinople would be severely affected by such a hazardous undertaking. But Callwell ignored the opinion expressed at the conclusion of the report that a combined operation might well be successful and that the arrival of German artillery men and ordnance was increasing daily the difficulty of getting through.[37]

In view of this and of the universal concurrence of General Staff appreciations on the need for surprise and for a joint attack, Callwell should have pressed for such an operation in January 1915 when he knew that a naval attempt would be made. Instead he mentioned his doubts to Robertson but added 'the naval attack *may* succeed and if it does will be a tremendous coup'.[38] Callwell was prepared to connive in the process of strategy by default which characterized the direction of military operations for several months to follow.

The question of attacking the Dardanelles was brought up by the First Lord of the Admiralty during a discussion on the defence of Egypt. Churchill's over-riding aim was to bring much needed support to the toiling Russians and his enthusiasm for his cause was such that he was subsequently saddled with most of the blame for initiating the fiasco at Gallipoli. Yet he received powerful, if hitherto unremarked, support in his crusade from the secretary to the War Cabinet, Sir Maurice Hankey. It was a memorandum by Hankey which first seriously raised the possibility of attacking Turkey in order to bring down the Central Powers rather than battering away at their lines in France. It also foreshadowed most of the points subsequently made on its behalf by the 'Easterners': the historical precedents for attacking an enemy's overseas territories, the possibility of opening communications with Russia via the Black Sea and thereby unlocking her supplies of wheat, which could be used to purchase munitions, and finally the heady prospect of mobilizing Serbia, Greece and Bulgaria on the Allied side.[39]

These were precisely the points taken by Lloyd George, then Chancellor of the Exchequer, in a paper written on New Year's Day 1915. To them he added a subtle and persuasive new argument: Kitchener's new armies would be ready by March and they added a new dimension to the direction of the war: 'if this superb army is thrown away upon futile enterprises, such as those that we have witnessed during the last few weeks, the country will be uncontrollably indignant at the lack of prevision and intelligence shown in our plans.'[40] The most fruitful operation that he envisaged was one directed against the Dardanelles.

It was at this point that the lowly position to which Kitchener had permitted the General Staff to sink became crucial. The General Staff should now have been called upon to produce a full-scale strategic appreciation of the question, or should have done so on their own initiative. In the absence of such guidance, the papers by Hankey, Lloyd George and others became an acceptable substitute and combined with Churchill's enthusiastic oratory to get the Dardanelles expedition under way. Kitchener helped it on its way by presenting the War Council on 8 January 1915 with 'the results of a preliminary examination in the War Office' which concluded that it would be fruitless to attempt operations in Italy or Salonica and that the most suitable objective appeared to be the Dardanelles.[41] In all probability this was the product of Kitchener's brain alone.

Of another scheme voiced early in February 1915 by Lloyd George, Hankey's biographer has written: 'The people whom Lloyd George really had to convince regarding the soundness of his proposals were of course Kitchener and his colleagues on the General Staff.'[42] In fact, the politicians when considering any military venture at this time had only to convince each other and since all agreed early in January 1915 that something must be done somewhere, the Dardanelles scheme commanded ready acceptance. Confronted by strong political demands for this course of action, Kitchener was prepared to accept it and then try to justify it afterwards. As a result everyone agreed to the venture for different reasons, and so sketchy was the strategic examination of the issue that it is hard to avoid the conclusion that all thought they were agreeing to different ventures. Thus Fisher, as First Sea Lord, felt a Fleet attack to be justified only as long as it forced a decision at sea.[43] Had this view been elicited and its implications appreciated somewhat earlier, Asquith might

not have experienced the embarrassing incident of the crusty old Admiral's resignation in May 1915, which severely weakened his own political standing. Kitchener, for his part obsessed by a fear of native insurgency in Egypt, thought the scheme an admirable prophylactic for this danger and the basis for some kind of campaign on the plain of Hungary. Callwell felt that naval bombardment alone could effect a political change in Turkey, and after it had begun could be myopic enough to write:[44]

> the Dardanelles affair is getting on very nicely and, *if the Navy will only go very cannily and not rush things*, I believe the Turks will drift off out of the Gallipoli Peninsula and its occupation will be a fairly simple matter.

At this stage, Callwell's advice would scarcely have been worth having even if he had been asked to give it, which he was not.

Further papers from Balfour and Lloyd George in February 1915 came out in favour of a Dardanelles operation but they were surpassed by a highly professional paper from Hankey. In it he listed five major strategical arguments and four economic advantages for action in the Dardanelles, all of which boiled down to the necessity of opening up communication with Russia through the Straits, as well as a number of minor benefits such as the removal of any threat to the Suez Canal.[45] The paper was terse and convincing, in fact exactly what the General Staff might have been expected to produce.

Churchill's exuberant self-confidence waned during February so that by the 26th he was prepared to disclaim all responsibility if disaster occurred as a result of an insufficiency of troops to back up the navy. The War Council were becoming slowly acclimatized to the idea of military operations at Gallipoli, quite foreign to the original conception, and Hankey aided that progress. By 1 March he was optimistically considering the capture of Constantinople and the necessary diplomatic terms to accompany it. This paper also bore all the hall-marks of a Hankey product: clear setting out of aims and methods, considerable strategic detail, the enumeration of secondary objectives and a clear military course to be followed. To his credit Hankey recognized that such an operation demanded collated planning of an extremely high standard; his solution was not however to demand that the General Staff resume its true functions and prepare plans jointly with the naval War Staff for consideration by the War Council, but to suggest the formation of a special joint committee. In this instance Asquith appears not to have followed his advice.[46]

The first landings at Gallipoli signally failed to effect an occupation, and Kitchener's response to the consideration in May 1915 of reinforcing the troops there shows all too clearly how he was even less capable of independent strategic thought and was becoming transfixed by gloom. He paraded all the customary arguments—Hankey's arguments—about helping Russia and gave as his final reason for favouring reinforcement the need to gain an asset which could be used in the discussion of peace terms to bargain against 'any gains on the Continent which Germany may still hold'. It was not on military grounds but on political ones that he opted for pushing on and making what progress was possible. Such a course had much to commend it:[47]

> It avoids any immediate blow to our prestige; it keeps the door open to Balkan intervention; it ensures our hold on a strategical position of great importance, which rivets the attention of the Turks and in all probability limits active operations on their part against Egypt, or in Mesopotamia, or the Caucasus.

This was the last appreciation of strategy produced by the War Office before Wolfe Murray was replaced as CIGS on 25 September 1915. Hankey now had the field virtually to himself.

By 4 June a strong military attack at the Dardanelles had failed yet again to break the Turkish lines but for a number of reasons things were set fair for the Dardanelles.[48] Again it was two crucial memoranda from Hankey which provided the reinforcement for the Cabinet's decision to go on. In the first he considered the possibilities of cutting Turkish supply routes at the Bulair Lines or at Kum Kale and opted for the latter. In the second paper, both more lengthy and broader in perspective, Hankey provided a study of the war to date and of future strategic options. His conclusions were that a combined Allied offensive in France and Flanders would not be possible until 1916 and that every effort must first be made to equip Russia. To do this the opening of the Dardanelles was 'absolutely essential' and must be carried through in 1915. The paper was, like all Hankey's minutes, polished and persuasive. Unlike the others it advocated a positive step to retard the development of the General Staff: its first recommendation was that there should be a

discussion of the whole policy of the war as soon as possible with Sir John French. No mention was made of Wolfe Murray, Callwell or any other General Staff officer.[49] A memorandum produced by Kitchener on the same subject two days later was little more than a carbon copy of it, advancing the same strategic postulations and arriving also at the conclusion that the Dardanelles operation must be pressed to a successful end.

It must be emphasized that there were other memoranda being put forward in favour of the Dardanelles, most notably by Churchill. With the exception of Kitchener's gnomic utterances they were by politicians and were couched in terms of international politics with an admixture of heady rhetoric. Hankey's papers were cool, factual and detached assessments in strategic terms; presented with them the War Council and Dardanelles Committee felt no need to press for similar papers from elsewhere.

Significantly it was Hankey who was sent out to Gallipoli in August to bring back a full report. The result was a twenty-seven page paper which commenced with tactical considerations, Hankey making it clear that he thought the opportunities at Anzac Landing were good. Careful consideration was given also to requirements for a winter campaign—landing places, requirements in *matériel* and transport. Man for man he considered the allied forces equally matched by the Turks, though the latter were poorer in equipment and supplies. The paper concluded by considering withdrawal, technically difficult and involving considerable loss of prestige, negotiation, which would involve complex dealings with Russia, France and Italy, and going on. Hankey ended: 'The final decision . . . must depend upon a wider appreciation of the situation than is possible to one who for some weeks has been almost wholly out of touch with views of worldwide affairs.'[50] At the meeting of the Dardanelles Committee on 31 August which discussed this paper and the situation at Gallipoli, Hankey showed no hesitation when questioned by Curzon and Lloyd George in advocating retention of all three landing places and an attack from Anzac Beach. This meeting clearly showed him acting as military adviser to the committee, discussing geographical factors, technical points about the effects of long- and short-range fire and Turkish positions. The General Staff representatives stayed silent. Hankey remained an influential proponent of operations in the Dardanelles virtually up to the withdrawal, and wrote a memorandum to Bonar Law in an attempt to persuade him of the merits of staying immediately after Robertson's paper of 5 November.[51]

The provision of strategic advice on the conduct of the war had passed almost completely from the hands of the War Office, and the consequent 'living from hand to mouth' which marked the government's handling of the Dardanelles had not gone unremarked. In the spring of 1915 an attempt was made to redevelop the position of the General Staff and remedy the defects caused by its quiescence. It began in France with a demand by Sir William Robertson, then Quartermaster-General there, that the government make known to the High command in the field its future military policy since until it did so long-term military planning was impossible.[52] Shortly afterwards, Lord Haldane drew the attention of the Cabinet to the failure of the General Staff and naval War Staff to engage in any co-operative study. The absence of a 'General Staff mind' meant losing the advantages of the continuous and systematic study of problems and the chance to look ahead for developments which might be escaping public observation.[53] But how could the Secretary of State for War be convinced that he must resuscitate the General Staff?

The way to affect Kitchener's policy frequently lay in a personal appeal. Sir Ian Hamilton was shortly to use it successfully to avoid being reinforced by Ewart, on the ludicrously trivial grounds that the latter officer was too fat to squeeze into some of the trenches.[54] Esher now made just such an advance. He suggested the recall of three highly experienced General Staff officers—Wilson, DuCane and Macready—to strengthen the War Office, coupled with the creation of an 'Assistant Secretary of State for War'.[55] The value of advice other than Kitchener's, particularly that of Sir William Robertson, had even percolated as far as the throne; the King wrote to Asquith urging 'strongly' that if French be brought back to consult with the Cabinet then Robertson should come too.[56] These moves totally failed to effect any change in Kitchener's attitude towards the General Staff and Asquith, faced with the issue of compulsory service, was content to let the opportunity pass by.

By late summer 1915 dissatisfaction with the higher direction of the war was growing in certain quarters, and this was par-ticularly the case with regard to the position of the General

Staff. Haldane complained, somewhat querulously, to the Foreign Secretary:[57]

> The General Staff organization which ought to be at work simply does not exist. There are fragments for which individual ministers are responsible, but there is no one to coordinate the work . . . the confusion is disconcerting. General Staff work is a thing which requires training and watching over, and no one takes sufficient interest in it to insist on the co-ordination of the necessary elements.

He made similar observations to Esher, remarking on the want of '*mind*' and the bad choice of men. In fact it was difficult, though not impossible as Asquith's biographers have maintained, to find General Staff officers of sufficient authority to hold their own with Kitchener and to be taken seriously as independent organs of opinion.[58] And until such a person could be found to fill the office of CIGS the redevelopment of the General Staff was stultified.

The chance to revive the General Staff came on 22 September 1915. Curzon afterwards held that the Cabinet were ignorant of the lack of a proper General Staff until a Cabinet committee was appointed in August 1915 to consider the introduction of compulsory service; it was not until then that he and his colleagues 'discovered exactly the nature of the deficiency'.[59] Certainly as the operations at Gallipoli progressed, it became clear that professional advice was sadly wanting. Yet no one yet dared to challenge Kitchener openly; advantage was taken of his absence from the War Council on the 22nd to exert a unanimous pressure on Asquith to reconstitute and reinforce the General Staff.[60]

The Prime Minister wrote that same day to Kitchener reporting the feeling that, because of the Secretary of State's immense responsibilities, it had become essential that he and the Cabinet should have 'the best intelligence that the army can supply for our common purpose'.[61] Asquith suggested that Sir Archibald Murray be made CIGS immediately; that he have as assistants 'three or four of the best Staff Officers who have seen service at the front'; and that a systematic interchange between staff officers at headquarters and at the front be instituted. Since these details are absent from the Cabinet report they may have been entirely Asquith's; certainly it was only when the whole Cabinet pushed that he moved decisively.

Lieutenant-General Sir Archibald Murray was appointed CIGS on 25 September 1915. This complied with Asquith's first suggestion and he heard of its successful application 'with relief'. Esher wrote to Fitzgerald that 'The news about Archie Murray is *excellent*. It will make all the difference. I am sure of this.'[62] Had Kitchener accepted the other suggestions made by Asquith this might have proved accurate; as it was, Esher was far too sanguine of the prospects. Kitchener made no great effort to implement the other changes and Asquith did not press them. Hence an apparent development of the General Staff was really only a substitution of heads. Moreover Archibald Murray had to deal with attitudes and personalities which in a very real sense hindered the development of the General Staff.

On the eve of Wolfe Murray's replacement Hankey produced a thirteen-page memorandum of the preparations at the Dardanelles for a winter campaign. It was as usual clear, concise and well constructed and gave in detail the state of supplies, labour, fuel, transport material, medical arrangements and water-supply. The result was impressive, and Hankey's belief that everyone on the spot was happy with the arrangements and that little more could be done in England acted as a support for that section of the Cabinet which held that Gallipoli must be brought to a successful conclusion.[63] Equally there was the persuasive voice of Churchill, now chancellor of the duchy of Lancaster, raised to demand that a new general be sent out to report whether the Dardanelles could be forced and what troops would be required.[64] Both helped prevent the redevelopment of the General Staff: Hankey by presenting very good appreciations of a General Staff type, Churchill and others by suggesting courses which circumvented the main question of whether the Dardanelles was any longer strategically a desirable or useful operation.

In the face of these and other obstacles Murray made a determined effort to revive the place of the General Staff in Cabinet government. He attended his second meeting of the Dardanelles Committee as CIGS on 30 September and took a very active part in discussion on all the main topics, in strong contrast to his predecessor. He also lost no time in putting his views on paper in a general strategic review of the war. In it Murray considered all the major theatres from the point of view of whether or not it was desirable to open another one in the Balkans. His views anticipated those of Robertson when he became CIGS and reveal him as the first 'Western Front' CIGS. Foreshadowing arguments with which politicians were to become all too familiar in 1916 and 1917, Murray told the Dardanelles Committee that Germany could not hope to increase her total strength in the West to any great extent, whereas Great Britain and Russia still had considerable resources in manpower. Germany was therefore engaging in the traditional pursuit of trying to persuade her enemies to disseminate their forces and thereby lose what was otherwise an undeniable superiority in France. His conclusion was direct:[65]

> The General Staff are of opinion that the defeat of the German Army in the western theatre of war is still the main strategical objective and that, as long as this is so, the balance of advantage is against the employment of any Allied troops in the Balkan theatre which could possibly be thrown into the scale in France, unless it can be shown that the defeat of Serbia would more than counterbalance success by the Allies in the main theatre and that such defeat cannot be delayed without the employment of Allied forces in the Balkans.

Of the validity of the latter view Murray was patently unconvinced.

The appearance of this memorandum represented a number of important innovations in the development of the General Staff. It was the first wide-ranging and critical strategic appreciation made by the General Staff without subservience to Kitchener; it was also the first completely 'Western Front' recommendation. In form it represented an ideal, lacking dogmatism and reaching a reasoned conclusion without appeal to lurid language. Robertson was not to depart radically from the line proposed by Murray.

There followed a gradual change in attitude towards the General Staff; even Churchill became anxious to have it consider various strategic options.[66] It was in this atmosphere that the CIGS won an early success in the first use of a General Staff appreciation to reach a decision in the Dardanelles Committee. On 6 October he prepared an estimate that Austrian munitions might reach Gallipoli in mid-November whereas Allied reinforcements could not reach the Aegean until mid-December. It was this which brought the War Committee to face a possible abandonment of Gallipoli and resulted in the revolutionary recommendation that the General Staff be requested, in conjunction with the

Naval War Staff, to prepare an appreciation on the possibilities of retaining Gallipoli if Germany and Austria opened up through-communication with Constantinople 'and to advise as to the military action to be taken, either to avert this contingency, or to safeguard our Eastern Empire, if it should occur'.[67]

The importance of this move was not lost on Murray. The joint appreciation was signed by him and Admiral H. B. Jackson, First Sea Lord, two days later. It pointed to the advantage of Germany's strategic position to switch troops from the Western Front to the Balkans and back more rapidly than could the Allies, and to the possible peripheral nature of combat at Salonica. The conclusion was that the risks attendant on detaching 150,000 men to Serbia to attempt to prevent the passage of German munitions were too great to justify such an operation. The most hopeful course was to reinforce Gallipoli and renew the attempt, but only, and this was heavily emphasized, if such forces were not more urgently needed or could not be better used elsewhere. Murray reiterated his belief in France and Flanders as the main theatre of operations and added the condition that troops could be spared only if a big offensive was not to be tried again in France for three months and if French troops could relieve those of Britain. He did not think that such a contention should in any case be made.[68]

At the same time the structure of the political leadership of the war was undergoing a change which was to highlight the need for a redevelopment of the General Staff and thus to aid Robertson. A recent study of the strategy of the 1914–18 war has remarked upon the collapse of war by Cabinet government in 1915, and the procession of committees has aptly been described as 'the reaction of an inadequate system to situations as they arose'.[69] There are signs that Asquith recognized the ground-swell of discontent: on 17 October he wrote an unusually stilted letter to Kitchener warning of a plot by Curzon, Lloyd George and others to split them up and insisting that 'So long as you and I stand together, we carry the whole country with us. Otherwise, the Deluge!' He was remarkably perceptive, for on 22 October Crewe reported to the King the unanimous conclusion that the War Council was too large to be effective, an act which Roy Jenkins, in his biography of Asquith, has castigated as 'most unfair'. It certainly forced Asquith's hand, for he announced on 11 November the formation of the five-man War Committee.

It was in this atmosphere that Murray continued to press a 'General Staff view' on all strategic questions. His criticism of French intentions *vis-à-vis* Salonica was blunt: their only aim was to support French troops already there without regard to the difficulties involved. His greatest effort came with a paper written in late November on the issue of partial evacuation of Gallipoli. It was designed as a direct confrontation with and refutation of Kitchener's views in so far as they were known.

Murray confirmed at the outset that the General Staff foresaw a success of possibly decisive proportions in Flanders the following spring if a vigorous, concerted and continued effort were made there. Kitchener's favourite argument of the possible loss of prestige following the evacuation of Gallipoli, reaching perhaps disastrous proportions, was deemed conjectural and in any case outweighed by the results which would follow were the British to be driven off the peninsula. On the effects of possible withdrawal on Russia, Australia and New Zealand, Murray admitted that there was room for 'serious doubt'. Much less valid was the accepted thesis that the position contained and inflicted losses upon large Turkish forces.

The CIGS also advanced the idea that the Turks might be as effectively discouraged, and internal order preserved, by the presence of troops in Egypt, and that the retention of Helles alone would certainly invite heavy and repeated attack. His conclusion had a pungency to which the War Committee were unaccustomed:[70]

> The arguments in favour of retaining our positions on Gallipoli are based mainly on conjectures as to the effect on the East of withdrawal, and on questions of Imperial and military sentiment. The arguments on the other side are based on cold calculations of military strategy.

No one in the War Committee could have any delusions now that Kitchener's strategic pronouncement had tacit support from his colleagues at the War Office.

The weight of the House of Commons was shortly to be added to the move to redevelop the General Staff, and thereby to add to the pressure upon Asquith. Captain Leo Amery raised the topic in a debate on the naval and military situation on 2 November, pointing out the unfortunate decision of employing as Secretary of State for War a soldier who lacked experience of the revised system in operation after 1904. He sharply criticized the failure to remedy the 'bleeding white' of the General Staff which had occurred in the summer of 1914, and wound up by advocating as essential:[71]

> that the Government should have at its side a Chief of Staff, with an adequate staff below him, giving direct and responsible advice, not advice submitted through the Secretary of State for War in memoranda, liable to be re-edited and changed.

Similar points were made by a number of his colleagues including the Foreign Secretary, Sir Edward Grey, during the day.

Lack of confidence in the system was sufficiently apparent for Asquith to attempt to calm the fears of the House on this score a week later. Speaking during the vote of Credit, he reassured members that in the CIGS they possessed 'a very distinguished general' who had able senior assistants and some twenty-six staff officers with experience of the present war. As was becoming increasingly the case, Asquith's reassurances had little effect.

The major debate came on 18 November. During question time a demand was made that the government set up special committees to comb the Territorial and New Armies for officers suitable for General Staff work, and that Lord Haldane be recalled to undertake the organization of 'a great national General Staff service'. Bonar Law replied that there were no grounds for adopting 'the specific suggestion contained in the questions'.[72] The House proved far from satisfied with these glib assurances and later in the day as it debated the Consolidated Fund Bill it became clear that there was a consensus of opinion that the direction of the war was not in as professional hands as it might be, and a particular call for an enquiry into the Dardanelles Campaign. Law, left to answer for the government, tacitly admitted that a full-scale enquiry might well be made in the future and promised that in making decisions on the Dardanelles the government would be influenced by 'what, in the best military opinion they can get, they believe to be the wisest course'. General Sir Ivor Herbert then rose to make the longest speech on the subject of the role of the General Staff since the outbreak of the South African War.

Herbert's speech anatomized the government's failure to assure itself of a proper source of strategic advice and laid the blame squarely at the door of the Secretary of State for War. He was amazed, he said, that after fifteen months of war the Prime Minister should have to call for greater liaison between the General Staff, Admiralty and other departments. Co-ordination had been evident in the transportation of the Expeditionary Force and had ceased—the culprit was Lord Kitchener:[73]

> It is just as if you took a fireman from the footplate of some passing locomotive and put him in charge of the highly organized machinery of a battleship. He might be the best stoker in the world, but he is unfit to take charge of such a highly complicated machine.

The new War Committee offered the chance, Herbert felt, of obtaining much greater success than hitherto, but only if the military and naval experts were not overpowered as the General Staff had been 'by a personality assuming the attitudes of Commander-in-Chief'. He concluded with an exhortation to return to the earlier and much more flexible Army Council system set up by Balfour in 1904 as the best means of organizing the national effort for victory. The harrying which Asquith suffered when next he appeared at question time indicated that Herbert was far from being the sole advocate of a reform of the General Staff.[74]

The pressure increasingly being put on the government to resolve the dilemma posed by the Gallipoli operation and the growing demand for a revivification of the General Staff were two of the strands which led to the momentous changes of December 1915. The third, which came to be of equal importance, occurred contemporaneously with the rise in strategic counsels of Sir William Robertson. Robertson ensured while he was in France that Callwell kept him informed of whatever strategic ideas were current, and by August 1915 was secretly in correspondence with the King through his equerry, Clive Wigram. He first appeared at a meeting of the Dardanelles Committee on 11 October 1915 in his capacity as Chief of Staff to the BEF. The meeting was important both because Robertson gave a blunt appraisal of the chances of the Dardanelles, something to which the committee were unaccustomed, and because Asquith made his most decisive intervention to date in refusing to countenance evacuation. Instead, circumlocuting the CIGS, he recommended that either Kitchener or Douglas Haig be sent out to decide where on the peninsula additional troops should be employed.[75]

Robertson returned to France and confided to Haig his doubts about the General Staff under Murray. The failure of the Loos offensive made them determined to replace Sir John French. By 24 October 1915 the two most formidable soldiers in France had formed a united front to oust French and replace Murray with Robertson.[76]

Robertson strengthened his candidacy as a future CIGS in a letter to the Prime Minister in which he pressed the urgent need for joint planning with the French.[77] It was confirmed by a masterly paper presented to the Cabinet on future military policy early in November. In a crisp ten-page memorandum he established from the outset the basis of Allied strategy as he saw it: the defeat of the Central powers, which could only be obtained by the defeat or exhaustion of the predominant partner, Germany. Considering each theatre of war in turn he concluded that France offered the most reasonable chance of securing the main aim:[78]

> It is not of course possible to say that the next great attempt which we and the French may make will succeed in breaking through the enemy's successive lines, but judging from past experience there is a reasonable certainty of obtaining such a measure of success as will add greatly to the cumulative effect of past successes.

His view of the Dardanelles campaign was stark: it was an operation without an object, a drain upon resources, and evacuation was the logical answer.

Robertson went on to ask the Cabinet to decide whether it intended to make France the main theatre of operations, and if it did to concentrate its efforts there. And he urged not only that such decisions be taken but that the machinery be created to give effect to them:[79]

> We are now conducting four distinct campaigns, and we hold in England large disposable reserves. It is essential in these circumstances that there should be one military authority responsible for advising His Majesty's Government regarding military policy in all theatres.

The paper showed Robertson at his best, concise and convincing. It also tilted directly at the monolithic obstacle of Lord Kitchener. Lord Selborne afterwards remarked that to challenge Lord

Kitchener would have involved saying publicly that one did not regard him as a competent adviser.[80] Robertson was one of the first of those who now began to do so.

The pressure on Asquith to reform the General Staff, and with it the higher direction of the war, was becoming intense. Esher, who had formed a favourable impression of Robertson's cool judgment, now pressed the latter's claims as part of a speeding up of decision-making and the improvement of liaison with the French. Murray, though a 'dear good fellow', did not possess the confidence of the army as did Robertson; the post of CIGS was Robertson's right place.[81] Very similar sentiments had previously been impressed on him by Haig, who had himself written to Asquith and Bonar Law.[82]

Law was himself instrumental in altering the attitude of the War Council to professional General Staff advice at this time. He was, as has been accurately recorded, hesitant to support any policy which conflicted flatly with military opinion.[83] Rather, the War Council should accept advice from the General Staff as its true source of military expertise and not from anyone who thought himself qualified to offer it. It was this which was behind his reluctance to continue the Dardanelles venture.[84] In a memorandum he wrote for the Cabinet early in December he emphasized that, despite his belief that the retention of even one of the three beaches at Gallipoli was unwise, 'I do not urge my colleagues to take any steps which are not recommended by our military advisers.'[85]

Against this must be set the continuing attachment to amateur strategy of various members of the Cabinet, and the role played by Hankey. The tendencies of the former to regard their own opinions as strategically indisputable was best shown at the Cabinet of 24 November. When Asquith reported the decision of the War Committee, based on a General Staff appreciation, to evacuate Gallipoli Curzon objected strongly and with support from Lansdowne and Crewe got the discussion adjourned. Curzon then circulated a memorandum in which he challenged the decision to evacuate on military, as well as political grounds. Never before, he thundered, except in the case of Afghanistan, 'have the British run away from an Asiatic enemy'.[86] A second paper recommended replacing and reinforcing the troops on the peninsula. Both were marked by the lack of any overall strategic design—precisely the grounds on which Curzon criticized the military planners—and by language which at the consideration of withdrawal became extremely lurid.

At the same time Hankey was contriving to produce polished and persuasive memoranda which lessened any inclination to look to the General Staff for strategic appraisals. A typical paper examined in detail the supply situation at the Dardanelles and concluded that, apart from certain problems connected with the health of the troops which could easily be solved, the forces there were well supplied for a winter campaign. And as late as 29 November he was advising holding on to Gallipoli or, better still, taking the offensive.

While the Cabinet and the War Committee wrangled with one another over whose opinion should be sovereign, the future of the General Staff was suddenly and radically resolved. By 1 December Asquith and Kitchener agreed that Robertson should replace Murray as CIGS. Asquith's resolution must have been hardened by a letter from the King urging the replacement of Murray as highly desirable:[87]

> His Majesty does believe that important advantages would be secured by the transfer of Sir W. Robertson to the post of C.I.G.S. making him responsible only to the *War Council* for whose information and advice he and his staff would deal with all matters of strategy and the conduct of war.

This suggestion bore a remarkably close resemblance to Robertson's own proposals. The close relationship between George V and Haig has often been remarked upon; what is less often realized is that, at this moment certainly, Robertson too enjoyed the confidence of the King. It is quite possible that this may have been the deciding factor in his success.[88]

On the afternoon of 4 December Kitchener asked Robertson how he would view the status and duties of the CIGS in the event of his being appointed to that office. He received in reply a lengthy but characteristically blunt appraisal. The main conditions Robertson laid down as essential for the successful conduct of military operations were more power for the War Council—which should become the supreme directing authority to formulate policy—and much greater autonomy for the CIGS. He should become the one authoritative channel through which the War Council received all advice on military operations:[89]

It is his function, so far as regards military operations, to present to the War Council his reasoned opinion as to the military effect of the policy which they propose, and as to the means of putting this approved policy into execution. The War Council are then free to accept or reject the reasoned advice so offered.

Robertson aimed to escape almost entirely from the supervision of the Secretary of State, who would be connected with actual military operations on no more intimate footing than that of any other member of the War Council.

Kitchener, by now eager to hand over the burden of responsibility which he could not carry, took these proposals to Asquith with the recommendation that they be accepted. He was not, however, prepared to retain the responsibility of Secretary of State 'without any executive work as regards the war' and hinted to Robertson that he might shortly resign in favour of Lord Derby.[90] Asquith found it 'curious' that Kitchener accepted Robertson's proposals; in truth, behind Kitchener's impassive façade, he was out of his depth and knew it.[91] The Prime Minister himself was sufficiently alarmed at the implications behind the proposals to turn to Curzon for his opinion of them.

The Lord Privy Seal did not much relish the prospect of Robertson or his scheme, and drew Asquith's attention to the danger that the new CIGS would become 'the real Commander-in-Chief in the sense understood in the foreign countries'. He felt grave misgivings about raising the status of the War Council *vis-à-vis* the Cabinet, and also about the problem of what to do with Kitchener:[92]

> With a Chief of the Staff thus enthroned in England and with another great luminary, General French in London ... I cannot see how K. can very well remain in this country. Where would he sit? What would be his office? Who would be under him and what would he do?

Although prepared to accept Robertson's suggestions, Kitchener was not prepared to remain himself to work within them. Asquith wanted the best of both worlds—Kitchener to remain and the new system to be brought into effect together. There was only one man with the right qualities to effect such a delicate negotiation and he duly called on Lord Esher to attempt it. Esher, always at

his best in such situations, succeeded. He convinced Robertson
that the Secretary of State could not avoid remaining constitutionally responsible for the army, and persuaded Kitchener that
with modifications the scheme would be both acceptable and
desirable.[93]

As a result of Esher's loquacious diplomacy Robertson agreed
to modify his scheme so that orders from the War Council would
be issued by the CIGS under the authority of the Secretary of
State. He also felt confident that having subscribed to the
conditions Kitchener would not attempt to escape from them—
thus calming another of Asquith's apprehensions. Esher himself
supported the retention of Kitchener since French confidence
would be severely shaken were such a *point fixe* to disappear.
Even Kitchener was wholly behind the new scheme; he wrote
to Asquith that:[94]

> I feel he [Robertson] and I can work quite well together and
> his presence at the W.O. as C.I.G.S. will relieve me of a
> good deal of work and improve the relations of the office to
> the troops in the field besides giving great confidence.

All was now for the best in the best of all possible worlds. The
obstruction in the way of the General Staff was dissolved;
Kitchener would stay on but would accept the assistance of a
professional body of strategic advisers. Robertson took over as
CIGS on 23 December 1915, and it became immediately apparent
that the role of that officer had undergone a sudden and complete
transformation. In a note for the War Committee dated the same
day he concurred in the conclusion previously reached by Murray
that Flanders was the main theatre of operations and that
commitments to all other theatres should be reduced to a minimum. But he went a step further. He requested that the War
Committee either approve his statement of policy or formulate
a new policy of their own; on the latter, he had no suggestions
to make.[95]

In the War Committee that day the new CIGS supported his
predecessor's conclusion that the whole of the Gallipoli Peninsula
must be abandoned and reminded the gathering that such had
been the recommendation of the Chantilly Conference of 4
December, which had included a Russian delegate. The discussion began to drift, with Balfour challenging the General
Staff estimate that the number of Turks held at Gallipoli was

immaterial and the naval representatives pressing for the retention of Helles, when Robertson brought it up short. He gave a crisp reminder that concentration of forces was essential, and that withdrawal from the Dardanelles in the future might be impossible without even greater loss. The result of his un-compromising review of the strategic possibilities was that the War Committee recommended the Cabinet to order the immediate evacuation of Cape Helles, the last foothold on the Gallipoli Peninsula.[96]

Robertson had won a major victory on his first day in office, and from that time onwards the role of the General Staff was virtually secure. He made the forecast changes in the structure of the General Staff, in the process reducing it from seventy-six to sixty-seven officers. Major-General R. D. Whigham became Deputy CIGS and Callwell, who had injudiciously remarked to Robertson how much he disliked doing General Staff apprecia-tions for the Cabinet, was replaced by Sir Frederick Maurice. Major-General G. M. W. Macdonogh, well qualified by his experience in MO5, became the first Director of Military Intelligence and proved able at his task. The new team combined to give a much more professional approach to General Staff work than had hitherto been the case.

Within the War Committee, discussion began to hinge closely around General Staff appreciations, and at the decisive meeting on 28 December 1915 Robertson effectively controlled proceed-ings. He stood implacably by his written statements, with support from Kitchener, and as soon as the discussion began to drift, which it rapidly did into whether or not General Delmé-Rad-cliffe's estimation of available Italian manpower was correct, Robertson reminded the committee that an immediate decision was necessary if Flanders offensive proposed for March 1916 was not accepted. As a result the Cabinet accepted his major premise, that from the point of view of the British Empire Flanders was the main theatre of operations.

The convictions of the General Staff were embodied in a paper on the Western Front written on New Year's Day 1916. In a concise four-page memorandum Robertson argued that it would take a considerable time for the full resources of the *entente* powers to become available; equally a successful attack would need an advance on a wide front of a minimum of 20,000 yards. Of three such attacks so far Neuve Chapelle in March 1915 had been carried out 'to raise the offensive spirit of our troops', Festubert in May had been to support the French whose left flank had collapsed, and the Loos attack had been planned by Joffre. Failure did not negate the basic principles, which were held still to apply: 'sufficient force should be employed to exhaust the enemy and force him to use up his reserves, and . . . then, and then only, the decisive attack, which is to win victory, should be driven home.'[97] Although prospects were reasonably hopeful, Robertson warned that 'we must anticipate prolonged fighting, a great expenditure of ammunition and heavy losses, even when his defensive lines have been penetrated'. Having now placed its entire confidence in Robertson and the strategic specialists of the General Staff, the Cabinet accepted this advice without question. Thus the way was opened for the costly offensives of 1916 and 1917.

Notes

1 Maurice Papers. Robertson to Maurice, 1 December 1932.
2 S. W. Roskill, *Hankey: Man of Secrets*, vol. 1, London, 1970, p. 229.
3 Maurice Papers. Birdwood to Rawlinson, 15 December 1914.
4 Bonar Law Papers. Asquith to Bonar Law, 2 August 1914. Beav. Lib. B.L. 34/3/3.
5 Viscount Esher, *The Tragedy of Lord Kitchener*, London, 1921, p. 29.
6 M. V. Brett and Viscount Esher, *Journals and Letters of Reginald Viscount Esher*, vol. 4, London, 1934–8, p. 142.
7 Minutes of War Council, 6 August 1914, Cab. 43/1/3.
8 H. R. Moon, 'The Invasion of the United Kingdom: Public Controversy and Official Planning 1888–1918', vol. 2, Ph.D. thesis, London, 1968, pp. 490, 501–2.
9 *Contra* P. Guinn, *British Strategy and Politics: 1914 to 1918*, London, 1965, p. 32.
10 Minutes of Meetings of Military Members of Army Council, 4 August 1914. W.O. 163/44.
11 Brett and Esher, *Journals and Letters*, vol. 3, p. 178. For a similar impression of Douglas *see* Sir N. Macready, *Annals of an Active Life*, vol. 1, London, n.d. [1924], p. 135.
12 Home Defence, 23 September 1914. W.O. 32/5226.
13 Arnold Forster Diary, 10 November 1905. B.M. Add. MSS. 50352.
14 Dardanelles Commission, Minutes of Evidence Q.2605. Cab. 19/33.
15 Kitchener to Asquith, 22 August 1915. P.R.O. 30/52/76. *See also*: Asquith Papers. Letters between Kitchener, Crewe and Asquith, 21–23 August 1915. Bodl. MS. Asquith 14.

16 Kitchener to Esher, 22 February 1915. P.R.O. 30/57/59.
17 Minutes of War Council, 27 August 1915. Cab. 42/3/17.
18 Kitchener to French, 2 January 1915. P.R.O. 30/57/50.
19 W.O. 158/21, *passim.*
20 Rawlinson to Kitchener, 23 February 1915. P.R.O. 30/57/51.
21 Birdwood to Kitchener, 3 and 10 March 1915. P.R.O. 30/57/61.
22 Minutes of War Council, 31 August 1915. Cab. 42/3/20.
23 Dardanelles Commission, Minutes of Evidence Q.3661. Cab. 19/33.
24 Roskill, *op. cit.,* p. 219. Diary entry, 23 September 1915.
25 Dardanelles Commission, Minutes of Evidence Q.25094. Cab. 19/33.
26 Cd 8490, Dardanelles Commission: First Report, p. 4.
27 Dardanelles Commission, Minutes of Evidence Qs 23110–15. 23128. Cab. 19/33.
28 Minutes of War Council, 12 June 1915. Cab. 42/3/2.
29 *See* Cd 8490, *op. cit.,* pp. 10, 29.
30 Cmd. 371, Final Report of the Dardanelles Commission, p. 86.
31 Roskill, *op. cit.,* p. 212.
32 Dardanelles Commission, Statements A—C, 'Summary of Proposed Evidence of Major General Charles Callwell', n.d. Cab. 19/28.
33 Sir C. Callwell, *Experiences of a Dug-Out 1914–1918*, London, 1920, p. 211.
34 Scheme for Attack of the Defence of the Dardanelles, 11 July 1907, p. 4. W.O. 106/1461.
35 Unheaded memorandum, 3 September 1914, p. 1. W.O. 106/1463.
36 Callwell, *op. cit.,* p. 91.
37 Question of Passage of the Straits, 30 August 1914. W.O. 106/1462. In view of Callwell's various pronouncements to say, as Gilbert does, that he felt an attack on the Dardanelles would be justifiable seems too simplistic. M. Gilbert, *Winston S. Churchill*, London, 1971, vol. 3, p. 203.
38 Robertson Papers. Callwell to Robertson, 30 January 1915. K.C.L. Robertson 1/8.
39 Unheaded memorandum, 28 December 1914. Cab. 37/122/194. Hankey's biographer does not allot him any significant role in initiating the plan; *see* Roskill, *op. cit.,* pp. 152–3.
40 Suggestions as to the Military Position, 1 January 1915. Cab. 24/1/G2.
41 Minutes of War Council, 8 January 1915. Cab. 42/1/12.
42 Roskill, *op. cit.,* vol. 1, p. 155.
43 Bonar Law Papers. Fisher to Bonar Law, 31 January 1915. Beav. Lib. B.L. 36/2/57.
44 Robertson Papers. Callwell to Robertson, 30 January, 25 February and 1 March 1915. K.C.L. Robertson 1/8.
45 Attack on the Dardanelles, 2 February 1915. Cab. 24/1/G8.
46 Lloyd George Papers. Hankey to Lloyd George, 19 March 1915. Beav.Lib. Ll. G. C/4/19/4.
47 The Dardanelles: Notes by the War Office, 28 May 1915, p. 6. W.O. 106/1466.
48 R. R. James, *Gallipoli*, London, 1965, pp. 215–16.
49 The Future Policy of the War, 24 June 1915. Cab. 37/130/26.

50 The Dardanelles: Memorandum on the Situation, August 30, 1915. Cab. 24/1/G19. *See* Roskill, *op. cit.*, pp. 206–8.
51 Bonar Law Papers. Hankey to Law, 6 November 1915. Beav.Lib. B.L. 51/5/14. For Robertson's paper *see* below p. 324.
52 Memorandum, 23 March 1915. W.O. 158/17.
53 The Future Relations of the Great Powers, 8 April 1915. Cab. 37/127/17.
54 Dardanelles Commission, Evidence D—L. Telegram, Hamilton to Kitchener, 16 June 1915. Cab. 19/29.
55 Esher to Kitchener, 7 June 1915. P.R.O. 30/57/59.
56 Asquith Papers. George V to Asquith, 23 June 1915. Bodl. MS. Asquith 4.
57 R. B. Haldane Papers. Haldane to Grey, 6 September 1915. N.L.S. MS. 5912.
58 J. A. Spender and C. Asquith, *Life of Herbert Henry Asquith, Lord Oxford and Asquith*, vol. 2, London, 1932, p. 189.
59 Dardanelles Commission, Minutes of Evidence Qs 23129, 23178, 23180. Cab. 19/33.
60 Asquith to George V, 23 September 1915. Cab. 41/36/45. Dardanelles Commission, Minutes of Evidence Q.23183. Cab. 19/33. By telescoping together this event and the appointment of Robertson as CIGS in December, Asquith's latest biographer somewhat overestimates his subject's contribution to the development of the General Staff. R. Jenkins, *Asquith*, London, 1967 [Fontana edition], pp. 429–31.
61 Asquith to Kitchener, 23 September 1915. P.R.O. 30/57/76.
62 Esher to Fitzgerald, 27 September 1915. P.R.O. 30/57/59.
63 Preparation for a Winter Campaign at the Dardanelles, 22 September 1915. Cab. 24/1/G22.
64 Dardanelles, 15 October 1915. Cab. 37/136/12.
65 Robertson Papers. Appreciation by the General Staff of the actual and prospective military situation in the various theatres of war, 2 October 1915, pp. 3, 4. K.C.L. Robertson 1/9.
66 Memorandum, 5 October 1915. Cab. 37/135/4.
67 Minutes of Dardanelles Committee, 7 October 1915. Cab. 42/4/4.
68 Robertson Papers. An Appreciation of the Existing Situation in the Balkans and Dardanelles, with remarks as to the relative importance of this situation in regard to the general conduct of the war, 9 October 1915, esp. p. 9. K.C.L. Robertson 1/9.
69 P. Guinn, *British Strategy and Politics: 1914 to 1918*, London, 1965, p. 115; J. Ehrman, *Cabinet Government and War 1890–1940*, Cambridge, 1958, p. 61.
70 Summary of Arguments for and against the complete or partial evacuation of Gallipoli, 22 November 1915, p. 11. W.O. 106/1467.
71 Hansard, 5th series, vol. LXXV, 2 November 1915, cols 601, 602.
72 *Ibid.*, 18 November, cols 2009–11.
73 *Ibid.*, col. 2013.
74 Hansard, 5th series, vol. LXXVI, 24 November 1915, col. 302.
75 Minutes of Dardanelles Committee, 11 October 1915. Cab. 42/4/6.

76 R. Blake [ed.], *The Private Papers of Douglas Haig 1914–1919*, London, 1952, pp. 108, 109.
77 Asquith Papers. Robertson to Asquith, 31 October 1915. Bodl. MS. Asquith 15.
78 Memorandum on the Conduct of the War, 5 November 1915, p. 3. Cab. 24/1/G33.
79 *Ibid.*, p. 6.
80 Dardanelles Commission, Minutes of Evidence, Q.23380. Cab. 19/33.
81 Asquith Papers. Esher to Asquith, 29 November 1915. Bodl. MS. Asquith 15.
82 Blake, *op. cit.*, pp. 113–15.
83 R. Blake, *The Unknown Prime Minister: The Life and Times of Andrew Bonar Law 1858–1923*, London, 1955, p. 285.
84 Here I disagree somewhat with Roskill's interpretation; *see* Roskill, *op. cit.*, vol. 1, p. 190.
85 Memorandum, 4 December 1915, p. 2. Cab. 37/139/12.
86 The Evacuation of Gallipoli, 25 November 1915. Cab. 37/138/12.
87 Asquith Papers. Stamfordham to Asquith, 3 December 1915. Bodl. MS. Asquith 4.
88 *See* Robertson Papers. Wigram to Robertson. 9 and 10 December 1915; Robertson to Wigram, 11 December 1915. K.C.L. Robertson 1/12.
89 Robertson Papers. Memorandum, 5 December 1915. The revised version of this memorandum is reproduced in Sir W. R. Robertson, *Soldiers and Statesmen: 1914–1918*, vol. 1, London, 1926, pp. 168–71.
90 Robertson Papers. Kitchener to Robertson, 7 December 1915. K.C.L. Robertson 1/13.
91 Roskill, *op. cit.*, vol. 1, p. 237.
92 Asquith Papers. Curzon to Asquith, 8 December 1915. Bodl. MS. Asquith 15.
93 M. V. Brett and Viscount Esher, *Journals and Letters, of Reginald Viscount Esher*, vol. 3, London, 1934–8, pp. 294–6.
94 Kitchener to Asquith, 10 December 1915. P.R.O. 30/57/76.
95 Robertson Papers. Note for the War Committee by the Chief of the Imperial General Staff, with reference to the General Staff paper dated 16 December 1915, 23 December 1915. K.C.L. Robertson 1/6.
96 Minutes of War Committee, 23 December 1915. Cab. 42/6/13.
97 The Question of Offensive Operations on the Western Front, 1 January 1916, p. 3. Cab. 24/2/G47.

Bibliography

1 Primary Sources

Official papers consulted during the preparation of this book comprised the following: Cabinet Office, War Office and Colonial Office records, at the Public Record Office; General Correspondence of the Australian Department of Defence and Correspondence of the Chief of the Australian Section of the Imperial General Staff, at the Commonwealth Archives Office, Canberra; and the Correspondence of the Canadian General Staff, at the Public Archives of Canada, Ottawa. In addition, the Ministry of Defence provided the minutes of War Office Directors' Meetings 1906–13.

Manuscript collections consulted were:

ARDAGH Papers (Public Record Office, P.R.O. 30/40).
ARNOLD FORSTER Papers (British Museum, Add. MSS. 50300–53).
ASQUITH Papers (Bodleian Library, Oxford).
BALFOUR Papers (British Museum, Add. MSS. 49683–962).
BALFOUR Papers (Public Record Office, P.R.O. 30/60).
BONAR LAW Papers (Beaverbrook Library).
CAMPBELL-BANNERMAN Papers (British Museum, Add. MSS. 41206–52, 52512–21).
DAWNEY Papers (Imperial War Museum).
EDMONDS Papers (Centre for Military Archives, King's College, London).
ELLISON Papers (Private).
ESHER Papers (Private).
EWART Papers (Private).
GREY Papers (Public Record Office, F.O. 800).
HAIG Papers (National Library of Scotland, Edinburgh).
J. A. L. HALDANE Papers (National Library of Scotland, Edinburgh).
R. B. HALDANE Papers (National Library of Scotland, Edinburgh).
HAMILTON Papers (Public Record Office, T.168).
HARCOURT Papers (Private).
HOWELL Papers (Centre for Military Archives, King's College, London).
HUTTON Papers (British Museum, Add. MSS. 50078–113).
KIGGELL Papers (Centre for Military Archives, King's College, London).
KITCHENER Papers (Public Record Office, P.R.O. 30/57).
LLOYD GEORGE Papers (Beaverbrook Library).
LYTTELTON Papers (Private).
MARKER Papers (British Museum, Add. MSS. 52276–8).
MAURICE Papers (Private).
MIDLETON Papers (Public Record Office, P.R.O. 30/67).
MIDLETON Papers (British Museum, Add. MSS. 50072–7).
ROBERTS Papers (Ogilby Trust, Ministry of Defence).
ROBERTS Papers (Public Record Office, W.O. 105).

ROBERTSON Papers (Centre for Military Archives, King's College, London).
ROYAL ARCHIVES (Windsor Castle).
SEELY Papers (Private).
SYDENHAM Papers (British Museum, Add. MSS. 50831–41).
WILKINSON Papers (Ogilby Trust, Ministry of Defence).
WILSON Papers (Private).

2 Parliamentary Papers

Cd 1789   Report of His Majesty's Commissioners appointed to inquire into the military preparations and other matters connected with the War in South Africa, 1903.
Cd 1790   Minutes of Evidence taken before the Royal Commission on the War in South Africa, vol. I, 1903.
Cd 1791   Ibid., vol. II, 1903.
Cd 1792   Appendices to the Minutes of Evidence taken before the Royal Commission on the War in South Africa, 1903.
Cd 1932   Report of the War Office (Reconstitution) Committee (Part I), 1904.
Cd 1968   Ibid. Part II, 1904.
Cd 2002   Ibid. Part III, 1904.
Cd 2200   Treasury Minute dated 4th May as to Secretariat, 1904.
Cd 2251   Order in Council of 10th August 1904 defining Duties of the Army Council.
Cd 3404   Published Proceedings and Precis of the Colonial Conference 15th to 26th April 1907.
Cd 3523   Minutes of Proceedings of the Colonial Conference, 1907.
Cd 3524   Papers laid before the Colonial Conference, 1907.
Cd 4475   Correspondence relating to the Proposed Formation of an Imperial General Staff, 1909.
Cd 4948   Correspondence and Papers relating to a Conference with Representatives of the Self Governing Dominions on the Naval and Military Defence of the Empire, 1909.
Cd 5741   Imperial Conference 1911: Precis of Proceedings.
Cd 5745   Minutes of Proceedings of the Imperial Conference, 1911.
Cd 5746   Imperial Conference 1911: Papers laid before the Conference.
Cd 8490   Dardanelles Commission—First Report, 1917.
Cmd 371   Final Report of the Dardanelles Commission, 1917.
C. 11969   [Australia] Defence: Imperial General Staff—Correspondence relating to proposed formation, 1909.

3 Unpublished Manuscripts and Theses

ANON., 'Staff Duties Directorate 1870–1903', n.d., W.O.Lib. A.O.11.14.
ASHLEY, J. G., 'The Old War Office and Other Humours', 1928, W.O. Lib. A.O.11.1.

CAMERON, L. R., 'Constitution of the Army and Militia Councils and the Creation of the Imperial and Canadian General Staffs', Ottawa, n.d., Department of National Defence, Canada.

DAWSON, D. W., 'British Defence Strategy 1906–1914', M.A. Manchester, 1966.

ISAACS, W. V. R., 'History of the M.I. Directorate', 1957, W.O.Lib. A.O.11.14.

—— 'F.-M. Sir William Robertson', n.d., W.O.Lib. A.O.11.14.

KELL, LADY, 'Secret Well Kept: The Life of Sir Vernon Kell', n.d., in private possession.

MOON, H. R., 'The Invasion of the United Kingdom: Public Controversy and Official Planning 1888–1918', 2 vols, Ph.D. thesis, London, 1968.

D'OMBRAIN, N. J., 'The Evolution of British Defence Strategy 1904–1914: A Study of Supreme Command in an Age of Transition', M.A. thesis, McGill, 1965.

PEDLEY, A. C., 'Notes on the Days that are Past 1877–1927', n.d., W.O. Lib. A.O.11.1.

STEARNS, S. J., 'The War Office 1874–1904', M.A. thesis, Columbia, n.d. [1962].

SUMMERTON, N. W., 'The Development of British Military Planning for a War Against Germany 1904–1914', Ph.D. thesis, London, 1970.

4 Memoirs and Biographies

ADYE, SIR J., *Soldiers and Others I Have Known*, London, 1925.

AMERY, L. S., *My Political Life*, vol. I, London, 1953.

(ARNOLD FORSTER, MARY), *The Right Honourable H. O. Arnold Forster: A Memoir*, London, 1910.

ASH, B., *The Lost Dictator: A Biography of Field Marshal Sir Henry Wilson*, London, 1968.

ASQUITH, H. H., *Memories and Reflections*, vol. I, London, 1928.

ASTON, SIR G., *Memories of a Marine*, London, 1919.

—— *Secret Service*, London, 1930.

BLAKE, R., ed., *The Private Papers of Douglas Haig 1914–1919*, London, 1952.

—— *The Unknown Prime Minister: The Life and Times of Andrew Bonar Law 1858–1923*, London, 1955.

BONHAM CARTER, V., *Soldier True: The Life and Times of Field Marshal Sir William Robertson*, London, 1963.

BORDEN, H., ed., *Robert Laird Borden: His Memoirs*, London, 1938.

BRACKENBURY, SIR H., *Some Memories of My Spare Time*, Edinburgh, 1909.

BRETT, M. V. and ESHER, VISCOUNT, *Journals and Letters of Reginald Viscount Esher*, 4 vols, London, 1934–8.

BRIDGES, SIR T., *Alarms and Excursions: Reminiscences of a Soldier*, London, 1938.

BRODRICK, ST. J. (as Lord Midleton), *Records and Reactions 1856–1939*, London, 1939.

BUCKLE, G. E., ed., *Queen Victoria's Letters 1886–1901*, 3 vols, London, 1930–2.

CALLWELL, SIR C. E., *Experiences of a Dug-Out 1914–1918*, London,1920.

—— *Stray Recollections*, 2 vols, London, 1923.

—— *Field Marshal Sir Henry Wilson: His Life and Diaries*, 2 vols, London, 1927.

CHURCHILL, R., *Winston S. Churchill Vol. II: Young Statesman 1901–1914*, London, 1967.

CHURCHILL, W. S., *The World Crisis 1911–1918* (Odhams ed.), 2 vols, London, n.d.

CLARKE, SIR G. S. (as Baron Sydenham), *My Working Life*, London, 1927.

COLLIER, B., *Brasshat: A Biography of Field Marshal Sir Henry Wilson*, London, 1961.

DAWSON, R. M., *William Lyon Mackenzie King: A Political Biography*, vol. I, Toronto, 1958.

DILKS, D., *Curzon in India, 1: Achievement*, London, 1969.

DUGDALE, B. E. C., *Arthur James Balfour: First Earl of Balfour 1894–1905*, London, 1939.

EVELYN, G. P., *A Diary of the Crimea*, London, 1954.

FRENCH, E. G., *The Life of Field Marshal Sir John French, 1st Earl of Ypres*, London, 1931.

—— ed., *Some War Diaries, Addresses and Correspondence of Field Marshal the Right Honble. The Earl of Ypres*, London, 1937.

FRENCH, SIR J. D. P. (as Viscount French), *1914*, London, 1919.

GILBERT, M., *Winston S. Churchill, Vol. III*, London, 1971.

GLEICHEN, LORD EDWARD, *A Guardsman's Memories*, Edinburgh, 1932.

GOLLIN, A. M., *Proconsul in Politics*, London, 1964.

GOUGH, SIR H., *Soldiering On*, London, 1954.

HAIG, COUNTESS, *The Man I Knew*, Edinburgh, 1936.

HALDANE, SIR A., *A Soldier's Saga*, Edinburgh, 1948.

HALDANE, VISCOUNT, *Before the War*, London, 1920.

—— *Richard Burden Haldane: An Autobiography*, London, 1929.

HAMILTON, I. B. M., *The Happy Warrior: A Life of General Sir Ian Hamilton*, London, 1966.

HANKEY, LORD, *The Supreme Command 1914–1918*, London, 1961.

HARRISON, SIR R., *Recollections of a Life in the British Army*, London, 1908.

HOLLAND, B. H., *The Life of Spencer Compton, eighth Duke of Devonshire*, 2 vols, London, 1911.

JAMES, D., *Lord Roberts*, London, 1954.

JENKINS, R., *Asquith* (Fontana ed.), London, 1967.

LEE, SIR S., *King Edward VII: A Biography*, vol. II, London, 1927.

LYTTELTON, SIR N. G., *Eighty Years: Soldiering, Politics, Games*, London, n.d. [1927].

MACDIARMID, D. S., *The Life of Lieut. General Sir James Moncrieff Grierson*, London, 1923.

MACMUNN, SIR G., *Behind the Scenes in Many Wars*, London, 1930.
MACPHAIL, SIR A., *Three Persons*, London, 1929.
MACREADY, SIR N., *Annals of an Active Life*, 2 vols, London, n.d. [1924].
MAGNUS, SIR P., *Kitchener: Portrait of an Imperialist*, London, 1958.
MARDER, A. J., *Fear God and Dread Nought: the correspondence of Admiral of the Fleet Lord Fisher of Kilverstone*, 3 vols, London, 1952–9.
MAURICE, SIR F., *The Life of General Lord Rawlinson of Trent*, London, 1928.
—— *Haldane 1856–1915: The Life of Viscount Haldane of Cloan*, London, 1937.
PONSONBY, SIR F., *Recollections of Three Reigns*, London, 1951.
REPINGTON, C. à C., *Vestigia*, London, 1919.
—— *The First World War 1914–1918: Personal Experiences*, 2 vols, London, 1920.
REPINGTON, MARY, *Thanks for the Memory*, London, 1938.
ROBERTSON, SIR W. R., *From Private to Field Marshal*, London, 1921.
—— *Soldiers and Statesmen: 1914–1918*, 2 vols, London, 1926.
ROSKILL, S. W., *Hankey: Man of Secrets*, vol. 1, London, 1970.
SEELY, J. E. B. (as Baron Mottistone), *Adventure*, London, 1930.
SKELTON, O. D., *Life and Letters of Sir Wilfred Laurier*, 2 vols, London, 1922.
SOMMER, D., *Haldane of Cloan: His Life and Times 1856–1928*, London, 1968.
SPENDER, J. A., *Life of the Right Hon. Sir Henry Campbell-Bannerman*, 2 vols, London, n.d. [1923].
—— AND ASQUITH, C., *Life of Herbert Henry Asquith, Lord Oxford and Asquith*, vol. II, London, 1932.
SWINTON, SIR E. D., *Over My Shoulder*, Oxford, 1951.
VERNER, W., *The Military Life of H.R.H. The Duke of Cambridge*, 2 vols, London, 1905.
WATERS, W. H.-H., *Secret and Confidential*, London, 1926.
—— *Private and Personal*, London, 1928.
WOOD, SIR E., *From Midshipman to Field Marshal*, 2 vols, London, 1906.
YOUNG, K., *Arthur James Balfour*, London, 1963.

5 Contemporary Works

ARNOLD FORSTER, H. O., *The War Office, the Army and the Empire*, London, 1900.
CLARKE, SIR G. S., *Imperial Defence*, London, 1897.
DILKE, SIR C., *The Present Position of European Politics*, London, 1887.
—— AND WILKINSON, S., *Imperial Defence*, London, 1897.
[REPINGTON, C. à C.], *Imperial Strategy: by the Military Correspondent of The Times*, London, 1906.
VON SCHELLENDORFF, B., *The Duties of the General Staff*, London, 1905.

WILKINSON, S., *The Brain of an Army: A Popular Account of the German General Staff*, London, 1890.

6 Secondary Sources

BOND, B. J., *The Victorian Army and the Staff College 1858–1914*, London, 1972.
Cambridge History of the British Empire vol. 3, Cambridge, 1959.
CLARKE, SIR G. S. [as Baron Sydenham], *Studies of an Imperialist*, London, 1928.
CLARKE, I. F., *Voices Prophesying War 1763–1884*, Oxford, 1966.
CLODE, C. M., *The Military Forces of the Crown*, London, 1869.
COBDEN, R., *The Three Panics*, London, 1884.
DUNLOP, J. K., *The Development of the British Army 1899–1914*, London, 1938.
EHRMAN, J., *Cabinet Government and War 1890–1940*, Cambridge, 1958.
ESHER, VISCOUNT *The Tragedy of Lord Kitchener*, London, 1921.
―― *The Influence of King Edward and Essays on Other Subjects*, London, 1915.
ELLISON, SIR G., *The Perils of Amateur Strategy*, London, 1926.
FORTESCUE, J. W., *A History of the British Army*, vol. XIII, London, 1930.
GODWIN-AUSTEN, A. R., *The Staff and the Staff College*, London, 1927.
GORDON, D. C., *The Dominion Partnership in Imperial Defence 1870–1914*, Baltimore, 1965.
GORDON, H., *The War Office*, London, 1935.
GRAHAM, G. S., *The Politics of Naval Supremacy*, Cambridge, 1965.
GUINN, P., *British Strategy and Politics: 1914 to 1918*, London, 1965.
HALPERN, P., *The Mediterranean Naval Situation 1908–1914*, Harvard, Mass., 1971.
HAMER, W. S., *The British Army: Civil-Military Relations 1885–1905*, Oxford, 1970.
HANKEY, LORD, *Government Control in War*, Cambridge, 1945.
―― *Diplomacy by Conference: Studies in Public Affairs 1920–1946*, London, 1946.
HIGGINS, T., *Winston Churchill and the Dardanelles*, London, 1963.
HOWARD, M. E., ed., *The Theory and Practice of War: Essays presented to Captain B. H. Liddell Hart*, London, 1965.
―― *Studies in War and Peace*, London, 1971.
―― *The Continental Commitment*, London, 1972.
JAMES, R. R., *Gallipoli*, London, 1965.
JOHNSON, F. A., *Defence by Committee*, London, 1960.
JUDD, D., *Balfour and the British Empire*, London, 1968.
KEMP, P. K., *The Papers of Admiral Sir John Fisher*, vol. 2, Navy Records Society, 1964.
KENDLE, J. E., *The Colonial and Imperial Conferences 1887–1911: A Study in Imperial Organization*, London, 1967.

LUMBY, E. W. R., ed., *Policy and Operations in the Mediterranean 1912–1914*, Navy Records Society, 1970.

LUVAAS, J., *The Education of an Army: British Military Thought 1815–1940*, London, 1965.

MACKINTOSH, J. P., *The British Cabinet*, London, 1962.

MARDER, A. J., *The Anatomy of British Sea Power* (Archon edition), Hamden, Connecticut, 1964.

—— *From the Dreadnought to Scapa Flow, I: The Road to War*, Oxford, 1961.

MONGER, G. E., *The End of Isolation: British Foreign Policy 1900–1907*, London, 1963.

OMOND, J. S., *Parliament and the Army 1642–1904*, Cambridge, 1933.

PRESTON, R. A., *Canada and 'Imperial Defense'*, Durham, N.C., 1967.

(REPINGTON, C. à C.), *Imperial Strategy, by the Military Correspondent of The Times*, London, 1906.

ROBINSON, R. and GALLAGHER, J., *Africa and the Victorians*, London, 1961.

STANLEY, G. F. G., *Canada's Soldiers 1604–1954*, Toronto, 1954.

STEINER, Z., *The Foreign Office and Foreign Policy 1898–1914*, Cambridge, 1969.

STOFFEL, BARON, *Rapports militaires écrits de Berlin*, Paris, 1870.

THORNTON, A. P., *The Imperial Idea and its Enemies: A Study in British Power*, London, 1959.

TYLDEN, G., *The Armed Forces of South Africa*, Johannesburg, 1954.

TYLER, J. E., *The British Army and the Continent 1904–1914*, London, 1938.

WEIGLEY, R. F., *History of the United States Army*, London, 1968.

WHEELER, O., *The War Office Past and Present*, London, 1914.

WILLIAMSON, S. R., *The Politics of Grand Strategy*, Harvard, Mass., 1969.

WOODWARD, SIR E. L., *Great Britain and the War of 1914–1918*, London, 1967.

7 Articles and Pamphlets

BAKER, H. T., 'Lord Haldane', *Army Quarterly*, vol. XVII, 1928–9.

CAILLARD, M., 'The War Office fifty years ago', *Army Quarterly*, vol. LXXI, 1955–6.

CALLWELL, SIR C. E., 'War Office reminiscences', *Blackwood's Magazine*, vol. CXC, August 1911.

DENING, B. C., 'The future of Intelligence in the Army', *Army Quarterly*, vol. IX, 1924–5.

EDMONDS, SIR J. E., 'Four generations of Staff College students: 1896', *Army Quarterly*, vol. LXV, 1952–3.

ELLISON, SIR G. F., 'Lord Roberts and the General Staff', *The Nineteenth Century and After*, vol. CXII, December 1932.

—— 'From here and there', *The Lancashire Lad: Journal of the Loyal Regiment*, 1931–9.

GIBBS, N. H., 'The Origins of Imperial Defence' [Lecture:] Oxford, 1955.

HELMREICH, J. C., 'Belgian concern over neutrality and British intentions 1906–14', *Journal of Modern History*, vol. 36.

HOWARD, M. E., 'Lord Haldane and the Territorial Army', *The Haldane Memorial Lecture 1966*.

IRVINE, D. D., 'The origin of Capital Staffs', *Journal of Modern History*, vol. 10, 1938.

MACKINTOSH, J. P., 'The role of the Committee of Imperial Defence before 1914', *English Historical Review*, vol. LXXVII, 1962.

MAUD, P. D., 'Lord Haldane's reorganisation of the British Army 1905–1912', *Army Quarterly*, vol. XL, 1947.

POLLOCK, A. W. A., 'The Army and the Esher scheme', *The Nineteenth Century and After*, no. CCCXXVII, May 1904.

TRAINOR, L., 'The Liberals and the formation of imperial defence policy 1892–5', *Bulletin of the Institute of Historical Research*, vol. XLII, 1969.

TUCKER, A. V., 'Army and society in England 1870–1900: reassessment of the Cardwell reforms', *Journal of British Studies*, vol. II, 1963.

—— 'Politics and the Army in the Unionist Government in England 1900–1905', *Report of the Annual Meeting of the Canadian Historical Association*, 1964.

—— 'The issue of Army reform in the Unionist Government 1903–5', *Historical Journal*, vol. 9, 1966.

WELLS, S. F., 'British strategic withdrawal from the Western Hemisphere, 1904–6', *Canadian Historical Review*, vol. XLIX, 1968.

8 Newspapers and Periodicals

Annual Register, 1890–1914
Army Quarterly, 1920–68
Army Review, 1911–14
Hansard, 1890–1916
Journal of the Royal United Services Institution, 1890–1914
Morning Post, 1901–14
The Times, 1890–1916

Index